1966

THE GROWTH OF
THE BRITISH PARTY SYSTEM
VOLUME II
1924–1964

IVOR BULMER-THOMAS

The Growth of
the
British Party System

VOLUME II
1924–1964

NEW YORK
HUMANITIES PRESS

*First published
in the United States of America 1966
by Humanities Press Inc.
303 Park Avenue South
New York 10, N.Y*

Library of Congress Catalog Card No. 66–15527

Printed in Great Britain

CONTENTS OF VOLUME II

PART FOUR
CONSERVATIVE—LABOUR
CONFRONTATION

22

LABOUR IN OFFICE
1924

Labour and Liberals combine to defeat the government—the King sends for MacDonald—who forms a minority Labour government —and is subject to much carping criticism from within his own party—the liaison committee between back-benchers and minis- ters—weakness of the Liberal position—MacDonald's successes in the foreign field—but the Conservatives combine with the Liberals to turn out the government over the Campbell case—the King grants a dissolution—and the Zinoviev letter greatly damages the Labour party—big Conservative victory in a heavy poll—despite a greatly increased Labour vote—Liberals reduced to forty mem- bers—MacDonald resigns and Baldwin forms a Conservative government

IT was clear that the electors had not given Baldwin a mandate for protection, and even clearer that they had not given the Labour party a mandate for socialism. It was more difficult to say for what, if anything, they had given authority. The House of Commons being divided between three fairly equal parties, no party could hope to command a majority except in a coalition; but in 1923 coalition was a dirty word.

When the results came in, Baldwin's government was still in office, and the urgent question was whether ministers should resign immediately or wait to meet Parliament. Baldwin would have re- signed immediately, but at that time the King took the view that "the Sovereign ought not to accept the verdict of the Polls except as expressed by the representatives of the electorate across the floor of the House of Commons".[1] Baldwin acquiesced, and at the same time made clear that he was unwilling to conclude an alliance with the Liberals merely to keep Labour out. This coincided with the King's own view of the proprieties of the situation.

The view was not generally shared among Conservatives. The thought that Ramsay MacDonald might become Prime Minister at the head of a socialist government was so alarming that St. Loe Strachey, editor of the *Spectator*, suggested a "government of national trustees"[2] who should hold office for two years. Younger thought that Baldwin might agree to serve in a coalition under Asquith, Long held that Asquith should be assured of Conservative support if he would form a Liberal administration, while Derby believed that the Conservatives should remain in office with Balfour as Prime Minister in place of Baldwin. When confronted by Stamfordham, Balfour thought that if Baldwin resigned the King should first look to someone in the same party, mentioned Neville Chamberlain, and did not absolutely refuse a hint that he might himself undertake to form a government; later, in correspondence with Birkenhead and in conversation with Horne, he thought that Baldwin should try to come to terms with Asquith.

For a moment Baldwin entertained the idea of a coalition with Asquith, but only to dismiss it. As his biographer, G. M. Young, says:[3]

"To make overtures to the Liberals would have been in direct contradiction to the principles by which he always directed his dealings with the Labour party. Sooner or later, he knew, they must come into power, and so into office. Therefore they must be given the opportunity of acquiring the art and science of constitutional administration. In no circumstances would he have entered into any combination with Lloyd George; and a coalition with the Old Believers, the faithful remnant under Asquith, would either have been, or would have been viewed by the opposition as being, a Party of Order to keep the working classes in their place."

Asquith was firmly of the same opinion. On 18th December he told a meeting of Liberal members that it was a novel experience for him, after being for seven years the favourite target for Tory and coalition vituperation, to be suddenly acclaimed in the same quarters as a potential saviour of society. He went on to say:[4]

"There have been no overtures of any kind from or to the leaders of the two other parties. As far as we are concerned, they are free; as far as they are concerned, we are free. That freedom I intend to preserve uncompromised and unfettered.

"The days of the present government are of course numbered. It seems to be generally assumed that, as the second largest party in the House of Commons, the Labour party will be allowed to assume the responsibility of government. Well, this may reassure some trembling minds outside: If a Labour government is ever to be tried in this country, as it will be sooner or later, it could hardly be tried under safer conditions."

Lloyd George and Simon approved, and the advice was accepted by the party. The King opened the new Parliament on 15th January 1924, and on the 21st Labour and Liberals combined to defeat the government by seventy-two votes. The next day Baldwin handed in his resignation. The King, who was quite clear that in such circumstances it was his constitutional duty to send for the leader of the next largest party in the House of Commons, and was not in the least deterred by the fact that the next largest party was the Labour party, refrained from asking Baldwin's advice—though the advice would have coincided with his own judgement. There was one preliminary to be done. The Cabinet is a committee of the Privy Council, and MacDonald was not a privy councillor. Soon after noon the King held a Council at which MacDonald was sworn a member. The King then invited him to form a government, which MacDonald agreed to do. That evening the King wrote in his diary:[5]

"Today 23 years ago dear Grandmama died, I wonder what she would have thought of a Labour Govt.."

Clynes, who had accompanied MacDonald to the palace, was equally seized of the historical importance of the occasion. He wrote in his *Memoirs*:[6]

"King George sent for Mr. MacDonald. Arthur Henderson, J. H. Thomas and myself accompanied our leader to Buckingham Palace, to that fateful interview of which we had dreamed, when a British Sovereign should entrust the affairs of the Empire to the hands of the people's own representatives.

"As we stood waiting for his Majesty, amid the gold and crimson magnificence of the palace, I could not help marvelling at the strange turn of fortune's wheel, which had brought MacDonald the starveling clerk, Thomas the engine-driver, Henderson the foundry labourer and Clynes the mill hand, to this pinnacle beside the man whose forebears had been Kings for so many splendid generations. We were making history!"

In the light of events some in the Labour party have held that MacDonald should have declined to form a minority government. He had no doubt himself that it was his duty to accept, nor did anyone else in a responsible position in the Labour party have any hesitations at the time.[7] The prospect had its obvious limitations and pitfalls, but Labour would never have been allowed to forget the day if it had shied away from the responsibility of governing the moment the chance came. The cry "Is Labour fit to govern?" was being given wide currency, not least by Churchill, and if Labour had declined it would have been hailed as an acceptance of the taunt. MacDonald, in whom ambition was then running stronger than socialism, may even have welcomed the opportunity of governing in conditions which put a curb upon his extreme followers.

The fear in the Labour movement at the time was that the party would be denied the place to which it was entitled by its performance at the polls. When the King sent for MacDonald, he drew his attention to words used by Lansbury at Shoreditch Town Hall earlier in the month. Lansbury had alleged that certain circles, and even the leaders of the main parties, were bringing pressure on the

King to keep Labour out of office, and he ominously added: "Some centuries ago a King stood against the common people and he lost his head."[8] The King told MacDonald that he was not affected by these personal attacks, but he took exception to the idea of intrigues at Court. With the exception of his private secretary, part of whose duty was to keep the King informed about the views of men in the various schools of political opinion, and of the assistant-secretaries, he did not discuss these matters with anyone but formed his own judgement. It was a theme that was to recur in Labour history.

King George V was fully aware of the dangers, and, although he was conservative by instinct and dreaded many of the things for which Labour stood, he went out of his way to show consideration to his new ministers, and behaved in a manner that was not only constitutionally correct but exemplary. His consideration showed itself in such matters as an easing of the regulations about Court dress and invitations for ministers' ladies to Court ceremonies. The King's courtesy was reciprocated by MacDonald, and relations of mutual confidence, never to be broken, were quickly established.

At their first meeting the King had taxed MacDonald about the singing of the *Red Flag* at an Albert Hall meeting under his chairmanship. MacDonald asked the King to understand the difficult position in which he stood in relation to his own extremists; if he had tried to prevent the singing of the *Red Flag* on that occasion a riot would have taken place. There had been a serious possibility of the *Red Flag* being sung in the House of Commons, and it had required all his influence to prevent this taking place. Twenty-one years later the melancholy dirge (words by an Irishman to the German tune *O Tannenbaum*) was sung in the House of Commons and shivers ran down Conservative spines.

One early problem in the relations of the Labour government to the Crown harked back to a famous political crisis. As few members of the Labour party felt any desire or qualification to fill the household posts, MacDonald suggested that the practice of making them political appointments should be abandoned, and that the King should himself appoint such Court officials as he thought fit. The King felt that it would be wrong to surround himself entirely with his personal friends, and that some household officials should be drawn from the Labour party. Stamfordham recalled the passions roused by the Bedchamber Question in 1839, and suggested that the leaders of the two older parties should be consulted. Balfour favoured keeping the appointments political, Asquith was willing to see them abolished, and in the end a compromise was reached by which only the three political lords-in-waiting and the three officers of the House of Commons (Treasurer of the Household, Comptroller and Vice-Chamberlain) were to be selected by the Prime Minister.

Though these appointments played a big part in the mind of a

Sovereign meticulous in matters of protocol, they were hardly the most crucial that MacDonald had to make. The formation of the first Labour government presented peculiar difficulties, for in the nature of the case no one on the Labour front bench had held office before; and constitutionally it was necessary to have some ministers in the Lords, where Labour was totally unrepresented. MacDonald did not add to these inherent difficulties by regarding the Parliamentary Labour party, or even his senior colleagues in it, as being entitled to any say in the distribution of offices. It is one of the most remarkable happenings in the evolution of the party system that when Labour was called upon to provide a government it was neither given, nor did it claim, any control over the allocation of ministries; and MacDonald behaved exactly as any of his Conservative or Liberal predecessors with a mandate from the sovereign had done, treating the choice of ministers as entirely a matter between himself and the King. In December 1923 when it seemed likely that Labour would soon be called upon to form a government, MacDonald, Snowden, Henderson, Clynes, Thomas and Webb had met to discuss what course should be followed, and according to Snowden,[9] "Nothing was said about the allocation of ministerial offices beyond that this should be left to the Prime Minister, Webb urging that we should follow in this respect the usual constitutional practice." Thus did the constitution mould the revolutionary party to itself. Henderson, indeed, expressed some misgivings immediately after the meeting about leaving the appointment of ministers to MacDonald, and his misgivings were shared by Snowden when MacDonald retreated to Lossiemouth and began to draft his list of ministers in the greatest secrecy; but no attempt was made to limit MacDonald's freedom of choice.

The difficulty about Labour's lack of representatives in the Lords was eased by three peers not previously associated with the Labour party agreeing to take office. The former Liberal, Lord Haldane, whose removal from the Woolsack still rankled a little even in that philosophic mind, accepted an offer to return to that seat. The former Tory, Lord Parmoor, High Church lawyer and pacifist, became Lord President. The former Viceroy of India, Lord Chelmsford, took the Admiralty. Parmoor and Chelmsford were both Wykhamists, and their acceptance of office started the tradition by which Winchester has become a breeding-ground for the Labour front bench almost as conspicuously as Eton for the Tory front bench. These three appointments not only gave the new administration an air of respectability, but enabled MacDonald to raise a mere trio to the peerage, and those unencumbered by male heirs—the Fabians Olivier and Arnold and General C. B. Thomson, who had shown himself a friend to Labour. The Labour peers won the name of "the thin red line" more by their thinness than by their redness.

The biggest of MacDonald's decisions was to take the Foreign Office himself. The King, mindful of Salisbury at the beginning of the century, queried whether he could combine both offices, and in retrospect the Labour party has blamed the vanity of MacDonald, who was unable to see Henderson filling the bill. He is allowed by impartial historians to have made a notable, even a brilliant, success of his tenure of the Foreign Office, for which he had long trained himself, and in which he saw the chief possibility of a minority Labour government making a mark; but his doubling of the offices took a permanent toll of his powers of concentration and expression, and enhanced the tendency to rhetorical diffuseness already noted in his Bristol election speech. It also made it more difficult for him to maintain the contacts with his followers which a leader should have. Henderson, who had a greater capacity for losing seats than anyone except Masterman, was compensated with the Home Office. Snowden had no rival for the Exchequer, and among the other notables of the party Clynes was made Lord Privy Seal, J. H. Thomas became Colonial Secretary and Sidney Webb President of the Board of Trade. Attlee, with a creditable record as a battalion officer in the Middle East, was given junior office as Under-Secretary for War. The composition of the government was designed to allay suspicion. John Wheatley at the Ministry of Health, Charles Trevelyan at the Board of Education and F. W. Jowett at the Office of Works were the only advanced socialists to be given office.

There was no little resentment in the Conservative party that it found itself in opposition, when it might have had several years of power, as a result of Baldwin's precipitate decision against strong advice to raise again the question of protection, and all the more so in that this had brought the Labour party into office for the first time. It was clearly desirable to give the party an opportunity of saying whether it wished him to continue as leader or not, and this was done at a specially convened meeting in London on 11th February 1924 of Conservative peers, members of Parliament and candidates who had been defeated at the general election.[10] Though not formally a meeting for the re-election of the leader, Baldwin could hardly have survived if there had been a critical vote at the meeting. He took the chair himself, and after admitting that the electors had expressed themselves clearly against protection, he said he did not feel justified in advising the party to renew the proposal for a general tariff until there was clear evidence that the public was disposed to reconsider its judgement. In the meantime the party must strive its hardest for imperial preference and imperial development, and think out a policy for agriculture. He asked the party to give its attention to the pressing problems that had presented themselves since the war—problems of housing, education and the relationship between master and man. This speech disarmed criticism, and Balfour thereupon moved: "That this meeting, having heard the statement by the leader of the party, desires to express its confidence in him and its agreement with the policy he has outlined." Austen Chamberlain supported Balfour's motion, and in his speech pleaded with his hearers not to be tempted into trying to control executive actions as many in the Labour party wished to do.[11]

"Do not weaken the hand of the man whom you choose for your leader, and do not ask of him or of any of us that we should remit executive decisions to be debated in public meetings. That way confusion and disaster lie. That has been the practice of the Labour party, and unless their arrival in power leads to a direct breach with their past traditions, leads to their giving their leaders a confidence, a responsibility, and a power that they have never been entrusted with so far, they will come to an early and speedy disaster.

"Mr. Clynes in the last Parliament, in two speeches which I recall of great wisdom and of great courage, warned them of their danger. Do not let us at this hour, with all our traditions, with all our experience behind us, fall into the error which that new party has committed, and of which it is trying to shake itself free."[12]

This was a generous speech, for Baldwin had done as much as any man alive to destroy Chamberlain's position as leader. The rank and file followed the lead given by Balfour and Chamberlain, and passed the resolution with acclamation and the singing of "For he's a jolly good fellow". It was not merely that Baldwin had convinced them at the meeting. The issue had been settled before it assembled, for in a paradoxical way the losing of the election had given him a greater status in the country than he had ever possessed before. Here, it was felt, was an honest Englishman who would rather lose an election than break a pledge. This was not always to be the feeling of the nation, especially after the Fulham by-election of 1933, but it prevailed in 1924, and Tory candidates knew it. "The instinct of self-preservation alone," as his biographer says, "compelled the body of the party to range themselves under the only leader who could restore them to office."

The first Labour government began its life warily, like a mouse watched by two cats. MacDonald took the precaution of announcing that he would not resign if defeated on a minor issue, but would require defeat on a major issue or on the question of confidence before relinquishing office. He was obliged to keep a watch not only on the Conservatives and Liberals on the opposition side of the house but on his own followers on the benches behind him. Many of them wished to press for the socialist millennium without paying any attention to the realities of the parliamentary situation, and they expected to control their leaders as they had done in opposition, but this ran up against the principle of ministerial and Cabinet responsibility as it had evolved throughout the centuries. The device of a liaison committee, consisting of twelve private members and three ministers, was adopted to serve as a link between the parliamentary Labour party and the government. It was used as a means of bringing pressure to bear on ministers and enforcing changes of policy; and it was itself subject to extra-parliamentary pressures from the national executive and the general council of the Trades Union Congress.

In practice, MacDonald had to counter three oppositions, two in front and one behind him. In a revealing discussion during a Cabinet, reported by Sidney to Beatrice Webb, MacDonald,[13] after eight months in office, said he was sick of it; the party had behaved so badly, the parliamentary executive regarding themselves as a court-martial and the *Daily Herald* queering his pitch perpetually. "It would be a grave misfortune," he added, if the next election gave the party a majority as it was not "fit to govern." As there was no possibility of socialist legislation being passed, MacDonald made it his aim to build a good reputation, or as would now be said to create a good image, for the Labour party by administrative action at home and an easing of tension abroad. The only substantial measure passed in that Parliament was Wheatley's Housing Act; whereas Chamberlain's Act of 1923 provided subsidies for houses to be built by private builders for sale, Wheatley's Act of 1924 gave subsidies for houses to be built by local authorities for renting. The difference in emphasis marked a basic difference in outlook between the Conservative and Labour parties, but the Tories allowed the bill to pass. There had been angry scenes early in the session over Wheatley's annulment of the regulations imposed by Chamberlain on the Poplar Board of Guardians, and Asquith was particularly indignant; but he decided that it was too early to throw out the government, and the issue was one on which they might have considerable support. Clynes and Snowden, in their different offices, nibbled at the problem of unemployment, and Trevelyan initiated a programme of new school building and an increase in grants. Apart from the support of "Poplarization" there was little to offend the Liberals, and Snowden's budget, in which the McKenna duties protecting the motor industry were swept away and many other duties reduced, was wholly Liberal.

Yet it soon became evident that the triangular situation threatened the position of the Liberal party more than that of Labour or the Conservatives. Asquith had hinted that when Labour proved its incompetence and was dismissed, it would not be constitutionally proper to grant a dissolution so long as a government commanding a majority in the House of Commons could be found, that is, a Liberal government supported by the Conservatives. But Labour hated the ignominy of being kept in office on Liberal sufferance, and was not at all disposed to regard Liberals and socialists as two wings of one radical or progressive party. A common bond of feeling began to unite the Labour party and the Conservatives on the subject of the Liberals, and each saw the possibility of great profit in the destruction of that party. The way feeling in the country was running was well shown by a famous by-election in the Abbey division of Westminster. There was an official Conservative in the field, but Winston Churchill thought this too good an opportunity to miss and stood as an Independent Anti-Socialist with the backing of Balfour, Birkenhead and Austen Chamberlain as well as all the publicity of Rothermere and Beaverbrook's newspapers. He lost by forty votes, but in so doing took a notable stride back towards the Conservative fold. The glamour of his fight did not conceal another significant feature of the result. The Liberal candidate secured only a handful of votes, being well beaten even in this West End division by Fenner Brockway of the Independent Labour party.

In his conduct of foreign affairs MacDonald was helped by an able department and the tradition of national support for the Foreign Secretary, as also by the fall of Poincaré in France, but it would be churlish even in his bitterest enemies not to recognize the immense easing in tension among the powers that he brought about by the force of his personality and the single-mindedness of his exertions. Pre-eminent among his triumphs was to secure the French evacuation of the Ruhr and the acceptance of the Dawes report on German reparations; and though his "Protocol for the pacific settlement of international disputes" did not get Conservative support at home, it was signed by France and nine other countries before the Assembly of the League of Nations dispersed and might have been the prelude to a successful disarmament conference.

Though the Labour government's most conspicuous successes were gained in the field of foreign affairs, it was the conduct of foreign relations that was to prove its undoing. The resumption of free economic and diplomatic relations with Russia had been included in the Labour election manifesto, and soon after assuming office MacDonald recognized the Soviet government as the legal government of Russia and invited it to enter into negotiations for a trade agreement. The Russians sent Rakowsky to London for that purpose, and on the British side the negotiations were conducted by the Under-Secretary of State, Arthur Ponsonby, son of Queen Victoria's private secretary, who had been a Liberal member of Parliament—a type of the men whose accession was giving respectability to the Labour party in the eyes of the country. On 5th August Ponsonby informed the House of Commons that the negotiations had broken down. The very next day he announced, not only that negotiations had been resumed, but that two treaties were ready for signature, and that a third, enabling the Soviet government to raise a loan on the London market, would be negotiated once British claims

B

against Russia had been met. Conservatives and Liberals were suspicious that pressure from outside Parliament had compelled the government to resume and conclude the negotiations; and they were particularly angered about the provision for raising money because as recently as June MacDonald had said there was no intention of making a loan to Russia.

About the same time the Campbell case exposed the government to further criticism both from its own followers and from the opposition. An article by J. R. Campbell published in the *Workers' Weekly* on 25th July incited soldiers not to obey when ordered to act against strikers. The Public Prosecutor drew the attention of the Attorney-General, Sir Patrick Hastings, to the article, and Hastings instituted proceedings for sedition under the Mutiny Act. He did not consult the Home Secretary, Henderson. Many Labour members were furious at the prosecution, recollecting that MacDonald himself had in days gone by led the protest against a similar prosecution of Tom Mann. MacDonald himself was angry as soon as he heard of the charge. He sent for the Attorney-General and the Public Prosecutor, as he told the King later, and gave them a bit of his mind. It was conveniently discovered that Campbell had a good war record, and the prosecution was withdrawn. Unfortunately for the government the Communists insisted on making it known that the withdrawal had been made under left-wing pressure, and particularly because they had threatened to call MacDonald as a witness so as to subject him to cross-examination.

Parliament adjourned, and in the recess feeling against the Russian loan grew in the Conservative and Liberal parties. MacDonald's self-confidence was undermined by universal discussion of the "Biscuits scandal" in which he had become involved. It had come to light that earlier in the year he had been presented with a Daimler motor-car by his friend Alexander Grant, chairman of the biscuit manufacturers McVitie and Price, together with 30,000 shares in the company to pay for the running costs. It might have been possible for him to ride the resulting storm if he had not rather imprudently recommended Grant for a baronetcy in the June honours. It was ungenerous to grudge a Prime Minister without personal means the gift of a motor-car, and Grant's other benefactions justified the honour bestowed on him, but in the light of the Labour attitude at the time of the "honours scandal" and the setting up of the Political Honours Scrutiny Committee it was inevitable that MacDonald should be subjected to some scorn and much derision. By the time Parliament met again at the end of September he was rattled.

The purpose for which Parliament had been called together was to pass the Irish Boundary Commission Bill, but although it was contentious even the peers allowed it to go forward for the royal assent without amendment rather than allow the government a fall on this issue. On account of the Liberal respect for freedom for the press, Asquith was not happy about making the Campbell case the *casus stantis aut cadentis*. The general expectation was that Liberals and Conservatives would combine to bring the government down over the guarantee for a Russian loan. It was MacDonald himself who demanded that a debate on the Campbell case should be held as soon as possible, and it was fixed for 8th October. At question time that day he had to admit that a week earlier he had misled the house in saying that he had not been consulted. The debate took place on a Conservative vote of censure moved by Horne. Rising after Horne, Sir Patrick Hastings made such a convincing defence of his own actions that two Tory lawyers announced they intended to vote with the government. There were wider issues at stake, however, than mere legal correctness, as was shown when Sir John Simon moved a Liberal amendment for a select committee to inquire into the circumstances in which the prosecution had been withdrawn. It was, in the words of one hearer,[14] "a vicious and cynical defamation on the Prime Minister". MacDonald in reply announced that if either the motion or the amendment was passed it would be "the end of what has been a high adventure". His combative reply won back the cheers of his supporters. Then Asquith rose to make what was to prove the last and not the least memorable of his speeches in that arena where he had so often excelled. He twitted MacDonald with pronouncing the funeral oration before the doctor had pronounced life extinct. The Liberals would not ask for places on the committee so that there could be no suggestion of a packed jury. His rôle of peacemaker was in vain. For the government J. H. Thomas wound up the debate with a defiant attack on the Conservatives for deserting their own motion in favour of the Liberal amendment. There was now nothing left but to go through the division lobbies, and there voted for the Liberal amendment 364, against 198.

In reporting to the King the end of the first experiment in Labour government MacDonald fairly said:[15]

"The Prime Minister himself does not think that he will offend against the canons of modesty if he puts forward certain claims in regard to the work of the government. They have shown the country that they have the capacity to govern in an equal degree with the other parties in the house ... They have also shown the country that patriotism is not the monopoly of any class or party. Finally, they can justly claim that they have left the international situation in a more favourable position than that which they inherited."

These words are a good summary of the aims which MacDonald set before himself in assuming office, and their achievement was to prove of climacteric importance in the history of party by establishing in the eyes of a great part of the electorate that Labour was "fit to govern".

MacDonald asked for an immediate dissolution, which the King was no less reluctant to grant to him in 1924 than to Baldwin in 1923. It was still good constitutional doctrine that the fall of a government did not necessarily entail the end of the Parliament. The King deplored the dislocation of trade and the fact that the election could not take place on an issue more vital than that which had brought down the administration, and suggested that the parties might come back in the same relative strengths, which would solve nothing; but he had already ascertained that neither Baldwin nor Asquith was able or willing to form a government, and he could hardly refuse to a Labour Prime Minister what he had granted to a Tory the year before. Polling was fixed for 29th October.

The Labour party went to the polls in high confidence that the injustice of their defeat would be remedied by the electorate. MacDonald embarked on a great electioneering campaign all over the country, speaking not only at big meetings in halls but for a few minutes here and there at railway stations and in the open air. It was, said MacNeill Weir[16] who accompanied him from London to Glasgow, "a triumphal tour on the modern American campaigning model". It was also the first election in which the leaders broadcast to the whole nation. MacDonald's speech to a large audience in Glasgow was a failure over the broadcasting system because he did not then know that he had to speak into the microphone. Baldwin, reading a manuscript quietly in the privacy of a room in London, made a much better impression. A new element in the age-old strife of parties had arrived. The party leader of the future would need to project his personality sympathetically over the radio. It was not yet so necessary that he should also look glamorous, or MacDonald would have had the advantage over Baldwin.

The "high adventure" was to contain one further act of drama before the curtain was finally rung down on Labour's first show. The Campbell case was properly relegated to a minor place, and the election was fought on what had always been the real issue—the Russian treaties and particularly the proposed loan. Both Tories and Labour were content to have it so. The Labour party was proud of having established relations with the new proletarian rulers of the vast Russian lands. In the eyes of the Tories, as MacNeill Weir graphically put it, "here was this Labour government conspiring with foreigners, and Communists at that, to hand over good British money to a gang of bloodthirsty revolutionaries".[17] Winston Churchill, who had so far progressed in his return to the Tory party as to be standing at Epping as a "Constitutionalist and Anti-Socialist" with no Conservative opponent, said that the government was preparing to "shake hands with murder".

Though it was the third election in two years, the campaign was fought on both sides with greater keenness than any election since

1905. It was in this atmosphere that the "Zinoviev letter" burst upon the country. MacDonald was on his electoral tour when there came into the possession of the Foreign Office, on 10th October, a copy of a letter to the British Communist party marked "Very secret" and purporting to be signed by the President of the Praesidium of the Third Communist International, Zinoviev, and countersigned by "McManus" (Arthur McManus, a British member of the Praesidium), and the secretary, Kuusinen. After noting that "the time is approaching for the Parliament of England to consider the treaty concluded between the governments of Great Britain and the S.S.S.R.", the letter went on to say :[18]

"The proletariat of Great Britain, which pronounced its weighty word when danger threatened of a break-off of the past negotiations, and compelled the government of MacDonald to conclude the treaty, must show the greatest possible energy in the further struggle for ratification and against the endeavours of British capitalists to compel Parliament to annul it.

"It is indispensable to stir up the masses of the British proletariat, to bring into movement the army of unemployed proletarians, whose position can be improved only after a loan has been granted to the S.S.S.R. for the restoration of her economies and when business collaboration between the British and Russian proletariats has been put in order . . .

"Armed warfare must be preceded by a struggle against the inclinations to compromise which are embedded among the majority of British workmen, against the ideas of evolution and peaceful extermination of capitalism. Only then will it be possible to count upon the complete success of an armed insurrection."

The dilemma of the officials of the Foreign Office as they studied this letter was to know whether it was genuine or a forgery. It said exactly what the leaders of international communists would be expected to say, but that was a reason for caution. Imitation of their style was child's play, and there were many such documents in circulation, put out by White Russians with the object of discrediting the Bolshevik régime. It was only a copy—to this day nobody has claimed to have seen the original—and it was suspicious that "McManus" had used only his surname for signature in the continental manner. The officials do not appear to have taken the letter seriously at first, for it did not reach the higher levels of the department until the 14th. It was then sent after MacDonald on his electoral tour. It is a little curious that it was not first submitted to Ponsonby, who had been conducting the Russian negotiations, or to Haldane, who was deputizing for the Prime Minister in London. MacDonald read the document among other Foreign Office papers just before or just after midnight on 15th/16th October. He asked for the greatest care to be taken to establish whether the letter was authentic or not, and in the meantime a draft note of protest should be prepared to be published simultaneously with the letter if its authenticity was proved.

The draft note was sent to MacDonald on the 21st, but owing to his movements it did not reach him until the 23rd, when he was in his own constituency, Aberavon. He was by that stage physically exhausted with electioneering. The following day he made some alterations in the draft and sent it back to the Foreign Office without further comment or instructions, and without initialling it. Sir Eyre Crowe, the Permanent Under-Secretary at the Foreign Office, received it the same day. By then he had been told that the *Daily Mail* had also received a copy of the letter and intended to publish it in the next issue. He took the view that it would be damaging to the government, and to the Prime Minister personally, if the impression were given that this "incriminating document" had been in the possession of the Foreign Office for some time without any action being taken. Without attempting to consult MacDonald in Aberavon, or Haldane or Ponsonby in London, he sent the protest to Rakowsky, and gave both the letter and note to the press. Next day, Saturday the 25th, with only four more days to go before polling, every newspaper reader in Great Britain knew of the Zinoviev letter. The country was in an uproar.

The King's shrewd comment was:[19]

"Under the circumstances Crowe was quite right to publish the letter, though it has certainly put the P.M. and his Party in a hole & their opponents will make great capital out of it. But it would have been much worse if the *Daily Mail* had published it & the F.O. had remained silent.

"I suppose there is *no doubt* that Z's letter is *genuine*? I see the Communists say it is a forgery."

J. H. Thomas on opening his newspaper had slightly varied the King's metaphor with a graphic "We're bunkered".[20] He and Snowden at once telephoned to MacDonald at Aberavon to get some guidance, but the only reply they received was that he did not attach great importance to the letter, was uncertain about its authenticity, was making inquiries and would in due course refer to it in a speech. Throughout the week-end Labour candidates waited anxiously for the word from MacDonald that never came. The Tories were naturally making the utmost out of the letter—proof, they argued, that Labour was trying to do a deal with people whose avowed aim was to promote revolution in Britain. MacDonald's first inclination was to blame the Foreign Office for publication. In response to his query why the draft letter of protest was published he was told: "You initialled it."[21] In fact he had not, but it would be a quibble to stand on this point as he had sent it back with changes in his own hand. On Monday, the 27th, he made his first public reference to the document, but the time-table of events that he then set out left his followers more confused than ever. The only way in which MacDonald could have mitigated the damaging force of the letter was by a categorical denial of its authenticity. As his parliamentary private secretary later commented: [22]

"The effect of the publication by the Foreign Office of the Zinoviev letter and MacDonald's note of protest was a tremendous blow to the Labour party. Coming as it did, just at the psychological moment, it did the maximum amount of damage. MacDonald, for several critical days, kept the party completely in the dark as to why he had put this weapon in the hands of his opponents. The election was being fought on the Russian loan, and the Prime Minister was accepting as genuine a letter from Russia which was an attempt to stir up revolution in this country."

MacDonald could not deny the authenticity of the letter for two reasons, firstly, because that would be to throw over the senior officials of the Foreign Office without any adequate reason that he could set against theirs, and secondly, because in his heart of hearts he wanted to believe in its genuineness. The constant stream of calumny from Moscow directed at himself made him willing to believe that the Russian government was bent on creating revolution in England; and by accepting the letter as genuine and sending a stiff protest he would strengthen that reputation for patriotism that he had been at so much pains to create.

The effect of the Zinoviev letter was to send into the polling booths on Wednesday, 29th October, over a million voters who might otherwise not have bothered to turn out. The electorate had increased by 800,000 since the past election, but about two million more voted than in 1923; the percentage of electors voting increased from 70·8 to 76·7. The benefit of the swollen poll was chiefly felt by the Conservative party, whose total vote rose from 5,559,690 to 7,864,402; the number of Conservative candidates returned was 413 (compared with 258 at the previous election), and to them must be added seven Constitutionalists—among them Churchill at Epping—so that Baldwin had a following of 420, giving him the massive majority of 225 over all others. Baldwin's gamble the year before had eventually paid a handsome dividend.

It was galling to the Labour party to find that although it polled over a million more votes than in the previous year—5,508,482 instead of 4,347,379—it secured the return of only 150 candidates against 191. The greater poll is mainly explained by the larger number of candidates put into the field, 515 against 428. Though left in a hopeless minority compared with the Tories, the Labour party had no reason to be ashamed of its performance. It must have held almost all who had voted for it the year before, and if it had not been for the flood of Tory reinforcements brought out by the

Zinoviev letter it would have won many more marginal seats; it is indeed possible that the high hopes of victory entertained by Labour on the eve of the poll might have been justified. Labour even made a dent in the hitherto impregnable Unionist citadel of Birmingham. One of the "safe" Tory seats was captured, and in the Ladywood division Neville Chamberlain himself scraped home after three re-counts with a majority of only seventy-seven over Oswald Mosley. The product of Winchester and Sandhurst, and heir to an old baronetcy, Mosley had sat as a Conservative from 1918 to 1922 and as an Independent from 1922, but had now thrown in his lot with the Labour party.

The real casualty in the 1924 election was the Liberal party, and for it defeat was almost total and almost final. It is ironical that at a time when the party was again united in its appeal to the country its total vote should drop from 4,251,573 to 2,929,571, and its members from 157 to a mere forty. It was blamed by one section of the country for putting the Labour party into office and by another for turning it out. Of its leading figures only Lloyd George, safe in his mountain fastnesses, Simon and Mond were returned. Simon was helped by the absence of a Conservative candidate, but Asquith, though similarly assisted at Paisley, crashed before his Labour rival. In the grim struggle provoked by the aims of international com-munism, the country was clearly deciding that there was no half-way house between Conservatism and Socialism. After a period of confusion the two-party system was again reasserting itself, with the Labour party taking the place of the Liberal as the alternative government to the Tories. Apart from the 420 Conservatives, the 150 Labour members and the forty Liberals, there were in the new house only one Irish Nationalist and four Independents to blur the straight edges of the picture.

In such a parliamentary situation it was inevitable that MacDonald should hand in his government's resignation, but he de-layed for a few days in order that the authenticity of the Zinoviev letter might be investigated by a Cabinet committee consisting of himself, Haldane, Parmoor and Henderson. They did not succeed, and announced that they "found it impossible on the evidence be-fore them to come to a conclusion". Their Conservative successors reached the conclusion that it was genuine, but really had no more definite evidence. The Labour party continued to smart under the injustice of the letter, and some years later MacDonald even moved, unsuccessfully, for a full inquiry. To this day the question is still open, but the balance of probabilities is that the letter was not authentic. No one has at any time claimed to have seen the original, and Mr. J. D. Gregory, head of the Northern Department of the Foreign Office at the time of publication, wrote later in a book of memoirs:[23]

"Why this particular rag should have been considered such a singularly tasty morsel, I have never been able to explain to myself. People could at any time have had a whole meal off Zinoviev letters if they had wished. But the October 1924 brand seems to have been responsible for a vast amount of indigestion."

If it was a forgery, the probabilities point to authorship by a group of Russian *émigrés* anxious to discredit the Bolsheviks. The Conservatives certainly exploited the letter to the full, but no responsible person has ascribed it to the Tory party, and the party's worst enemies would never admit that it could be so clever as to concoct such a brilliant election winner. The charge of a conspiracy between officials of the Foreign Office and the *Daily Mail* has been made and needs closer examination. There is no evidence that the *Daily Mail* had anything except a copy of the purported letter, and the probabilities are that it was "planted" on the newspaper as likely to be receptive. In retrospect some of Eyre Crowe's actions look curious, but they can all be explained in the circumstances of the time. He was not so familiar as the head of the Northern Department with the literary *genre* of which the letter was a type, and he may well have thought it so important that the Prime Minister rather than Haldane or Ponsonby ought to deal with it personally; and as a diplomatist of the old school he would not have thought of using the telephone to consult MacDonald in Aberavon when he learnt of the intention of the *Daily Mail* to publish. He acted for what he thought to be the best, but the incident is one of many that could be adduced to show how ministers and parties are at the mercy of innocent actions on the part of their permanent civil servants. The King came blamelessly out of the affair. Against his natural instincts he had given the Labour government full constitutional support, and his parting comment on MacDonald was: "I like him, and have always found him quite straight."[24]

The inescapable upshot of these dramatic events was that Labour was out and the Tories in. On 4th November at 5.30 p.m. the King accepted MacDonald's resignation, and at 7 p.m. he sent for Baldwin and invited him to form a new administration.

23

TORIES *versus* SOCIALISTS
1924–1929

Baldwin re-unites the Conservative party—and gives Churchill the Exchequer—Labour re-elects MacDonald—trade unions assert themselves—Labour dissociates itself from the Communists— Lloyd George becomes the Liberal leader in the House of Commons —but his political fund comes under attack—two tendencies competing in the Conservative party—return to the gold standard—the general strike—Liberal divisions reopened—Trade Disputes and Trade Unions Act—new understanding of industrial workers among Conservatives—Labour moves to the right—final break with Communist party—deteriorating relations with the I.L.P.— Labour and the Nation—closer relations with the Cooperative party—adult suffrage for women

O N the morrow of the election Baldwin's position was unassailable, and he used his position to heal the old wounds in his party, though in doing so he created a few new ones. Austen Chamberlain was brought back to the Foreign Office, and Curzon was left to nurse the grief of his declining years in the dignified position of Lord President; when he died a year later the opportunity was taken to bring in Balfour. Salisbury became Lord Privy Seal. "The little man has given me India," a surprised Birkenhead told his secretariat.[1] Worthington-Evans and Gilmour were given the War and Scottish Offices respectively. Churchill was summoned and asked if he would become Chancellor. He assumed that it must be the modest post of Chancellor of the Duchy of Lancaster, and when he realized that he was being offered the second or third post in the government tears welled into his eyes. This meant that Horne could not be given the Exchequer, and he was hurt by his total exclusion from the government. The Conservative party was again visibly united in Parliament and in the country.

Though there was much criticism of MacDonald's aloofness in office and his handling of the Zinoviev letter, his leadership of the Labour party was confirmed. The Clydesiders had by this time regretted the way they cast their votes in 1922, and Maxton proposed

Lansbury as leader, but he did not get a single vote. The humiliating experiences of the past eighteen months led to demands that Labour should never again form a minority government, and also led to a decline in the importance of the parliamentary party in comparison with the Trades Union Congress. The new mood was expressed by a resolution that Ernest Bevin moved on behalf of the Transport and General Workers' Union at the Liverpool conference of the Labour party in 1925, "that in view of the experience of the recent Labour government, it is inadvisable that the Labour party should again accept office whilst having a minority of members in the House of Commons". MacDonald spoke strongly against the motion, and in reply Bevin said MacDonald's speech was "enough to make Keir Hardie turn in his grave". Bevin's motion was heavily defeated.[2] At the same conference the party took further steps to dissociate itself from the Communists. Though ineligible to become members of the Labour party, Communists were sometimes appointed by trade unions to be delegates to the conference or to local parties. The National Executive recommended that this should no longer be done, and a move by William Gallacher, himself a Communist, to secure the reference back was overwhelmingly defeated.

It was in the Liberal party that heart-searching was deepest. On the morrow of Asquith's defeat the King offered him an earldom, and after taking some months to consider the matter he consented to go to "the charnel house", as he once described the House of Lords.[3] It shows the bitterness of party strife that his revival of the title of Oxford, even though coupled with his personal name as Oxford and Asquith, provoked fierce criticism; and when he was nominated as a candidate for the chancellorship of the University of Oxford on the death of Curzon, this also was made a party issue, and the electors of that venerable institution preferred the worthy but totally undistinguished Lord Cave who had just been elevated to the Woolsack. Though out of the House of Commons, the Earl of Oxford and Asquith, as we must now call him, continued to be leader of the Liberal party because a substantial element was not prepared to have Lloyd George. The Liberal failure was largely attributed by defeated candidates to the failure of Lloyd George to throw his political fund into the common pool, and they were out for his blood. In 1923 the trustees of the fund had contributed about £100,000 to election expenses, but in 1924 only about half that sum. Not being satisfied with the efficacy of the party machine and the quality of the available candidates Lloyd George had declined to part with more. Within a fortnight of the election about a hundred candidates assembled at the National Liberal Club and strong words were used about Lloyd George. On 2nd December the Liberal M.P.s met at the House of Commons, and it was proposed that Sir Godfrey Collins, the chief whip and a follower of Asquith, should act as chairman at party meetings until Asquith should obtain a seat. An amendment to appoint Lloyd George was carried. The following day ten Liberal M.P.s, with Walter Runciman as their leader, formed a "Radical Group" pledged not to compromise either to right or to left. In 1925 a trust with Lloyd George, J. T. Davies, C. A. McCurdy, W. Edge and H. Fildes as trustees was constituted for the administration of the "National Liberal Political Fund", but it continued to be a grievance among Liberals until Lloyd George's death and beyond, and for Lloyd George himself it was a source of moral weakness as much as of financial strength.[4]

Within the soul of the governing Tory party two tendencies struggled for the mastery after the great victory of 1924; they can be seen competing even within the bosom of the Prime Minister, the Chancellor of the Exchequer and the Minister of Health. Some would have had the Conservative majority use their power to consolidate an authoritative and repressive attitude towards the working classes; others recognized that changed conditions called for an equal and honourable partnership between employers and employed. In some moods Tory statesmen sought to extend the principles of social security so as to remove the spectre of want from all homes in the land; in others, they urged a policy of "sound finance", meaning deflation, which could only bring about the conditions which social reform aimed at ameliorating. It took a bitter struggle between capital and labour before both the main parties learnt the necessity of shedding their extremes and treading the paths of moderation. It was in the general strike of 1926 that the modern parties took their shape.

These two principles struggling for possession of the Tory party may be called the tough and the gentle. They may both be studied in the Prime Minister. The gentle was shown in a memorable speech that he made early in the session, one Friday in March, in resisting a move by a private member, F. A. Macquisten, to reopen the question of levies upon trade unionists for the political funds of the Labour party. In simple but telling phrases Baldwin said:[5]

"I want my party today to make a gesture to the country . . . and to say to them : 'We have our majority; we believe in the justice of this bill which has been brought in today, but we are going to withdraw our hand, and we are not going to push our political advantage home at a moment like this . . . We, at any rate, are not going to fire the first shot . . . We believe we know what at this moment the country wants, and we believe it is for us in our strength to do what no other party can do at this moment, and to say that we at any rate stand for peace.' . . . Although I know that there are those who work for different ends from most of us in this house, yet there are many in all ranks and all parties who will re-echo my prayer : 'Give peace in our time, O Lord.' "

Fourteen years later these words were still so vivid in the mind of the fiery Clydesider, Kirkwood, that he wrote to Baldwin:[6] "It seemed to me, this evening, that in your speech you made flesh the feelings of us all, that the antagonism, the bitterness, the class rivalry were unworthy, and that understanding and amity were possible." Yet all the while this same Baldwin, displaying his tough side, was taking no risks, and was quietly making preparations to defeat the general strike which he thought likely sooner or later. One of his first acts as Prime Minister in 1923 had been to revive the Supply and Transport Committee which was responsible in the war for the provision and carriage of essential commodities. It had been used to break the railwaymen's strike of 1919, but had been allowed to run down after 1921. Some of the Labour ministers who followed appear to have been aware of the revival but not to have appreciated its significance. When Prime Minister again, Baldwin saw that the preparations went ahead; but in 1925 the committee was still not a serviceable instrument. In judging Baldwin's actions it must be remembered that there had been no little revival of syndicalist thought and that talk of "direct action" was common.

The other, gentler side of Baldwin was also shown in 1923 by his decision to set up a committee to consider the future of national insurance. Out of office, Conservative leaders continued their researches, and when they came back in 1924 they were ready with a scheme. Within a fortnight of the election Baldwin invited Chamberlain and Churchill to proceed to put it on the statute book. Churchill insisted on making the financial provisions an integral part of his first budget in 1925, but it was Chamberlain who was really the architect of the Widows', Orphans' and Old Age Contributory Pensions Act and who carried it through the house. The act of 1908 had provided non-contributory pensions of up to 5s. a week at the age of seventy, and the acts of 1911 had set up a contributory insurance scheme for certain classes of persons in sickness and unemployment. Under the act of 1925 contributory pensions of 10s. a week were provided for men and women at the age of sixty-five, with pensions for the widows of insured persons and for orphans. The Labour party naturally welcomed the extension of benefits, but was opposed to the introduction of the contributory principle. Chamberlain claimed of the bill that it marked "the greatest measure of social reform that has ever been introduced by any party in any country".[7] The Liberal Unionist philosophy had by now thoroughly permeated the Conservative ranks and Tories had travelled far from their opposition to stamp-licking in 1911. Henceforth the advancement of social security was to prove a matter of rivalry rather than of opposition between the parties.

The same budget speech in which Churchill outlined these social reforms included the fateful announcement of the impending return to the gold standard at the pre-war parity with the dollar which was to prove the cause of so much misery, to bring about a direct clash between Conservatives and the Labour movement, and once again to split the Liberal party. It must be said at once that no statesman intended these consequences and few persons anywhere understood the workings of the financial mechanism. Finance was still treated as a great mystery to be approached only by the initiated. The gold standard was held in reverence by the Treasury, the Bank of England, the City and almost all academic economists; and although it was admitted as unavoidable in time of war that the requirement of meeting obligations in gold should be abandoned, a constant and increasing pressure was brought on the government to return to it as soon as possible, especially by Montagu Norman, the Governor of the Bank. In the spring of 1925 the government yielded, and by a still more fateful error decided to return to the gold standard at the old pre-war parity with the dollar. Although the pound sterling had been rising in value in relation to the dollar, there was still a gap, and the decision was equivalent to putting two shillings on the cost of every pound's worth of British exports. If manufacturers were to hold their own in the markets of the world, it was necessary for them to cut their costs, and almost the only way in which they could cut their costs quickly was to reduce wages. Thus the Tory party again became committed to the deflationary policies which it had pursued in the grim years after Waterloo. Once again the old adage seemed to be justified that we learn nothing from history except that we learn nothing from history. The warmest admirers of Churchill's genius will readily concede that he understood less of the workings of finance than of any of the other great departments of state over which he presided; but in fairness to him it must be conceded that among eminent men only Keynes and Lloyd George saw the dangers of the policy and made public protest. Keynes, who was beginning to formulate the views that have now ousted the old orthodoxy, exposed the fallacies in a series of articles expanded into a pamphlet entitled "The Economic Consequences of Mr. Churchill".[8] Lloyd George, who had been savaged by Keynes in 1919, had learnt from his tormentor. With the resources of his political fund to back him, he picked the brains of Keynes and other young economists and embarked on a series of economic studies—*Coal and Power* and *Land and the Nation* were the earliest—in which he sought to give the Liberal party a new orientation. In this spirit he readily appreciated the dangers of a policy that overnight priced British goods out of many of the markets of the world.

The consequences of "looking the dollar in the face" were immediate and severe. The coal industry suffered first and suffered most, for not only was it Great Britain's chief exporting industry but demand had been artificially inflated by the French occupation of the Ruhr, which had caused a big decline in German exports. It was a piece of bitter irony that MacDonald's success in securing the evacuation of the Ruhr should hit the British miners who were the mainstay of his support. Now the return to the gold standard dealt them an even more grievous blow. In order to maintain exports, the mine owners demanded a reduction in wages and a lengthening of the working-week. The Miners' Federation appealed to the whole Labour movement for support, and in July a national conference of trade union executives ordered an embargo on the movement of coal and authorized the General Council of the Trades Union Congress to call a general strike.

At this dangerous point the government offered a subsidy—previously declared to be out of the question—for nine months while a Royal Commission investigated and made recommendations. The owners' notices terminating the men's employment were withdrawn.

In a later year Baldwin's future biographer, G. M. Young, asked him directly: "Why did you give that subsidy in 1925?" Baldwin's immediate reply was: "We were not ready."[9] He gave the same answer to the Cabinet. The Supply and Transport Committee was not yet perfected; and so Baldwin bought time. Lloyd George charged him with yielding to intimidation and said: "Democracy is doomed if it surrenders to the compulsion of a minority";[10] but Baldwin knew what he was doing.

The commission, presided over by Sir Herbert Samuel, reported in March 1926. It advocated the nationalization of coal royalties, but rejected nationalization of the mines in favour of voluntary amalgamation with compulsory powers in reserve; of more immediate relevance, it advocated that the miners should be given a choice between severe wage-cuts with the existing hours or less severe cuts with an increase in the working day. The government offered to act as recommended by the report if it were accepted by owners and miners; both owners and miners rejected the report. The miners, under the leadership of their secretary, A. J. Cook, then the "humble disciple of Lenin", took as their war cry "Not a penny off the pay, not a second on the day", and the owners announced that unless the federation gave way they would refuse to negotiate nationally and would seek district settlements. They served notices which expired on 30th April. By that time the government's preparations for emergency services were ready. The Trades Union Congress failed to secure a renewal of the subsidy, and when the government broke off negotiations, following the refusal of the *Daily Mail* staff to print a leading article criticizing the unions, they called a general strike. On Monday, 4th May, the greater part of British industry was paralysed.[10]

Nine days that might have ended in civil war passed with restraint and even with good humour. The fundamental qualities of the British people were again called into play and were again equal to the occasion. Churchill was put in charge of the *British Gazette*, the government newspaper printed on the machines of the *Morning Post*. On 10th May Samuel offered to mediate. The General Council of the T.U.C. accepted his good offices, and on the 12th the general strike was called off. As on "Black Friday" in 1921 a quarrel broke out between the Trades Union Congress and the men most directly involved. The General Council considered that the men who had struck in sympathy with the miners had a right to say on what terms a settlement should be brought about, but the Miners' Federation insisted that it was for the miners alone to say on what terms they would resume work, and they continued the strike alone. The government's retort was to repeal the Seven Hours Act and make a working day of eight hours permissible. A grim test of endurance ensued. In October the first returns to work began in the Midlands. A Labour member of Parliament, G. A. Spencer, undertook to get the best terms he could for the Nottinghamshire miners, and was duly expelled from the party. In November the miners' conference recommended the districts to get the best terms they could. On 26th November a delegate conference called off the strike.

The general strike acted as a crucible in which the parties were transformed. The most immediate consequences were felt by the Liberals.

On 6th May, the third day of the general strike, Sir John Simon argued from the Liberal benches in the House of Commons that it was illegal, that every workman who had struck in breach of his service of contract was liable to be sued in the county court for damages, and that every trade union leader who advised and promoted this general course of action was liable in damages to the uttermost farthing of his personal possessions.[11] It says much for the respect in which law is held in Great Britain that these propositions made an immediate impression on the whole country and contributed not a little to the collapse of the strike. Serious revolutionaries would hardly have been deterred by the thought that what they were doing was illegal. Simon went on to argue that trade unionists could not be required to obey unlawful orders as a condition of receiving benefits, and on the merits of the dispute he said the general strike was a tragic blunder from the point of view of the future of trade unionism.

Until Simon's speech the Liberal party had not taken a decisive line. On the opening day of the strike, 4th May, the Liberal "shadow Cabinet" had agreed that while the government must be upheld in resisting the strike, they themselves bore a large share of the responsibility for it; Asquith spoke in that sense in the House of Lords the same afternoon, and in the House of Commons Lloyd George made a plea for a further effort to reach a settlement. After Simon's speech both Asquith and Grey supported the government in demanding the unconditional withdrawal of the strike notices as a condition for further negotiations. On 10th May there was another meeting of the "shadow Cabinet", but Lloyd George excused himself from attending on the ground that the party had been committed to a point of view from which he dissented. "I, therefore," he wrote to the chief whip, Sir Godfrey Collins,[12] "cannot see my way to join in declarations which condemn the general strike, while refraining from criticism of the government, who are equally, if not more, responsible."

Asquith, in despair, reproached Lloyd George with disloyalty, but Lloyd George retorted that it was he who had remained faithful to the original decision of the "shadow Cabinet". On 1st June Asquith wrote to Collins to say that by refusing to attend the "shadow Cabinet" Lloyd George had in effect resigned from it, and he concluded poignantly:[13]

"I am this month completing forty years of service to the Liberal party. For a considerable part of the time I have been its leader, and I have honestly striven during the last two years to recreate and to revive the broken fabric of Liberal unity. It has been a burdensome, and in some of its aspects a thankless task. I will not continue to hold the leadership for a day unless I am satisfied that I retain in full measure the confidence of the party."

On the same day twelve of his colleagues in the "shadow Cabinet", headed by Grey and Simon, wrote to assure him of their support and added:[14] "We have done our best in the interests of Liberalism to work with Mr. Lloyd George in the councils of the party, but we cannot feel surprised at your feeling that confidential relations are impossible with one whose instability destroys confidence."

The hard-won Liberal unity had not lasted long, but in the end it was Asquith who went. In June his health broke down, and early in October he circulated to his colleagues a secret memorandum on the disintegration of the Liberal party since 1918. The extent to which Lloyd George's political fund was a source of grievance is shown in the following passage:[15]

"We have now for nearly three years been trying the experiment of 'Liberal reunion'. There is not one of us that does not know that in practice it has turned out to be a fiction, if not a farce. The control of the party has throughout been divided between two separate authorities: the Liberal Central Office and Mr. Lloyd George's rival machine—the former very scantily, and the latter very richly, endowed. Things came very nearly to a crisis a year ago when the 'Land policy' as embodied in the Green Book was let loose,

C

and followed up by an intensive and expensive propaganda. I insisted upon its being submitted to a representative conference before it was incorporated in the party programme. Prolonged negotiations between Sir Donald Maclean and Mr. Phillipps on the one side, and Mr. Lloyd George on the other, showed that he regarded his accumulated fund as at his own disposal, to be given to, or withheld from, the central office of the party, as a dole, upon such conditions as he thought fit to impose. I was driven myself last December to the humiliating task of making a personal appeal to the better-to-do among our followers to come to the rescue and provide us with a wholly independent fund of adequate amount. Many generous contributions were made, but the fact remains that at this moment our central office is faced in the near future with the certainty of serious and perhaps fatal financial stress, in relief of which it is idle, in the present condition of the party, to expect that a repetition of last year's appeal or any other expedient would meet with a substantial response.

"Meanwhile, the rival organization, well supplied with material resources, is being enlarged in every direction, and has been recruited at its headquarters quite recently by an influx of skilled wirepullers and propagandists."

At the conclusion of this narrative Asquith, now in his seventy-fifth year, stated his decision to lay down the leadership. His resignation was publicly announced in a letter sent to the heads of the English and Scottish Liberal federations on 14th August, and he amplified the reasons in a speech which he was booked to make at Greenock the following night. "The fortunes of the Liberal party," he told his audience,[16] "may fluctuate . . . but there is only one way in which it can ever be killed, and that is by suicide." The reason he gave for this confidence was that : "Liberalism means two things— the preservation and extension of liberty in every sphere of our national life, and the subordination of class interests to the interests of the community." He argued that "the appearance of the Labour party on the scene has done nothing to invalidate, or render obsolete, the mission of Liberalism"; but though the suicidal, or rather fratricidal, impulses of the Liberal party after 1916 must be fully acknowledged, it may be doubted whether, after the decision of the Labour party to pursue its independent course, even a fully united Liberal party could for long have avoided the fate of being ground between the upper millstone of Conservativism and the lower millstone of socialism.

The sequel to Asquith's resignation is curious, for it was Lloyd George who was elected to succeed him as leader of the Liberal party. To have the leader in the Lords had been an exceptional step justified only by Asquith's exceptional prestige. On his resignation, it was inevitable that the leadership should revert to the Commons, and almost equally inevitable that the choice should fall on Lloyd George, already chairman of the party in the Commons. But the knives that had been drawn were not sheathed. Lloyd George's stipulation that in return for subventions from his fund there should be changes in the persons employed at the party headquarters provoked resentment, and on 23rd December Grey called a meeting of like-minded Liberals which included Gladstone's sons Herbert and Henry, Asquith's daughter Lady Violet Bonham Carter, Walter Runciman, Donald Maclean and Vivian Phillipps. It was agreed that an association, to be known as "The Liberal Council", should be formed within the party "to enable Liberals who desire to uphold the independence of the party to remain within it for the furtherance of the aims of Liberalism".[17] Grey accepted the presidency and remained in that office until his death in 1933. Asquith died in 1928, lamented as "the last of the Romans".

The effect of the general strike upon the Conservative party was at first to strengthen the hands of those who wanted strong action against the industrial workers. The general strike, which appeared to those taking part in it as an act of sympathy with the miners, was regarded by most Conservatives as a conspiracy to coerce the government. The immediate consequence was the Trade Disputes and Trade Unions Act of 1927. This measure declared to be illegal all strikes which extended beyond a single industry and were "designed or calculated to coerce the government either directly or by inflicting hardship upon the community". Severe restrictions were placed on the right of peaceful picketing. Civil servants were forbidden to join trade unions with political objects. In practice the most important provision of the measure was that which substituted "contracting in" for "contracting out". Baldwin did not repeat his objection to the change MacQuisten had sought. Under the 1913 act trade unions were authorized, subject to a majority vote of their members, to take part in all lawful forms of political action, provided that electoral and similar activities were financed out of a special political fund from which those who objected could "contract out", that is, decline to pay. The 1927 act laid down that the political fund could be financed only by those who specifically agreed to "contract in", that is, who signed a form agreeing to pay the political levy. Human nature being what it is, many thousands of trade unionists who had paid the political levy when they could avoid it only by "contracting out" and so drawing attention to themselves, now declined to go to the trouble of "contracting in". The affiliated members of the Labour party dropped from 3,388,000 in 1926 to 2,077,000 in 1927, and although a small part of the decline can be attributed to the disaffiliation of the civil service unions the bulk was due to the substitution of "contracting in" for "contracting out". Strong theoretical arguments can be used for either "contracting in" or for "contracting out", and the issue cannot be settled as a matter of political philosophy; it was, however, a question of the utmost practical consequence to the financing of the Labour party, and the act of 1927 was a source of bitter grievance until repealed nineteen years later. In 1929 the income of the Labour party from affiliation fees was only three-quarters what it had been in 1927, and owing to the depletion of their funds trade unions had also to restrict their financing of candidates.

Though the immediate consequence of the failure of the general strike and the crushing of the miners' resistance was to strengthen the authoritarian elements in the Conservative party, ultimately it led through greater understanding, and through the working of human compassion to a new sympathy with the aims of the labouring masses. Just as the Roman patricians dreaded a revolt by the slaves, so the Conservative party had conjured up a vision of the fearful possibilities of direct industrial action. When it was proved that an attempt to coerce the government by industrial action had little support and could easily be defeated and when it was shown that in a direct clash between the state and the trade unions the state was bound to win, Conservatives breathed more freely and were prepared to think more kindly of labour. Having first made sure they could knock labour down, Conservatives readily offered it a helping hand to get up again. This accorded with the natural instincts of the Prime Minister, and Baldwin wove into Conservative philosophy a new respect for the dignity of labour and the rights of the working classes. The new mood found expression in the conversations proposed by Sir Alfred Mond, now become a Conservative, and a group of other large employers to the Trades Union Congress with a view to improving industrial relations. They were accepted by Ben Turner as chairman of the General Council, and the Mond–Turner proposals, as they became known, were embodied in an interim report issued in July 1928.

The change in the Conservative attitude was made the easier because the Labour party and the whole Labour movement went through a transformation after 1926 which may be described in the language of the continent as a move to the right. From the outbreak of the Russian revolution in 1917 to the general strike of 1926 the Labour movement had been ambiguous in its attitude to the question of using violence to achieve the overthrow of the existing order. After the general strike the Labour leaders went to great pains to free the party and movement from such imputations. During the period between the general election and the general strike the Parliamentary Labour party had taken a back seat. Discredited by its failure in office, it had left the initiative to the trade union leaders, and the parliamentary leaders played virtually no part in the events leading to the general strike. Though MacDonald had been present at the delegate conference that took the decision to strike, and though he had made an eloquently ambiguous speech which was taken by his audience as throwing in his lot with the strikers, in fact he was then and always had been opposed to the notion of sympathetic strike action. When the strike collapsed, the parliamentary party began to recover its prestige in relation to the trade unions, and MacDonald's personal inclination to moderate courses soon found expression in a more rigorous proscription of Communists and in a deepened breach with the Independent Labour party.

Communist parties throughout the world were weakened in 1927 by Chiang Kai-shek's overthrow of the Chinese Communists, and the British party was no exception. The British Labour movement did not approve of the government's raid on the Russian trading agency in London—"Arcos"—and the severance of diplomatic relations with the Soviet Union, but it was resolved to crush "subversive activities" within its own ranks, and a number of local trades councils and Labour parties which insisted on maintaining Communist connexions were disaffiliated. A controversy then broke out between those Communists who still believed in trying to achieve a "United Front" with the Labour party and those who favoured outright opposition. This was sharpened in 1928 when the Communist International ordered national parties to abandon United Front tactics and attack Social Democratic parties. The majority of the central committee of the Communist party of Great Britain clung to the policy of the United Front, but in 1929 they were ousted by the minority led by Harry Pollitt and Palme Dutt. One of the decisions then taken was to set up a daily newspaper, and the *Daily Worker* came into existence in 1930. The breach with the Labour party was by this time complete and final.

After the fall of the first Labour government the Independent Labour party proceeded to work out a policy of "Socialism now" or "Socialism in our time" as it came to be called. This was adumbrated in a series of reports to the party conference in the years 1925–8, and the party committed itself especially to the principle of the "living wage", that is, to the doctrine that the provision of a minimum income adequate for a satisfying life should be made a first charge on the national product, and that all other matters should be subordinated to this objective. In 1927 the I.L.P. delegates sought to win the endorsement of the Labour party conference for this view. MacDonald had already dismissed the I.L.P. proposals as "flashy futilities",[18] and the I.L.P. in revenge refused to nominate him as party treasurer or even as a delegate to the conference, so that he was compelled to secure nomination from his local party at Lossiemouth. This was the end of his effective connexion with the I.L.P., and Snowden actually resigned from it a few months later. At the conference the national executive avoided a show-down by proposing that the I.L.P. proposals be examined in conjunction with the trade unions. It soon became clear that the trade unions were divided on the question of children's allowances, which was an essential element in the I.L.P. programme, and the proposals were again raised at the 1928 and 1929 conferences without finality.

In the meantime the differences had extended over a much wider field, including such varied topics as working-class resistance to war, the emancipation of India, withdrawal from Egypt, nationalization of the banks and birth control. It became evident in 1927 that the Labour party was moving in an opposite direction from the I.L.P. when it set out to produce a new programme to supersede *Labour and the New Social Order*. After MacDonald had moved a resolution at the party conference authorizing the preparation of a new election programme, Bevin asked for "a short programme of immediate objectives that Labour could really hope to accomplish"; then they would be able to go back and say: "At least we have done what we said we would: we have delivered the goods."[19] What eventually emerged was *Labour and the Nation*. In a preface MacDonald said "the Labour party, unlike other parties, is not concerned with patching the rents in a bad system, but with transforming capitalism into socialism"; and the document itself described the Labour party as "a socialist party"; but the only definite commitments in this direction were to nationalize the land, coal and power, transport and communication services and life insurance, and to make the Bank of England a public corporation. The document consisted for the most part of a series of sonorous general principles. When the draft was submitted to the party conference at Birmingham Maxton and Wheatley and other I.L.P. speakers urged that it was neither a declaration of socialist aims nor an immediate programme for the next election; it might take fifty years to achieve, and at the end the result would not be socialism but controlled capitalism. There was point in the criticism. MacDonald had no wish to enter an election bound by a programme that would frighten electors, and therefore sought only to depict Labour's "conception of society" so that he and his immediate colleagues could be free to draw up a practical election programme when the occasion arose. In the light of subsequent events it is significant that the questions of currency, banking and credit were dealt with only in a supplement. In debate Snowden said that although he favoured in principle nationalization of the joint stock banks the time was not ripe for it so long as the greater part of trade and industry remained in private hands; and Pethick-Lawrence urged that public ownership of the Bank of England would make it unnecessary to take over the joint stock banks. Various amendments were made to the draft, but they did not alter its general character, and *Labour and the Nation* became for the next few years the official statement of the party's aims. The I.L.P.

can hardly be blamed for regarding it as a retreat from, rather than a statement of, socialist objectives.

The same Birmingham conference which endorsed *Labour and the Nation* also approved a statement on party loyalty which among other things laid down that "members of political parties declared by the annual conference or by the national executive committee in pursuance of conference decisions to be ineligible for affiliation to the Labour party" were thereby ineligible as delegates to national or local Labour party conferences or meetings.[20] It was the beginning of the list of proscribed organizations by which the Labour party sought to prevent infiltration by Communists.

As the Labour party moved away from the Communists and the I.L.P. Cooperators began to feel less hesitation about their alliance. The Cooperative Congress of 1925 approved a resolution favouring a working arrangement with Labour party in the matter of candidates and elections; and an agreement drawn up by a joint committee of the Labour and Cooperative parties was accepted at the Cooperative Congress of 1927, though only by the narrowest of margins. Under the same agreement local Cooperative parties became eligible for affiliation to divisional Labour parties. From 1925 the Cooperative party was permitted to hold its own annual conference, though still kept subordinate to the Cooperative Congress. One large society, the Royal Arsenal, decided in 1927 to affiliate directly to the Labour party instead of belonging to the Cooperative party; the fear of this happening on a large scale made Cooperators readier to accept the Labour party's terms for electoral arrangements, but the example of the Royal Arsenal was not followed.

The closing years of this Parliament were uneventful so far as the party system is concerned. Neville Chamberlain's mind was thoroughly at home in the recasting of the finance of local administration that was eventually embodied in the Local Government Act of 1929. His brother Austen had won a personal triumph in 1925 by the conclusion of the Locarno agreements for regional security in western Europe, but these were not matters of party conflict except in so far as they were a substitute for the Geneva Protocol. Foreign policy became an issue between the parties in 1927 when the measures taken by the government to protect British interests in China against the nationalist forces led to fierce denunciation by the Communists and the I.L.P., and more restrained protests by the Labour party. This was not wholly to the taste of Labour members, for one of them, Haden Guest, resigned his seat and fought a by-election, unsuccessfully, in support of the government.[21] In the same year Lord Cecil of Chelwood, as Lord Robert Cecil had now been made, resigned office—he was Chancellor of the Duchy—because he found his instructions as principal representative on the Disarmament Commission at Geneva unpalatable. It was the last office he held and marked a permanent estrangement from the Conservative party to which his family had so signally contributed. It marked, moreover, the beginnings of a running dispute between the League of Nations Union, of which Cecil was president from 1919 to 1945, and the Tory leadership which was to play a major part in politics in the years ahead.

One of the government's acts towards the close of the Parliament was to carry a bill extending the vote to women at the age of twenty-one—the "flapper vote", as it was nicknamed in one section of the press. The act of 1918, it will be recalled, had given the vote to women at the age of thirty. Thus was completed the process begun in 1832, and adult suffrage was at last achieved. The Representation of the People Act, 1928, added seven million voters to the register and brought the total number of electors to twenty-eight millions. It was expected by Baldwin that the newly enfranchised women would be a Conservative force in politics, and on the whole the expectation has not been unjustified; but on the first occasion that the younger women had the chance of casting a vote he was disappointed.

24

SECOND LABOUR
GOVERNMENT
1929–1931

*General election of 1929—Liberal bid for power—Baldwin urges
"Safety first"—Labour and unemployment—appearance of
Nationalist candidates—Labour the largest party in the new house
—MacDonald forms his second government—cleavage in the Conservative party over India—Churchill's denunciation of Baldwin's
policy—Beaverbrook and Rothermere's campaign for Empire free
trade—Baldwin's triumph—balance of power held by the Liberals
—humiliating life of Labour ministers—Simonite Liberals break
with Lloyd George—and drop their insistence on free trade—the
deepening economic crisis—Mosley's break with the Labour party
—the I.L.P.'s attempt to be "a party within a party"*

THE Parliament elected in the autumn of 1924 was allowed to
run out almost the whole of its allotted span of five years. To
have waited the whole period would have been to risk the danger
of an election at some unpropitious moment, and in the spring of
1929 Baldwin decided that the right hour had come. He asked for a
dissolution, and polling was fixed for 31st May.

Now at last the acknowledged leader of the Liberals, Lloyd
George threw the full weight of his fund into the contest, and 512
Liberal candidates took the field, more than had done so for many
years or were ever to do so again. In his biography[1] Mr. Frank
Owen reckons that in 1927 the fund contributed £300,000 towards
the expenses of the forthcoming election, in 1929 a further £20,000,
and between 1927 and 1930 a further £60,000 for the expenses of
the Liberal headquarters, a total of £380,000. The Liberal candidates
fought on a carefully prepared policy which had advanced beyond
the Liberalism of Asquith in the direction of state intervention as
far as Asquith's Liberalism had gone beyond that of Gladstone. A
team of brilliant economists whom Lloyd George had gathered
round him—Maynard Keynes, Josiah Stamp, Walter Layton and
Hubert Henderson among them—carried out a series of searching
inquiries into the economic problems of the day, and a stream of
scintillating reports made the intellectual appeal of the Liberals

higher than that of any other party. *Coal and Power* and *Land and the Nation* were followed by *Towns and the Land* and *Britain's Industrial Future* (the "Yellow Book"), and all culminated in the Liberal election programme with the confident title *We Can Conquer Unemployment* (the "Orange Book"). The main element in the remedy was a massive programme of public works financed by budget deficits. It was the forerunner of Roosevelt's "New Deal" in the United States.

Though the economists supplied the ideas and Lloyd George the money and the dynamism, all was not well in the Liberal ranks. Runciman and his radical group remained discontented, while Grey and his council looked askance at the new doctrines and new methods. Simon was with them in spirit, but from 1927 to 1930 he was deeply engaged, and much out of the country, as chairman of the statutory commission to inquire into the working of the system of Indian government set up by the Montagu–Chelmsford reforms; among the six other members of the Commission was Attlee from the Labour side. It was a gracious act on Baldwin's part, as well as a sign of closer collaboration to come, that he induced the Conservative candidate, David Maxwell Fyfe, not to stand against Simon in the Spen Valley.[2]

Baldwin correctly divined that the real challenge would come from the Labour party rather than the Liberals, but was so confident of continuing in office that he speculated about the changes he would make—Neville Chamberlain for the Exchequer, if Churchill would take India, if Birkenhead would go back to the Woolsack, which Birkenhead was not prepared to do. His uninspiring formula for keeping the socialists out was "Safety first". It was the opposite strategy from the reckless plunge that lost him the 1923 election, but electorally just as disastrous. The great problem of the day, as Lloyd George sensed, was unemployment, and those who suffered from it, as well as those who feared they might, were ready to try new, even desperate, remedies. With fluctuations up and down, the number of permanently unemployed had kept well above the million mark, and the problem had become chronic.

The Labour party, like Lloyd George, knew that the electors were demanding a cure for unemployment, and its spokesmen made no secret of their claim to possess it. They claimed that *We Can Conquer Unemployment* was culled from *Labour and the Nation*, which was regarded by the extremists as proof of the identity between MacDonaldism and capitalism. At the last moment G. D. H. Cole was asked to write a Labour counterblast, *How to Conquer Unemployment*. Though the intellectual backing of the Liberal proposals was greater, Labour had captured the emotional support that once sustained the Liberal party. It fought the election on a more massive scale than ever before, with 571 candidates for the 608 contested seats.

In pursuance of its new policy, the Communist party opposed Labour vehemently. As it could not field more than twenty-five candidates, it used them especially to fight Labour leaders regarded as peculiarly obnoxious—MacDonald, Clynes, Morrison, Margaret Bondfield and Attlee among them.

A novel feature of the election was the appearance of Nationalist candidates in Wales and Scotland. *Plaid Cymru*, "the party of Wales", was founded in 1925, largely by Saunders Lewis, lecturer in Welsh language and literature at the University College, Swansea. It is curious that the leader of the nationalist movement in a country where Protestant Nonconformity was still a major force should have been a Roman Catholic. The National party of Scotland was founded in 1928 and later became known as the Scottish Nationalist party. It was formed by some members of three earlier bodies—the Scottish Home Rule Association, the Scots National League and the Scottish National Movement (itself a breakaway from the League)— and in due course the three older bodies disappeared. The National party had fought a by-election in North Midlothian early in 1929.[3]

Polling brought out the vagaries of the British electoral system. Conservative candidates obtained 8,666,243 votes but only 260 seats, whereas Labour candidates with rather fewer votes in total, 8,360,883, secured 288 seats. Liberal candidates polled 5,301,000 votes, but only fifty-nine of them were successful. No Communist was elected and most of them lost their deposits, as did the Nationalist candidates in Wales and Scotland. The Speaker and seven Independents completed the membership.

Conservatives were disappointed, and Labour more successful than it had dared to hope. This was mainly because electors who might have been expected to vote Liberal gave their vote to the Labour candidate. The belief that under the British system "a Liberal vote is a wasted vote" was beginning to have a fatal effect on the fortunes of the party. This time there was no last-minute scare such as the Zinoviev letter had been, and the fine weather of a spring election was favourable to a maximum Labour poll at a time when motor transport was still mainly in the ownership of the "capitalist classes" and not so restricted in its use as it was later made.

Though Labour had come back the largest party, it was only a minority of the whole house, but despite all the talk after 1923 of "never again" no suggestion was made that Labour should not take office. The possibility of a stalemate had been canvassed in advance, but no form of coalition was practicable. A Tory–Liberal coalition was out of the question, not only because Baldwin would have nothing to do with Lloyd George but because the Liberals would require a pledge of no general tariff and a reform of the electoral system. A Liberal–Labour coalition was ruled out because Lloyd George was not prepared to "carry the ladder and hold it in its place for five years whilst the socialists are up on the scaffolding doing all the building".[4]

The King's government had to be carried on, but by whom? In 1923 the King had taken the view that the Conservatives should remain in office until defeated in the House of Commons, but in 1929 he agreed with Stamfordham that the people had spoken directly, and made no demur when Baldwin came to Windsor to hand in his government's resignation. Stamfordham saw MacDonald the same day and sensed that there were some difficulties, but within twenty-four hours MacDonald agreed to form an administration. His chief difficulty was that he wanted J. H. Thomas at the Foreign Office, as the King did, but Henderson would no longer be denied that department. MacDonald again contemplated doubling the parts, and seriously offered to stand down as Prime Minister and to be Foreign Secretary alone, but that was unacceptable to his colleagues. In other respects MacDonald had an easier task in forming a government than in 1924, for fifteen members of his previous Cabinet were available. It is significant of the rightward trend of his views that Wheatley, Jowett and J. C. Wedgwood were dropped, and even more remarkable was the appointment as Attorney-General of Sir William Jowitt, who had only just been elected as a Liberal at Preston. Jowitt resigned his seat, fought the by-election as a Labour man and won; Lloyd George after some thought did not put up a Liberal against him, but months later in the House of Commons he got his own back by labelling him among those "genuinely seeking work".[5] The ex-Liberal Christopher Addison, who had been elected at Swindon as a Labour candidate, was given office for the first time in a Labour administration in the modest post of Parliamentary Secretary to the Ministry of Agriculture. The only concession to the left wing was the appointment of Lansbury to the harmless post of First Commissioner for Works, but Lansbury successfully used this office to lever himself into the Cabinet.

The years 1929–39 were climacteric in the British party system, and all the parties were transmuted. It is convenient to deal first with the Conservatives.

The loss of the 1929 election, like that of 1923, was very quickly to prove of great advantage to the fortunes of the Tory party, for each led to a huge majority at the next election and a long period of effective rule, but it was not seen in this light at the time. If the loss of these elections had been deliberately planned, Baldwin would have stood out as a supremely cunning political strategist, but in fact he was doing his best to win and he lost. There was much recrimination, and those who differed from him over major questions of policy did their utmost to remove him from the leader-

ship. Two major cleavages developed, over India and over Empire
free trade.

Baldwin had long accepted the need for a steady development of
self-governing institutions in India. In 1925 when a successor to
Reading as viceroy had to be appointed, the King suggested Edward
Wood.[6] Baldwin's immediate reaction was, "I cannot spare him,"
but on reflexion he decided that: "India must have the best that we
could send." Lord Irwin, as Wood now became, had a close approxi-
mation of ideals and views to Baldwin and by his patent honesty
won the respect of the Indian leaders. Nearly two years in advance
of the period stipulated by the India Reform Act of 1919 Baldwin
appointed the Simon commission to consider the lines of further
constitutional advance. The fact that membership was confined to
British peers and members of Parliament provoked a boycott in
India; and the chairman's legal mind was better adapted to analysing a given situation and finding the objections to any course of
action rather than to cutting through the difficulties to an instinctively recognized solution.

The commission was still at its task when the Conservative
government fell and Wedgwood Benn succeeded Birkenhead as
Secretary of State. Benn summoned Irwin home for consultations,
and the Conservative viceroy had no difficulty in persuading the
Labour minister that there should be a round-table conference
attended by representatives of the United Kingdom, the Indian
States and British India. In 1927 he had opposed Indian membership
in the Royal Commission, but experience had shown him that there
could be no progress without Indian participation. It was made to
appear that the suggestion had come from the Simon commission.
This was not all. Irwin asked for authority to say that the British
government recognized the goal as being dominion status, which by
that time meant that India would be in no way subordinate in any
aspect of its internal or external affairs to Great Britain. Permission
was readily given, and back in India on 31st October 1929 Irwin
not only announced the round-table conference but made the historic declaration:[7]

"In view of the doubts which have been expressed both in Great
Britain and India regarding the interpretation to be placed on the
intentions of the British government in enacting the statute of 1919,
I am authorized on behalf of his Majesty's government to state
clearly that in their judgement it is implicit in the declaration of
1917 that the natural issue of India's constitutional progress, as
there contemplated, is the attainment of dominion status."

A thrill ran through politically minded India, but the members of
the commission were dismayed, feeling that the ground had been
cut from under their feet, and a large section of the Tory party was
angry. As the Conservatives were now in opposition, the natural

tendency was to suppose that the socialist government had imposed the policy on the viceroy. It came to light in due course that Baldwin had been consulted. While he was on his annual holiday in France a private secretary from Downing Street had presented himself and had asked for his concurrence in the issue of the announcement about dominion status "in the event of the Simon commission being consulted and agreeing and the consent of all parties being obtained". Baldwin agreed, on these conditions. A similar approach was made to Reading, and he also agreed, on the same conditions; Lloyd George as the leader of the Liberals was prepared to follow his advice. The Simon commission was not in fact consulted, and the viceroy was authorized to make the statement. In the subsequent exchanges in the House of Commons Lloyd George taunted Benn, a physically small man, with being a "pocket edition of Moses" and drew the damaging retort: "But I never worshipped the golden calf."[8] Even ex-Liberals could not forget that political fund.

Though Baldwin had made his concurrence subject to consultation with the Simon commission, he was wholly behind Irwin, and the realization that this was so produced a grave split in the Conservative ranks. At a meeting of the "shadow Cabinet" Birkenhead, with a lawyer's precision, launched a scathing attack on the use of the phrase "dominion status", but his death in the following year removed this formidable critic. He was supported by Austen Chamberlain and Salisbury, but Baldwin found valuable aid for his and Irwin's ideals in Hoare. In December, while the round-table conference was in session, Churchill denounced the Indian claims as "absurd and dangerous pretensions"; and from that point he emerged as the strongest critic of the Irwin–Baldwin policy. He opened a campaign within the Conservative party which had momentous consequences for himself, his party, the country and indeed the world.

When the Simon commission formulated in June 1930 its principal recommendation, provincial autonomy, it was already outstripped by the movement of Indian opinion. The first session of the round-table conference in November made notable progress even though boycotted by Gandhi—dismissed by Churchill as a "half-naked fakir"—and the Congress. During the session it became clear that nothing short of an all-India federation would be acceptable. The conference adjourned in January until 7th September 1931—the date was later to assume unexpected importance.

The Conservative "shadow Cabinet" had not met since its discussion of Irwin's statement, but in its place there had been frequent meetings of a small "business committee". Hoare gave it as his view to the committee that the demand for an all-India federation should be accepted, but he found that Churchill resented any proposals for responsibility at the centre, however carefully safe-guarded. Churchill resigned from the "business committee" and began a campaign of systematic and relentless opposition against the Irwin–Baldwin–Hoare policy which was his major preoccupation for the next four years and put him in conflict with the Conservative leadership for much longer. He was out of office and forced to play the rôle of a lone Cassandra when his services were most needed by the state and by the whole free world. It says much for the loyalty of his constituents and the tolerance of the Conservative party that he was able to sustain this rôle of critic within the party for so long, but it was a national disaster that he should have excluded himself from high office at a time when Hitler and his National Socialists were rising to power in Germany; for while there is something in Hoare's later argument that "his action, by separating him from his Conservative colleagues, left him free and untrammelled to fight his great campaign of resistance to Hitler, and to become, amidst general acclamation, the alternative Prime Minister when Chamberlain resigned",[9] how much better it would have been if he had been in a position to strangle National Socialism at the first signs of danger. The tragedy is all the greater in that history has proved him to have been thoroughly wrong in his judgement of India—and in years to come he was destined to offer India far more than he would have refused in 1931. It is also strange, as Sir Evelyn Wrench has noted,[10] that the old Liberal who had shown his sympathy with the Boers and taken a prominent part in Irish peace-making, should have thrown in his lot with the "die-hards" over India. The strong romantic element in Churchill's constitution prevailed on this occasion over the rational. Echoing words that his father had used as Secretary of State for India, he could not bear the thought of "casting away that most truly bright and precious jewel in the crown of the King, which more than all our other dominions and dependencies constitutes the glory and strength of the British Empire".[11]

India was not the only front on which Baldwin had to fight, nor Churchill the only enemy with whom he had to contend in these critical years. Beaverbrook and Rothermere conducted through their newspapers a virulent campaign against him, both on the subject of concessions to India, and on their own pet topic of Empire free trade. At the mass meeting following the party conference in November 1929 Baldwin had held out an olive branch to Beaverbrook—"I think we owe a word of gratitude to one—not always a supporter of our party—Lord Beaverbrook—for bringing before the country the idea ... of a United Empire"[12]—and in speaking to the party's central council in March 1930 he came out in favour of an empire economic conference to be followed by a referendum if an agreement involving a tax on food was reached. Beaverbrook was satisfied for the time being, but Rothermere continued his attacks, Beaverbrook resumed his, and in June Baldwin summoned a meeting of members and candidates at the Caxton Hall. He compared the action of the two noblemen with that of the Trades Union Congress in trying to impose a policy on the government of the day in 1926, and accepted their challenge to run candidates all over the country. He accused Beaverbrook of changing his mind, but for Rothermere he had worse to come. Drawing a letter from his pocket he read: [13]

"I cannot make it too abundantly clear that, under no circumstances whatsoever, will I support Mr. Baldwin unless I know exactly what his policy is going to be, unless I have complete guarantees that such policy will be carried out if his party achieves office and unless I am acquainted with the names of at least eight, or ten, of his most prominent colleagues in the next ministry."

With consummate artistry Baldwin drew a picture of himself saying to the King: "Sire, these names are not necessarily my choice, but they have the support of Lord Rothermere." A more preposterous and insolent demand, he added, was never made on the leader of any political party. He won a great ovation in the House of Commons that afternoon, but the cheers lasted longer on the Labour benches, and he felt it prudent to warn Irwin that the party could not accept any responsbility for repetition of the term "dominion status" at that stage.

Beaverbrook and Rothermere kept up their campaign throughout the summer. Neville Chamberlain, who had succeeded Davidson as chairman of the party organization in June 1930, was put in a difficult position as his sympathies were all with taxes on foreign food and he knew he was the most likely successor. A party meeting to decide whether or not to go on under Baldwin's leadership, which was attended by peers, M.P.s and candidates, was held at the Caxton Hall, London on 30th October, and Colonel J. Gretton's resolution declaring a change in the leadership of the party to be in the national interest was defeated by 462 votes to 116. Another engagement had been won, but the struggle to remove Baldwin continued relentlessly, and was sharpened when the round-table conference brought the difference over India into the open. In the House of Commons, Baldwin censured the government for refusing to consider the offers to extend empire trade made by the Dominions, and Thomas said the Canadian offer was " 'umbug". [14]

Baldwin's most dangerous hour came in February when Sir Robert Topping, the general director of the central office, wrote to Chamberlain, [15] "From practically all quarters one hears the view that it would be in the interests of the party that the leader should reconsider his position"—in plain English, that he should resign, or so Baldwin understood it when, after much hesitation and consultation, Neville Chamberlain showed it to him after the omission of some wounding phrases. He first thought of retiring to Astley, but a visit from Bridgeman, "like an admiral in a gale",[16] brought back the fight in him. The languid, indolent Baldwin of the popular legend disappeared, and in his place there stood a fighting tiger. The death of Worthington-Evans had created a vacancy in the representation of St. George's, Westminster. A former minister, Moore-Brabazon, who had been expected to become the official Conservative candidate was unacceptable as he had declared that he could not support Baldwin's policies. Sir Ernest Petter, a blameless West Country manufacturer, offered himself as an independent Conservative with strong backing from the Beaverbrook and Rothermere press. "Gandhi is watching St. George's" was their slogan. In these circumstances Baldwin told Chamberlain that he intended to apply for the Chiltern Hundreds and offer himself as a candidate in the by-election. The dramatic proposal appalled Chamberlain, Topping and others, and no more was heard of it. Duff Cooper stepped into the breach at St. George's. At Newton Abbot on 6th March Baldwin supported the government in seeking to continue the round-table conference, and Duff Cooper echoed him. Three days later the India committee of the Conservative party welcomed "the decision of Mr. Baldwin that the Conservative party cannot be represented at any further round-table conference to be held in India",[17] and it looked as though he had been repudiated by his party. In the House of Commons on the 12th he explained that Conservatives would not send a delegation to a conference in India, but would welcome another session in London; there were differences in the Conservative party, but unless all parties cooperated the Indian problem would prove insoluble. If his critics were in a majority, he demanded that they should choose a new man to lead them, but if not he asked them to refrain from throwing difficulties in the way of those who had undertaken an almost super-human task. He won a great parliamentary triumph, and it was followed by an even greater public triumph in a speech at the Queen's Hall in support of Duff Cooper's candidature. A charge that he had proved his incapacity to govern by losing his father's fortune gave him his opening, and he said:[18]

"The papers conducted by Lord Rothermere and Lord Beaverbrook are not newspapers in the ordinary acceptance of the term. They are engines of propaganda for the constantly changing policies, desires, personal wishes, personal likes and dislikes of two men.... What the proprietorship of these papers is aiming at is power, and power without responsibility, the prerogative of the harlot throughout the ages."

At last his opponents had to acknowledge defeat. Duff Cooper was returned by a majority of over five thousand, and Baldwin

D

received no further challenge to his leadership. Chamberlain decided to escape from "an acutely difficult position"[19] and gave up the chairmanship of the party organization in April. (He was succeeded by Lord Stonehaven.) Within six months Baldwin had the whole Conservative party behind him in cooperating with MacDonald in a "National" government, but it will be hard to understand how this startling change could have come about if the mutual understanding between the two men on the subject of India over the previous two years is not first appreciated. Baldwin, like Irwin, knew that the "die-hard" policy of retaining the control of Indian affairs in London was impracticable, morally indefensible and the negation of British policy since 1917. He found himself far more in sympathy with the leader of the Labour party than with the "die-hard" section of his own party, which then, by one of history's ironies, was led by Churchill. His victory over his critics brought about a permanent transformation in the Conservative party.

Though only fifty-nine in number, or fifty-eight after Jowitt crossed the floor, the Liberals held the balance in the House of Commons and so enjoyed an importance out of all proportion to the benches they occupied. The 289 Labour members could not hope to carry any measure against the opposition of the 260 Conservatives without at least the abstention of the Liberals; nor could the Conservatives defeat the government without Liberal support. It was the last occasion on which the Liberals were to enjoy the semblance of power; and Lloyd George, sustained by the return of his son Gwilym for Pembroke and his daughter Megan for Anglesey, set out to make the most of it.

In fact, he was able to make little use of the balance of power. Baldwin was not disposed to take the smallest step to court or conciliate him, and MacDonald was only too glad of an excuse to avoid anything that looked like socialist legislation. There was an ugly episode early on when Lloyd George opposed a Coal Mines Bill requiring district quotas and minimum prices because it offended too much against the principles of free trade, but the government were allowed to scrape home on second reading by eight votes. Samuel on behalf of the Liberals insisted successfully that proposals for the compulsory amalgamation of mines should be added. Later in the bill's progress Lloyd George was assailed by a new Welsh member for wanting, not cheap coal, but cheap colliers, and was visibly shaken because, so one commentator said, in Aneurin Bevan he was "confronted with the ghost of his own angry youth"; but he still led the Liberals into the lobby against the government.

The Coal Mines Act did eventually find a place on the statute book, but two measures on which Labour set equal store were not so fortunate. One was a Trade Disputes and Trade Unions (Amendment) Bill, which was intended to restore the legal position before the 1927 act, though Sir Stafford Cripps, the Solicitor-General, for whom a seat had just been found at East Bristol, created confusion in the ranks behind him by his opinion that the general strike would have been illegal under it though legal under the measure being amended. Lloyd George and MacDonald had a private talk, and enough Liberals voted for the second reading for it to be sent to committee, but it was there so emasculated that the government abandoned it. This is exactly what Churchill had predicted when he painted a picture of MacDonald saying to Lloyd George:[21] "Just look at the monstrous bill the trade unions and our wild fellows have foisted on me. Do me a service, and I will never forget it. Take it upstairs and cut its dirty throat." The other measure was an Education Bill which would have raised the school-leaving age to fifteen. John Scurr, a veteran Roman Catholic, who was chairman of the Parliamentary Labour Party's consultative committee which maintained liaison with the government, moved an amendment at the report stage to postpone the operation of the bill until another act had been passed authorizing expenditure out of public funds to cover the costs of non-provided schools in meeting the requirements. Thirty-five Labour members voted against the government, and the government was defeated by 282 votes to 249. MacDonald, who had given a warning that the amendment would "knock the bill to smithereens", now said it involved no vital principle. Churchill taunted him as "the greatest living master of falling without hurting himself".[22] The bill went to the House of Lords and was there thrown out.

Life under such conditions was not easy for ministers, and from the first months of the administration efforts had been made to ascertain the terms on which Liberals would give support in the lobbies. The price was electoral reform. As the principal sufferers from the British system of "first past the post", the Liberals had come to see virtues in proportional representation, or in default the alternative vote, which few of them had noticed when in power. Towards the end of 1929 Viscount Ullswater, the former Speaker, was asked to preside over a three-party conference on electoral reform. In the following July he threw in his hand, saying that no agreement was likely to be reached and that the conference could at best submit a few resolutions carried on party lines which would not fulfil the purpose for which it was appointed. It was the Labour representatives, according to Snowden's later account,[23] who blocked any change, but Snowden himself was convinced of the desirability of proportional representation, both on theoretical grounds and on the grounds of the ultimate interest of the Labour party, and after some bargaining, in which he, Henderson and Arnold took part for Labour and Samuel, Ramsay Muir and

Archibald Sinclair for the Liberals, he persuaded the Cabinet to introduce an Electoral Reform Bill. University representation and plural voting (except in the City of London) were to be abolished and restrictions placed on the use of motor-cars in return for the alternative vote, but the bill never reached the statute book.

Though no formal treaty with the Labour party was ever made, it was evident that Lloyd George's sympathies were with the government far more than with their Tory opponents. In June 1930 MacDonald tried to get a three-party conference on unemployment; the Tories declined to attend, and the fact that Lloyd George, Lord Lothian and Seebohm Rowntree were closeted for months with MacDonald, Snowden and Vernon Hartshorn confirmed the impression that the Liberals under his leadership were drifting into socialism. So strong was this impression that Lansbury, the only out-and-out socialist in the Cabinet, wrote to Lloyd George in February 1931 urging him to join the Labour party and put a little vitality into its leadership. The invitation was considered not unsympathetically, but declined on the ground that going over would antagonize millions of Liberals with traditional loyalties who would gladly support any government from another party putting through a real policy of reconditioning Britain. As late as July 1931 Lloyd George was toying with an alliance under which Labour would drop some of its ministers and he would take the Foreign Office or Treasury under MacDonald as Prime Minister.[24]

This flirtation with the Labour government was not at all to the liking of a considerable section of the Liberals extending far beyond Runciman and Grey, whose hostile attitude to Lloyd George had not changed. At the end of October 1930 Simon, whose prestige among the right wing of his own party and among the Tories had risen considerably by his attitude to Indian reform, wrote a letter to Lloyd George claiming freedom of action.[25]

"The Labour government [he wrote] has been in office for nearly seventeen months, and has proved a complete failure in all departments. All your well-meant efforts to help it to do something effective and to get a more satisfactory understanding have produced no result, except that Liberals are exposed to the reproach that they are keeping in friendly contact with the socialists in an effort to save their own skins. We are in danger of carrying offers of assistance to the point of subservience."

Simon added that he gathered the government's principal measure of the session would be to reverse the law governing trade unions. He remained of the opinion he expressed in 1927, and served notice: "If, therefore, the question arises as to confidence in the government, I shall feel obliged to vote in such a way as will show that I, at any rate, have no confidence in it."

This was open revolt, and it was heightened by the resignation at

the same time from the post of Liberal chief whip of Sir Robert
Hutchinson, who was succeeded by Sir Archibald Sinclair. Hutchinson thereafter acted with Simon, and this was the beginning of a
new and permanent split in the Liberal body. Simon spoke and
voted against the trade union measure as he had threatened, and
again diverged from Lloyd George over Snowden's proposal in the
Finance Bill of 1931 to put an annual tax of a penny in the pound
on all land values apart from purely agricultural land. Lloyd George
saw this as a revival of his own proposal for the taxation of land in
1909 and gave it his backing. To Simon's mind there was a pro-
found difference in that the budget of 1909 had proposed to tax the
unearned increment on land values but the budget of 1931 sought to
tax all land values and was thus a discriminatory tax aimed at a
particular form of property. Simon discovered a further ground for
dissenting from Snowden's proposal in that it involved the un-Liberal
principle of double taxation inasmuch as land already bore a
property tax. For a while it seemed that on this issue Simon would
carry the party with him, and Lloyd George wavered, but eventually he reached a compromise with Snowden which enabled him to
go on supporting the government. This was too much for Simon,
especially as Snowden made his concessions in a manner calculated
to inflict the maximum humiliation on the Liberals, and on 26th
June 1931 Simon, Ernest Brown and Hutchinson informed Sinclair
that they no longer wished to receive the official whip. When the
bill came up for third reading in the Commons on 3rd July there
was a notable clash between the rebel and his former leader. Simon
made a reasoned statement of his objections, to which the Tories
listened with approval, but Lloyd George turned savagely on him
and trounced him mercilessly as the erstwhile "guardian of the doctrine" who had turned heretic.[26]

Lloyd George realized, and made it plain in his speech, that the
land tax was not the only issue dividing Liberals, and that Simon
and his friends were preparing to abandon the historic Liberal doctrine of free trade. In guarded words at Manchester as early as the
previous 3rd March Simon had shown the way his mind was working. To understand the circumstances which reconciled an important section of the Liberal party to the imposition of a tariff—and
so opened the way to alliance with the Conservatives—it is necessary to go back to the formation of the Labour government.

Labour could not have resumed office at a more unfortunate
time. The sweets of victory turned sour in its mouth, and Baldwin
had every reason to be thankful that he had lost the election,
though his followers showed little gratitude to him for so doing.
The second Labour government had some notable achievements to
its credit in the field of foreign affairs—the London naval conference of 1930 is outstanding, and Snowden's insistence at The

Hague reparations conference on British rights was acclaimed at the time—but in almost all other directions it was hamstrung by the parliamentary situation and paralysed by the world economic depression of which the most evil consequence was mass unemployment.

The American boom came to an end soon after Labour resumed office, and the consequences of reduced American buying were soon felt all over the world. The number of registered unemployed in Great Britain was 1,163,000 at the count in June 1929 following Labour's victory; a year later the number was 1,912,000; and by the end of 1930 it was 2,500,000. The cost of maintaining the unemployed was rising heavily, partly through the increase in their numbers and partly through more generous rates and conditions of benefit; the deterioration in the balance of payments threatened the position of sterling as a world currency; and the failure to find productive employment for such a large body of workers, especially in the depressed areas, constituted a social and moral as well as an economic problem of the utmost magnitude. Mass unemployment dominated everything else in Labour's second term of office.

In a country so dependent on external trade as Great Britain no government could have wholly insulated itself against a world depression on the scale of that which began in 1929; but certain remedial measures could have been taken, and they were not taken. When the storm rages round a house, it may not be possible to quell the violence of the wind and the rain, but there are actions that can be taken to shelter the inmates. Among the leaders, Snowden was the only one to claim any understanding of the financial mechanism, and his mind had set in such a pattern of rigid orthodoxy as to be impervious to the ideas that might have ameliorated the problem. Among the rank and file, there was a large section, imbued with the ideas of Karl Marx, who had been taught to regard the collapse of capitalism as inevitable and saw no reason why they should try to take any steps to prevent it. Only a few had grasped the new ideas which Keynes was formulating, and they were powerless to influence the course of events.

At the outset the minister responsible for co-ordinating schemes to deal with unemployment was the Lord Privy Seal, J. H. Thomas. He had three ministers to help him—George Lansbury as First Commissioner of Works, Sir Oswald Mosley as Chancellor of the Duchy of Lancaster and Thomas Johnston as Under-Secretary for Scotland. Though Thomas was nominally the minister for dealing with unemployment, there was in practice little he could do without the approval of the Chancellor of the Exchequer; and Snowden judged every proposal made to him by the tests of free trade, a balanced budget, maintenance of the gold standard and the upholding of sterling in the foreign exchanges.

The combination never worked. Lansbury and Mosley pressed schemes for providing work on Thomas, but he, according to Henderson, was "completely rattled and in such a state of panic that he is bordering on lunacy".[27] Early in 1930 Mosley put his own ideas into a memorandum. The basic thesis was to expand purchasing power in the home market by a liberal credit policy secured by public control of banking, the development of social services and higher pensions, benefits and allowances; and to reduce British dependence on oversea supplies by controlling imports, either through tariffs or through quotas, by developing home agriculture and by rationalizing industry under public control. It was supported by Lansbury, who put it before the Cabinet. Thomas was apparently by-passed. Under Snowden's lead, the Cabinet rejected it out of hand because it offended against the sacred canons. In retrospect much of it makes sense, and not a little of it is to be found in the wartime coalition government's white paper in 1944. On 21st May in reply to a Conservative vote of censure—these were almost regular events—Thomas churned out the same old arguments and a disgusted Mosley resigned.[28] Unobtrusively Attlee took his place.

With the freedom of a private member Mosley then carried the fight upstairs to the meeting of the parliamentary party. His arguments carried conviction to many of those present, but he made the fatal mistake of pressing to a division what was in effect a vote of censure on the party leaders. Loyalty and self-interest made the average member's mind close with a snap, and Mosley could muster only twenty-nine votes with more than two hundred against him. Undaunted, he stumped the country and planned to make a great appeal in October to the final tribunal of the party conference at Llandudno. By that time unemployment had risen above two millions, and MacDonald was under heavy fire. He drew out all the stops of his oratory and won a great triumph that not even the rancours of subsequent years have effaced from the minds of those who were present. Yet two days later the conference listened with growing sympathy while Mosley pleaded that if the government must die, let it die like a man in the field, not like an old woman in bed. The resolution supporting his economic policy was lost by the narrow majority of 1,046,000 to 1,251,000. He was himself elected to the National Executive Committee in preference to Thomas.

In December Mosley put his ideas into a manifesto along with some significant additions—a supreme Cabinet of five and a national planning organization capable of acting much more quickly than was possible under normal parliamentary procedure. It was the first hint of dissatisfaction with parliamentary institutions. Even so, the manifesto was signed by seventeen Labour M.P.s, among them two young men well on the left, Aneurin Bevan and John Strachey. In January Bevan, with Mosley's support, moved at the party meeting a resolution asking for a special national conference on unemployment. It was defeated by ninety-seven votes to thirteen. On 24th February another document, giving warning of an impending attack on the social services, was issued. Mosley was helped in its preparation by Bevan, Strachey, W. J. Brown and Allan Young. On the day before publication *The Observer* told its readers with all the air of authority that Mosley intended to break with Labour and form a new party. Mosley had given no hint of his intention to his associates in the writing of the document, but the report turned out to be true. Only five members of Parliament followed Mosley into the New party, as it was simply called—his wife Lady Cynthia Mosley (daughter of Curzon), Oliver Baldwin (son of the Conservative leader), W. J. Brown, John Strachey and Robert Forgan, and of these Baldwin and Brown were out within a day and Strachey within a few months. Aneurin Bevan wholly declined to follow Mosley on the new path.

The career of Oswald Mosley shows once more the importance of the unexpected in party history. In his protest against the failure of the government to cope with unemployment he had a large section of the party with him. In the main lines of his proposed solution he is now realized to have made a strong case. If he had contented himself with a critical speech on resignation and had bided his time, it is probable that before long the party would have turned to him in its distress. "Has MacDonald found his superseder in Oswald Mosley?" asked Beatrice Webb, and with apparent reason.[29] He had birth, education, wealth, a lovely wife, good looks, a commanding presence, fluency of speech, a capacity for hard work and the will to be great. No one would have predicted when Mosley resigned in 1931 that the next Labour Prime Minister would be the quiet little man who slipped into his place as Chancellor of the Duchy. It has since become fashionable to detect in Mosley fundamental defects of character that ought to have been evident to such men as Bevan and Strachey. Few other than Beatrice Webb noted them at the time. It is more credible that at the critical moment Mosley took a wrong step and was carried from one to another until he became lost in the follies of the Fascist movement. No country is so rich in public life that it can afford not to lament the tragic way in which Oswald Mosley squandered his gifts and opportunity.

Though the immediate cause of Trevelyan's resignation in 1931 was the rejection of his Education Bill, he was thoroughly disillusioned over a wide range of policy, and in sympathy with the Independent Labour party in its running fight with the leadership. The I.L.P. by this time was completely under the dominance of the wild but lovable Maxton, especially since the death of Wheatley in 1930. Maxton had become alarmed at the deviation of the Labour party from the strict paths of socialism at the time of the Mond–Turner talks in 1928, and the "Cook–Maxton manifesto"[30] which he issued with the miners' leader was a counter-blast calling for "unceasing war against capitalism". As he had put his name to it without consulting his colleagues, he was challenged in the national administrative council of the I.L.P., and escaped censure by only one vote; but in 1929 he was elected chairman of the party by an overwhelming majority. At the same time there was passed a resolution requiring all candidates for Parliament sponsored by the I.L.P. to give an undertaking that they would, if elected, carry out the policies laid down by the I.L.P. conference, though it was realized full well that this might bring them into conflict with a majority of the Parliamentary Labour party. Charles Buxton argued in vain that it was impossible for the I.L.P. to be a party within a party.

Out of the 288 successful Labour candidates in the ensuing general election thirty-seven were sponsored by the I.L.P. The Birmingham conference of 1930 declared[31] that the I.L.P. was "an independent socialist organization, making its distinctive contribution to Labour party policy and having its distinctive position within the party". It was unreasonable, the conference statement added, "to ask members of the party to accept without question all the proposals of the government when those proposals are not themselves subject to the decisions of the parliamentary party, and in many instances do not comply with the programme authorized by the Labour party conference". The complaint brings out the extent to which the Labour party had been quietly assimilated to the parliamentary model. It was hopelessly unrealistic of the I.L.P. to think that a government's proposals should be debated at a party meeting before submission to Parliament. The Birmingham conference finally demanded that in future only members accepting the I.L.P. policy should be eligible as members of the I.L.P. parliamentary group. A letter to I.L.P. members of Parliament carrying out this instruction laid down that they were to pledge themselves to the policy documents, *Socialism in our time* and *Internationalism in our time*, and that they were to act against the Labour party if necessary. The national executive of the Labour party retorted by deciding to endorse no more I.L.P. candidates until a settlement was reached, and in pursuance of this decision it withheld support in November 1930 from the I.L.P. candidate at a by-election in East Renfrew.

25

FALL OF THE SECOND
LABOUR GOVERNMENT

*May report—the Cabinet adopts £56·4 million of economies—the
opposition leaders raise the question of unemployment allowances
—economies of £76 million including a cut of ten per cent in unemployment benefit suggested—the Bank of England consults New
York—the King asks Baldwin and Samuel to see him—in the event
the reply comes from New York—the Cabinet divided—and
ministers place their resignations at MacDonald's disposal—the
King sees the three party leaders—and presses on them the desirability of a National government—they agree—MacDonald informs
his Labour Cabinet colleagues—only three agree to serve—he forms
a "National" government—Labour accusations of a plot by
MacDonald—a "bankers' ramp"—the King's part*

IN the light of the parliamentary balance and the internal dis-
sensions related in the previous chapter it is not surprising that
the second Labour government fell, but rather that it lasted as long
as it did. The sequence of events in the crowded sixty-three weeks
preceding the disintegration can now be disentangled beyond serious challenge; their interpretation is still a matter of some dispute,
for after the lapse of a third of a century they are still capable of
stirring deep passions.[1] To find a parallel for the swiftness of the
collapse, the bitterness created and the transformation wrought in
the British political scene it is necessary to go back to Peel's break
with the Conservative party in 1846; and in many respects Mac-
Donald's breach with the Labour party, or the Labour party's
breach with MacDonald, whichever way it is regarded, is the more
outstanding.

The collapse of the United States boom led to the reduction of
American short-term credits in Europe, and this in turn led to the
failure in May of the Kredit Anstalt bank in Austria and in July to
the failure of German banks and to pressure upon sterling. On 22nd
July the Bank of England had lost £22 million in gold, and on the
following day the bank-rate, which had stood at the low rate of $2\frac{1}{2}$

per cent to stimulate employment, was raised to $3\frac{1}{2}$ per cent. A week later it was raised to $4\frac{1}{2}$ per cent, and on 1st August credits amounting to £50 million were obtained from the Federal Reserve Bank of New York and the Bank of France in equal shares. Any good these might have done was immediately undone by the almost simultaneous publication of the May report.

In February, under Liberal insistence, the government had set up a committee under the chairmanship of Sir George May, who had recently retired as secretary of the Prudential Assurance Company, to consider what reductions in national expenditure could be made consistent with efficiency. On the day that Parliament rose for the summer recess, 31st July, the May report was published. It predicted a deficit of £120 million by the end of the financial year, and recommended that £24 million should be found by new taxation and that economies of £96 million should be made by cuts in official salaries, the salaries of civil servants and teachers, the pay of the services and expenditure on unemployment. This last item was to account for £66·5 million and was to include a twenty per cent cut in the standard rates of benefit. In a minority report the two Labour members of the committee rejected the proposals for dealing with unemployment. The Cabinet appointed a committee, which came to be known as the Cabinet Economy Committee, to consider the report. It consisted of MacDonald, Snowden, Henderson, Thomas and Graham. Strong hostility to the May report developed at once throughout the Labour party in the country.

The May report caused alarm in foreign countries about the state of British finances. The rate at which funds were being withdrawn from London increased, and the credits obtained from France and the United States were being quickly exhausted.

Warned by Snowden of the gravity of the situation, MacDonald returned to London from Lossiemouth, arriving on 11th August. In consequence of information they had received, Baldwin returned from France and Chamberlain from Scotland, both arriving on the 13th. In Chamberlain's case the information seems to have come from the deputy governor of the Bank of England, Sir Ernest Harvey; the governor, Montagu Norman, was ill and played no part in the crisis. Lloyd George was also ill, convalescing after a severe operation; he had collapsed on August bank holiday with prostate gland trouble. Samuel was leading the Liberals in his place and had returned to London on the 12th, and in his case also it is known that he came in response to a telegram from the Deputy Governor of the Bank. It may be presumed that Snowden or MacDonald authorized Harvey to inform the opposition leaders.

The first meeting of the Cabinet Economy Committee was held on 12th August. Snowden gave warning that the budgetary deficit the following April would be £170 million, £50 million more than was estimated by the May committee. During the morning of 13th August MacDonald invited Samuel to see him, and in the afternoon Baldwin and Chamberlain. The week-end having arrived, MacDonald and Chamberlain returned to Scotland and Baldwin to Aix. On Monday, 17th, and Tuesday, 18th, the Economy Committee met again. There was a division of opinion about how much revenue should be raised from additional taxation and how much from cuts in expenditure, and the suggestions put before the full meeting of the Cabinet called for Wednesday, 19th, were in Snowden's words "only tentative proposals suggested for consideration".[2] Whereas the May committee had recommended a cut of twenty per cent in the standard rates of unemployment benefit, and a Treasury memorandum considered by the Economy Committee included for consideration a cut of ten per cent, the Economy Committee itself made no proposal to the Cabinet for a cut in the rates of benefit. It was, however, proposed to raise £48·5 million by cutting down the cost of unemployment in other ways, and this was the biggest item by far in savings of £78,575,000 which it was proposed to make towards the deficit of £170 million. The £48·5 million was made up of £15 million from increased contributions, £8 million from a reduction in the period of insurance benefit, £20 million from a reduction in the Exchequer contribution to transitional benefit and £5·5 million from two lesser devices.

The full Cabinet met on Wednesday, 19th August, as arranged, and sat from 11 a.m. to 10.25 p.m., with only brief intervals for lunch and dinner. Agreement was provisionally reached on economies amounting to £56,250,000, which included £22 million for unemployment insurance. The question of cutting £20 million from transitional benefit was referred to a committee of four with instructions to report back. An important new proposal not raised by the Economy Committee was a revenue tariff. Opinion among economists had been veering in favour of such a tariff, and there were many Labour leaders, formerly opposed to it, who would have swallowed a tariff in preference to cuts in unemployment benefit; but Snowden was an out-and-out free trader and the discussion was adjourned.

When the Cabinet dispersed late that evening there were no definite measures for stopping the rot but also no talk of a break up or resignation, and it seemed as though the ministerial machine would slowly grind out some agreed compromise. The next day, Thursday, 20th August, was critical. At 10 a.m., in accordance with a decision of the Cabinet, MacDonald, Snowden and Thomas met the available opposition leaders—Chamberlain and Hoare for the Conservatives, Samuel and Maclean for the Liberals. They were told that towards a deficit now estimated at £170 million the Economy Committee had made tentative proposals for economies amounting to £78·5 million, which did not include any cut in the standard rates of unemployment benefit. Chamberlain expressed the view that to produce economies less than the total suggested in the May report was wrong, and that if unemployment benefit was left untouched the contemplated economies would be jeopardized. He and Hoare formed the impression that MacDonald and Snowden agreed, the latter saying that if account was taken both of the fall in the cost of living and the rise in benefits the unemployed were thirty-six per cent better off than in 1924. The opposition leaders asked for an adjournment to consider further what they had been told.

At 11 a.m., while the opposition leaders were still at Downing Street, seven members of the consultative committee of the Parliamentary Labour party arrived for a discussion with the Economy Committee. This had been decided at Monday's meeting of the committee. According to notes made by Chuter Ede after the meeting, it was gathered from MacDonald that the Conservative and Liberal parties insisted on the cost-of-living cut in unemployment benefit; the seven members consulted together afterwards and formed the view that if the government attempted to meet the conditions said to be laid down, "it was very doubtful if they would get any other votes from our party other than the lawyers".[3]

At 3 p.m., also as arranged at Monday's meeting, the members of the Economy Committee went to a joint meeting of the General Council of the Trades Union Congress and the National Executive of the Labour party. MacDonald made a speech on the general situation and Snowden spoke more particularly on the proposals being considered by the government. Later it was claimed by Citrine, Henderson and others that he had said there would be no cut in unemployment benefit; it seems more probable that after giving the Cabinet's provisional decision to increase contributions and reduce the period of insurance benefit he stated that no decision had been taken in regard to the standard rates of benefit. This did not imply that it had been ruled out, but there was a genuine misunderstanding on the part of some of his hearers. The curious thing is that Henderson seems to have been among those who took him to mean that there would be no cut in the standard rates.

At the conclusion of the joint meeting, the General Council and the National Executive held separate meetings to consider what they had been told. At the meeting of the executive Henderson, in reply to questions, emphasized what Snowden had said in regard to cuts in unemployment benefits, and the executive, largely composed of ministers, decided to leave matters to its members in the Cabinet.

The General Council, in a discussion lasting four hours, found the proposals under consideration by the government totally unacceptable apart from the cuts in the salaries of ministers and judges.

According to Snowden, the General Council opposed any interference with the existing terms and conditions of the unemployment insurance scheme, including the limitation of statutory benefit to twenty-six weeks, and said the trade unions would oppose cuts in teachers' salaries and in the pay of the fighting services, and any suggestions for reducing expenditure on works in relief of unemployment. This agrees with Citrine, who said the General Council decided it "must oppose the whole thing".[4] A crisis of the utmost gravity immediately opened before the Labour leadership, for if it went on it would challenge the main source of its power, while if it retreated it would be accused of submitting to outside dictation and running away from the serious economic problem threatening the nation. The General Council realized that it was not enough merely to oppose, and as an alternative offered a four-fold plan: (1) a graduated levy on profits, incomes and earnings in place of unemployment insurance contributions from the worker, the employer and the state; (2) new taxation upon fixed-interest securities and unearned income; (3) suspension of the sinking fund; and (4) consideration of a revenue tariff. It seems that this last proposal took at least half the four hours of this decisive meeting, and even then the council refrained from a definite conclusion.

The Cabinet met at 8.30 p.m. to hear reports of the day's meetings, and at 9.30 p.m. the Economy Committee received a deputation to communicate the General Council's refusal to cooperate in the proposals under consideration. The deputation consisted of Arthur Hayday, Walter Citrine, Ernest Bevin, Arthur Pugh and A. J. Walkden. Members of the Cabinet went uneasily to bed knowing that the General Council thought the proposals went much too far while the opposition leaders thought they did not go far enough. "The General Council are pigs," Passfield told his wife according to her diary.[5]

In the morning of Friday, 21st August, the General Council met again, and Citrine was instructed to send to the Prime Minister a letter giving the council's adherence to the views expressed by the deputation. The Cabinet met morning and afternoon for five hours, and in reply to Citrine the Prime Minister said the General Council's scheme would not reduce expenditure but increase it; accordingly, the Cabinet had decided to go ahead with its examination of the scheme discussed with the joint meeting as otherwise the situation would worsen and unemployment rapidly increase. At the same meeting the Cabinet finally rejected the suggestion of a revenue tariff. Fifteen members had expressed themselves in favour of a ten per cent tax on imports of manufactured and semi-manufactured goods, with five against. On the suggestion of a duty on all imports, including food and raw materials, the figures were reversed—five in favour and fifteen against. As there was no unanimity and the

Cabinet would have broken up, the project was dropped; and MacDonald clinched the argument by saying the Liberals would oppose. The Cabinet as a whole confirmed its acceptance of £56·4 million of economies, almost exactly the same figure as provisionally agreed, and there was a long discussion of a cut in unemployment benefit, but as a substantial minority opposed it this and other proposals relating to unemployment insurance were not persisted in. The opposition had clearly been strengthened by the General Council, and to Lansbury at least Henderson appeared to have changed his mind.[6] It was understood by Henderson that the Cabinet would face Parliament with these proposals, prepared for defeat and a Conservative government. What did happen was very different and the source of bitter recrimination.

At 5 p.m. that same Friday, with the knowledge and approval of the Cabinet, MacDonald and Snowden saw the opposition leaders for the second time. In the meantime Chamberlain and Samuel had held consultations within their own parties, and both came back prepared to say (in Samuel's words[7]) that the proposals of which they had been told "represented a very bold scheme, and a courageous attempt to grapple with the realities of the situation, but we doubted whether such a large sum of savings could be effected with regard to unemployment without a diminution in the scale of unemployment allowances, and we determined to raise this point at the next conference". If measures of that kind were laid before Parliament, they would give a general assurance of support. Samuel and Chamberlain were taken aback when told that of the proposed economies amounting to £78·5 million only £56·4 million had in fact been approved by the Cabinet. They had come to ask for larger economies to be achieved by a reduction in unemployment allowances, and found that their starting-point had been reduced by a third. They asked for an adjournment of a few hours to consult, and Samuel included the invalid Lloyd George in his consultations. During this interval it appears probable from the account later compiled by ex-ministers that MacDonald and Snowden saw "the bankers", presumably Harvey and Peacock of the Bank of England. "The bankers" would undoubtedly have impressed on them the rapidly growing financial difficulties.

At 9.30 p.m. the opposition leaders returned for their third conference with the Prime Minister and the Chancellor of the Exchequer. Chamberlain opened by saying that if economies amounting to £56·4 million were the government's final proposals, the opposition would turn them out immediately the house met; that in their view a financial crash would come before that date; that they considered it to be the Prime Minister's bounden duty to avoid that crash; and that they were ready to give him any support in their power for that purpose, either with his present or in a reconstructed government. Samuel followed in the same vein. As a result of their *démarche*, MacDonald appears to have mused whether to resign or to break with his dissidents, but to have come to no definite conclusion.

It had been planned that the King, who had been at Sandringham, should leave London for Balmoral on the 21st. He suggested that he should stay in London, but MacDonald advised against so doing on the ground that it would disturb confidence. The King arrived at Balmoral early on Saturday, 22nd August.

Baldwin had been informed by Chamberlain of the deepening crisis and decided to return from Aix. He spent the Friday night in Paris and arrived in London during the Saturday.

The Cabinet met at 9.30 that Saturday morning, and MacDonald and Snowden reported on their talks with the opposition leaders. They left members of the Cabinet with the impression that the opposition leaders had demanded further cuts of £25 million to £30 million, the bulk of which must come from the unemployment, as a condition of their support. Later Samuel and Chamberlain denied that there was a "demand" or that precise figures were mentioned or a specific cut in unemployment benefit required, but it is hard to see how MacDonald and Snowden, and the Cabinet in turn, could have avoided forming this impression from the language they used.

The Prime Minister and Chancellor also warned the Cabinet that owing to the rate at which funds were being withdrawn from London a moratorium would be inevitable by Wednesday unless further credits could be obtained. Such credits would have to be obtained by the government as the Bank of England could raise no more. Soundings for a loan of £80 million had been made since 13th August, and the Federal Reserve Bank of New York had explained that as it was precluded by its charter from lending money to a government the best procedure would be to seek aid from a consortium of New York banks. It was made clear from the outset that if such a large credit was to be arranged, the lenders would wish to be satisfied about the British financial position. A balanced budget would be a necessary condition, and the proposals for bringing this about, and their acceptability to the opposition parties, would have to be considered.

This brought a new element into a picture sufficiently confused already, and Henderson made it clear that he favoured the resignation of ministers as they were being asked to handle a situation that it would be impossible for them to carry through. Passfield was of the same opinion: "Let the Tories come in and stand the racket," he told his wife.[8] Henderson could not have pressed the point, or did not win support, and there appears to have been some discussion of a question that was soon to assume major importance—the formation of a coalition government or a National government drawn from all three parties. The evidence comes from Beatrice Webb's diary, and she adds: "This, he [MacDonald] intimated, was what the King desired and might propose."[9] It was apparently not the first time such a suggestion had been ventilated. A tantalizingly brief note in the memorandum drawn up by ex-ministers says that at the Cabinet meeting on 19th August: "The Prime Minister adumbrated the possibility of a National government."[10] There was little support at the Saturday meeting for the idea, and as the Cabinet was not then prepared either for resignation or for reconstruction it proceeded to consider how it could meet the opposition. After a heated discussion the Cabinet authorized the Prime Minister and the Chancellor to see if economies amounting to £76 million, including a cut of ten per cent in the standard rate of unemployment benefit, would secure opposition support; but this was to be done without any commitment of the Cabinet as a whole.

The Cabinet adjourned soon after noon. Chamberlain and Hoare, Samuel and Maclean were invited to Downing Street during the lunch hour for the fourth occasion. They expressed the view that Parliament might accept the proposals, but as they could not say whether they would be adequate to restore confidence they suggested that "the bankers" should be consulted. The Cabinet met again in the afternoon, and agreed that the Bank of England should be consulted. Harvey and Peacock said they would immediately seek the opinion of Mr. George L. Harrison, chairman of the Federal Reserve Bank of New York. It was arranged that the Cabinet should meet again at 7 p.m. the following day, Sunday, 23rd August, by which time the reply from New York was expected.

Baldwin arrived in London during the Saturday evening, and gave Hoare the impression that the last thing in the world that he wished was either a return to office or the end of his holiday. Chamberlain was a man of sterner temperament and saw "politically, how urgent it was to get an all-party agreement and, tactically, how desirable to split the Labour party". He urged Baldwin to try to work with the Labour moderates, whatever the Liberals might do.[11]

Scarcely had the King arrived at Balmoral than he decided he ought to return, and he did so by the night train, arriving in London early in the morning of Sunday, 23rd September. He had received a telephone message from MacDonald saying that his presence in London might be necessary after all, but the decision to return was his own. He asked the Prime Minister to see him at ten o'clock that same morning. MacDonald told him of the inquiry being made in New York, and warned him that some of his leading colleagues in the government might not agree to the economies being tentatively put to the American bankers and might resign. In that case the resignation of the whole government would be inevitable. An official

E

announcement after the interview stated that "on the Prime Minister's advice the King has asked Mr. Baldwin and Sir Herbert Samuel to see him, because his Majesty wishes to hear from them themselves what the position of their respective parties is".[12] Though this is formally correct, and the King would not have summoned Baldwin and Samuel if his Prime Minister had not approved, it appears from a telephone call from his private secretary, Clive Wigram, to the editor of *The Times*, Geoffrey Dawson, that he had already made up his mind on the desirability of seeing the opposition leaders.[13]

Normally, the King would have seen Baldwin, as the leader of the larger party, before Samuel, but he could not be found. He had not "strayed off into the streets", as was for long thought, but had gone to see Geoffrey Dawson, with whom he afterwards drove to the Travellers' Club.[14] When Baldwin could not be located, Wigram asked Samuel to the Palace. The accidental transposition is of some importance, for Samuel put before the King what his Majesty regarded as a clear and convincing case for a National government. Wigram later recorded:[15]

"Some time after the crisis, in discussing it with the King, I was impressed by the fact that His Majesty found Sir Herbert Samuel the clearest-minded of the three and said that he had put the case for a National Government much clearer than either of the others. It was after the King's interview with Sir Herbert Samuel that His Majesty became convinced of the necessity for the National Government."

Samuel's own record of his advice to the King, as given in the note he made at the time, is as follows:[16]

"If Mr. MacDonald, with this, or a reconstituted, Labour Cabinet, was able to propose economies, which were really adequate, that would be the best solution ... If that solution proved to be impracticable, then a National government of members of the three parties would be the next best alternative. It would be preferable that Mr. MacDonald should be the Premier, unless he found that he could not carry with him a sufficient number of his colleagues. We deprecated a purely Conservative government, as we thought it would have great difficulty in securing popular support for the necessary measures. If, however, his Majesty found that no other solution could be reached, we should of course support the government of the day in the steps immediately necessary to save the financial situation. I said nothing as to the possibility of a Conservative–Liberal or Labour–Liberal administration, and the King did not raise the point."

Samuel added that a National government should be "for the single purpose of overcoming the financial crisis".[17]

Baldwin was eventually found, and he saw the King at three o'clock. The King asked him whether he would be prepared to serve in a National government under MacDonald, and he answered that he would be ready to do anything to assist the country in its crisis. Even if MacDonald insisted on resignation, he would be prepared to carry on the government if he could be assured of the Liberal party's support in making the necessary economies. In that event, once the crisis had been surmounted, he would ask for a dissolution. The King agreed.

When the Cabinet assembled at seven o'clock, the expected message from New York had not arrived. Harrison had given a personal opinion that "if the programme was approved by all three parties it would be possible to raise a loan",[18] but he thought that the inquiry should be made through the government's agents, J. P. Morgan and Company. Harvey had sent off the message on the Sunday morning, and members of the Cabinet went out into the garden while awaiting the reply.

At 8.45 p.m. a telephone message said that the reply had been received at the Bank and Harvey was on his way to Downing Street with it. The Cabinet reassembled. MacDonald took the decoded telegram from Harvey, re-entered the Cabinet room and read it to the ministers around the great table. As he came to the end, Harvey waiting in the ante-room thought that "pandemonium had broken loose".[19]

Morgans emphasized that they could give no assurances that day, but said that if the suggestion were for a public loan, they were confident that until Parliament took action they could not give a favourable opinion. If the suggestion were for a short-term Treasury operation, that would be less difficult and they would give an answer by the next day's closing. They asked to be told the government's desires after the Cabinet meeting, and concluded: [20]

"Are we right in assuming that the programme under consideration will have the sincere approval and support of the Bank of England and the city generally and thus go a long way towards restoring internal confidence in Great Britain? Of course, our ability to do anything depends on the response of public opinion particularly in Great Britain to the government's announcement of the programme."

It was presumably the inquiry about the approval of the Bank of England and the city generally that released pandemonium. The American bankers, it was clear to ministers, though not stated in set words, would not be satisfied with anything less than the £76 million of economies, including the ten per cent cut in unemployment benefit, calculated to save £12.5 million. MacDonald thereupon appealed to the Cabinet to accept this total of economies, including the cut in benefit. He was well aware that the reduction of unemployment benefit would cause much resentment among Labour supporters, but he was confident that the majority of the party would support him if he were able to lay all the facts before them. If the unemployed were not touched while other sections of the community were asked to bear great sacrifices, the Labour party would lose moral prestige. He must therefore ask the Cabinet to agree to a cut of ten per cent in unemployment benefit, and if any senior ministers felt it necessary to resign it would entail the resignation of the whole government.

The crunch had come. One by one ministers made their attitude known. When the opinions were collected, eleven were in favour of acceptance (apart from MacDonald himself) and nine were against. The nine dissentients were Henderson, Clynes, Graham, Lansbury, Greenwood, Alexander, Johnston, Adamson and Addison.[21] The Prime Minister said he proposed to inform the King at once of what had passed and to advise him to summon Baldwin, Samuel and himself to a conference the following morning. The ministers placed their resignations at the Prime Minister's disposal.

MacDonald reached the Palace at 10.20 p.m., looking "scared and unbalanced" according to Wigram, who added:[22]

"The King impressed on the Prime Minister that he was the only man to lead the country through this crisis and hoped that he would reconsider the situation. His Majesty told him that the Conservatives and Liberals would support him in restoring the confidence of foreigners in the financial stability of the country."

The King agreed to meet the three party leaders together the following morning, and before leaving the Palace MacDonald sent messages inviting Baldwin and Samuel to meet him immediately at No. 10 Downing Street. Chamberlain was also present, and for the earlier part of the meeting Josiah Stamp and two of the directors of the Bank of England.

According to Chamberlain's diary, MacDonald said he would help the Conservative and Liberal leaders to get the proposals through, though it meant his death warrant, but it would be of no use for him to join a government. Chamberlain asked him to consider that, even if he should not command many votes in the house, he might command much support in the country. Would not a government including members of all parties hold a much stronger position? Had he considered the effect on foreign opinion?[23]

MacDonald's response is not known, but Chamberlain stated in a public speech soon afterwards that he went to bed expecting Baldwin to be commissioned to form a government. Snowden in his autobiography recorded the same impression, and this was the general expectation of the members of the Cabinet. Malcolm MacDonald, who recorded his father's conversations at this time immediately after the event, has testified that he was fighting as hard as he could to keep the Labour government in office.[24] When he feared that he would not carry enough of his colleagues with him, what he contemplated was the resignation of the whole government. He also expected, his son records, that Baldwin would immediately become Prime Minister and that he would probably be back in Lossiemouth two or three weeks afterwards, more or less in retirement. If this is so, the only puzzling thing is why he proposed to advise the King to summon himself as well as Baldwin and Samuel to a conference; and it is also puzzling why his Cabinet colleagues read no significance into this statement. Perhaps he wished to keep all avenues open as long as possible; perhaps their minds were more preoccupied with the cut in the dole than with the constitutional niceties of how to surrender office.

What took place at the Palace the next morning, Monday, 24th August, cannot be better told than in the words of the memorandum that Wigram wrote the same day: [25]

"At 10 a.m. the King held a Conference at Buckingham Palace at which the Prime Minister, Baldwin and Samuel were present. At the beginning, His Majesty impressed upon them that before they left the Palace some *communiqué* must be issued, which would no longer keep the country and the world in suspense. The Prime Minister said that he had the resignation of his Cabinet in his pocket, but the King replied that he trusted there was no question of the Prime Minister's resignation: the leaders of the three Parties must get together and come to some arrangement. His Majesty hoped that the Prime Minister, with the colleagues who remained faithful to him, would help in the formation of a National Government, which the King was sure would be supported by the Conservatives and the Liberals. The King assured the Prime Minister that, remaining at his post, his position and reputation would be much more enhanced than if he surrendered the government of the country at such a crisis. Baldwin and Samuel said that they were willing to serve under the Prime Minister, and render all help possible to carry on the Government as a National Emergency Government until an emergency bill or bills had been passed by Parliament, which would restore once more British credit and the confidence of foreigners. After that they would expect His Majesty to grant a dissolution. To this course the King agreed. During the Election the National government would remain in being, though of course each Party would fight the Election on its own lines."

From this narrative of events it is clear that the King's appeal was the decisive factor in persuading MacDonald to remain at his post, and although Wigram does not specifically mention the fact he must have agreed there and then. The King withdrew, leaving the party leaders to settle the terms of the press announcement. On returning the King congratulated them and pointed out that "while France and other countries existed for weeks without a Government, in this country our constitution is so generous that leaders of

Parties, after fighting one another for months in the House of Commons, were ready to meet together under the roof of the Sovereign and sink their own differences for a common good". A memorandum drawn up by Samuel while the conference was still in session confirms some of the points in Wigram's account and brings out that the proposed National government would not be a coalition in the ordinary sense but "a cooperation of individuals".[26] The statement made to the press said very simply:[27]

"His Majesty the King invited the Prime Minister, Mr. Stanley Baldwin and Sir Herbert Samuel to Buckingham Palace this morning, and the formation of a National government is under consideration."

MacDonald left the Palace for the last meeting of the Labour Cabinet, which had been convened for noon. It will be recalled that ministers expected to be told that they were all out of office and that Baldwin was about to form a government. Great was the surprise when MacDonald informed them that he would be forming a government of individuals drawn from the three parties to deal with the emergency. It is difficult to reconstruct exactly what took place at this meeting from the conflicting accounts of those who were present, but it seems probable that no general invitation to join the new administration was given. At the end MacDonald invited Snowden, Thomas and Sankey to join him in the new government. Snowden thought it was essential that he should remain Chancellor until the crisis was tided over, and consented, but with misgivings. Sankey thought the work he was doing for the India round-table conference obliged him to accept. Thomas had no hesitations.

At 2.30 that same day MacDonald met the junior ministers and the ministers not in the Cabinet. He had no wish, he assured them, that they should accompany him into the wilderness; they were young men and must consider their future careers. "Most of the junior ministers," Sir Harold Nicolson drily observes, "followed, but without much subsequent gratitude, this unselfish advice."[28]

At four o'clock MacDonald was once more at the Palace, this time to tender his formal resignation as Prime Minister of the Labour government. He immediately received, and accepted, an invitation to form a National administration and kissed hands on his appointment as the new Prime Minister. He who went in as a Prime Minister also came out a Prime Minister. There is no more astounding story in the whole history of the British party system, and it has been necessary to tell it at some length.

It is not surprising that many legends have sprung up about the fall of the Labour government, but they can be disposed of more briefly.

One is that MacDonald had long plotted the formation of a

National government. It was given currency soon afterwards by Webb,[29] who wrote of "the whole unfolding within sixty-three days of a single drama, in all its development foreseen in advance, it is safe to say, only by the statesman who was at once its author, its producer and its principal actor". Snowden in his autobiography a few years later endorsed the same conclusion. In the light of what happened, his colleagues found a significance in earlier statements that they had not noticed at the time. One such statement was contained in his first speech in the new Parliament of 1929 when he said:[30]

"The thought must be occurring to the minds of everyone who is aware of the very serious problems that this country has to face, problems at home and problems abroad, I wonder how far it is possible, without in any way abandoning any of our party positions, without in any way surrendering any item of our party principles, to consider ourselves more as a Council of State and less as arrayed regiments facing each other in battle."

This sentiment was natural in the parliamentary situation left by the election, which gave no party a majority, and it is not necessary to read any deeper significance into it. Garvin had asked for a National government in *The Observer* on 25th January, 1931, but there is no reason to think MacDonald had connived in it. The evidence is conclusive that MacDonald's mind was converted to the suggestion only in the last hours, and especially by the King's appeal. It need not be denied that disillusionment with many of his colleagues made his mind receptive to the idea.

A stronger form of the legend accuses MacDonald of an act of deep treachery to the Labour party. It would, indeed, be strange if, despite much provocation, he had wished to destroy the party he had personally done so much to create. The balance of evidence is that he hoped to maintain the unity of the Labour party under his leadership almost to the end, and expected the National government to be a matter of short duration, after which normal party government would be resumed.

A weaker variant of the legend is that he was a vain man whose love of high society had put him out of touch with the rank and file and with most of his colleagues. This does not rest solely upon his words to Snowden, "Tomorrow every duchess in London will be wanting to kiss me," and the significance of that remark depends on whether it was said "gleefully", as Snowden records, or ruefully, as it may well have been.[31] This is, however, a side of MacDonald's character that had long been noted, not only by such a connoisseur of snobbery as Beatrice Webb, and there is not a little truth in the charge that he had lost touch with the party, the trade unions and the working classes from which he had sprung. He enjoyed aristocratic society, and an appeal from the King was to him a royal command. Owing to his isolation from his party, he failed until the last moment to realize the extent to which his actions would be repudiated, and probably thought he would carry a substantial section of the party with him. It is only fair to add that if he was a vain man, he had something to be vain about.

An alternative to the legend that the overthrow of the Labour government was a MacDonald plot is the theory that it was a "bankers' ramp". This was the favourite explanation in the Labour party at the time, and may still frequently be heard; it is, indeed, accepted history in the Labour party. "The first Labour government had been destroyed by a Red Letter, and the second by a Banker's Order," Dalton told the first parliamentary party meeting after the crisis; and the dictum was so acceptable that it was widely repeated in the party's literature.[32]

Though it was a message from the Bank of England that brought Chamberlain and Samuel to London, it is not suggested that the deputy governor did this on his own responsibility; almost certainly he was requested or at any rate authorized to do so by the Prime Minister or Chancellor of the Exchequer. The charge could mean that there was no real crisis, but that the alarm was deliberately manufactured by "the bankers". It is undoubtedly the case that the country's financial difficulties were aggravated by publication of the May report, but this was not the responsibility of "the bankers". It was the Liberal party which demanded the committee, and although Snowden could not have prevented the demand or prevented publication, he bears a responsibility for the tone of the Treasury evidence and for the publication of the report just as Parliament was rising. He could, if he had wished, have counteracted the influence of the report with a statement of his own, but the fact is that he thoroughly endorsed the report and its recommendations, and wanted it to have the maximum effect. In examining this aspect of the matter, we must be careful not to use the benefit of hind-sight. In retrospect we can see that the government was "crucified upon a cross of gold", but in the context of the beliefs held by the Chancellor of the Exchequer, the Treasury, the Bank of England and everyone else in a position of responsibility in the summer of 1931 there was a real crisis. Gold was being lost at an alarming rate, and it was a matter of days before the Bank of England would be obliged to close its doors.

In the last resort the charge that the government's fall was brought about by a "bankers' ramp" rests upon the message from Messrs. J. P. Morgan and Company read to the Cabinet on that fateful Sunday evening. It is more than likely that Morgans did not realize the explosive effect that the words "Bank of England and the city generally" would have upon a Labour Cabinet. The names of these highly respectable institutions, as they seemed in New York, had become dirty words in the Labour party. But what did the answer given by Morgans amount to? The British government, thinking itself to be in a desperate strait, wished to borrow a large sum of money from American investors, and Morgans merely observed that before lending the money those investors would want some assurance that they would see it back. In the light of what the British government was itself proclaiming from the roof-tops of Whitehall about the parlous state of the nation's finances this does not seem unreasonable.

There is, finally, the legend that the King acted unconstitutionally in the part he played in bringing about the formation of the new government. Mr. Leonard Wolff made this charge soon after the government was formed, and it was developed later by Harold Laski.[33] There can be little doubt that the King played a great, and perhaps even a decisive part, in persuading MacDonald to attempt to form a National government, and without MacDonald at its head no government would have had even the semblance of being national; but there can be equally little doubt that the King acted with strict constitutional propriety as the conventions of the constitution were understood in 1931. The charge was answered by Samuel in his *Memoirs* with great clarity:[34]

"Mr. MacDonald's resignation was the necessary consequence of an irreconcilable division in his Cabinet. The King then acted in strict accordance with precedent in following the advice of the outgoing Premier: that was to bring into consultation the spokesmen of the two parties which together could furnish a majority in the House of Commons able to sustain a new administration. The invitation to the Prime Minister to return to office, and to form a new administration on an all-party basis, was the course advised by them. So far as I was myself concerned, neither directly nor indirectly, did any expression reach me of any personal opinion or wish of his Majesty. In every particular the principles and practice of our democratic constitution were scrupulously observed."

Once more the sequence of events has brought out the importance of the word "if" in the history of party. If Lloyd George had not been out of action, if Churchill had not quarrelled with his party, if Baldwin had left a telephone number behind when he went to see Geoffrey Dawson, the story might have been very different.

It might also have been different if the chief participants had realized how few in the Labour party would follow MacDonald's lead.[35] When the new government was formed, that could only be guessed; but the truth was soon to be apparent, and stultified the claims of the third MacDonald administration to be a National government in the full sense of that term, or indeed in any real sense; for that reason it seems best to call it the "National" government.

LABOUR ROUT
1931

Party balance in the "National" government—Labours goes into opposition under Henderson's leadership—Great Britain forced off the gold standard—demands for a general election—and the Cabinet decide to go to the country as a "National" government—a "doctor's mandate"—Lloyd George comes out against the government and breaks with Samuel—Liberal National party formed by Simon—National Labour party improvised—a bitter campaign— Snowden's attack on the Labour party—only forty-six Labour candidates returned—Liberal factions in the new house—overwhelming Conservative majority

ON Tuesday, 25th August, MacDonald settled the posts in the new government in consultation with the other party leaders. The Cabinet consisted of only ten members. Labour was given four places, the Conservatives four and the Liberals two. MacDonald, Snowden, Sankey and Thomas retained their old offices. For the Liberals, Samuel went to the Home Office and Reading to the Foreign Office. Of the Conservatives, Baldwin became Lord President, Neville Chamberlain returned to his old desk at the Ministry of Health, Sir Philip Cunliffe-Lister became President of the Board of Trade and Hoare was given the crucial post of Secretary of State for India. The knowledge that the round-table conference was to reassemble on 7th September had been a major factor underlying the crisis and had reinforced the urgency of finding a solution; and, as already indicated, the identity of views between Baldwin and MacDonald on this important issue greatly facilitated the formation of the government.

The problem of putting three pints into a pint pot, or rather, owing to the reduction in size of the Cabinet, into a half-pint pot was eased by the swelling of a patriotic feeling that this was no time for selfishness. Two problems arose in filling the offices outside the Cabinet. Rousing himself on his sick-bed Lloyd George would not hear of Samuel's proposal to bring in Simon and his associates, and the Liberals were confined to those who accepted his leadership. MacDonald found great difficulty in persuading any more of his old colleagues to accept office. In his first list Lord Amulree, Secretary of State for Air, was the only one. Eventually Jowitt, Craigie Aitchison and G. M. Gillett agreed to resume office, and MacDonald's son Malcolm was brought in.

Though Labour had a high share of posts in the Cabinet, and it remained to be seen how far Labour voters in the country approved of what had been done, it soon became evident that MacDonald had failed to carry more than a tiny element of the organized Labour movement with him. After a joint meeting of the three main party committees held on 26th August the following resolution was passed:[1]

"That this joint meeting of the Trades Union Congress General Council, the National Executive of the Labour party, and the Consultative Committee of the Parliamentary Labour party, having considered the position created by the formation of the new government, is unanimously of opinion that it should be vigorously opposed in Parliament and by the movement throughout the country; they express their approval of the action taken by the ministers of the late government in declining to render their support to the new administration; and recommend the Parliamentary Labour party to constitute itself the official parliamentary opposition."

There was some criticism of ministers, even though they had not followed MacDonald, who had shown themselves willing in Cabinet to agree to economies and taxation of which the General Council disapproved. By this time Thomas had made it known that a majority of the Cabinet had agreed to the full programme of economies. Once again the failure of the parliamentary party led to the General Council taking the reins more firmly in its own hands, and this became clear on 27th August when a joint manifesto of the three bodies accepted the contention of the General Council that the crisis was a "bankers' ramp" and denounced the new government with bell, book and candle.

The Parliamentary Labour party met on 28th August, and the meeting was attended, not only by the National Executive, as provided for by the rules, but by the General Council, which was a significant innovation. Both MacDonald, who had gone to Scotland, and Snowden sent apologies for absence.[2] Thomas did not attend and did not write. Sankey and Malcolm MacDonald were present. In a speech heard with respect Sankey said he believed MacDonald had saved the country but Henderson had saved the soul of the Labour party. He explained his own preoccupation with the forthcoming round-table conference on India. The meeting approved the joint manifesto with only six or seven votes against and thus decided to go into opposition. It proceeded to elect officers for the session. Henderson wanted Clynes, who had been the deputy, to become leader in place of MacDonald, but Clynes himself nominated Henderson, who was obliged to accept. Clynes and Graham were chosen deputy leaders.

In the course of the next few days it was seen that only about eleven Labour back-benchers would support the new government. In almost all cases resolutions were passed by their local parties calling upon the member to resign or withdrawing his selection as prospective candidate. MacDonald was expelled from the Hampstead Labour party. Thomas resigned as political secretary of the National Union of Railwaymen and had his endorsement as prospective candidate at Derby withdrawn. Snowden announced that he would not seek re-election, but was nevertheless censured by the Colne Valley party for his action. Not one divisional Labour party supported the new government, though in some cases the decision was not unanimous; nor did any other affiliated organization.

The taking up of positions on the Labour side was completed on 7th September when the Trades Union Congress met at Bristol. In his presidential address Arthur Hayday set the tone of much subsequent Labour criticism when he declared:[3] "At the bidding of irresponsible and uncontrolled financial interests whose very existence is hardly known to the public the social policy of this country, which has set an example to the rest of the world, is to be violently reversed." The organized Labour movement thus took up almost immediately an attitude of solid, or, as it would now be called, monolithic hostility to the new government, and its claim to be a National government could not be rested on the support of all the main parties. Whether it would ever have come into existence if this solid opposition on the part of Labour had been foreseen must remain a matter for conjecture. Though the opposition was unyielding, criticism of the former Labour leaders at this stage was still muted. The ties of old friendship, the hope of reconciliation when the crisis was over and the fact that too many potential critics were themselves implicated in the proposed economies acted as restraining influences.

The Liberal members of Parliament, like the Labour members, met on 28th August. It was a rare example of Liberal unity. Grey attended for the first time since the war in order to demonstrate his emphatic agreement with the action of the Liberals who had joined the government, and even the excluded Simon sent a message of support from Scotland. Reading conveyed from Lloyd George a message saying that he was "in complete accord with what is being done".[4]

The Conservative members also met the same day. Behind the scenes there had been some criticism of Baldwin and Chamberlain for not seizing the opportunity to form a purely Conservative

government and seek authority for tariffs. Amery had put the point
in a letter to *The Times* that morning. With this in mind, Baldwin
told the meeting that after the budget was balanced Parliament
would be dissolved and "you will then have a straight fight on
tariffs and against the socialist party".[5] His decision to take part in
the formation of the government was approved unanimously.

When the House of Commons met on 8th September the normal
procedural motion to go into a Committee of Ways and Means was
treated as a vote of confidence. MacDonald and Henderson justified
their respective actions, and Churchill disclosed that he was far
from happy about the formation of the new government. Some
might think, he said, that it would have been better to have given
the most complete assurances of support to the socialist administration in respect of all the economies and financial measures they
were willing to take, and he added: "Now that the largest party in
the house is in irreconcilable opposition, it is true that the term
'National government' can no longer be properly used." This was
little comfort to the benches opposite, however, for his main contention was that "there will be no restoration of confidence at home
or abroad until the socialist party has been again decisively defeated at the poll". The old free trader insisted that there could be
no revival of industry without a tariff, and so, with more con-
sistency, did Amery.[6]

At the end of the day the government secured their vote of confidence by 309 votes to 249. The majority was made up of 242
Conservatives, fifty-two Liberals, twelve Labour and three Independents. (One Labour member more than expected voted with the
government.) The minority consisted of 240 Labour, four New
party, three former Labour members sitting as Independents and
two Irish Nationalists. Twelve Labour members were absent un-
paired, and of these five are known to have abstained deliberately
from voting.

Snowden brought in on 10th September his emergency budget
providing for economies and new taxation on the expected scale,
and in the debate a new bitterness in the attitude of the opposition
was discerned by commentators. The credits of £80 million had
been duly obtained by the new government, but withdrawals of
funds from London had never ceased, though they had diminished.
On 15th September the men serving in the ships of the Royal Navy
at Invergordon sent a reasoned letter to the Admiralty protesting
against the cuts in pay and announcing their decision to refuse to
sail under the new rates, though willing to accept a cut which they
considered reasonable. The Admiralty ordered all ships of the
Atlantic Fleet already at sea to return to their home ports for an
investigation of complaints, but the Invergordon "mutiny", as it
became known, had an immediate and damaging effect on British

credit throughout the world. Withdrawals of funds from London accelerated sharply. The credits of £80 million were nearing exhaustion, and on 21st September by an act passed through all its stages in one day the Bank of England was relieved of its obligation to sell gold at a fixed price. The bank-rate was raised to six per cent.

The dreaded moment had come, and men waited anxiously for the disaster. As the hours and then the days passed it dawned on them at last that there was not going to be a disaster. As the days turned into weeks and months, they found that they had unwittingly and through *force majeure* taken the essential step for recovery. The pound sterling, left to find its own value in the exchanges of the world, sank from the artificial value figure at which it had been pegged to nearly one-third less. This meant that foreigners for the same amount of their own currency were able to buy more British goods, and British exports received a much-needed stimulus. Conversely, the British public had to pay more in sterling for imports of foreign goods, and devaluation served in place of the revenue tariff so widely advocated. Many economists' faces went red in the autumn of 1931. Only one, Hugh Dalton observes, the author of *Essays in Persuasion*, "can claim any intellectual or political credit in the crisis of 1931"; and after he had told a meeting at the House of Commons on 16th September what he would do if he were Prime Minister, Simon expressed the general view by saying that it was "tragic to see how Keynes had completely taken leave of his wits".[7]

There had been, as we have noticed, a desire among some Conservatives for an early general election. Until 21st September a powerful argument against such a course had been the danger to the gold standard. After 21st September the argument was no longer valid, and the pressure for a general election increased. When the government was formed, the most explicit assurances had been given that it was formed for the sole purpose of coping with the financial emergency, and that once the emergency was over there would be a dissolution. It had then been generally expected that this would be a relatively short time sufficient to ensure the passage of the emergency legislation. The legislation had been passed, and though it was not so obvious that the emergency was over the case for an early election was pressed.

Equally explicit assurances had been given that when the appeal to the country was made it would be made on a party basis. The parties would bow to their partners, so the phrase ran, and then return to their places. In the meeting at Buckingham Palace between the King and the party leaders preceding the formation of the administration it had been agreed, we may recall, that "during the election the National government would remain in being though of course each party would fight the election on its own lines".[8]

There had been many similar public utterances by Conservative leaders, notably by Hailsham on 3rd September:[9]

"The National government was formed for one purpose and one purpose only, to balance the budget. It is absolutely essential to finish that task quickly, to do nothing else, and to have an immediate dissolution and an appeal to the country on the Conservative party's reconstructive programme. The country could not be saved by economies alone."

There were others, not committed by these pledges, who saw the matter differently. Pre-eminent among them was Geoffrey Dawson, who wrote in a leading article in *The Times* of 16th September:

"Is there any real reason why the appeal to the country, whenever it may come, should not be made—on a broad programme of reconstruction which will include a tariff—by the National government as such? The notion that after the events of the last month, and in the face of an emergency which still persists, it can merely dissolve in the chaos of the old three-party system is altogether too light-hearted to bear examination."

The idea had already won much support among the Conservative party managers. Three weeks of working with MacDonald had impressed them with his honesty and utility. As the Parliamentary Correspondent of *The Times* explained on 17th September: "One of the great assets of the present National government is the faith which large masses of electors who voted for Labour candidates at the last election have in Mr. MacDonald, Mr. Snowden and Mr. Thomas." On the 21st, the same day that Great Britain went off the gold standard, the Conservative back-benchers in the 1922 Committee asked unanimously for the immediate imposition of an emergency tariff and for an early general election on the basis of a national appeal by the National government. Three days later the business committee of the party considered the same question, and according to Neville Chamberlain's account in his diary:[10]

"All were in favour of the national appeal by a National government under MacDonald, provided the programme embodied the full tariff. All agreed that the election should be at the earliest moment. All agreed that, if we went to election with R[amsay] M[acDonald] as P[rime] M[inister], we must accept him as P[rime] M[inister] when we come back ... Truly, the Conservative party is a wonderful embodiment of good sense, patriotism, and honesty."

At some point about this time Baldwin told Snowden that his party's request placed him in a dilemma. He was very anxious to stand by the conditions upon which the government had been formed, but party pressure was too strong.

Samuel was strongly opposed to an election, not only because it meant breaking his word but because it was likely to raise the question of tariffs and so bring into the open the differences among

Liberals. Simon had come out definitely in favour of the abandonment of free imports in a speech on the budget resolutions on 15th
September; and on the 21st, the day that Great Britain abandoned
gold, twenty-two Liberal M.P.s organized by Hore-Belisha and Ernest
Brown dispatched a memorial to the Prime Minister promising to
support him in whatever measures he and the majority of his
Cabinet colleagues might think necessary to maintain the financial
stability of the country and to restore the balance of trade; no one
doubted that they meant tariffs.[11] On the 23rd a meeting of Liberal
M.P.s asked Samuel to convey to the Prime Minister their strong
opposition to an election.

MacDonald was the key man in the situation and he was divided
in his mind. On 28th September Wigram wrote to the King, "He
does not like the idea of smashing up the Labour Party at the head
of a Conservative organisation,"[12] but on that same day the
National Executive of the Labour party took an action which hurt
and angered him. It decided that all members and supporters of the
"National" government ceased from that moment automatically
and immediately to be members of the Labour party.[13] Henderson,
it is worth noting, voted against the decision.[14] MacDonald felt all
the more hurt because on that same day also he had caused, or
allowed, to be circulated a memorandum which said:[15]

"It could safely be assumed that if there was an immediate
general election Mr. MacDonald would not lend himself to the plans
of any one party. The more he considered the situation the more he
was convinced that what was required above everything else was
national unity ... What the Prime Minister really wanted was a
'doctor's mandate' to deal with the position in which the country
now finds itself."

The term "doctor's mandate" caught the imagination and provided a basis on which an appeal to the country could be made.
MacDonald seems to have decided at this time in favour of an election if a formula could be found that would keep the three parties
together. The protectionist Tories were not at all anxious to keep all
the three parties together, and much of their energy was expended
in finding a formula which would enable them to retain MacDonald
as a figurehead while shedding Samuel and the other Liberal free
traders. The keenest among them was Amery, but Chamberlain
does not seem to have been far behind. "We were all agreed,"
Amery wrote in his diary, "as to the present importance of pitching
our tariff demands high enough to make sure of getting rid of
Samuel and Reading"; and on 30th September he was able to add:
"Neville produced a formula which he thought would serve to dis-
pose of Samuel. His view is that MacDonald is the key and that it is
essential to get him and no less essential to keep Samuel out." "Into
the sandy arena," says Chamberlain's own biographer, "Chamber-

lain threw a formula, asking for a free hand and indicating that the
new government would consider tariffs." At half past ten on the
night of 1st October, during a division in the House of Commons,
Amery heard with dismay that "Samuel had swallowed the formula,
'hook, float and sinker', and that there was no way of getting rid
of him", but at midnight the news was more cheerful with Samuel
being given till half past two the following day to say yes or no.[16]

It was not only his Cabinet colleagues whom Samuel had to
consider, but the formidable invalid at Churt for whom he was
deputizing. Lloyd George would have been willing to consider
tariffs if the election were postponed to a date at which he could
take part in it, but if there were to be an immediate election he
proposed to drape himself in the free trade flag; he had never even
in the great days of Liberalism felt strongly about free trade as a
principle, but he thought that his presence in counsel was essential
if Chamberlain and his friends were to be restrained from turning
the government into a purely Tory administration. When the
Cabinet met in the afternoon of 2nd October, Samuel, with the telephone from Churt still buzzing in his ears and fortified by a hastily
summoned meeting of Liberal members of Parliament, told his
colleagues that the formula was unacceptable and needed amendment, but the ground was slipping under his feet. Runciman speaking that night at Penzance said he was prepared in the matter of
tariffs to support any steps found necessary to restore the balance
of trade, and in *The Times* next morning there was a letter from
Grey urging that it would be unreasonable for free traders to stipu-
late that tariffs should be excluded.[17]

MacDonald was distressed by these turns and felt like throwing
his hand in, but the King, who had returned in the normal course
from Balmoral on 29th September, stiffened his resolution. The
King, who did not understand the semi-religious devotion of the
Liberals to free trade, at this juncture found Samuel "quite impossible, most obstinate",[18] but he was as convinced as ever that
MacDonald was essential at the head of the government. He urged
him to "brace himself up to realise that he was the only person who
could tackle the present chaotic state of affairs", and told him that
he would refuse his resignation if it should be tendered.[19] Such
words were balm to the tortured soul of MacDonald, and he
returned to the task.

On Sunday, 4th October, Samuel paid a visit to the oracle at
Churt. Lloyd George expressed himself strongly against any lasting
alliance between the Liberal party and the Conservatives, and
added: "If I am to die, I would rather die fighting on the left." He
enjoined Samuel to stand out against an election. On the way home
Samuel's eye caught a signpost, "Keep left—one way only", and he
telephoned the story to Lloyd George.[20]

F

The stream of visitors to the convalescent at Churt culminated on 5th October with the Prime Minister himself. If MacDonald sought Lloyd George's support, he failed to get it. He told Lloyd George he was still uncommitted, but the veteran was suspicious, and on his departure telephoned to Samuel to keep him up to the mark.

The Cabinet met that evening for a final decision. Samuel and Reading made a strong appeal that there should be no early election, but gave in when it became clear that the Cabinet would break up if the postponement of an election was insisted upon. MacDonald also capitulated. The deadlock over tariffs continued. It continued for a long time until someone, it may have been Snowden,[21] had an inspiration: instead of a joint manifesto signed by representatives of the three sections let each party draft its own manifesto, and let the Prime Minister sign an individual manifesto. This would free Liberals from the necessity of signing a statement referring to the possibility of tariffs, while MacDonald was an adept at making general statements committing no one to anyone. Samuel thought he had done reasonably well in difficult circumstances; but Lloyd George was furious and never forgave him.[22]

Polling was fixed for 27th October, and the campaign preceding it was the most virulent known since the first Reform bill. The results also were the most astonishing in the history of the British party system.

The Conservative party was solidly united against Labour, even if some members were lukewarm about the government combination. Amery recorded his own feelings in these words:[23]

"I disliked the whole humbug about a National government above party, and feared that a clear national verdict for the causes for which I had worked so long would be weakened and frittered away in order to hold together a coalition which had no other object than to perpetuate its own unnecessary existence ... I had no doubt that we could have secured an ample majority for a purely Conservative government on a straight issue."

Amery was, however, exceptional in the purity of his Conservative creed, and most Conservatives instinctively realized that to go to the country as a National government was very much to the party's advantage. Not only would they be able to deal a crushing blow to their chief opponents but there was a high probability that tariff reform might follow in its train. In his diary on 24th September Chamberlain had asked himself:[24]

"What would have been the astonishment of the socialist executive, if it could have overheard the Conservative executive agreeing to allow the man, who has all his life actively opposed them, now to have the credit of carrying out their own policy just when the whole country has come round to it."

The Labour answer would not have been the one Chamberlain

gave. It would have been that the Conservatives were using Mac-
Donald to win working-class votes that would not be given to the
Conservative party alone, and that when he had achieved their purpose they would discard him. As the number of Liberal and Labour
candidates available to support the government was limited partly
by their fewness and partly by finance, and as the candidates
already adopted in constituencies held by the Labour party were
mostly Conservatives, inevitably the great majority of the government candidates were Conservatives. Even after a fair number of
Conservatives had withdrawn to make way for Liberal or Labour
supporters of the government, no fewer than 519 Conservatives
were entered.

The Liberal party was shattered by the election into three sections
which never united with each other again. Both the Samuelites
and the Simonites supported the government, but as the Simonites
had come out openly in favour of the view that tariffs were a
necessary part of the British armoury they would not sign the
manifesto that appeared over the names of Samuel, Reading, Crewe,
Maclean, Sinclair, Lothian, Ramsay Muir and Lady Acland. These,
who were supported by Grey, kept the name of the Liberal party.
They put 121 candidates into the field. It is unlikely that many of
them received help from the Lloyd George fund, though Lloyd
George stated that the fund would be at the disposal of Liberals
who were unequivocal free traders.

Simon and the twenty-three Liberal M.P.s who acknowledged his
leadership hastily formed a new organization under the name of the
Liberal National party. He himself became its chairman, and Hore-
Belisha chairman of the executive committee; Geoffrey Shakespeare
gave much help. They fielded forty-one candidates. Many of them
were able to carry their local Liberal associations with them. Simon
recalled in his autobiography:[25]

"Few political organizations have ever got into fighting trim so
quickly. The election was upon us, but before the campaign began we
had not only established headquarters and staff, but had collected
an adequate fighting fund and gathered a large body of adherents."

Lloyd George's section of the party fought as Independent
Liberals. Only seven were nominated. Two of them were his son
Gwilym and his son-in-law Goronwy Owen, who gave up their
minor posts in the government; and a third was his daughter
Megan. Regarding the election as "a partisan intrigue under the
guise of a patriotic appeal",[26] Lloyd George came out strongly—for
the first time in his life, it was maliciously said—as a free trader.

Those members of the Labour party who had followed MacDonald
had rapidly to improvise an organization. A National Labour
committee was formed soon after the dissolution with Lord De La
Warr as its chairman. Twenty-one candidates were nominated. As

all the local Labour organizations had taken the same line as the party headquarters, they had to make their own arrangements in the constituencies. However greatly they may have welcomed Conservative votes, it would have roused fatal prejudice to have relied solely upon the Conservative organization.

The main body of the Labour movement maintained an impressive unity against the government, and 489 candidates were entered for the contested seats. The former Labour members were not spared, but on the contrary every effort was made to run candidates against them. Attention was specially concentrated on MacDonald's seat at Seaham and Thomas's at Derby. There were eleven straight fights between Labour and National Labour, and one three-cornered fight in which both were involved. Yet even in this desperate hour the quarrel with the Independent Labour party could not be resolved. The 489 Labour candidates included twenty-three put forward by the I.L.P. who gave the necessary pledge in regard to the standing orders, but nineteen other I.L.P. candidates stood without any official Labour support. There were eight other Labour candidates who must be labelled independent because they refused to give the pledge. This makes 516 Labour candidates in all.

Of the minor parties, the Communists ran twenty-six candidates and the New party twenty-four. Mosley had vaunted that he would have 400 candidates in the field. *Plaid Cymru* nominated two candidates, the Scottish Nationalist party four.

There were sixty-seven uncontested seats, of which the Conservatives enjoyed fifty-six, the Liberal Nationals none, the Liberals five and Labour six. Efforts were made to prevent government supporters from fighting the same seat, but they were not wholly successful. There were, in fact, about seven hundred government candidates for 548 seats. This was no coupon election. The Liberal National and National Labour candidatures had been kept low partly in order to prevent a splitting of the government vote, and the Liberals, still hoping to keep their position as a great party, were the main victims. The Conservatives gave Liberal candidates a clear field in only twenty divisions, of which eight had formerly been held by Liberals. Resentment was specially felt at the insistence of the local Conservatives in opposing Samuel and Maclean. Baldwin publicly deprecated the opposition to Samuel. In fairness to the Conservatives it should be noted that Ramsay Muir, chairman of the Liberal Federation, had addressed a letter to associations and candidates in which he said:[27]

"We need not look for any arrangement with the Conservatives. They will do their best to destroy us, except possibly in the constituencies where we alone have any chance of defeating Labour. There will be no pact and no coupons."

There was, in fact, in the 1931 election a fight within a fight. The minor, though not unimportant, issue was free trade *versus* tariffs. It was a confused fight because it took place in the context of the greater struggle between the "National" government and the Labour party. In 1931 there were no fewer than 373 straight fights between Labour candidates (including the I.L.P. and the independents) and candidates supporting the government (Conservative, Liberal National and National Labour). As the campaign proceeded, this aspect dominated everything else, and in the end it almost narrowed to a quarrel between the Labour party and its former leaders. It was the first election in which broadcasting by the leaders played a considerable part,[28] and the B.B.C. allocated seven talks to the government side and four to the opposition, given in the order MacDonald, Baldwin, Clynes, Lloyd George, Simon, Snowden, Graham, Samuel, Baldwin, Henderson, MacDonald. Not only did the government speakers have a greater share of time than the opposition but they used it far more effectively, and the experiment brought out that a new and potent factor had come into the party struggle.

There were several incidents in the campaign that rankled in the minds of Labour voters. One was the spectacle of MacDonald brandishing a handful of German mark notes from the inflation before his audiences and saying that was what would have happened in Great Britain if he had not acted as he had done. Another was the "Post Office scare". Henderson had asked whether depositors in the Post Office Savings Bank had the slightest fear that their savings were imperilled because they were held by a public service. Runciman commented that he happened to know the Labour government had been anxious about Post Office savings because a substantial part had been lent to the insurance fund. Snowden in turn observed:[29]

"Mr. Runciman's warning to depositors in the Post Office Savings Bank and other thrift societies is well founded. The Labour leaders when they ran away were well aware that I had warned them of the peril which threatened the savings of the poor. That peril is passed, due to the measures which the National government has taken. There is now no danger, but if the Labour party, with its programme of huge borrowing and increased taxation were returned it would at once become a real danger again."

Snowden appalled his old colleagues, and even some of their opponents, by the sustained venom of his attacks upon them. "Every day from the first day of the election campaign to the eve of the poll," as he later recalled in his autobiography,[30] he attacked them ferociously. He used the newspapers to expose their inaccuracies and repudiation of former commitments, but his greatest effect was achieved by the broadcast talk that he gave on 17th October:[31]

"I hope you have read the election programme of the Labour party. It is the most fantastic and impracticable programme ever put before the electors. All the derelict industries are to be taken over by the state, and the tax-payer is to shoulder the losses. The banks and financial houses are to be placed under national ownership and control, which means, I suppose, that they are to be run by a joint committee of the Labour party and the Trade Union Council [sic]. Your investments are to be ordered by some board, and your foreign investments are to be mobilized to finance this madcap policy. This is not socialism. It is Bolshevism run mad."

What made the impression on the country was not what Snowden said so much as the fact that it was he who said it. The government held most of the winning cards in their hand before the game opened, but they played with incomparably greater skill than their opponents. It was wise on Baldwin's part to choose the rôle of dummy and allow MacDonald and Snowden to play the hand. The response of Henderson and his friends was one of injured innocence, and at the end the score-sheet showed a little slam. Only forty-six Labour candidates were successful. Every Cabinet minister except Lansbury lost his seat. Apart from five under-secretaries the only other ministers to scrape home, and they by narrow majorities in what had been safe seats, were Attlee and Cripps. Never had such a massacre been seen in British political history, not in 1906, not in 1830. Of the forty-six, no fewer than twenty-three were ex-miners sponsored by the Mineworkers' Federation; other trade unions secured the return of nine; only thirteen were sponsored by divisional Labour parties, only one by the Cooperative party. In experience and in debating strength Labour in the new House was as weak as in numbers. Even if there be added the three I.L.P. candidates who were successful (Maxton, McGovern, Wallhead), the two Independent Labour members who were sponsored by trade unions but would not sign the pledge (Kirkwood, Buchanan) and the Independent (J. C. Wedgwood) who sat with them, the total Labour force amounted to only fifty-two. With them as occasional but fitful allies could be counted the Lloyd George family party of four (himself, Major Gwilym Lloyd George, Miss Megan Lloyd George, Major Goronwy Owen), making a maximum opposition strength of fifty-six. No Nationalist, no Communist and no New party candidate was successful.

On the other side the Liberals and Liberal Nationals (Samuelites and Simonites), were returned in almost equal numbers, thirty-three and thirty-five respectively; but the Samuelites had made a much greater effort and the result was tantamount to an electoral rebuff. By limiting candidatures as far as possible to places where they were assured of Conservative support and likely to win the Simonites obtained the maximum result for the minimum of effort. The number of Simon's followers actually increased by eleven whereas those of Samuel remained at practically the same level as in the last Parliament. The Liberals lost nine seats in three-cornered fights with Conservative and Labour opponents, whereas the Liberal Nationals lost only two in similar circumstances. Both Samuel and Maclean survived their three-cornered trials, and Simon had an easy passage in Spen Valley, but the three-cornered contests caused the disappearance of one Liberal National and two Liberal Ministers.

National Labour, like the Liberal Nationals, had concentrated its scanty forces in the first place in support of sitting members and otherwise as far as possible in places where it was assured of Conservative support and had a fair chance of winning. By these tactics it lost only two seats on balance and was able to claim thirteen members in the new house. Its greatest triumphs were the return of MacDonald at Seaham and Thomas at Derby, for the Labour party had made supreme efforts to ensure their defeat. There were not enough Tories and Liberals in either of these places to carry the day, and it would appear that enough Labour voters remained loyal to them to ensure their return. The extent to which normal Labour voters supported the government can never now be known, but it must have been a factor. At Burnley the Labour vote was exceptionally steady in falling by only a little over a thousand, but even so Henderson lost his seat.[32] There were two cases, Everton and Southeast Essex, where National Labour candidates had to compete with Conservative as well as Labour men for the favours of the electorate, and they polled respectably. Clearly the Labour strongholds that were lost would not have been lost if many normal Labour voters had not given their suffrages to the government candidate. Even the redoubtable Ernest Bevin fighting Gateshead for Labour was not able to prevent a majority of 16,700 from being turned into a debit of 12,938.[33]

If a visitor to the House of Commons asked where the real victory lay, he had only to look around. The answer lay in the 473 Conservatives (including two labelled as National) who overflowed the government benches and occupied most of the seats on the Speaker's left as well. Many of them had not the slightest expectation of being returned to the House of Commons, but there they were, and one man's vote was as valuable as another's. No Conservative member lost his seat, and Conservatives made 210 gains. With a majority of 331 over all others combined, they could afford to dispense with allies, and the omens for the Samuelite Liberals and the cause of free trade were not good. Nevertheless they had allies, and with them the government strength came to 554, a majority over all others of 493. There should be little danger of defeat.

A few moments' analysis, however, showed that in accordance with the British system party strengths in the House of Commons were distorted, and on this occasion grossly distorted, in comparison with the votes cast in the country. The electorate had increased by about a million since 1929, but despite the unusual circumstances and the immense publicity the poll dropped by almost the same figure. Clearly many of the electors were too puzzled to know how to cast a vote. The total vote cast for government supporters was 14,532,519, and for all others 7,123,854; and even when we allow for the fact that sixty-one government candidates were unopposed and only six opposition candidates the disparity between votes cast and seats obtained is striking. Conservative candidates obtained 11,978,745 votes (and there were forty-nine Conservative candidates who had no contest); there were 6,649,630 votes for Labour candidates (of whom six were unopposed). The Conservative vote rose by 3,322,272 compared with 1929, but the Labour vote fell by only 1,739,882. The success of the government coalition masked the fact that Liberal votes had fallen from 5,308,510 in 1929 to 2,212,404 in 1931, distributed between 1,403,102 for Liberal candidates and 809,302 for Liberal National candidates. Though it has to be borne in mind that the electors had fewer Liberal candidates to vote for in 1931, the movement of the country towards a two-party system was undeniable. The explanation of the immense success of the government coalition in 1931 is quite simple. In most constituencies Conservative, Liberal and a substantial number of normal Labour voters combined to vote against the Labour candidate; and as most of the government candidates were Conservatives, the total vote for Conservative candidates was swelled far in extent of its normal size.

On the morrow of the election Beatrice Webb wrote in her diary:[34] "This Parliament will last four or five years; and the Labour party will be out of office for at least ten years." She was right in the first part of her prediction and very nearly right in the second.

27

"NATIONAL" GOVERNMENT 1931–1935

The Conservatives secure tariffs—resignation of Liberal ministers and Snowden—Lloyd George's new deal—MacDonald succeeded by Baldwin—the Labour party in opposition—final break with the I.L.P.—campaign for a "united (socialist) front"—Mosley forms the British Union of Fascists—Labour reshapes its policy—the unemployment problem—the means test becomes an issue between Labour and Conservatives—but they are united on marketing schemes—and on Commonwealth questions—India causes a rift among Conservatives—Japanese aggression and the rise of Hitler—the East Fulham by-election—rearmament and the Peace Ballot—Lansbury deposed as Labour leader and Attlee takes his place

F EW administrations have been required to cope with such grave and such pressing problems as those that crowded upon the ministry reconstructed by Ramsay MacDonald on the morrow of the general election of 1931. The crisis in the balance of payments may not have been in reality so great as it appeared at the time, and the most essential step in coping with it had already been unavoidably and unwittingly taken; but the magnitude of unemployment and the method of treating the unemployed harassed the government all through its life. Under cover of alleviating the economic distress, the main body of government supporters demanded and obtained a reversal of the historic policy of free trade and secured a policy of imperial preference. Almost as soon as the administration was formed ministers were required to reformulate the relationships of the United Kingdom with India and with the self-governing dominions in a manner that amounted to a complete new philosophy of its imperial mission. These would have been tasks sufficient to engage the ablest minds for many years, even if they had not been overshadowed by a breakdown of the delicate fabric of maintaining international order precariously established by the Treaty of Versailles. While Great Britain was at the hustings, Japanese troops were pushing the Chinese forces out of Manchuria and the new military dictatorship of Japan openly flouted the League of Nations.

In January 1933 Hitler became Chancellor of Germany and in the following October the German delegation walked out of the World Disarmament Conference at Geneva, which quickly petered out in failure. The assassination of the Chancellor of Austria, Dollfuss, in 1934 forboded an act of aggression, and in 1935 the dictator of Italy, Mussolini, made no secret of his intention to launch an attack upon Ethiopia, a fellow-member of the League. This sequence of events compelled both government and opposition to rethink their attitude towards national defence and the maintenance of international order. It was a painful process for both, and it is against this grim background that the party struggle in these years has to be viewed.

Although MacDonald decided after the election to revert to the normal size of Cabinet, he did not find it easy to allocate the available places among the parties. The readiness to subordinate personal claims was no longer as conspicuous as it had been in August, though Austen Chamberlain, Reading, Crewe and Amulree made the task easier by offering to retire in favour of younger men.

Snowden, now wearing the ermine of a viscount, was not eligible for the Exchequer and became Lord Privy Seal, but Sankey and Thomas remained Lord Chancellor and Dominions Secretary respectively. National Labour thus kept four of the highest offices, and although its proportion of places had diminished it was far in excess of the party's standing in the country. Malcolm MacDonald was brought in as Parliamentary Secretary for the Dominions.

As Lloyd George had gone into opposition, there was no longer need to pay attention to his ban on the Simonites, and both Liberals and Liberal Nationals were included. Of the former, Samuel remained at the Home Office and Maclean was given the Board of Education, while Sinclair was made Secretary of State for Scotland; of the latter, Simon stepped into Reading's place at the Foreign Office and Runciman became President of the Board of Trade. The Liberal share of government posts flattered their membership of the House of Commons, but was not so disproportionate to their votes in the country.

Inevitably the lion's share of the places went to the Conservatives, though they did not claim all that they would have been entitled to demand by their membership of the house or their share of the popular vote. Baldwin remained Lord President, and with the prestige of such a victory behind him his leadership henceforth was unassailed. It is hard to recollect that only a few months earlier he had been fighting for his political life. Neville Chamberlain moved up to the Exchequer, Hoare remained at the India Office and Conservatives made a clean sweep of the Service departments. A feature of the appointments was the number of able Conservatives, given minor office for the first time, who were later to play a big part in the national life—Anthony Eden, Oliver Stanley and Duff Cooper among them. It was perhaps ominous for the future that such tigers as Churchill and Amery were roaming about outside the camp; but the moderate Conservative element in the government was notably reinforced in 1932 when Irwin returned from his historic mission to India. A place was found for him as President of the Board of Education, which had then become vacant by the resignation of Sir Donald Maclean in circumstances now to be described.

The first task facing the Liberals after the election was the delicate one of choosing a leader, and a meeting was called for 4th November. Simon immediately showed his intention of going his own way by evading an invitation from Samuel to meet for a discussion on India, and he and his followers did not attend the meeting. The day before it was due to be held, Samuel received a chilly letter from Lloyd George declining to attend "what I am informed will in fact be a section only of the Liberal members elected to this Parliament". He added: "It may therefore ease matters, and at any rate save embarrassment to my friends, if I write to tell you that I am not a candidate for election to any office in the group."[1] In the absence of competition, Samuel was himself elected leader.

Lloyd George's final separation of himself from the main Liberal body raised anew the question of his fund. By this time the original gifts had certainly been exhausted, and it could fairly be claimed, as Lloyd George did in a letter to Reading in 1929,[2] that the fund as it then stood had almost entirely been created by him through his remarkably successful handling of newspaper properties. In 1931 he changed the name from "National Liberal Political Fund"—no doubt because this was liable to confusion with Simon's organization—to "Lloyd George Political Fund", and laid down that on instructions from himself, approved by the trustees, grants should be made for "political purposes which would advance Liberalism in this country". Sinclair made a brave show of welcoming the fact that the whips' office would no longer receive £2,000 a year from the fund towards their annual expenses of £3,000.

A more serious problem even than Lloyd George's fund was soon to harass the Liberals. Many influential Tories had made clear that in their view a general tariff was the only instrument that could effectively cure the depression, and when the election put their party in a position to enforce their demands they were not to be baulked. Their minds, and in some cases their words, were closely studied abroad. The expectation that Great Britain would soon adopt tariffs led to a sudden flooding of British markets in order to escape duty. To cope with the situation, an Abnormal Importations Bill was rushed through all its stages in November, and under it duties of as much as fifty per cent were imposed on a wide range of goods. By a bitter irony it was no Tory but the Liberal National Runciman, with an erstwhile reputation for the purity of his devotion to free trade, who had the task of piloting the measure. Snowden and the Liberals thought he showed too much relish in the task, but felt obliged to acquiesce in what was on the surface a temporary expedient. They also acquiesced in a bill to raise a fund to help wheat-growers by a charge on each sack of flour.

Their heart-searching was deeper when the Cabinet appointed a committee to make an inquiry into the desirability or otherwise of a permanent tariff. Neville Chamberlain presided over it, and Snowden and Samuel were members, but it soon became clear that a large majority would come out in favour of protective tariffs as part of the permanent financial mechanism of the country. Samuel was particularly disappointed to find that Runciman had been won over completely. On the eve of the poll Chamberlain had said,[3] "All these matters are going to be examined carefully, thoroughly, exhaustively, impartially, by the National government when it is formed again," but in the view of Snowden and Samuel the examination was perfunctory and led to a predetermined conclusion.

Early in the new year, on 21st January 1932, the Cabinet considered the report of the committee, and Snowden, Samuel, Maclean and Sinclair announced that if the proposals were adopted they would resign. The Prime Minister asked for a decision to be suspended till the following day, and in the evening at Snowden's flat he tried to talk them round. It was in vain. The following morning they were preparing to take their leave when Hailsham proposed that the minority should not resign but should be allowed to oppose the measure, even to the point of speaking and voting against it in Parliament. Independently the same suggestion had occurred to Chamberlain. It was an astounding proposal from the constitutional point of view, violating the doctrine of collective responsibility that had prevailed in the Cabinet for over a hundred years. The last issue over which members of the Cabinet had "agreed to differ" was Roman Catholic emancipation in the period 1809–27. Snowden and Samuel were taken aback, but after a brief adjournment saw no sufficient reason to reject the proposal. A fortnight later Chamberlain introduced into the House of Commons the Import Duties Bill providing for a duty of ten per cent on all goods except those on a free list, those already subject to duty and the products of colonies and mandated territories. It was a proud moment for the son of Joseph Chamberlain to be standing before the dispatch-box and persuading the house to accept that permanent system of tariffs for which his father had campaigned as far back as 1903 and which the nation had decisively rejected at the polls in 1906 and in 1923. His words were equal to the occasion:[4]

"There can have been few occasions in all our long political history when to the son of a man who counted for something in his day and generation has been vouchsafed the privilege of setting the seal on the work which the father began but had perforce to leave unfinished. Nearly twenty-nine years have passed since Joseph Chamberlain entered upon his great campaign in favour of imperial preference and tariff reform. More than nineteen years have gone by since he died without having seen the fulfilment of his aims and yet convinced that, if not exactly in his way, yet in some modified form his vision would eventually take shape. His work was not in vain. Time and the misfortunes of the country have brought conviction to many who did not feel that they could agree with him then. I believe he would have found consolation for the bitterness of his disappointment if he could have foreseen that these proposals which are the direct and legitimate descendant of his own conception, would be laid before the House of Commons, which he loved, in the presence of one and by the lips of the other of the two immediate successors to his name and blood."

Attlee opposed the bill for the Labour party, and Amery spoke in support, as his record fully justified him in doing. Samuel then rose from the front bench, and there followed an incident unprecedented in the memory of any living parliamentarian—a Home Secretary speaking against a bill introduced by the Chancellor of the Exchequer. The division was taken on the third day, and there voted for the bill 413 Conservatives, thirty-two Liberal Nationals and nine National Labour, a total of 454. There voted against, forty-five Labour, thirty-two Liberals and one Independent, a total of seventy-eight. When the "agreement to differ" was subsequently challenged on a vote of censure, Baldwin calmly said: "We have collective responsibility for the departure from collective action."[5]

The innovation kept the Liberals in the government for the time, their number soon reduced by the death of Maclean—at this point Irwin was brought in—but Chamberlain and his friends quickly advanced from a general tariff applicable to all oversea goods to imperial preference with discrimination against foreign countries in favour of the dominions. A conference of Commonwealth representatives met at Ottawa in July and reached a series of agreements for preferential duties. On 8th September the Liberal members met and decided in favour of resignation. Apart from their general hostility to tariffs, and their particular dislike of discriminatory tariffs, they foresaw that the Ottawa agreements would wreck the World Economic Conference due to meet in London in 1933 with the object of reducing tariffs and other barriers to trade. MacDonald urged Samuel to stay on the ground that if he should go:

"The government will become purely party: politics will become purely party ... Whatever use I may have rests on the fact that I represent a combination. If you go, I am no longer the head of a combination. The *nature* of the government has changed."[6]

MacDonald wrote in a similar sense to the King:[7]

"I cannot hide from Your Majesty my apprehensions of the result of resignations at this time. The patched up Government will in reality be a new government, it will not be the one brought into being by the General Election, the country will have a shock, the Opposition Parties a score, and the outside world will see cracks in our national unity. The new Government will also be to all intents and purposes a single party administration, and I think Your Majesty will find that a Prime Minister who does not belong to the party in power will become more and more an anomaly, and as policy develops his position will become more and more degrading."

Samuel was not dissuaded. On 28th September the ten Liberal ministers and Snowden announced their resignations. Snowden had been given an additional grievance by the repeal of his tax on land values before it came into operation. A letter signed by Grey, Crewe and Reading supported the Liberal ministers' action; but when Samuel broadcast his explanation, the reply came from Simon. The Liberal split was never healed. The Liberal Nationals, while retaining a separate organization, moved more and more into the position of a wing of the Conservative party. It was impossible for the most critical eye to distinguish any difference in policy between a Liberal National and a Conservative. Chamberlain, rejoicing in the departure of the Samuelites as likely to make the government more homogeneous, looked forward to "the fused party under a National name which I regard as certain to come".[8]

Though Samuel had now left the government that he had done so much to create, Lloyd George was never reconciled and played no further part in official Liberalism. As fertile in ideas and as dynamic in energy as ever, the old warrior made frequent forays into the political arena, and his influence remained potent almost to his death; but they were henceforth the incursions of a free-lance.

One such foray caused some degree of alarm to the government. At the end of 1934 he adumbrated a British New Deal for conquering unemployment, developing the national resources and giving a new inspiration to youth. "Of course," admits his biographer, Mr. Frank Owen,[9] "it was another bid for power." It impressed many leading people, and MacDonald and Baldwin were urged to take him into the Cabinet. They would as soon have welcomed a whirlwind. It was then that MacDonald made his celebrated remark, never to be forgotten by the cartoonists, that he preferred to go "up, up and up and on, on and on, without experiencing the disastrous effects of sudden breaks in continuity".[10] It was Neville Chamberlain, however, who was the biggest obstacle. He said flatly that he would never sit in a Cabinet with Lloyd George. Perhaps his dismissal in 1917 still rankled. On his seventy-second birthday in January 1935 Lloyd George opened a public campaign on behalf of the New Deal. It made such a favourable public impression that in March Mac-

Donald invited him to submit his proposals, and he was cross-examined by a Cabinet committee. The meetings were studiously pleasant, Lloyd George said later, "but they knew in their hearts that they were going to knife me", and he added: "What they didn't know was that I had a dagger in my sheath for them too."[11] This was the Council of Action for Peace and Reconstruction, which was launched on 1st July as a non-party (or all-party) movement for influencing politics. He was joined by many Nonconformists led by Dr. John Scott Lidgett, and by a number of Conservatives, Liberals and Labour men of an independent cast of mind. Among them was a rising Tory, Harold Macmillan, who had already shown in a book called *Reconstruction: A Plan for a National Policy* his readiness to embrace new solutions.[12]

MacDonald's forecast of the consequences of the resignation of Snowden and the Liberals proved wholly accurate. Though the name "National" continued to be used until the wartime coalition was formed in 1940, from September 1932 it was indisputably a Conservative government carrying out a Conservative policy. The presence of a few National Labour and Liberal National members in it, supported by small contingents in the House of Commons, could no longer mask the fact that it was a Conservative administration resting upon a huge Conservative majority in Parliament. Mac-Donald himself became more and more of a figurehead, and the reality of power was in the hands of Baldwin long before Mac-Donald was compelled by ill-health and failing powers of concentration to resign in the summer of 1935. In the meantime MacDonald had not only to endure the charges of treachery from the Labour leaders who regarded him as having deserted the working-class movement; he had not only to suffer from the venom of Snowden, whose feelings of personal dislike found release after being pent up during the years of enforced collaboration; he had not only to witness the perfunctory toleration or open ingratitude of the Conservatives whom he had helped to the greatest victory in their history; but beyond all other trials he was tortured by the doubt whether he had after all done the right thing. In a discussion with Harold Nicolson about the 1931 crisis some years later he said:[13] "Any man in my position at the time, knowing all that I did, would have acted as I acted. However, I wish sometimes that someone else had been in my position at the time." From one quarter support never failed. The King who had called him to assume such onerous responsibilities sustained him with confidence and friendship to the end.

Whatever had been the case before, from September 1932 the political scene had reverted to a struggle between the Conservative and Labour parties. It is time to look more closely at the principal contenders.

The forty-six Labour members who returned to Westminster re-elected Henderson as their leader, but as he was out of the house they selected Lansbury to be chairman of the Parliamentary Labour party—which meant that he was acting leader. It was an inevitable choice as no one else had Cabinet experience. If Clynes had been available, he would undoubtedly have been preferred, and after him Graham, and perhaps others, but they were not available. Of the other two ministers of rank who survived, Attlee had sat in Parliament since 1922, whereas Cripps had entered only a few months earlier and was still regarded by the trade unionists with the suspicion that successful lawyers often excite. It was equally inevitable that Attlee should be vice-chairman, which carried the responsibilities of deputy leader. Maxton could not be nominated as he was no longer technically a member of the Labour party, and no one at that time would have thought of the young Aneurin Bevan, though later he was to be hailed as a leader. The choice turned out to be more important than it seemed at the time, for the forty-six had no thought that they were choosing the next Labour Prime Minister. Dalton has noted[14] that of the ex-ministers elected to the parliamentary executive in September just before the general election the casualties included, in the order of precedence established by the votes given to them by their colleagues, Henderson, Clynes, Graham, Johnston, himself, Greenwood, Addison, Alexander, Pethick-Lawrence, Shinwell and Lees-Smith; and of ex-ministers not on the executive, Morrison. It is fair to assume that in November the parliamentary party would have selected its leader and deputy leader from this list, and probably in that order according to availability. Neither Attlee nor Cripps was then a member either of the national or of the parliamentary executive. This is apart from any consideration of what might have happened if Mosley had not broken with the Labour party. If only he had kept his head and his seat, this would have been his hour.

Though only one-thirteenth of the total membership of the house, and with small experience of high affairs among them, the little band of Labour members strove gallantly to fulfil all the duties of an official opposition. The task was all the greater in that many of the Labour members who survived were in the nature of things older men sitting for safe mining divisions, and not able, as Attlee gently recalls, to "contribute much beyond their votes".[15] In practice the task of debate in the house and scrutiny in committee had to be undertaken by no more than thirty men, reinforced by the five I.L.P. members. Lansbury was by nature an individualist and the "hot gospeller" of the Labour movement rather than the leader of a team, but he strove with much success to adapt himself to his new rôle and won the admiration of the front bench opposite. The work was hard—Attlee tells us he normally left home at nine in the morning and seldom returned until after midnight—and had to be distributed, so that members became specialists on unfamiliar subjects, for example, the miner Tom Williams on agriculture. This stood the party in good stead in later years. For the fact that the forms of parliamentary democracy were preserved in Great Britain at a time when they were suppressed or cynically misused in many parts of the continent, the greatest credit belongs to the tiny band led by Lansbury.[16]

It might have been thought that in their reduced circumstances the Labour party and the I.L.P. would have patched up their quarrel, but it was intensified to the point of a final break. Discussions between Maxton and Henderson failed to break the deadlock over the Labour party's standing orders, and the national administrative council of the I.L.P. decided to report the matter to the I.L.P. annual conference at Easter. At that conference Maxton proposed that the I.L.P. immediately disaffiliate itself from the Labour party, but the motion was defeated by 183 votes to 144. Frank Wise spoke in favour of continued affiliation and acceptance of the Labour party's standing orders, but this also was defeated, by 214 votes to ninety-eight. David Kirkwood asked the conference to agree to continued affiliation on condition that the standing orders were amended, and this was carried by 250 votes to fifty-three. Approaches were accordingly made again to the Labour leaders, but the only concession the parliamentary party would make was to agree that the standing orders might need redrafting when Labour again found itself in office. (This was because the I.L.P. criticism that MacDonald had gone against Labour conference decisions was now conceded to have force.) The administrative council of the I.L.P. thereupon called a special conference in July at Bradford and recommended disaffiliation. This was carried by 241 votes to 142, and I.L.P. members were ordered to withdraw from local Labour parties and from Labour groups on local authorities. The I.L.P. thus resumed the position of a separate party which it had held from 1893 to 1900.

Though it meant a continuance of the schism in the Labour movement at a time of great weakness, from the long-term point of view the Labour leaders were right in refusing to allow the I.L.P. to continue to hold the position of a party within a party. In 1931 the Labour party had to be built up again almost from the foundations, and it was well to have no further truck with the special pretensions of the I.L.P., which had been a source of great embarrassment for many years. This was all the more necessary in that the I.L.P. had adopted at Easter, and amplified in July, a more militant policy calling for an intensified class struggle and throwing doubts on the adequacy of parliamentary methods. Maxton may have thought that a time when "MacDonaldism" was discredited was propitious for building up the mass membership of the I.L.P. as a separate

G

party on a left-wing programme, but he was soon disillusioned. At the end of 1931 the I.L.P. had 653 branches; a year later it had 452; thereafter no figures were given, and the I.L.P., cut off from the Labour party, soon ceased to play any significant part in the political life of the country, though nominally it is still in existence.

The I.L.P. had gone, but the Socialist League arose in its place and was to trouble the Labour leadership for several years. Frank Wise, who left the I.L.P. after the decision to disaffiliate, was the main founder, and he brought with him many other I.L.P. members who had no wish to leave the Labour party. They made approaches to two bodies which had been formed while the Labour government was still in office—the New Fabian Research Bureau and the Society for Socialist Inquiry and Propaganda. G. D. H. Cole was the leading spirit in both and he persuaded Bevin to accept the chairmanship of the society. The New Fabian Research Bureau had been created because the Fabian Society had sunk into a torpor. It declined Wise's overtures, and in 1939 was able to secure control of the Fabian Society and to rejuvenate it. The Society for Socialist Inquiry and Propaganda agreed to a fusion, and the Socialist League was brought into existence in 1932 with Frank Wise as its chairman. Bevin was not acceptable to the old I.L.P. element and played no part in the league. On Wise's death in 1933 control passed into the hands of Sir Stafford Cripps, who was largely responsible for financing it and now emerged as the leader of the Labour's left wing. The Socialist League was preoccupied from its foundation with the question what the next Labour government should do on assuming office to prevent sabotage by financial interests, and drew up an emergency programme including such items as the abolition of the House of Lords to cope with the imagined dangers. This was exasperating to the leaders and managers of the party, who were concerned to ensure that Labour did get back into office and saw in the Socialist League's effect on public opinion a serious impediment to so doing. They were particularly incensed by a speech in which Cripps, after saying that the Labour party would have to act rapidly when it came into power and deal with the House of Lords and the influence of the City of London, added: "There is no doubt that we shall have to overcome opposition from Buckingham Palace and other places as well." In his diary Dalton noted: "Cripps is a problem . . . He has no political judgement at all."[17]

The most serious friction between the Labour party and the Socialist League arose over the question of a united socialist front. The growth of unemployment and the cuts of 1931 gave the Communists an opportunity which they exploited to the full. The National Unemployed Workers' Movement led by Wal Hannington, a Communist, made itself the spearhead of agitation on behalf of the unemployed, and "hunger marches" focused public attention on their problems. In 1933, after Hitler came to power in Germany, the Communist International called on Communist parties throughout the world to convene conferences with the object of forming a united front against fascism. The British Communist party addressed a request to the Labour party, the Trades Union Congress and the Cooperative party, and the I.L.P. also issued an appeal for a united front and reached an agreement with the Communists. At this point the British Labour movement, following the lead of the Labour and Socialist International, took a step that was as courageous as it was wise, and one which greatly helped to rehabilitate its fortunes in the eyes of the electorate. The National Joint Council of the Labour movement declined the overtures from the Communists and the I.L.P. and issued a manifesto, *Democracy versus Dictatorship*, in which it equated Nazi dictatorship in Germany with Communist dictatorship in Russia, and proclaimed the historic task of British Labour to be the upholding of the principles of social democracy against dictatorship of every kind. The manifesto was approved at the Hastings conference of the party in 1933, but the Socialist League continued to agitate for a united front, or its wider successor, a popular front, and the issue harassed the Labour party until the Second World War made it irrelevant.

Until 1932 the Communist was the only form of these two dictatorships directly canvassing support in Great Britain. In that year Mosley went to Italy to study the "modern movements", came away deeply impressed, and transformed the New party into the British Union of Fascists. He was its leader, Forgan its director of organization and deputy leader. The British Union took to the streets and was involved in frequent clashes with Communists. These were the days when Ronald Knox asked:

> Whose is the face shall launch a thousand ships
> Sir Oswald Mosley's or Sir Stafford Cripps?[18]

and the *mot* ran through the democratic parties: "A plague on both your blouses."

The reaction against "MacDonaldism" was so strong in these years that even the leaders of the Labour party were sometimes carried away. At Hastings in 1933 Clynes moved on behalf of the National Executive and the conference passed a resolution laying down the conditions on which a Labour government should next be formed. The final decision as to the steps to be taken was to rest with the parliamentary party, but this body was to have before it the considered views of the National Joint Council which should consult the bodies represented in it. Three members of the parliamentary party were to be elected to advise the party leader on the choice of ministers, and the secretary of the party was to be associated with them in the task. The Prime Minister was to be subject to majority decisions of the Cabinet, and should recommend the dis-solution of Parliament only on the decision of the Cabinet con-firmed by a meeting of the parliamentary party. It may be added at once that when next Labour was in a position to form a government these decisions were completely ignored and perhaps forgotten.

Despite such occasional aberrations, the Labour leaders knew that their task was the re-presentation of social democracy in such a form that it was likely to persuade a majority of the electors to vote for them; and they knew also that after their crushing defeat and the loss of leaders this would be no easy task. As early as December 1931 the National Executive appointed a committee under its chair-man, George Latham, to frame a complete new policy for the party. Morrison and Dalton were leading members of the committee, and the object was to produce a series of reports on particular subjects which would convince the nation that Labour had a practical policy and serve as a better basis for Labour's policy when in office than *Labour and the New Social Order* or *Labour and the Nation* had done. Four reports were ready for presentation to the party con-ference at Leicester in 1932—on finance, agriculture, transport and electricity. There was a set-back to the report on finance, com-mended by Dalton, when Wise, supported by Cripps, moved an amendment asking for the nationalization of the Bank of England as well as the joint stock banks; and although Bevin and Pethick-Lawrence both brought their guns to bear against it the amendment was carried. It may be observed that despite six years of subsequent Labour government the joint stock banks are still not nationalized.

These reports raised the form that nationalization should take, and largely under Morrison's guidance, against the opinion of Bevin, the party came out in favour of ownership by a public board rather than direct state ownership on the Post Office model. It was held that the commercial freedom of such corporations and their effici-ency would be impaired if they were made directly responsible to a minister who could be questioned in Parliament about their day-to-day operations. There was a demand that certain members of the board of a nationalized industry should be appointed after consulta-tion with the trade unions having members employed in the in-dustry, but Morrison argued that if this were conceded it would be impossible to avoid the representation of other interests and eventu-ally persuaded the party to leave the appointment of members to such boards in the unfettered discretion of the minister. The issue arose in the first place over transport, and a decision was postponed at the Leicester conference, but in due course the Labour party's declared aim of industrial democracy was tactfully ignored.

These special reports led up to a more general document entitled *For Socialism and Peace*, which was presented to the Southport con-ference in 1934. It was intended to take the place of *Labour and the*

Nation as a programme of action, and it summarized Labour's aims as being:

"(*a*) To establish peace, freedom and justice by removing from among the nations the root causes of international disputes, by conciliation and arbitration, by renouncing war as an instrument of national policy, by disarmament, by political and economic co-operation through the League of Nations, and by agreement with states which are not yet members of the League.

"(*b*) To secure to every member of the community the standards of life and employment necessary to a healthy, independent and self-respecting existence, and to give equality of opportunity, both political and economic, to men and women alike.

"(*c*) To convert industry, with due regard to the varying needs and circumstances of different sections, from a haphazard struggle for private gain to a planned national economy owned and carried on for the service of the community.

"(*d*) To extend rapidly and widely those forms of social provision —education, public health, housing, pensions, and maintenance during unemployment—in the absence of which the individual is the sport of economic chance and the slave of his environment.

"(*e*) To adjust taxation in such a way that due provision is made for the maintenance and improvement of the material apparatus of industry, and that surpluses created by social effort shall be applied for the good of all."

What readers, both Conservative and Labour, looked at most closely was the section on economic reorganization. This laid down:

"Economic reorganization and control will take many forms, but the public ownership and control of the primary industries and services is an essential foundation step . . . The method of approach in any particular case will, of course, depend on the nature of the industry concerned.

"Banking and credit, transport, water, coal, electricity, gas, agriculture, iron and steel, shipping, shipbuilding, engineering, textiles, chemicals, insurance—in all these the time has come for drastic reorganization, and for the most part nothing short of immediate public ownership and control will be effective.

"The public acquisition of industries and services will involve the payment of fair compensation to existing owners . . . The suggested basis of compensation, broadly, is the net reasonable maintainable revenue of the industry concerned."

The Socialist League, asking for "a decisive advance within five years towards a Socialist Britain",[19] put down no fewer than seventy-five amendments, but the document emerged substantially unchanged and was approved as a whole by 1,519,000 votes to 673,0000. It thus became the official policy of the Labour party. It was amplified and expounded by Dalton in a book *Practical*

Socialism for Britain, published in 1935, which did much to convince middle-class voters that the Labour party had a programme
which was practical and not too socialist.

This was, however, a programme for a future Labour government. In Parliament the exiguous Labour party had to recognize
that power was in the hands of a government of a very different
complexion.

Clashes between Conservatives and Labour over the problem of
unemployment were frequent and bitter. The purely financial crisis
was soon resolved. The budget deficit was cut, the bank rate was
brought down to two per cent and the money borrowed from the
United States and France was repaid. In 1934 Chamberlain was able
to budget for a surplus. *Bleak House*, he said, was over and *Great
Expectations* had opened.[20]

Though the financial crisis was resolved—so quickly as to increase the suspicion on the left that it had been imagined or even
manufactured—the bleakness remained in the field of employment.
For the first few months of the "National" government the number
of those permanently or temporarily out of work actually increased.
The peak figure of 2,995,000 was reached in January 1932. Thereafter it began slowly to decline. The departure from the gold
standard and the tariff gave a needed stimulus to British manufacturers, and eventually under the genial impact of Roosevelt's
New Deal prosperity began to radiate out once more from the great
trading nation where the depression had started. But the average
number of unemployed never fell below two million in any year of
the Parliament. The percentage of the total Labour force out of
work, which had been 10·4 in 1929 and rose to 21·3 in 1931 and 22·1
in 1932, was still 19·9 in 1933 and 16·7 in 1934. Labour speakers
bitterly accused Conservatives of wishing to keep a large reservoir
of unemployed for the sake of disciplining those who were lucky
enough to have work. It was an unfair charge, for the government
were doing their utmost, if only for the sake of their own repute
and prospects at the next election, to find a solution, but Chamberlain's mind was impervious to unorthodox remedies. He was, it was
alleged, an inverted Micawber always looking for something to turn
down.

The figures of unemployment for the whole country concealed
great disparities between relatively prosperous areas, such as the
Midlands and London, and the Depressed or Distressed Areas—
tactfully renamed the Special Areas—such as South Wales and the
North-east Coast. In these regions whole communities seemed to be
dying without hope. The fact that unemployment was so concentrated and related to particular industries is an indication that it was
a technical rather than a political problem, but it was naturally in
these areas that Labour's strength and Communist hopes were

highest, while Conservative rule was most acceptable in Chamberlain's own Midlands and in the south. England had again become, what Disraeli had dreaded, a land of two nations.

The treatment of those who were unemployed caused recrimination as bitter as the fact of unemployment. The system of unemployment insurance, as formulated in 1911, remodelled in 1920 and amended by later acts, was incapable of dealing with the number of those now out of work and the length of time for which they were unemployed. What was to happen when a man exhausted his insurance benefit? The problem had been met in the past by the expedients of "uncovenanted", "extended" or "transitional" benefit subject to certain conditions on which local committees advised the employment exchanges. Among the victims the cry of "Work or maintenance" was strong. If they were denied access to the means of production, they said, in words that they had picked up from Marxist textbooks, the state had an obligation to provide them, if not with the equivalent of a working wage, at any rate with the means to live a life of self-respect. Such a philosophy was repugnant to Chamberlain's mind, not only on the ground of the cost to the public funds, but because he held it to be demoralizing to the recipients. He was also deeply conscious of the pressures upon local authorities and ministers and the danger of making the relief of the able-bodied unemployed a matter of auction between the parties.

The outcome of his cogitation was the Unemployment Act of 1934. The cuts made in 1931 were restored, so that the insurance benefit for an adult male again became 17s. a week, and for an adult female 15s., but every claimant was made to prove that he had paid thirty contributions in the two years preceding his claim, which had the effect of striking out about half those who had been claiming benefit. For those who had exhausted their benefit, or had no title to it, the Act provided for "unemployment assistance" to be administered on a non-contributory basis out of funds provided from the Exchequer by an Unemployment Assistance Board; and "unemployment assistance" was to be subject to a test of need, or, as it came to be universally called, a "means test".

The means test at once became the subject of fierce controversy between the Labour and Conservative parties and dominated domestic politics for many years to come. The most vulnerable feature of the test was that not only the applicants' means but the means of other members of his family had to be taken into account. It was, in other words, not a personal but a household means test. The authors of the act pointed to the need to retain a sense of family responsibility, while the opponents drew attention to the bad blood created among brothers and sisters, parents and children, and to the splitting up of families for the purpose of avoiding it. The Conservatives were able to cite a circular issued by Arthur Greenwood while

Minister of Health requiring the income and means from every source available to the household to be taken into account in assessing the amount of poor-law relief, but poor-law relief still had a stigma which it was felt should not attach to those genuinely seeking work. The Conservatives also made full use of the fact that the Labour Cabinet had agreed to save £5 million by imposing a means test for transitional benefit, but this concession under pressure was not felt to justify the permanent statutory provision of 1934.

More than anything else, the treatment of unemployment and the unemployed is the key to the relations between the Labour and the Conservative parties in the years between the fall of the Labour government in 1931 and the formation of the wartime coalition in 1940. The picture of the Conservative party as "grinding the faces of the poor" again found favour, and as the minister chiefly responsible Chamberlain bore much of the odium. The positive actions of the government in appointing Commissioners for the Special Areas, in encouraging industry to move into those areas, in setting up training centres and rehabilitation centres for the unemployed, and in creating trading estates for new factories in places of high unemployment counted for nothing against failure to deal with the main problem.

The bitterness between the Conservative and Labour parties did not extend to the whole area of domestic policy. In one field, that of agriculture, there was a significant harmony. The Tory and the socialist are agreed in not accepting the principle of *laisser faire*. For both, state intervention in the economic process may be desirable and even essential. In this respect they share a common outlook which puts them both in contrast with the Liberal, though in the present century even the Liberal has been forced to recognize many limitations of the principle of *laisser faire*. The Tory, Liberal and socialist should not be pictured as three points on a Euclidean straight line with the Liberal always between the other two, but rather as three points on a circle, with each intermediate between the other two or opposite to the other two according to the way things move.

In no field was this more evident than in agriculture in the nineteen-thirties. The Labour government in 1931 secured parliamentary approval for an Agricultural Marketing Act, which enabled the producers of any agricultural product to draw up a scheme, to be administered by a board, for the marketing of the product. Such arrangements were, in effect, combinations of producers to enable them to obtain better terms from consumers than would be obtainable in free competition; though they could bring advantages to consumers in such matters as quality and regularity of supply. The "National" government not only accepted the principle but extended it by the Agricultural Marketing Act, 1933, which gave the

Board of Trade power to regulate the import into the United Kingdom of any commodity subject to an agricultural marketing scheme; it provided also for the compulsory regulation of sales of home-produced agricultural products. Schemes were brought into operation for the marketing of milk, bacon, pigs, potatoes and hops without anything more than formal opposition or detailed criticism from the Labour party. The identity of view between the Labour and the Conservative parties then established has been maintained to this day and has lifted agriculture out of the depression into which it had sunk, but naturally at the cost of consumers, partly in the form of higher prices, but also in the form of direct subsidies. The agricultural marketing schemes led to misgivings in the Co-operative party, which is more concerned with the interests of consumers than of agricultural producers; and friction with the Labour party still occurs.

The identity of outlook in such matters between the main parties has been extended from time to time to industrial products, notably iron and steel, and it has led right-wing critics of the Tory party to taunt it with Conservative-socialism and left-wing critics of the Labour party to sneer at its state-capitalism. The historian of the Tory party and biographer of Neville Chamberlain, in writing of the 1932–5 government, says frankly:[21] "It was then a Conservative administration, using all the means of nineteenth-century socialism." The truth seems to be that the Conservative and the Labour parties both rest to a large extent upon the interests of producers, the former through the support of employers of labour and the latter through the trade unions of employed persons. The Liberal party in its hey-day rested upon the promotion of trade and commerce, which are in the common interest of producers and consumers, and the Cooperative party in the nature of things stands for the interests of consumers; but its political influence even within the Labour party has been small. Until the First World War the interests of consumers prevailed; since 1931 the producers have had their day. Which is more in the interests of the nation is a subtle question for the economic historian rather than the student of party.

The community of outlook between the Conservative and Labour parties extended also to relations with the other parts of the British Commonwealth. Two problems of great magnitude awaited the "National" government as soon as it took office.

One was a statutory definition of the relationship between the United Kingdom and the self-governing dominions. Balfour had presented to the Imperial Conference of 1926 a report which described the dominions as:

"Autonomous communities within the British Empire, equal in status, in no way subordinate one to another in any aspect of their domestic or external affairs, though united by a common allegiance to the Crown, and freely associated as members of the British Commonwealth of Nations."[22]

After the formula had been examined by legal experts the Imperial Conference of 1930 asked that it should be embodied in legislation and that the reserved powers and prerogatives still possessed by the British Crown and Parliament in relation to the dominions should be renounced. In the event it fell to the "National" rather than to the Labour government to carry out this recommendation, but there was a complete identity of view. The Statute of Westminster, brought into the House of Commons on 12th November, received the royal assent within a month. The right of the Crown under the Colonial Laws Validity Act, 1865, to disallow legislation in a dominion when in conflict with that of the United Kingdom was taken away, and the principle established that the legislature of a dominion could pass what laws it wished without reference to the United Kingdom; conversely, it was laid down that the Parliament of the United Kingdom could not legislate for a dominion without the prior consent of the dominion legislature.

Even before the Statute of Westminster was introduced Hoare and Sankey were closeted with Gandhi in the second session of the round-table conference on India, and on this subject also there was little difference between the Tory and Labour parties. The opposition came not from the Labour party but from within the Conservative party iself. Continuing his Seven Years' War, as Hoare termed it,[23] Churchill conducted a relentless, brilliant and at times mischievous campaign, both in Parliament and in the country, against the inevitable march of India towards self-government. Never in the history of human oratory have so much resourcefulness in debate and such splendours of language been used to so misguided an end; and unfortunately, not only was the cause of independence thereby delayed, but Churchill put himself still farther out of touch with the party that desperately needed his guidance in other directions where his instinct did not betray him.

A third round-table conference was held at the end of 1932. Gandhi, imprisoned by Irwin's soldier-successor, Willingdon, was absent. The British government then announced its draft proposals, and these were examined by a joint select committee of Lords and Commons on which all three parties were represented, along with assessors from British India and the Princes. In the spring of 1934 Churchill made his most audacious attempt to wreck the bill taking shape. He accused the Secretary of State of a breach of privilege of the House of Commons in that, at a dinner given by Lord Derby, he had induced the Manchester Chamber of Commerce to withdraw evidence it had sent in to the joint select committee and submit other evidence. This was too much even for Churchill's friend Amery. Churchill, he said, was impelled by the irresistible motive,

Fiat justitia, ruat caelum, which in translation meant: "If I can trip up Sam, the government's bust."[24]

He did not trip up Sam, who proceeded to draft and pilot the Government of India Act, 1935, based on the principles of an all-India federation, provincial autonomy, and responsibility with safe-guards. Provincial autonomy was brought into effect in 1937, but the all-India federation, resolutely opposed by Congress, never came into existence. The time spent on discussing it was not wasted, for it had a great educative effect on party opinion in Great Britain and made the passage to full independence easier some years hence. It was in the handling of this bill that R. A. Butler won his spurs and his reputation for a moderate Conservatism, not far removed from socialism as coming to be understood by the Labour party, that he was later to stamp upon the Tory party; for when in 1932 Lothian felt obliged in common with the other Liberals to resign, Hoare had picked him as Under-Secretary in his place.

The Statute of Westminster, 1931, and the Government of India Act, 1935, mark a turning-point in British thought, and especially Conservative thought, towards the other countries of the Common-wealth and Empire. Together they solemnized, says Sir Harold Nicolson,[25] "the renunciation by England of an imperial mission, which in the course of centuries had brought much benefit to herself, her dependencies and the world". The lesson that cost the loss of the American colonies in 1776 had been learnt; and although no other countries were mentioned in the statutes, thoughtful people began to ask themselves how what had been conceded to India could at the right time be denied to other dependent terri-tories. For the Conservatives it meant the abandonment of that dream of dominion over palm and pine that had been a cardinal article of their faith since Disraeli. At the time the significance of the change was not fully appreciated because less emphasis was laid upon the loosening of the political ties than upon the forging of new economic links at Ottawa, but in the course of years it became clear that a change of fundamental importance had taken place. The British Empire had been transformed into a Commonwealth and Empire, and was on the way to becoming simply a Commonwealth. As the changing nature of Britain's imperial mission was noticed, Labour thinkers also began to revise their ideas and to think more kindly of the British Commonwealth and Empire than had been their custom. It was difficult in the light of the Statute of West-minster and the Government of India Act to regard the oversea territories of the Crown simply as fields for capitalist exploitation. They began to take an interest, and even a pride, in the oversea dominions; and when a Labour government achieved power in New Zealand in 1935, they even began to hold them up as models for the British electorate.

In the field of foreign affairs, and the related field of defence, both the main parties were compelled by Japanese and Italian aggression and by the menacing rise of Hitler to make a fundamental readjustment in their thought. There was bitter recrimination between them, but basically their reaction was the same—a reluctance to face unpleasant facts and a proneness to make party capital out of national necessity, with the result that what was done was too little and too late.

The first world struggle had been fought as the war to end war, and from 1919 to 1931 most of the British people basked in the happy delusion that peace was safe in the keeping of the League of Nations. British policy from 1919 had been based on the assumption that the British Empire would not be engaged in any great war for ten years, and in 1928 this assumption was retained with the rider that the ten-year basis should start from the present and advance from day to day. National armaments were allowed to run down almost to token size. The Japanese seizure of Manchuria and penetration deep into China should have destroyed the happy illusion, but the failure of the League to take action was mainly assigned by the Labour party to Simon's alleged sympathy with the aggressors and not to any inherent defects in its structure or to the absence of the United States from its membership. The Foreign Secretary's handling of the matter certainly suffered from excessive legalism, and in his public speeches he seemed unconscious of the gravity of the political and moral issues. He was said by the delighted Japanese delegate at Geneva to have put the Japanese case far better than he (Matsuoka) could have done![26] Simon's fundamental dilemma was that the League could rely only on national forces, that the burden would fall almost entirely upon Great Britain, that Great Britain had nothing like the forces needed to sustain a great campaign on the other side of the globe and that public opinion would be hostile to their employment even if she had. The tone of Labour comment was set by Cripps, who asked in the House of Commons in 1933:[27]

"Are we merely going to put ourselves into the position of performing what we would call the centuries-old ceremony of kowtowing to the bullies of the world, or are we going to say that the theory of sanctions is a real theory, and it, indeed, is a theory and practice that was invented for the purpose of assisting in keeping peace, and are we going to apply it?"

When Hitler's rise to power made rearmament essential, whether undertaken solely in the interests of national safety, or to enable the League to fulfil its obligations, the leadership both of the Conservative and of the Labour party resorted to a series of distressing equivocations. Among the political figures of the front rank two men, and perhaps only two men, Churchill in the Conservative ranks and Dalton in the Labour, could look back with any pride to their speeches and actions in "the years that the locust hath eaten", as Sir Thomas Inskip later called them in the striking figure of the prophet Joel.[28] The descendant of Marlborough was obsessed by the change wrought in Britain's island security by the "cursed, hellish invention and development of war from the air". In memorable speech after speech, supported by information at least equal to that possessed by ministers, he begged for a strengthening of British air defences. So complete was the control of the whips over the House of Commons, and so sunk in lethargy were the parties, he recalled later, that it was like being smothered by a feather-bed. Baldwin, oppressed by the thought that "the bomber will always get through", was slow to move.[29]

In October 1933 there took place at East Fulham a by-election which seems to have made Baldwin lose his nerve. A seat that had been held by the Conservatives in 1929 with a majority of 1,705, and in 1931 with a majority of 14,521, was captured by Labour with a majority of 4,840, a turnover of nearly twenty thousand in two years. The Labour candidate, John Wilmot, owed his success according to Dalton to "his advocacy, not of 'pacifism', but of collective defence through a strong League of Nations, and of a general disarmament treaty",[30] and to local and personal factors; but Baldwin took it as evidence of a pacifist wave sweeping the country, and he could cite words used by the victor after the poll: "British people demand ... that the British government shall give a lead to the whole world by initiating immediately a policy of general disarmament." Three years later, speaking to the House of Commons on 12th November 1936 as Prime Minister on a Liberal motion dealing with the private sale of arms he used these words:[31]

"I would remind the house that not once but on many occasions in speeches and in various places, when I have been speaking and advocating as far as I am able the democratic principle, I have stated that a democracy is always two years behind the dictator. I believe that to be true. It has been true in this case. I put before the whole house my own views with an appalling frankness. From 1933, I and my friends were all very worried about what was happening in Europe. You will remember at the time the disarmament conference was sitting in Geneva. You will remember at the time there was probably a stronger pacifist feeling running through this country than at any time since the war. I am speaking of 1933 and 1934. You will remember the election at Fulham in the autumn of 1933, when a seat which the National government held was lost by about seven thousand votes on no issue but the pacifist. You will remember perhaps that the National government candidate who made a most guarded reference to the question of defence was mobbed for it.

"That was the feeling in the country in 1933. My position as the leader of a great party was not altogether a comfortable one. I asked myself what chance was there—when that feeling that was given expression to in Fulham was common throughout the country— what chance was there within the next year or two of that feeling being so changed that the country would give a mandate for rearmament? Supposing I had gone to the country and said that Germany was rearming and that we must rearm, does anybody think that this pacific democracy would have rallied to that cry at that moment? I cannot think of anything that would have made the loss of the election from my point of view more certain.

"I think the country itself learned by certain events that took place during the winter of 1934–35 what the perils might be to it. All I did was to take a moment perhaps less unfortunate than another might have been, and we won the election with a large majority; but frankly I could conceive that we should at that time, by advocating certain courses, have been a greal deal less successful. We got from the country—with a large majority—a mandate for doing a thing that no one, twelve months before, would have believed possible. It is my firm conviction that had the government, with this great majority, used that majority to do anything that might be described as arming without a mandate—and they did not do anything, except the slightly increased air programme for which they gave their reasons—had I taken such action as my right honourable friend desired me to take, it would have defeated entirely the end I had in view."

On the strength of these remarks Baldwin has been accused of deliberately misleading the country in 1935 for the sake of winning the general election, but close examination of the whole speech shows that what he was referring to was not the general election of 1935 but a hypothetical election that might have taken place in 1933 or 1934.[32] The key words to understanding his meaning are "All I did was to take a moment perhaps less unfortunate than another might have been", and the interesting constitutional point is that he seems to have thought a "mandate" at a general election was necessary to carry out a programme of rearmament. The pre-1914 Liberal governments had not taken this view, and it does not seem well founded. No government needs the "mandate" of a general election to bring its forces to any state of efficiency required by the international situation. If Baldwin did believe rearmament was necessary in 1933, and that a "mandate" from the electors was needed to authorize it, and refrained from going to the country because East Fulham had convinced him he would let the Labour party in, his action would be a severe condemnation both of the working of the party system and of himself.[33]

The government, nevertheless, did in July 1934 embark on a modest measure of rearmament in the air—the Royal Air Force was to be increased by forty-one squadrons or approximately 820 machines over a period of five years. It is hardly likely that this frightened Hitler, but it provoked the Labour and Liberal parties into putting down in the House of Commons votes of censure. Moving the Labour vote, Attlee said: "We deny the need for increased air armaments ... We deny the proposition that an increased British Air Force will make for the peace of the world, and we reject altogether the claim to parity." Supporting him, Cripps said that Baldwin had "had his hands forced by the wild men like Mr. Churchill". For the Liberals, Samuel asserted: "Nothing that we have so far seen or heard would suggest that our present Air Force ... is not adequate to meet any peril at the present time from that quarter [Germany]." A few weeks earlier he had compared a speech of Churchill's advocating rearmament to "the language of a Malay running amok".[34]

Throughout the latter half of 1934 the League of Nations Union under the instigation of its president, Lord Cecil, organized a poll of public opinion open to all residents in Great Britain over the age of sixteen on the question of support for the League of Nations. According to the organizers, strenuous efforts were made from the outset to establish and sustain the non-party character of the Peace Ballot, as it was called, but the question-begging title shows the difficulty of so doing, and the effects were only partly successful; the Liberal and Labour parties gave their official approval to the ballot and were represented on its executive committee, but the Conservative party took no official position. The first results came in during November, and by the summer of 1935 over eleven million people had answered the questions. Five questions were asked, one in two parts, and the affirmative and negative answers were as follows:[35]

	YES	NO
1. Should Great Britain remain a member of the League of Nations?	11,090,387	355,883
2. Are you in favour of an all-round reduction of armaments by international agreement?	10,470,489	862,775
3. Are you in favour of the all-round abolition of national military and naval aircraft by international agreement?	9,533,558	1,689,786
4. Should the manufacture and sale of armaments for private profit be prohibited by international agreement?	10,417,329	775,415
5. Do you consider that, if a nation insists on attacking another, the other nations should combine to compel it to stop by		
(a) economic and non-military measures?	10,027,608	635,074
(b) if necessary, military measures?	6,784,368	2,351,981

The results can be variously interpreted. Cecil himself claimed that the administration had been unmistakably shown that in the support of the collective system they had behind them the overwhelming approval of the people of the United Kingdom.[36] Others found it significant that only sixty-seven per cent of those who supported economic sanctions would be prepared, if necessary, to go on to military measures. To Baldwin the Peace Ballot was evidence, like the Fulham by-election, that the country was wedded to disarmament. At a meeting in Glasgow in November 1934 he called it misleading.[37] He also drew attention to a leaflet used in a municipal election which read:

"The Unionist party wants war. Your husbands and sons will be cannon fodder. More guns and poison gas will mean dearer food. Register your disgust with the policy of the warmongers by voting Labour."

In March 1935 Hitler announced that he was introducing conscription in Germany in defiance of the Treaty of Versailles. The British government immediately published a white paper justifying rearmament. For the Labour party Attlee said "the policy as outlined here is disastrous".[38] Simon visited Berlin that same month and from Hitler's own lips heard that parity in the air with Great Britain had already been achieved. The Air Ministry refused to believe it, and Hitler may have been bluffing.

"Depend upon it, Sir," Dr. Johnson told Boswell, "when a man knows he is to be hanged in a fortnight, it concentrates his mind wonderfully." A general election has the same effect upon a political party, and the realization in the summer of 1935 that a dissolution must take place within the following twelve months had a remarkable effect in concentrating the thought both of the government and of the opposition.

MacDonald, now barely coherent in his public speeches, exchanged offices on 7th June with Baldwin, who proceeded to give a more attractive look to a government that had by now rather faded in public esteem. Simon had been under continuous fire at the Foreign Office and returned to the Home Office to which he had first been appointed twenty years earlier. His Liberal National colleague Runciman stayed at the Board of Trade. Sankey went out of the government altogether, but J. H. Thomas and Malcolm MacDonald at the Dominions and Colonial Offices kept up the National Labour representation. It was, however, unmistakably a Conservative government under a Conservative Prime Minister. Londonderry, protesting that at no time under his rule was air superiority over Germany lost, became Lord Privy Seal and Cunliffe-Lister took his place at the Air Ministry. Hailsham went to the Woolsack. Halifax became Secretary of State for War. Oliver Stanley was given his first taste of high office at the Board of Education. The most important change was the transfer of Hoare to the Foreign Office. Many persons on whose advice Baldwin relied thought that the same gifts of conciliation shown by Hoare in dealing with the rival communities in India could advantageously be used to reconcile the French claim for security with the German for equality. There were others who pressed the merits of Anthony Eden. Promoted from being Under-Secretary for Foreign Affairs to Lord Privy Seal in 1934, he had shown a remarkable aptitude for negotiation with other powers. At home, while other ministers were assailed for their lip-service to the cause of international order, he had won a reputation as the knight-errant of the League of Nations. His debonair presence ranked him with the best-known film-stars in the eyes of the new women voters, and on all counts he was a man calculated to restore the Conservative image in the eyes of voters. But he was still only thirty-eight, and regarded by the more conservative members of the Conservative party as too idealistic and emotional—too "starry-eyed"—to be entrusted as yet with the main direction of foreign affairs at a critical time. As a compromise there was created for him the post of Minister without Portfolio for League of Nations Affairs.

Hoare and Eden soon had to deal with the threatened attack by Mussolini on Ethiopia. Their first effort, to compensate Ethiopia for the loss of territory to Italy by ceding a strip of land in British Somaliland with access to the Red Sea, was ruined by premature disclosure by a parliamentary private secretary and fiercely denounced. Eden and Mussolini formed a mutual dislike of each other, and Hoare became sensitive to a hardening of public opinion against Fascist Italy. On 18th August he wrote to Chamberlain:[39] "I see myself the making of a first-class crisis in which the government will lose heavily if we appear to be repudiating the covenant." In Hoare's estimate the general feeling about the League at that time was defeatist, but "he determined to make a revivalist appeal to the Assembly". He prepared a speech that seemed to him "on the one hand to explain our double policy of negotiation with Italy and loyalty to the League, and on the other, to give the League a programme for an expanding future". Baldwin approved after a perfunctory glance, and on 12th September he delivered it at Geneva. He has recorded that he did not think he was saying anything that he had not said time after time in the House of Commons, but one sentence that he used roused his audience to a frenzy of enthusiasm and reverberated round the world.[40]

"In conformity with its precise and explicit obligations, the League stands, and my country stands with it, for the collective maintenance of the covenant in its entirety, and particularly for steady and collective resistance to all acts of unprovoked aggression."

Hoare paused after "covenant" to repeat the word "collective",

H

and the impression he sought to give was that "collective security must be really comprehensive". The impression left among the British electors by his words when reported was rather different. "Is Samuel also among the prophets?" they asked. Whatever hesitations there might have been in the past, guided by its new Foreign Secretary the government would take collective action through the League of Nations to restrain Mussolini from attacking Ethiopia.

A parallel movement had been taking place inside the Labour party. In May Dalton had become exasperated with the ostrich-like attitude of the Labour leadership in the House of Commons to the resurgence of Germany as a military power. He was still without a seat, but was a member of the National Executive of the party. On 21st May he told a joint meeting of the Parliamentary Labour party, the National Executive and the General Council that it was impossible to vote against an increase in the Air Force sufficient to keep parity with Germany. The trade union leaders Citrine, James Walker and Bevin supported him. Attlee disagreed, saying that armaments must be related, not competitively with any one country, but to the forces available to support collective security. "That means," Dalton retorted, "that you want to sponge on the Red Army."[41] The next day some of the parliamentarians were in cheerful mood because Hitler had just said he was a man of peace, and in the House of Commons the party voted against the increase in arms.

Nevertheless, Dalton had started a movement which in the course of a few months greatly clarified the Labour party's attitude to defence and in so doing swept the pacifist Lansbury out of the leadership. It is necessary to interrupt the story of defence for a short time to consider what arrangements had been made for the conduct of the party's business in Parliament.

Henderson, still out of the House of Commons, had asked in October 1932 to be relieved of the party leadership and Lansbury was then formally elected leader. In 1933 Henderson returned at a by-election, but by that time he was deeply absorbed in his duties as President of the World Disarmament Conference, for which he had been nominated while still Foreign Secretary, and he had no wish to displace Lansbury. He also resigned in 1934, though more reluctantly, the secretaryship of the Labour party, which he had held since 1912. The party decided that in future the secretaryship should be incompatible with membership of the House of Commons,[42] and chose James Middleton who had already served as assistant secretary to Henderson and MacDonald for thirty-two years. Henderson was then ailing and died in 1935.

An accident in 1934 put Lansbury out of action for a long time, and in that period Attlee led the party in his place. Lansbury returned to his duties in 1935 to find the party in the throes of a debate about sanctions. Mussolini's reaction to the Wal-wal incident made it highly likely that before the year was out he would launch a full-scale war of aggression against Ethiopia. In September the Trades Union Congress was due to meet at Margate, and the three executives of the Labour movement held a two-day meeting on the eve of the session to consider what action should be taken. There was presented to the joint meeting a resolution which "called upon the British government, in cooperation with other members of the League, to use all the necessary measures provided in the covenant to prevent Italy's unjust and rapacious attack upon a fellow-member of the League".[43] It was opposed by Cripps, who had so strongly called for sanctions against Japan, on the ground that collective action against Italy was bound to become an imperialist war, and more logically by Ponsonby, the party leader in the Lords, and two other pacifist peers. Cripps then went away and did not stay for the vote the following day. Lansbury, according to Bevin, acquiesced in the resolution, which was put to the congress and carried by the overwhelming majority of 2,962,000 to 177,000.

The same resolution was set down for the Labour party conference at Brighton a few weeks later. This put Cripps, Ponsonby and Lansbury in a dilemma. On 20th September Cripps resigned from the National Executive and Ponsonby from the leadership in the Lords. A special meeting of the executive committee was called for that afternoon, and Lansbury, who was not prepared either to resign on his own initiative or to give up speaking in the country against the policy of sanctions, begged the committee to solve his problem of conscience for him. This the committee preferred to leave to the parliamentary party.

At Brighton[44] the resolution calling for sanctions against Mussolini's Italy was moved by Dalton, who said the immediate question to decide was: "Do we stand firm in this crisis for the policy to which we have so often pledged ourselves, or shall we turn tail and run away, repudiate our obligations under the covenant of the League and signal 'All clear' to Mussolini in his barbarous and long-premeditated assault on Abyssinia?" Cripps opposed, arguing that so long as a capitalist government was in power he was not prepared to trust it with arms, and stigmatizing the League as "nothing but the tool of the imperialist powers". Lansbury, then seventy-six, was greeted on rising with a loud and affectionate applause, almost the whole conference rising to its feet. He made no attempt to deny that his position as leader was impossible. "I agree with those who think it quite intolerable that you should have a man speaking as leader who disagrees fundamentally on an issue of this kind ... And I should not consider an expression of opinion hostile to my continuance as leader as anything more than natural and perfectly friendly." But he made no concession to the new mood of the party.

"When I was sick and on my back, ideas came into my head, and one was that the only thing worth while for old men to do is at least to say the things they believe and at least to try to warn the young of the dangers of force and compulsion." As he sat down in a gust of emotion, Ernest Bevin made his ponderous way to the rostrum. Forgetting all claims of sentiment or personal attachment, he launched a savage attack on the old man who had preceded him.

"Let me remind the delegates that when George Lansbury says what he has to say today, it is rather late to say it ... I hope you will carry no resolution of an emergency character telling a man with a conscience like Lansbury what he ought to do. If he finds that he ought to take a certain course, then his conscience should direct him as to the course he should take. It is placing the executive and the movement in an absolutely wrong position to be hawking your conscience round from body to body to be told what you ought to do with it."

Ignoring the protests, Bevin drove home his points with a diary of the meeting at which the policy now condemned by Lansbury had been agreed; and when he had finished with the aged leader, he turned on Cripps with acknowledged bitterness in his soul and lashed him for running away from his responsibilities. To his simple trade union mind, both Lansbury and Cripps were blacklegs; they had violated the fundamental loyalties and deserved no mercy. His speech was a brutal but awe-inspiring performance. On the following day the conference voted by 2,168,000 to 102,000 for the resolution. "Lansbury has been going about dressed in saint's clothes for years waiting for martyrdom," said Bevin afterwards in self-justification, "I set fire to the faggots."

Lansbury was deeply distressed, not least by the failure of any of his colleagues to say one word in his defence, and on 8th October he resigned the leadership of the party. The choice of a successor was, of course, limited to members of the House of Commons. Greenwood had returned at a by-election in 1932, but it was felt that Attlee had done a competent even if not very inspiring job as Lansbury's deputy and almost inevitably, without enthusiasm but without opposition, he was moved up to the higher post. If the choice could have been delayed for five weeks the lot might have fallen differently; for by then Parliament had been dissolved and a general election held, and at least eight ex-ministers whose standing had been considered superior in 1931 were back in the house. One of them, at least, was not disposed to minimize his claim.

28

LABOUR'S AND CHURCHILL'S ROAD BACK
1935–1940

Baldwin goes to the country—Liberal failure—the election is essentially a straight fight between Conservatives and Labour—the Conservatives given a further lease of power—Churchill still excluded—Morrison challenges Attlee for the Labour leadership but is defeated—Sinclair elected Liberal leader—the Hoare–Laval pact—Eden made Foreign Secretary—Margesson's firm control at the whips' office—internal quarrels of the Labour party—the Spanish civil war—the abdication—Chamberlain succeeds Baldwin —Eden's resignation—Conservative rift over the Munich agreement—Labour divisions over rearmament—and over the "united" and "popular" fronts—Cripps, Aneurin Bevan and others expelled —attempt to depose Attlee—Labour and Liberals decline to serve in the War Cabinet—Churchill and Eden brought in—the electoral truce—Chamberlain falls—Labour and Liberals agree to serve under Churchill

B ALDWIN would have been less than human as a party leader if the spectacle of Labour divisions at the Brighton conference had not convinced him of the need to refresh the government's authority with an appeal to the country. It seems by this time to have become established constitutional doctrine that the sovereign would grant a dissolution within twelve months of the statutory term of a Parliament, though he might query an earlier request. The vote on sanctions at the Labour conference was taken on 2nd October, undeterred thereby Mussolini's forces attacked Ethiopia the following day, on 10th October by fifty votes to one the League decided on collective action against Italy, Parliament was dissolved on 25th October and the poll was fixed for 14th November.

The election was unmistakably a battle between the giants of the Conservative and Labour parties with their allies and the minor parties making little impression on the general picture; and both made fundamentally the same appeal to the electors. For once in a way foreign policy and defence were, on paper at any rate, the major issues at stake though "bread-and-butter politics" continued to sway the votes of millions to whom Wal-wal meant nothing. Both the Conservative and Labour party professed to base their policy on the League of Nations; and both were unrealistic in that the Conservatives discounted the need for any great increase in armaments, while the Labour party denied that any increase at all was necessary. Speaking in the House of Commons on 22nd October Attlee declared: "We are not persuaded in the least that the way to safety is by piling up armaments ... We think that you have to go forward to disarmament and not to the piling up of armaments."[1] Although Labour candidates made no scruple about attacking ministers as "warmongers", Baldwin's message was not so very different. He asked, indeed, for authority to rearm, but in an address to the Peace Society on 31st October he inserted, into a cloud of beautiful language about "the level evening sun over an English meadow with the rooks trundling noisily home into the elms", his bid for the peace-lovers' vote: "Do not fear or misunderstand when the government say that they are looking to our defences ... Do not fear that it is a step in the wrong direction. You need not remind me of the solemn task of the League—to reduce armaments by agreement. But we have gone too far alone and must try to bring others along with us. I give you my word that there will be no great armaments. We are 'bound over to keep the peace', and it may not be an easy task, but we accept it."[2]

The Labour party threw 552 candidates into the contest. Cheerfulness breaking through, Attlee forecast a great victory for the party, but Morrison "did not consider that the opinions he expressed in a series of speeches were forceful enough to ensure the success he envisaged".[3] Conservative and Unionist candidates numbered 521 (including six who called themselves National), but on this occasion effective arrangements were made for ensuring that the forty-four Liberal Nationals and the twenty National Labour candidates were not opposed by Conservatives, so that the total government list was 585. For all essential purposes the Liberal National and National Labour parties may henceforth be regarded as wings of the Conservative party. The Liberals under the leadership of Samuel contested 157 seats, and Lloyd George's family party stood again for the four seats they held. It had been announced that the Liberals would field four hundred candidates, but the hope was disappointed. Despite its good spring showing, Lloyd George's New Deal played no significant part in the election, and the Council of Action put up no candidates but confined itself to a *questionnaire* to candidates, advising electors to vote according to the answers. This did not work out wholly as Lloyd George intended. Simon inquired of Scott Lidgett what action a voter should take where confronted with a straight fight between a government and a Labour candidate, and from that reverend Nonconformist figure he received the welcome answer: "Vote for the government candidate." This may have secured for him the 642 votes needed to save his own seat in the Spen Valley. The Independent Labour candidates dropped to seventeen and the Communists could muster only two. The Scottish Nationalists put up six candidates, Plaid Cymru one. Two Irish Nationalists fought in Fermanagh and Tyrone with no intention of sitting.

This was in essence a straight fight between the government and the Labour parties, and when the smoke cleared it was seen that the government had 432 supporters (391 Conservatives, thirty-three Liberal Nationals, eight National Labour) while Labour had 154. It was a fair result, for while the government deserved to lose, Labour did not deserve to win. Though there was bound to be a Labour recovery from the débâcle of 1931, the party was caught in the throes of dissension and indifferently led. It was obliged to reconcile itself to another four or five years in the wilderness. One satisfaction granted to Labour was to pay off its old score with MacDonald. Opposed by Emanuel Shinwell, who thereby expiated the error of nominating him for the leadership in 1922, MacDonald went down at Seaham by over 20,000 votes.[4] His son Malcolm was also defeated, but Thomas romped home easily enough at Derby.

The Liberals were even more disappointed than Labour, for they could secure the return of only seventeen members, and their leader suffered defeat at Darwen. The Lloyd George family held its four seats. Four Independent Labour party candidates were returned—all of them opposed by official Labour—only one Communist, and no Welsh or Scottish Nationalist. The two Irish Nationalists headed the poll but did not sit. Even more than the line up of candidates, the floor of the House of Commons after the election showed that Great Britain had substantially reverted to a two-party system.

Although the electorate had increased by about two-and-a-half millions since 1929, the poll was smaller by over half a million. This may reflect the confusion in the minds of the public no less than the inclement weather of a November day. The government parties received 11,810,158 votes and Labour 8,325,491. This was 1,675,861 more than the rock-bottom figure of 1931, but 35,392 lower than the 1929 figure, despite the larger electorate. The Liberals again suffered from the electoral system. Their twenty-one seats (including the Lloyd George quartette) were a poor showing for the 1,433,112 votes given to them in the country. The Liberal Nationals managed their affairs more skilfully. They secured the return of thirty-three out of forty-four candidates for 866,624 votes, which must have been largely Tory votes. It was clear, however, that despite their small showing in the house the Liberals had a substantial following in the country. If 161 candidates could bring out 1,433,112 votes, what would 500 do?

Having reconstructed the government as recently as June, Baldwin had no need to make any major changes, but Londonderry now moved out of the government altogether and Halifax took his place as Lord Privy Seal; Halifax was in turn succeeded by Duff Cooper at the War Office. Both the MacDonalds were kept in the government while looking for seats, but Malcolm exchanged offices with Thomas as the latter had given offence to Ireland. The departure of Londonderry at a time when the green light had at last been given for a cautious measure of rearmament was ironic, for he had been a persistent advocate of rearmament all along. His unguarded disclosure about the disarmament conference in 1932,[5] "I had the utmost difficulty at that time, amid the public outcry, in preserving the use of the bombing aeroplane, even on the frontiers of the Middle East and India," became the stock in trade of Labour platforms for many years and figured in not a few election addresses.

Londonderry's departure was read by many in conjunction with the refusal to admit Churchill. That statesman had let it be known that his opposition to the Government of India Act ceased with the royal assent. "The growing German menace" made him anxious to lay his "hands upon our military machine", and he coveted his old post at the Admiralty.[6] With the changing temper of Labour, he even dreamed of a government that would be truly national. Baldwin soon made it plain that he had no intention of including him in the government. Perhaps he thought, and he would have rightly thought, that it would be incompatible with his pledge of "no great armaments". Perhaps he merely held that there cannot be two kings in Brentwood. Like Lloyd George a few months before, Churchill was obliged to accept his continued exclusion from any share in the direction of national affairs. While Baldwin kept the reins of power in the Conservative party firmly in his own hands and Attlee strengthened his grip upon the Labour party, and both parties stumbled incoherently along the road to disaster, the two greatest political geniuses of the century were left to kick their heels. It was the age of Strube's little man; and the parties could not escape from the national cult of mediocrity.

According to its custom, the Parliamentary Labour party proceeded to the election of officers for the session soon after the reassembly of Parliament. It had been generally assumed that the choice of Attlee at the end of the last Parliament in succession to Lansbury was provisional and did not commit the party for the future. Among ex-ministers who had returned to the house were Clynes, Dalton, Morrison, Alexander, Johnston, Lees-Smith, Pethick-Lawrence and Shinwell. Clynes, now sixty-seven, when approached by Dalton took the view that the leadership should go to a younger man, and had thought of Dalton himself, Morrison and Greenwood, but apparently not of Attlee. Dalton had already made up his mind not to stand, and was vigorously canvassing for Morrison. Himself the son of the King's tutor, an old Etonian and Kingsman, he was of the opinion that the leadership should go "to a man of working-class origin, who had not been to a public school or a university". Of the others, Cripps (he told Morrison) had completely cooked his goose, Alexander had only the sectional Cooperative outlook on many economic questions, Attlee was very small and Greenwood was not the man he used to be. Dalton was not the only man who was canvassing, and in his own account and Morrison's importance is attached to a meeting of a masonic lodge to which a number of Labour M.P.s and officials of Transport House belonged. Their favoured candidate was Greenwood, and they seem to have agreed that if Greenwood was knocked out they would transfer their votes to Attlee.[7]

At an early meeting of the parliamentary party Shinwell suggested that as the majority of members were new or had been out of Parliament for some time, the election should be deferred, Attlee being confirmed as temporary leader.[8] His motion was heavily defeated, and the meeting for the choice of leader was fixed for 26th November. At this meeting Attlee was in the chair as usual and when he invited nominations Greenwood, himself and Morrison were proposed and seconded in that order. A member asked whether all three were willing, if elected, to give their full time to the job. Attlee said, "If I'm elected I shall carry on as before," Greenwood simply said, "Yes," but Morrison said at some length that he would place himself in the hands of the party, and if members thought he should give up the leadership at County Hall he would do so. The Labour victory in the elections of 1934 to the London County Council had been a resounding success and a big step in Labour's climb back to power. Morrison was proud of the work he was doing at County Hall, where Labour's grip was not shaken even when the county council was itself merged in the Greater London Council, and was loth to leave it. There is pathos in the fact that the triumph which had marked him out as a potential leader was to contribute to his undoing, for his reply was not well received, and comments of "Very slick" brought out also that his cockiness in manner—he was a true Cockney—did not ingratiate him with many of his fellows.

Members filled in the ballot papers, and the tellers announced: Attlee, fifty-eight; Morrison, forty-four; Greenwood, thirty-three. This was not the end, for it had been agreed beforehand that the candidate with fewest votes in the first round should drop out and a straight vote be taken between the other two. The first vote showed what was happening. Attlee's supporters almost exactly equalled the number of Labour members in the last Parliament. It is not surprising that working together in the difficult conditions from 1931 onwards had given the little band a sense of solidarity, and they felt that to vote for someone other than Attlee would be an act of betrayal. Morgan Jones was heard to murmur, "Fancy putting up a new member for the leadership," forgetting that Morrison had first entered the House of Commons in 1923.

Papers were filled in for the second round, and the result was: Attlee, eighty-eight; Morrison, forty-eight. The total vote was one more than in the first ballot, which would be explained by Greenwood voting on the second occasion. Greenwood and his supporters numbered thirty-four, and unless there were some rapid changes of mind as between Attlee's and Morrison's supporters in the few minutes since the first round, which is unlikely, thirty of the Greenwood faction must have transferred their votes to Attlee and only four to Morrison. This is where the masonic meeting a few days previously becomes of historic importance. In the approved manner, Morrison then moved and Greenwood seconded that the election should be made unanimous, and so it was. Returning thanks, Attlee said that of course it was only for that session and if they wanted a change later he would not complain.

Invitations were then invited for the post of deputy leader, and at this point Morrison made a fatal mistake. He declined nomination. His explanation was that he was too busy with the London County Council, but others present, such as Shinwell, thought he declined out of pique. In so doing he lost many opportunities of impressing himself upon the party that would have fallen to him and probably threw away his chance of becoming leader at a later date.

Far from being of temporary duration, Attlee's leadership was to last until, loaded with honours and basking in his party's affection, he laid it down voluntarily in 1955; but it was not unchallenged. Right to the end it was the subject of continual criticism and intrigue. Morrison, who denies that he took any part in these intrigues, never concealed his belief that he would have made a better leader, and Shinwell notes that the ballot of 1935 "was the start of a quiet rivalry and not-always-concealed dislike between the two men which was to jeopardize party unity for the next twenty years".[9] Dalton changed his view. He noted in his diary after the ballot: "A wretched, disheartening result. And a little mouse shall lead them!" But as the years passed he perceived that Attlee grew in stature while Morrison surprised by his comparative lack of growth or growth in the wrong direction. Several times later he campaigned for a change in the leadership, but not again in favour of Morrison.

The success of Attlee in securing and holding the leadership of the Labour party for no less than twenty years is such a remarkable phenomenon that it deserves more than passing notice. "A modest little man," Churchill is credited with saying, "and with much to be modest about"; but in 1935 and for years afterwards there was such a reaction against MacDonald that modesty was an asset. "We don't want another *prima donna*", was a favourite saying in the party. At all material times he was "the man in the job", and the instinct in the Labour movement against victimizing the man in the job is strong. He could have lost this instinctive support by antagonizing powerful elements in the party or by forcefully pushing some policy in which he believed strongly, but he made no enemies and is not known ever to have initiated any departures in policy. His type of leadership was to find out what the party wanted and then to do it. Morrison has called it "leadership from the rear". After any upheaval in the party, he would still be found at its centre of gravity. It is a different type of leadership from that of a Peel, a Gladstone, a Lloyd George or a Churchill, not to mention a MacDonald, but it is the type of leadership that the Labour party wanted in those years. The party was afraid of greatness. In the last resort Attlee held his post at the critical times by his negative qualities. The objections to the stronger personalities from time to time suggested in his place— Morrison, Dalton, Cripps, Bevin—were more vehement than criticism of Attlee's own shortcomings. Echoing Charles II, as he ranged over the aspirants for his office he could reflect: "Nobody is going to kill me to make you leader."

The Liberal party had also to elect a leader after the 1935 election as Samuel decided not to seek re-election and went to the Lords. Lloyd George attended the meeting, but preferred to retain his independence and nominated Sinclair, who received a unanimous call to the leadership of the diminished band.

The field was now set for the battle, which was not long in coming. What follows must rank as the most amazing *volte face* in British political history.

The Conservative party election manifesto had contained the following passage which satisfied all that the most ardent member of the League of Nations could ask:

"The League of Nations will remain as heretofore the keystone of British foreign policy ... The prevention of war and the establishment of peace in the world must always be the most vital interest of the British people, and the League is the instrument which has been framed and to which we look for the attainment of these objects. We shall therefore continue to do all in our power to uphold the covenant and to maintain and increase the efficiency of the League. In the present unhappy dispute between Italy and Abyssinia there will be no wavering in the policy we have hitherto pursued."

In December Hoare, worn out by incessant work for four years, sought a skating holiday in Switzerland. Laval persuaded him to break his journey in Paris for a few hours, which became two days.

At the end of the two days he had agreed with Laval on a plan for settling the Italo-Ethiopian war by the cession of considerable Ethiopian territory to Italy, the cession to Ethiopia of a port in Italian Somaliland (or failing that, in British Somaliland) with a strip of connecting territory, and the recognition of an Italian monopoly of economic development in a large zone of Ethiopia. It was intended for submission to Rome and Addis Ababa, and then to the League as a practical plan for settling the dispute.

If Hoare and Laval had been living in the nineteenth century, the plan might have been considered an act of wise statesmanship in cutting Ethiopia's losses before they became too great. If there had been no policy of sanctions, it might have been considered a prudent move on the part of two statesmen troubled by the resurgence of German military might and anxious not to throw Italy into the arms of Germany or to involve Anglo-French forces in a Mediterranean conflict away from the main danger. But Hoare had used brave words at Geneva in September—"steady and collective resistance to all acts of unprovoked aggression"—the League had called upon its members to apply sanctions, and the first mild sanctions were already being applied.

The plan was leaked to the French press while Hoare was blissfully unaware in the night train to Switzerland. There was an immediate uproar at home, and he returned—a sick man with his nose broken from a fall on the ice after a black-out. The outcry was not confined to the opposition, and the apparent lack of scruple in saying one thing at Geneva and doing another in Paris shook the Conservative party deeply. The Cabinet had at first approved the plan, but on sensing the public storm, and the dismay of his own supporters, Baldwin decided that it must be abandoned. Hoare, knowing that neither the French nor the British government was prepared to go to war, or to do anything likely to involve military action, and believing that the plan was the best obtainable for Ethiopia in the circumstances, preferred to resign rather than abandon it, and made a dignified defence of his actions from the third bench below the gangway on 19th December.

Following him in the House of Commons that day, Baldwin, always a master in the art of parliamentary confession, said:[10]

"We thought the proposals went too far and we would have liked to modify them ... I was not at all surprised at the expression of feeling in that direction. I was not expecting that deeper feeling which was manifested by many of my honourable friends and friends in many parts of the country on what I may call the ground of conscience and honour ... It is perfectly obvious now that the proposals are absolutely and completely dead. The government is certainly going to make no attempt to resurrect them ... If there arose a storm when I knew I was in the right I would let it break on me, and I would either survive it or break. If I felt after examination of myself that there was in that storm something which showed me that, however unconsciously, I had done something that was not wise or right, then I would bow to it."

In the opinion of some of those who had the decision in their hands,[11] the government was in real peril at that time, barely a month after its triumph at the polls, faced first with the prospect of defeat in the house and then rejection at the ensuing election; but the newly elected leader of the Labour party made a false move. Attlee had challenged Baldwin's personal honour:[12]

"There is the question of the honour of this country, and there is the question of the honour of the Prime Minister. If, as is suggested in some quarters, the Prime Minister won an election on one policy and immediately after victory was prepared to carry out another, it has an extremely ugly look."

This drew the veteran Austen Chamberlain to Baldwin's defence. His exposure of the Hoare–Laval plan in the private meeting of Conservative M.P.s had swung the party against it, and in combination he and Attlee might have brought the government down. He did not spare the plan, but the attack on Baldwin's honour gave him and the Conservative party generally an excuse—it may have been a welcome excuse—for walking with the government into the lobby.

The ministry had escaped, but under modern conditions no sooner is one election decided than the campaign for the next opens, and the Hoare–Laval pact did lasting injury to the Conservative cause in the country. Austen Chamberlain was invited to return to the Foreign Office, and when he declined Eden was given the post for which he had so carefully groomed himself. It was taken as a good sign by the supporters of the League, but the end of misfortunes was not yet in sight. Early in May Badoglio rode into Addis Ababa on a white horse and the Emperor left for Bath. The sanctions imposed by members of the League had failed in their purpose, and were indeed bound to fail because they stimulated the will of the Italian fascists without doing any serious injury to their economy. No sanction on trading in oil was imposed and the Suez canal was not closed to traffic. Hitler, forming the opinion that the democracies would not fight, had reoccupied the Rhineland. In an address to the 1900 Club in June Neville Chamberlain grasped the nettle firmly and said that the continuance of sanctions would be "the very mid-summer of madness".[13] Sanctions were in due course abandoned, but not before Lloyd George in a debate in the House of Commons on 18th June had shaken the government even as it had not been shaken by the Hoare–Laval pact. All the magic of the war years returned, and the House of Commons sat spell-bound as the old wizard turned on his foe from Birmingham and reminded Chamberlain of his election saying: "The choice before us is whether we shall make a last effort at Geneva for peace and security, or whether by a cowardly surrender we shall break all the promises we have made and hold ourselves up to the shame of our children and their children's children." "Tonight," said Lloyd George, "we have had the cowardly surrender," adding, with a sweep of his arm that seemed to clear the government front bench, "and there are the cowards." [14]

The government's stock at this time fell to abysmal depths, but its great majority was never in peril. A heavy responsibility fell in these years on the government chief whip in the House of Commons, David Margesson. He held that post in all the stormy years from 1931 to 1940, and at no time in that long period did the critics of the government make any deep impression on the government's majority. Churchill might make speeches of superb reasoning, but Margesson could nearly always muster three or four hundred more decisive reasons in the government lobby afterwards. Never in all the long history of the office of Parliamentary Secretary to the Treasury had its duties been carried out with so much smooth efficiency. It might have been better for the nation if Margesson had been less efficient and had allowed more of his flock to stray into the wrong lobby. His job, however, was not to make policy but to see that the government's policy commanded a majority, and without any of the cruder means of persuasion open to his predecessors he did it superbly. Chief whips do their work behind the scenes, seldom write their memoirs and leave few documents for the benefit of posterity; but in the history of party the reign of Margesson at the whips' office is a factor of consequence.

The government escaped more lightly than it should have done by reason of internecine quarrels that tore the Labour party apart. One of such quarrels was brought about by the civil war in Spain that began on 18th July 1936. At first the sympathies of the Labour movement were wholly with the Republican government. The National Executive and the General Council proclaimed their warmest sympathy for their Spanish comrades and launched an appeal for funds to help them survive the revolt of the army leaders. It quickly became apparent, however, that this was not simply another *pronunciamiento* after the pattern of many in Spanish history. Russia was supplying arms to the Spanish government, fascist Italy and nazi Germany to the insurgents, and unless great care was taken the dreaded European war would break out on the soil of Spain; nor could the Republican government be regarded simply as an injured democratic administration in danger of overthrow by a military and fascist conspiracy, for it had failed to preserve law and order for many months before and was heedlessly or of set purpose slipping into communism. The Popular Front government which had come to power in France under the leadership of the Socialist Léon Blum quickly saw the danger and, having no wish to become involved in a quarrel in Spain while Hitler did what he pleased beyond their north-east frontier, announced a policy of non-intervention. The British government, supported now by Churchill, came to the same conclusion. Dalton went to Paris and was convinced by Blum that non-intervention was his policy, not one foisted on him by Eden, and was the right policy. At the meeting of the Trades Union Congress at Plymouth in September, the General Council, through Citrine, urged that non-intervention, "distasteful as it is to them and it will be to you, is the only practical policy which can be followed in the present position".[15] They obtained a vote of 3,029,000 to 51,000 for it.

This looked decisive, but a wave of emotional sympathy with the Spanish republicans soon endangered Labour's support for non-intervention. Young men who had vowed that in no circumstances would they fight for king and country now went off to give their lives in a Spanish quarrel of whose origins they knew little. In Michael Foot's analysis:[16] "Spain cut the knot of emotional and intellectual contradictions in which the Left had been tangled ever since Hitler came to power. Suddenly the claims of international law, class solidarity and the desire to win the Soviet Union as an ally fitted into the same strategy." Cautious warnings about the danger of dropping the match into the powder barrel were swept aside as mere fascist propaganda. The annual conference of the Labour party assembled at Edinburgh in October in a very different mood from the Trades Union Congress at Plymouth, and to add to the confusion as they gathered delegates read a letter from Cripps, widely reproduced from the Glasgow *Forward*,[17] asking that "every possible effort should be made to stop recruiting for the armed forces". This would probably lead, Cripps argued, to some form of conscription which would provide a most favourable platform upon which to fight the government. If Great Britain were conquered by Germany, it was likely that socialism would be suppressed, but if Great Britain won another imperial victory British fascism would be less brutal than German but the world situation would be no better. The National Executive groaned at the antics of the *enfant terrible*, which were not making it easier for them to convince the nation that Labour could provide an alternative government.

The executive's difficulties were increased by the fact that Morrison had now come out against non-intervention in Spain. A cautious resolution moved by Greenwood expressed the hope that non-intervention would reduce the danger of a general war in Europe, but that it should be supported only so long as it was loyally carried out. It was carried by 1,836,000 votes to 519,000, but later that week the conference heard the famous Spanish woman Communist Señora Isabel de Palencia, known as La Pasionaria.

Claiming a Scots mother, and speaking in English, she swept the delegates off their feet in a burst of eloquence. Attlee and Greenwood were promptly dispatched to London to discuss the Spanish situation with Chamberlain, and reported back on the last day of the conference. Dalton commented:[18] "A large number of the delegates were now wildly excited. They were wallowing in sheer emotion, in vicarious valour. They had no clue in their minds to the risks, and the realities, for Britain of a general war."

In the meantime there had taken place a debate on the general international situation and defence. The executive sought to carry a stage farther the realism of the Brighton conference a year earlier, and the key words of their resolution were that "the armed strength of the countries loyal to the League of Nations must be conditioned by the armed strength of the potential aggressors". Dalton moved it, but the good effect of his strong speech was largely undone when Morrison, ostensibly supporting the resolution, declared that "this government's armaments policy is a purely competitive national armaments policy, and we cannot vote for it in the House of Commons". Bevin accused him of "one of the worst pieces of tightrope walking I have ever seen in this conference". The resolution was carried by 1,738,000 votes to 657,000.[19]

In face of the emotional upsurge in the party, and the undeniable evidence that the insurgents were being supplied by Germany and Italy, Labour's support for non-intervention was abandoned the following October. Attlee and three other Labour members visited Spain in December 1937 as the guest of the Republican Prime Minister, Negrin. A battalion of the International Brigade was called in his honour the Major Attlee Battalion, and he ran into some trouble on his return for giving the clenched fist salute—at that time a Communist symbol, though the visitor to the palace of Westminster may see Charles James Fox striking the same attitude in his statue in St. Stephen's Hall.

At the depth of the fall in Baldwin's reputation a crisis in the monarchy called forth all his best qualities and enabled him to retrieve his fortunes and retire in a blaze of glory. The life of King George V had drawn "peacefully to its close"[20] in January 1936, and he was succeeded by his son Edward VIII, whom most persons would have judged *capax imperii, nisi imperasset*. The new sovereign's wish to take as his wife a lady married to another man from whom she was on the point of securing a divorce raised moral and constitutional issues that could end only in abdication. Chivalrously Churchill suggested a "morganatic" marriage, by which the King's consort would not become Queen, and there was a little mad talk of a party of "King's friends" to back it in the House of Commons, but it soon petered out. With only a few exceptions the parties were united in thinking that such a marriage was incompatible with the

Throne, and amid universal sympathy George VI succeeded to the crown that his brother had laid aside. The new monarch was crowned in May 1937, and before the month was out Baldwin presided over his last Cabinet. In the delicate situation created by "the King's matter" he had not set a foot wrong, but it had left him mentally and physically exhausted. With the garter and an earldom he passed to the upper house, vowing "never to spit on the deck and never to speak to the helmsman".[21] He had been leader of the Conservative party for fourteen years, longer than anyone since Salisbury. As had long been foreseen,[22] Chamberlain was summoned to be Prime Minister in his place, and three days later a conference was called to elect him leader. It consisted not only of Conservative M.P.s and peers, but of prospective candidates and members of the executive committee of the National Union. Candidates had been present for Bonar Law's election in 1922, but not for Baldwin's in 1923; the presence of the executive committee of the National Union in 1937 was an innovation. Mr. R. T. McKenzie[23] thinks it was probably due to Chamberlain himself, in view of his interest in the organization of the party outside Parliament. Halifax presided, and Chamberlain's election was proposed by Derby and seconded by Churchill. There was no other nomination.

Some consequential changes in the government were necessary. Simon took Chamberlain's place at the Exchequer, and the Liberal Nationals also provided Hore-Belisha for the War Office, Ernest Brown for the Ministry of Labour and Leslie Burgin for the Ministry of Transport. Runciman temporarily went out of the administration. Of the National Labour element, Ramsay MacDonald now left the government—and died, at sea, the following November—but De La Warr remained in as Lord Privy Seal, and Malcolm MacDonald at the Dominions Office. (A foolish indiscretion about the budget had terminated J. H. Thomas's political life in 1936.) No one could say that the Liberal Nationals and National Labour did not get their fair share of the loaves and fishes, and the government continued to be called "National", but the power lay with the Conservatives. What the public did not appreciate for some time was that behind the scenes there was a serious rift among the Conservative ministers.

Unlike his predecessor, Chamberlain was a masterful and determined man who knew precisely what he wanted and went straight for it without deviating to right or left. In the Cabinet his intimates were Halifax, who had taken MacDonald's place as Lord President, Simon, and Hoare, who had been brought back to the Cabinet via the Admiralty and was now given the Home Office. These four constituted an inner Cabinet, and the Foreign Secretary, Eden, did not enjoy the Prime Minister's confidence in the same degree. This would have mattered less if Chamberlain had shared Baldwin's distaste for foreign affairs, but he was resolved on exercising the Prime

I

Minister's right to control the country's foreign policy. The aim he
set before himself was "appeasement", a laudable objective which
did not have at the time the pejorative meaning it has since acquired
through failure. His scarcely concealed wish was to detach Italy
from Germany, and his unspoken desire to divert Hitler's ambitions
in an easterly direction. Unfortunately, the knowledge of foreign
affairs that he brought to his task was not equal to his zeal or self-
assurance. He would, complained Lloyd George, look at world
affairs through the wrong end of a municipal drain-pipe, and he
seldom saw the picture whole. In one respect he resembled his critic.
Just as Lloyd George had his own "garden suburb" of experts,
Chamberlain neglected the Foreign Office and relied for advice, so
far as he sought any advice, on the government's chief industrial
adviser, Sir Horace Wilson, who had been seconded for service with
the Prime Minister since 1935. The experienced Permanent Under-
Secretary at the Foreign Office, Sir Robert Vansittart, whose warnings of the German menace were regarded by Chamberlain as tire-
some iteration and vain repetition, was removed and dignified with
the title of Chief Diplomatic Adviser, but his advice was never again
asked.[24] Eden's was ignored. Once when he pleaded the need for
more arms, Chamberlain told him to go home and take an aspirin.

A hint from Mussolini through Grandi made Chamberlain hot to
reach agreement with Italy. He sent the Duce a personal letter, and
wrote in his diary: "I did not show my letter to the Foreign Secretary, for I had the feeling that he would object to it."[25] His sister-in-
law, Austen's widow—Austen died in 1937—took up residence in
Rome and sent him personal messages from Mussolini. Eden was not
unwilling to see negotiations open with Italy, but insisted that there
should first be some tangible proof of Mussolini's seriousness, such
as a withdrawal of volunteers from Spain or a cessation of anti-
British propaganda. In January 1938 a graver issue arose. The President of the United States offered to invite the representatives of
certain governments to Washington for a discussion of the international situation if this should have "the cordial approval and
whole-hearted support of his Majesty's government".[26] In the
absence of Eden in the south of France, and without consulting him,
Chamberlain rebuffed Roosevelt's offer. Ten years later Churchill
commented:[27] "That Mr. Chamberlain, with his limited outlook
and inexperience of the European scene, should have possessed the
self-sufficiency to wave away the proffered hand stretched out
across the Atlantic leaves one, even at this date, breathless with
amazement." The differences between the two men, differences of
method and of temperament, were unbridgeable. On 20th February
Eden resigned, and his Under-Secretary, Cranborne, went with him.
They based their resignations on not yielding to Mussolini's black-
mail and kept silent about Roosevelt's offer.

The country was shaken for a time, but Eden soon made it evident that he had no intention of leading a campaign to compass the fall of the government. Halifax took his place at the Foreign Office. He had already, through the pretext of attending Goering's hunting exhibition, met the Führer, and the policy of appeasement was now concentrated upon the German dictator, whose appetite was growing. Austria fell to him in March, and in May the Germans in the Sudetenland of Czechoslovakia were ordered to increase their agitation. In July Chamberlain sent Runciman to negotiate between the Czech government and the Sudeten leader, Henlein, who had no reason to be displeased with his suggestions. On 7th September *The Times* invited consideration of "the project, which has found favour in some quarters, of making Czechoslovakia a more homogeneous state by the cession of that fringe of alien populations who are contiguous to the nation to which they are united by race".[28] Henlein fled to Germany and demanded the annexation of the Sudetenland. Chamberlain sought an interview with Hitler at Berchtesgaden. He formed the impression that "here was a man who could be relied upon when he had given his word".[29] At a second interview at Bad Godesberg he was faced with a demand for the cession of the Sudeten areas within a time limit. This, Hitler said, was the last of his territorial ambitions in Europe. It looked like war, and Duff Cooper secured the Prime Minister's assent to mobilizing the Fleet. Then Chamberlain was assailed by misgivings. "How horrible, fantastic, incredible," he broadcast to the British people, "it is that we should be digging trenches and trying on gasmasks here because of a quarrel in a far-away country between people of whom we know nothing." At a third meeting with the German dictator at Munich on 29th–30th September he agreed to press upon the Czechs the evacuation of the Sudetenland. He came back to England waving a scrap of paper about the desire of the German and British peoples never to go to war again, which he had no difficulty in persuading Hitler to sign, and he declared : "This is the second time in our history that there has come back from Germany to Downing Street peace with honour. I believe it is peace for our time."[30]

Though there was relief that the prospect of war had receded, Chamberlain's optimism was not shared by all his countrymen. The Labour and Liberal parties naturally denounced the Munich agreement without exception save for the pacifist wing, and, more significantly, the Conservative party was cleft in twain. Churchill has vividly recalled the schism at that hour :[31]

"Among the Conservatives, families and friends in intimate contact were divided to a degree the like of which I have never seen. Men and women, long bound together by party ties, social amenities and family connexions, glared upon one another in scorn and anger."

The Cabinet, he also recalls, was shaken to its foundations, but the event had happened and they held together. Only one minister resigned, and at the opening of a three-day debate in the House of Commons, speaking without notes from the corner seat of the third bench below the gangway, Duff Cooper challenged the folly of "addressing Herr Hitler through the language of sweet reasonableness". Churchill described the agreement as "a total and unmitigated defeat".[32] Margesson and his whips surpassed themselves in their exertions in these critical days, and only 144 votes were mustered against the government's 366. Some thirty to forty Conservatives who shared the views of Churchill and Duff Cooper ostentatiously abstained from voting. They had to bear the consequences of independence in the following months, when the full weight of the party machine was brought against them in their constituencies. In many cases it was necessary for them to seek a vote of confidence from their local associations, and this was not readily given. Even Churchill in the Epping division obtained such an assurance of support by a majority of only three to two. Bitter as these months were, they held out the promise of restored unity among Conservatives, for the lesson universally drawn from Munich was, not "peace in our time", but the need to rearm quickly for a war that was ever becoming more likely, and after the total subjugation of Czechoslovakia in March 1939 certain.

The Labour party was unable to take full advantage of the Tory discomfitures in these unhappy years because it was itself deeply divided. While demanding collective action against aggressors, it continued to take an equivocal attitude towards the armaments needed for collective action. Fortunately Dalton, who had no illusions in this matter, was chairman of the Labour party from the Edinburgh conference in 1936 to the Bournemouth conference in 1937, and with the prestige of that position he brought about a more logical attitude. He was helped by his identity of view with Bevin, who was chairman of the Trades Union Congress that same year. Dalton was also instrumental with Bevin's good will in bringing about an important change in the Labour party constitution by which the constituency parties were allowed to elect their own representatives on the National Executive—previously they had been voted upon by the whole conference, which placed the decisive power in the hands of the trade unions—and the number of such representatives was increased from five to seven.

In July 1936 Dalton tried to get the Parliamentary Labour party to stop voting against the Army, Navy and Air Force votes in Committee of Supply. Members could point to Conservative precedents before 1914, but the practice could easily be interpreted as meaning that the party wished to denude the country of all arms, and was so interpreted in Conservative propaganda. In 1937, when the Labour party came out in favour of "Arms for Spain", it became still more illogical to vote against "Arms for Britain". In the executive Dalton had the support of only Alexander and Lees-Smith, but he took the issue upstairs to the party meeting and there carried the day by forty-five votes to thirty-nine in favour of abstaining from voting on the defence estimates. Morrison and others publicly expressed their disagreement, but when the service votes next came up in the House of Commons only six members of the Labour party voted against them, along with the four I.L.P. members and the one Communist.

The snake of pacifism was scotched, but not killed. The decision of the government to introduce conscription in April 1939 gave another opportunity for its manifestation. Chamberlain was reluctant to take this step on account of pledges he had given, but in his reassessment of the international outlook after the seizure of Prague he yielded to the forceful arguments of Hore-Belisha.[33] The Labour and Liberal parties remained unconvinced, and opposed the bill, but opposition was not carried into the country. At the Southport conference of the Labour party the following month an amendment calling for the complete cessation of all further support for all national service schemes, except air-raid precautions, initiated by the government was defeated by 1,767,000 votes to 729,000.

A second and even bitterer quarrel divided the Labour ranks almost to the outbreak of war. This was the revival of the proposal for a united front between socialists and communists, followed by a new proposal for a popular front with anyone prepared to oppose the government.

The Communist party renewed in 1935 its appeal for affiliation to the Labour party, but the National Executive rejected it the following January on the ground that "the fundamental difference between the democratic policy and practice of the Labour party and the policy of dictatorship which the Communist party had been created to promote was irreconcilable". For good measure the executive issued a report British Labour and Communism accusing the British Communists of wanting a united front because their membership had dropped to 7,000. At the Edinburgh conference a resolution urging acceptance of the Communist appeal for affiliation "on the conditions laid down in the party constitution" won the mineworkers' support, but was rejected by 1,805,000 votes to 435,000.[34]

The cry for a united front was now taken up by the Cooperative journal Reynold's News and soon found practical expression in the Left Book Club started by Victor Gollancz. In January 1937 the

agitation took a new turn when the Communist party, the Independent Labour party and the Socialist League issued a manifesto
calling for "unity of all sections of the working class ... in the
struggle for immediate demands and the return of a Labour government, as the next stage in the advance to working-class power". It
advocated "the adoption of a fighting programme of mass-struggle,
through the democratization of the Labour party and the trade
union movement" and drew up a long list of demands. Among
Labour signatories were Cripps, William Mellor, Harold Laski,
Aneurin Bevan and G. R. Mitchison. The National Executive replied
with a circular declaring united action with the Communist party to
be "incompatible with membership of the Labour party" and disaffiliated the Socialist League from the party. A large number of
members of the League were not at all anxious to lose their
membership of the Labour party, and the League met the situation
by dissolving itself. At the Bournemouth conference Cripps moved
the reference back of the section of the executive's report dealing
with this matter, and was supported by Laski and G. R. Strauss.
After Morrison had told them they had "had a good run for their
money", the reference back was heavily defeated.[35]

The movement for a united front of all the working classes had
sometimes been called a popular front movement in reference to the
French *Front Populaire* and the Spanish *Frente Popular*, but towards
the end of 1937 there began to appear in Great Britain a demand for
a popular front of all "anti-fascist forces" willing to combine in
getting rid of the Chamberlain government and in substituting for it
a government that would drop appeasement and resist the aggressor
nations. This was taken up by *Reynold's News* under the editorship
of S. R. Elliott, and at Easter 1938 it obtained the support of the
Cooperative party conference, but a few months later it was rejected by the Cooperative congress. The National Executive condemned the movement in a manifesto, *The Labour Party and the
Popular Front*. The public reaction to the Munich agreement
strengthened the cry for a popular front to overthrow the Chamberlain government, and in a by-election at Oxford the divisional
Labour party withdrew its candidate in favour of the Master of
Balliol, A. D. Lindsay, who although personally a member of the
Labour party stood as an "Independent Progressive". He was beaten
by Hailsham's son, Quintin Hogg, now entering Parliament for the
first time, but a few weeks later the Liberal Vernon Bartlett, also
standing as an "Independent Progressive" on a popular front programme, won Bridgwater from the Conservatives in a three-
cornered fight.

Cripps and Strauss had supported the popular front through their
weekly paper, *Tribune*, and in January 1939 Cripps took a more decisive line. Despite his united front activities he was still a member

of the National Executive, to which he had been re-elected in 1937 after his resignation two years earlier. He sent to the secretary of the Labour party a memorandum urging a popular front open to all who opposed the Chamberlain government. His proposal found only two supporters and he thereupon circulated it generally. This caused great resentment among most of his colleagues, who could not understand how his agile mind could so easily leap from the extremer forms of socialism to cooperation with Liberals, and the executive called on him to reaffirm his allegiance to the Labour party and withdraw his memorandum. When he refused, they expelled him from the party by eighteen votes to one, only Ellen Wilkinson supporting him. He gave notice that he would appeal to the conference, and in the meantime he launched a great nation-wide petition in favour of a popular front "to save Spain, to save China, to save democracy, to save civilization itself . . . to save our own people from fascism, war, poverty and unemployment".[36] As he was receiving the support of some prominent members of the party, in March the executive required Sir Charles Trevelyan, George Strauss, Aneurin Bevan, Lieutenant-Commander E. Young and Robert Bruce to withdraw within a week. They declined and were also expelled.

When the annual conference was held at Southport at Whitsun, Cripps was allowed to speak though no longer a member of the party. He made a poor impression by concentrating on the legalistic aspects of the executive's right to expel him instead of on the merits of the case. Dalton answered him more in sorrow than in anger, and the *coup de grâce* was given by a young delegate from St. Albans, George Brown, who declared: "We have spent nine blasted months in a pre-election year just doing nothing else but argue the toss about Cripps!"[37] This was the general feeling, and the reference back of the executive's report was lost by 2,100,000 votes to 402,000. In June Cripps wound up the campaign, Bevan and Strauss were readmitted to the Labour party in 1940; Trevelyan also returned in the war; Cripps remained out till 1945.

Attlee was taken ill while at the Southport conference and in June had two operations for prostate trouble. In his autobiography he laconically relates: "While I was ill it occurred to a few people that this would be a good opportunity to change the leadership of the party, but this move got little support." Dalton fills in the details.[38] On 4th June an article by Ellen Wilkinson in the last independent number of the *Sunday Referee* asked how Chamberlain would feel if he knew that from now on he would be confronted in the House of Commons by Herbert Morrison, that superb political organizer. In an anonymous article in *Time and Tide* on 3rd June, that same week-end, she noted that news of Attlee's illness had been received with due sympathy, but his absence from Southport made not the slightest difference to the conference. On 9th June in a signed article in the *Daily Herald* the editor, Francis Williams, wrote of the leadership of the Labour party without mentioning either Attlee or his deputy Greenwood, and praising "the commanding position in public respect which has been achieved by Herbert Morrison through the great qualities of courageous and imaginative leadership he has brought to the control of London". There followed an angry meeting of the parliamentary party on 14th June, when a vote of sympathy with Attlee in his illness was carried unanimously and a vote of personal confidence in him was carried *nemine contradicente*, Ellen Wilkinson not voting. Morrison told the meeting that he had not seen her article in advance, had not inspired it and would have advised against publication. "This," says Dalton, "had been a queer episode."

The hot breath of approaching war was already felt by the delegates at Southport. All parties supported the guarantee to Poland. On 1st September Hitler struck at his eastern neighbour. The British people braced themselves for the declaration of war, but it was strangely delayed, and in the evening of 2nd September Chamberlain made a temporizing speech in the house. It gave the impression to the whole house, Duff Cooper recorded, "that even at this late hour Great Britain was going to repeat the surrender at Munich". In Attlee's absence Greenwood was still leading the Labour party. As he rose, Amery, himself "almost speechless with fury", according to Dalton, called out "Speak for England".[39] Greenwood did not fail, and said what was exactly right for the occasion. In the lobbies afterwards, at the Savoy Grill and at Churchill's flat there were anxious meetings of Tory groups. They were prepared to bring down the government if the guarantee to Poland was not honoured. They need have had no such fears. The delay was connected with French mobilization. On 3rd September for the second time in a generation Great Britain was at war with Germany.

There had been moves as war approached to secure a truly National government. In March Churchill, Eden and some thirty other Conservatives had tabled a resolution in the House of Commons to that effect. Cripps, now an Independent, visited Churchill and various ministers to promote the formation of an "all-in government". Oliver Stanley in June wrote to the Prime Minister urging the need to do something which would bring home to Hitler the certainty that Great Britain would fulfil her obligations to Poland; he could "think of nothing which would be more effective, if it were found to be possible, than the formation now of the sort of government which inevitably we should form at the outbreak of war".[40] Nothing came of these moves, but on the very day that Hitler attacked Poland Chamberlain invited Churchill to join the War Cabinet he proposed to set up and made approaches to the

Labour and Liberal parties. The executive of the Parliamentary Labour party met that evening and was unanimous in declining the invitation. The decision was approved the following morning without discussion at a joint meeting of the parliamentary and national executives. After so many years of criticism and suspicion of Chamberlain the Labour party did not feel it was possible to go in and serve under him. With more hesitation the Liberal party came to the same conclusion. Both parties emphasized that they would support the war effort while reserving the right to criticize both publicly and privately in the national interest as they conceived it. The Parliamentary Labour party gave immediate proof that its attitude would not be captious. By fifty-one votes to fifteen it agreed to support the government bill extending conscription to men between the ages of eighteen and forty-one. In the light of Labour's attitude to the Military Service bill barely four months earlier it was a remarkable transformation.

Churchill and Eden did not feel the same invincible reluctance to serving under Chamberlain, and under the pressure of war the Conservative breach was healed. On 3rd September Chamberlain was able to inform Churchill that the Admiralty was at his disposal, and the signal went out to the Fleet: "Winston is back."[41] It was almost exactly a quarter of a century since he had sat in that chair. He had pressed on the Prime Minister "Eden's influence with the section of Conservatives who are associated with him, as well as with moderate Liberal elements",[42] and Eden was made Secretary of State for the Dominions; it did not carry membership of the War Cabinet with it, but as it was necessary to keep the Dominions informed Eden was present at all meetings of Chamberlain's War Cabinet.

In the early days of the war arrangements were made by which certain of the Labour leaders maintained liaison with ministers—Greenwood with Chamberlain, Alexander with Churchill, and so on—for the exchange of information and ideas. An electoral truce was arranged. Under this the Conservative, Labour and Liberal parties agreed "not to nominate candidates for parliamentary vacancies that now exist, or may occur, against the candidate nominated by the party holding the seat at the time of the vacancy occurring". A second clause provided that "the agreement shall hold good during the war, or until determined on notice given by any one of the three parties signatory hereto".[43] In a separate document it was further agreed that vacancies on local authorities should be filled by co-option.

Attlee returned from his convalescence on 19th September. At the party meeting on 15th November Greenwood, Morrison and Dalton were nominated against him for the leadership, Dalton without his own knowledge, but all three withdrew. Greenwood's stock had risen greatly by his handling of affairs at the beginning of the war, and if he had been disposed to seize the leadership there is no doubt that he would have been supported, but he was too loyal a colleague to intrigue, and Attlee remained at the helm.

The electoral truce was not a political truce, and the parties would have been free to carry on their organization and propaganda, but in the nature of things there was a damping down, and almost a cessation, of party political activity. The chief event of political interest in the "twilight war"—the phrase is Churchill's[44] —was the supersession in January 1940 of Hore-Belisha as Secretary for War. The Liberal and Labour parties were suspicious that he had been sacrificed to the "brass hats", but as Chamberlain's contemporary note recorded, "nothing could be worse than perpetual friction and want of confidence between the Secretary of State and the commander-in-chief in the field".[45] It was the Secretary of State who went.

In May the "twilight war" ended with Hitler's invasion of Norway and the discomfiture of the British expedition. The opposition asked for a debate on the war situation, and this was arranged for 7th and 8th May. It soon became evident that the "twilight war" had ended in the House of Commons also. Chamberlain's opening speech was rudely interrupted, and he was reminded of his boast a month earlier that Hitler had "missed the bus".[46] The hero of Zeebrugge, Sir Roger Keyes, wearing the uniform of an Admiral of the Fleet trounced the failure to capture Trondheim. Before the day was out there fell upon Chamberlain's ears harsh words from a fellow-Birmingham member of high standing in the Conservative party. With blazing eyes Leo Amery used to him the words with which Cromwell had addressed the Long Parliament:[47]

"You have sat too long here for any good you have been doing. Depart, I say, and let us have done with you. In the name of God, go!"

It needed more than words, even such terrible words, to shift Chamberlain, and what was needed came at the end of the second day. Morrison opened and announced the intention of the opposition to force a vote. Chamberlain rose angrily and said: "I do not seek to evade criticism, but I say this to my friends in the house— and I have friends in the house. No government can prosecute a war efficiently unless it has public and parliamentary support. I accept the challenge. I welcome it indeed. At least we shall see who is with us and who is against us, and I call on my friends to support us in the lobby tonight."[48] The unfortunate words were conveyed to Lloyd George in his own room behind the Speaker's chair by his daughter Megan. The old war-leader, now seventy-seven, had been uncertain whether to take part in the debate, but Chamberlain's appeal to personal friendship brought him down to the chamber. It was the last and deadliest blow he was to deal in his long conflict with the son of Joseph Chamberlain. He begged Churchill not to "allow himself to be converted into an air-raid shelter to keep the splinters from hitting his colleagues", and turned on Chamberlain:[49]

"It is not a question of who are the Prime Minister's friends. It is a far bigger issue ... He has appealed for sacrifice. The nation is prepared for every sacrifice so long as it has leadership ... I say solemnly that the Prime Minister should give an example of sacrifice, because there is nothing which can contribute more to victory than that he should sacrifice the seals of office."

In vain Churchill rose at the end of the day to defend Chamberlain. He did so with a loyalty equal to his previous strictures, and sometimes could not make himself heard above the hub-hub from the opposite benches. Members filed into the lobbies, and it was noticed that many Conservatives were remaining in their places while the "No" lobby was crowded, not only with Labour and Liberal members, but with young Conservatives in uniform. The figures were announced by the tellers: For the government 281, against 200. The government were not defeated, but their normal majority of about 240 had fallen to a third of that figure. Forty-three Conservatives voted with the opposition, and some seventy abstained. Chamberlain walked crestfallen to his room and told Churchill that someone must form a government in which all parties would serve, or the country could not get through.

Next day, 9th May, the Conservative dissidents formed themselves into a body with Amery as their chairman and Boothby as their secretary, but the organization had no need to remain in being for long. That afternoon Chamberlain asked Attlee and Greenwood to see him in the presence of Halifax and Churchill. He asked if Labour would serve under him. They replied that they could not commit themselves without consulting their friends, but they thought the answer would probably be in the negative. He then asked if they would serve in a National government under another Prime Minister, and was again told they would need to consult.

It so happened that the annual conference of the Labour party was about to be held at Bournemouth, and members of the National Executive left London for a preliminary meeting there the following day, 10th May. They left in the knowledge that the Germans were sweeping through Holland, Belgium and Luxembourg to France. It was resolved "to take our share of responsibility, as a full partner, in a new government, which, under a new Prime Minister, commands the confidence of the nation".[50] It was noted that this was a decision taken there and then, not merely a recommendation to the party conference to open in three days' time, and Attlee and Greenwood were asked to return forthwith for any negotiations that might arise out of it. As they were leaving, Chamberlain's secretary telephoned to ask if they could yet answer the Prime Minister's two questions. Attlee read the resolution over the telephone.

During the morning of that day Chamberlain had asked Halifax and Churchill to see him at No. 10 Downing Street. Sitting opposite them across the great table, he said he was satisfied that it was beyond his power to form a National government.[51] The question was, for whom should he advise the King to send when his own resignation had been accepted. At last Halifax broke the long silence and said it would be impossible for a peer to discharge the duties of a Prime Minister in a war like that one.

Chamberlain's first preference, according to his biographer, had been for Halifax; and even Dalton had told Butler after the critical vote in the house that in his view, shared by others, there was much to be said for Halifax.[52] Chamberlain seems to have thought that Churchill's brush with the Labour party in his defence indicated hostility between them, but Churchill's loyalty to his leader was not misinterpreted on the Labour benches.

About 5 p.m. Chamberlain received the telephone call from Bournemouth, and knew that the supposition on which he had based his interview with Churchill and Halifax was correct. Shortly before 6 p.m. he was at the Palace to hand in his resignation, and soon afterwards Churchill was summoned there and commissioned to form a government. When Attlee and Greenwood arrived in London to see the Prime Minister, they were directed to the Admiralty.

They learnt that Churchill was disposed to offer the Labour party rather more than a third of the places with two seats in the War Cabinet of five, or perhaps six. While asking Attlee to supply a list of names, he mentioned Bevin, Alexander, Morrison and Dalton as men whose services in high office were immediately required. He let them know that they must not put a veto on Chamberlain, as this would not be acceptable to the Conservative party, of which he remained leader; and Halifax was to remain at the Foreign Office. About ten o'clock he sent these five names for the Cabinet—himself, Chamberlain, Attlee, Halifax, Greenwood—to the King. He also made up his mind on the three Service chiefs—Alexander for the Admiralty, Eden for the War Office, Sinclair for the Air Ministry. He intended to be Minister of Defence himself.

Further talks took place next day, and Attlee spent much time on the telephone to Bournemouth. There was strong resistance to the retention of Chamberlain, but Attlee and Greenwood urged that to demand his total exclusion would create too much bitterness. Churchill gave way on his first proposal to make the ex-Premier Chancellor of the Exchequer, and offered him the Lord Presidency with the leadership of the House of Commons. Attlee and Greenwood demurred to having him as leader of the house, inasmuch as in a coalition the leader had to be generally acceptable, and with Chamberlain's ready consent Churchill added the leadership to his other duties, with Attlee as his deputy.

The desire for a purge of "guilty men" extended to Simon and Hoare. The latter was dropped—and sent in due course as Ambassador to Spain—but Simon was made Lord Chancellor and became a viscount. "There," Attlee told Bournemouth, "he will be quite innocuous."[53]

The Liberal party was wholly ready to join the coalition, but made difficulties about Sinclair accepting the post of Secretary of State for Air without a seat in the Cabinet, as it was thought to derogate from his position as party leader. Churchill was insistent that the Cabinet must be kept small, and the obstacle was overcome by a promise that he would be asked to the Cabinet whenever any matter affecting fundamental political issues or party union was under discussion; he was, in fact, usually present.

On the second day of government-making three Conservatives were given office. The Exchequer went to Kingsley Wood, and the Colonial Office to Lord Lloyd, while Duff Cooper was brought back to the government *via* the Ministry of Information, that grave of reputations. Two non-party men were given posts. The formidable civil servant, Sir John Anderson, held in awe by the departments as "Jehovah", who had entered Chamberlain's administration in 1938 as Lord Privy Seal, now became Home Secretary and Minister of Home Security; and Sir Andrew Duncan, the steel chief, went to the Board of Trade. Only one Labour appointment was made that day; without enthusiasm, Morrison accepted the Ministry of Supply.

On the third day, 13th May, Churchill was able to get the consent of Ernest Bevin to take the vital post of Minister of Labour and National Service. He had designated the burly trade union leader for this key office from the start, but Bevin thought it prudent to secure the agreement of the Transport and General Workers' Union, of which he was still secretary, before accepting. On the same day Churchill filled another key post with equal success by making Lord Woolton, not then associated with any party, Minister of Food. He made his old friend Amery Secretary of State for India and Burma, fully aware that the evolution of India would be accelerated during the war. No complaint seems to have been registered when he kept Malcolm MacDonald in the government as Minister of Health. Perhaps the Labour party decided that the sins of the fathers should not be visited upon the children indefinitely. The National Labour organization was in any case wound up about this time. Many of its members had already found their way back to the Labour party. The Edinburgh conference in 1936 had ruled that they must do so

through their divisional Labour party or some other affiliated organization, and with the endorsement of the National Executive. Jowitt
had returned *via* the Fabian Society and had been Labour member
for Ashton-under-Lyne since 1939. His appointment as Solicitor-
General (along with the corresponding office for Scotland) completed Churchill's government—but this is to anticipate. There were
two more days of government-making, but only a few of the names
require mention. Dalton was brought in to be Minister of Economic
Warfare, as he desired, and the Liberal National Ernest Brown was
made Secretary of State for Scotland. Lord Hankey, the former
Secretary of the Cabinet, who acknowledged no party, was retained
in the government as Chancellor of the Duchy, and Lord Beaverbrook, whose Conservatism always had an individual flavour, was
with some difficulty and against many resistances given the vital
new post of Minister of Aircraft Production. Otherwise, the remaining senior posts were filled by Conservatives. Cranborne came back
as Paymaster-General.

In the matter of the whips, so vital to parliamentary organization,
Labour was given equality with the Conservatives: Margesson
shared his rule henceforth with the ex-miner Charles Edwards. One
junior appointment calls for notice, that of Harold Macmillan to be
Parliamentary Secretary to the Ministry of Supply. The independent
views that he had expressed in earlier books had been further developed in 1938 in *The Middle Way*, a plea for an intermediate
position between *laisser-faire* capitalism and state socialism; and in
several notable speeches in the House of Commons he had again
manifested his firm conviction that unemployment and poverty
could be and ought to be terminated.[54] In matters of foreign policy
his disagreement with Baldwin and Chamberlain had led him to
open revolt against his leaders. He had voted in 1936 with the
Labour and Liberal oppositions for the motion of censure arising out
of the abandonment of sanctions against Italy, and in a letter of
explanation to Baldwin he said "it would perhaps be more satisfactory if I was no longer regarded as being one of the official supporters of the present administration".[55] Though he again received
the Conservative whip after a year or so as an independent, he was
one of the small band who voted with Churchill, and during the
Oxford by-election of 1938 he announced that if he were an elector
at Oxford he would unhesitatingly vote and work for the return of
Lindsay to Parliament. This was strong meat for the Conservative
Central Office to accept even from the son-in-law of the Duke of
Devonshire; but war overshadowed all else, and he was now reconciled to his party, though still very low in its hierarchy.

When the reconstruction was over, Churchill observed that he
had formed the most broad-based government that Britain had ever
known, extending from George Lloyd to Ellen Wilkinson.

There was one failure that Churchill had to acknowledge. He could not persuade Lloyd George to enter his government. After the great speech of dismissal to Chamberlain, the veteran architect of victory in the First World War seems half to have expected that it was he who would be asked to form a new government, but this could only have been an old man's dream, or the dream of his friends. Churchill made no attempt to include him in the first appointments, but in May Lloyd George was offered a place in the War Cabinet. Though he was no longer capable of his exertions in the First World War, his name was a symbol of the will to win. There was one snag. In view of the known feelings of Chamberlain, Churchill felt bound to make the offer subject to the Lord President's approval. At once the bristles went up. The offer could be considered only when it was made definite. Churchill obtained Chamberlain's adhesion, but it was given, according to his biographer, "in scepticism and dismay".[56] The offer was then made firm, and Beaverbrook added his persuasions, but after much cogitation Lloyd George declined. Seeing how much he had aged even in the few months while the matter was under discussion, Churchill did not renew it.

During the morning of 13th May the Labour party conference assembled at Bournemouth, and in his undramatic manner Attlee sought approval for what he and his colleagues had done. (Laski said afterwards that he felt as though the cook and kitchen-maid were telling them how they had sacked the butler.)[57] A debate far below the level of the occasion followed, but Will Lawther spoke out boldly for the miners in favour of going in, and it was approved by 2,450,000 votes to 170,000.

The new government met the House of Commons for the first time that afternoon. As Chamberlain entered, the whole Conservative party rose to its feet, waving order papers and cheering. It was the traditional British sympathy for the man who was down, but it showed the Labour ranks opposite how impossible it would have been to have insisted on his exclusion.

Borrowing the words of Garibaldi, Churchill, speaking for the first time as Prime Minister, told the house that he had nothing to offer but blood, toil, tears and sweat. The policy of the new government, he said, was to wage war; its aim was victory.[58]

ELECTORAL TRUCE AND LABOUR TRIUMPH 1940–1945

The I.L.P. refuses support for the war effort—Communist am-
biguity—restiveness under the electoral pact—the Common
Wealth party—a Scottish Nationalist elected—Labour achieves
some of its aims—Let us Face the Future—all-party agreement on
education, children's allowances and full employment—the Tory
Reform group—discharging the duties of the opposition in war-
time—opposition from within the Conservative party—Aneurin
Bevan's campaign against Churchill and his own Labour leaders—
the Labour party strains the coalition over social security—over
town and country planning—and over Greece—Churchill's hopes
for a post-war coalition frustrated—he forms a "caretaker govern-
ment" of Conservative and non-party ministers—personal animosi-
ties in the Labour party—Greenwood's defeat of Morrison for the
treasurership—Laski's attempt to dictate to Attlee—Cripps re-
admitted to the party on the eve of the election—and Labour gains
a huge victory

T HE electoral truce did not extend to the minor parties, and they
felt no obligation to diminish their political work. In the
summer months before the outbreak of war the National Administrative Council of the Independent Labour party, chastened by
experience of the wilderness, had reconsidered its attitude to the
Labour party and had recommended a new application for affiliation. A special conference of the I.L.P. was summoned for September to take a decision. Owing to hostilities, it was not held, and
by the time the normal annual conference met the following Easter
the Council had lost its enthusiasm for the project by reason of deep
disagreement with the Labour party over the war. True to its pacifist past, the Independent Labour party refused support for the war
effort. It organized a series of conferences under the title "War and
the Workers", in which the British and French governments were
denounced equally with the German as guilty of imperialist ex-

ploitation; and it called upon the workers to refuse help for any war not waged by a "workers' government". When the vote of confidence in the Churchill government was taken in the House of Commons, Maxton and Campbell Stephen, and they alone, opposed.

The Communist party's attitude to the war was more ambiguous. In a manifesto issued in September 1939 the party came out "in full support of all necessary measures to secure the victory of democracy over fascism". It declared:[1]

"The essence of the present situation is that the people have now to wage a struggle on two fronts; first, to secure the military victory over fascism; and second, in order to achieve this, the political victory over Chamberlain and the enemies of democracy in this country."

The secretary of the party, Harry Pollitt, wrote a pamphlet, *How to Win the War*, in which he completely identified himself with the national purpose. Within a few weeks, just about time to ascertain the views of Moscow, it turned out that he and the British party had seriously misjudged the character of the struggle. From a hastily written second manifesto it appeared that the armed conflict was not a struggle of democracy against fascism but an imperialist war which the workers should oppose. When the British and French governments rejected suggestions for peace that would have allowed Hitler to keep Poland, they and the Labour party were denounced as warmongers. Pollitt ceased to be secretary in October, but sang the new tune along with the others. It was not until 1941, when Hitler invaded Russia, that the contest became once more a war of democracy against fascism. The Communist party in December 1942 made a new application for affiliation to the Labour party, but the National Executive denied that the Communist party was independent.[2] The dissolution of the Comintern in May 1943 brought a renewed appeal for a meeting to discuss affiliation, but the National Executive flatly refused.

"It is common knowledge [wrote the executive in its report to the annual conference[3]] that the philosophies and methods of the two parties are incompatible. The Labour party has developed, to the great benefit of its people, under the influence of the British tradition of democratic consent. Its belief in parliamentary government is fundamental to its conception of orderly social change. The Communist party repudiates this political principle in the plainest language." At the party conference in 1943 Will Lawther on behalf of the miners moved to accept affiliation "provided that the Communist party agrees to accept and abide by the constitution of the Labour party". His proposal was defeated by 1,951,000 votes to 712,000, and the ban on local cooperation with Communists was also maintained.[4]

In the meantime both the Labour party and the minor parties had

K

become increasingly restive under the electoral pact. In the nature of things it operated to preserve the party *status quo* and therefore was disliked by the Labour party, which was under-represented in relation to its strength in the country, and by the minor parties which disliked the ganging up of the main parties against them. The pact operated differently for elections to local authorities and to Parliament. Local elections were suspended by statute, and each local authority was empowered to fill vacancies by co-option, it being understood that when a member died or retired his place would be filled by a member of the same party, in practice nominated by the local party chiefs. Parliament prolonged its own life year by year so as to avoid a general election, but no ban was imposed on by-elections. So far as Parliament was concerned, the electoral truce was no more than an agreement among the Conservative, Labour and Liberal parties not to put up an official candidate in a bv-election for a seat formerly held by a member of one of the other two parties. There was nothing to prevent a member of another party or an independent from contesting such a by-election, and between the outbreak of war in September 1939 and the formation of Churchill's government in May 1940 no fewer than eleven out of twenty-four by-elections were contested. The opposition candidates included two Communists and two from the Independent Labour party, one who described himself as a Pacifist and three who stood under the label "Stop the War", two Fascists, one Progressive, one National Independent and one Scottish Nationalist. None was elected, and few obtained many votes.

When Churchill formed his coalition he asked the Labour and Liberal party leaders whether they would be prepared to join with him at by-elections in giving the government candidate their joint endorsement. The old suspicions of "coupon" elections were at once revived. Attlee felt it necessary to consult his National Executive. That body authorized him to join with Churchill and Sinclair in signing statements supporting the candidate drawn from the party previously holding the seat, but would not go beyond such endorsement, either in giving help to Conservative and Liberal candidates or in seeking support for its own. It was influenced in this decision, it stated,[5] "by its anxiety to maintain party unity in the constituencies, and to secure a common policy to which all party members could give their adherence". Throughout the war Conservatives, Labour and Liberals stood under their own labels rather than as coalition or "National" candidates.

From the formation of the Churchill coalition to the end of 1940 there were twenty-three by-elections, and six were contested. Two Independent Conservatives won seats held since the general election by official Conservatives, and the other non-coalition candidates labelled themselves Communist, Fascist, Independent and "Stop the

War"; none was successful. In 1941 out of twenty-five by-elections ten were contested, the opponents of the government candidates being labelled I.L.P., Communist, Independent, "Bomb Berlin" and Pacifist; none was elected. There were twenty-five by-elections also in 1942; thirteen were fought, by candidates labelled I.L.P., Labour Independent, Christian Socialist, Scottish Nationalist and Independent, and at last four Independents were successful in winning seats previously held by Conservatives. A sense of frustration with the electoral pact was growing, and it would appear that in the absence of a candidate of their own colour electors normally prepared to vote Labour or Liberal were backing the Independent against the Conservative.

A new apparition rose in the political firmament in 1942 when Sir Richard Acland, until that time Liberal member for Barnstable, founded the Common Wealth party. There was an amusing exchange in debates on the Education Bill two years later when Acland challenged the Labour Parliamentary Secretary to the Ministry of Education, James Chuter Ede, with the words, "Does the right honourable gentleman believe that the age of miracles is still here," to which Chuter Ede replied: "Well, I haven't tried to found a new party."[6] The judgement was justified when the next general election took place, but during the war years Common Wealth flourished on the exasperation with the electoral pact widely felt in the Labour party and left of it. The programme of Common Wealth, as the name suggests, was socialistic, but heavily tinged with moralism. Its declared intention was to contest every by-election where a "reactionary" candidate was in the field. Out of twenty-two by-elections in 1943 only one was left uncontested. Common Wealth put nine candidates into the field and one of them was successful against a Conservative at Eddisbury. Another Conservative went down before an Irish Labour candidate in Belfast West. The other eleven opponents of government candidates, standing as I.L.P., Independent Socialist, Liberal Independent and Independent without qualification, were all defeated, but some of them polled well. The propaganda of Common Wealth on behalf of a middle-class Christian socialism was more than counter-balanced in the eyes of official Labour by its competition with the Labour machine in the constituencies, and in 1943 the National Executive, supported by the conference, placed it on the list of proscribed organizations.[7]

It seemed that the electoral truce might break down, but in 1944 there were fortunately only twelve by-elections; ten were contested. Common Wealth fought two of them and won a second seat from the Conservatives. An Independent also took a seat from a Conservative, but the challenge of the other anti-government candidates —labelled I.L.P., Christian Socialist, Scottish Nationalist, Independent Liberal and unqualified Independent—was successfully held off.

There were only five months of electoral truce in 1945, but what took place is sufficient proof that it could not have survived the strains upon it much longer. Out of seven by-elections from January to June, six were contested, and the government candidates were defeated in three of them. Common Wealth gained a third seat at the expense of a Conservative in Chelmsford, an Independent defeated a Liberal National for the Scottish Universities and, most startling of all, a Scottish Nationalist ousted Labour at Motherwell. It was the first time a Nationalist candidate had secured election outside Ireland. Communists doubtless voted for him, and many Conservatives, indignant at Labour voters' repudiation of the pact in practice, must have done likewise.

The electoral truce was inevitable at a time when no diversion of effort from the war was tolerable and when air-raids pin-pointed on the constituency might have made polling a gamble, but the dissatisfaction it created proves the deep-felt need for the ordinary party processes. It shows that if party did not exist, it would be necessary to invent it. The electoral truce gave an artificial stimulus to the minor parties and to the Independents, and their combined numbers in the House of Commons rose from nine after the opening of Parliament in 1935 to thirty-three at the dissolution in 1945. It was the hey-day of the Independent member. The general election of that year soon brought home the realities of political life.

The rank and file of the Labour party itself were far from satisfied with the electoral pact. Its leaders accepted it as a necessary corollary of their participation in a coalition government, but the ordinary members chafed under it and longed for the day when they could settle accounts with the Tories. In October 1939 the Labour party even overhauled its local organization to ensure that so far as possible it should be kept in good order during the war. Negotiations for closer working arrangements with the Cooperative party were suspended, but the Cooperators agreed to send observers to sit with the National Council of Labour; in 1941 this informal attendance was converted into formal membership.[8] D. N. Pritt was expelled from the party in 1940 for opposing the official attitude towards the Russian attack on Finland and henceforth sat as Independent Labour.

Total war meant that governmental direction and control of labour and resources was inevitable, and in addition Labour took advantage of its presence in the coalition to press for the remedying of old grievances. The Determination of Needs Act, 1941, followed by another act in 1943, substituted a personal needs test for the hated family means test, but the Conservatives would not agree to the repeal of the Trade Disputes and Trade Unions Act, 1927. This last aim was one that would have to wait until the advent of a Labour government, and as the danger of military defeat receded the

Labour leaders began to address their minds to this possibility. Early in 1942 what was described as "a report on the problems of war and peace reconstruction" of an "interim" character appeared under the title *The Old World and the New Society*. It was an adaptation of *For Socialism and Peace* to the changed circumstances brought about by the war and stood in the line of *Labour and the Nation*. After reaffirming Labour's belief in the necessity for achieving total victory over the enemies, the document stated Labour's aims in broad sweeps under the four headings reconstruction, a planned democracy, imperial questions (the term could still be used in 1942 even at Transport House) and the peace. Some of the keynotes sounded were: "The basis of our democracy must be planned production for community use." "A planned society must replace the old competitive system." "The Labour party is absolutely opposed to the colour bar in every shape or form." "The principle of collective security against aggression must be given its appropriate methods and institutions." In the next two years many detailed pamphlets filled in the outlines, and in April 1945 *Let us Face the Future: A Declaration of Labour Policy for the Consideration of the Nation* converted the generalities of the larger pamphlet into an election manifesto, though no decision had at that time been taken to end the coalition.

The electoral truce may have helped the Liberal party by keeping its members in the House of Commons stable, and it received some compensation for Sir Richard Acland's defection when a by-election at Berwick-on-Tweed provided Sir William Beveridge with a seat. Beveridge had been appointed by Greenwood to conduct a report into the social insurance and allied services, which turned out to be political dynamite. The Beveridge report served the Liberals as a policy document and election manifesto, and their enthusiasm for it counteracted the strong personal friendship between the Conservative and Liberal leaders that had existed ever since Sinclair had been Churchill's second-in-command in the 6th Royal Scots Fusiliers in Flanders in 1916.

The Conservative party was no less conscious than the Labour and Liberal parties that big changes would be inevitable in the social and economic structure of Great Britain as a result of the war, but in the nature of things was more cautious in its approach to them. It had come to be expected that war would be followed by educational advance, and it was a Conservative minister, R. A. Butler, who framed the Education Act of 1944. The passions of 1902 had died, and the 1944 act maintained the dual system with scarcely a murmur of opposition, while giving a clearer recognition to "syllabus" religious teaching and collective worship in state schools and providing new forms of financial help for church schools so as to enable them to comply with rising standards. It made provision for the raising of the school-leaving age to fifteen, with a further extension to sixteen when practical, and for compulsory part-time education in due course to eighteen; these two latter provisions have not yet been carried out. It made secondary education available for all children and abolished fees in all state schools. There was agreement also in the coalition on the subject of children's allowances. As already noticed, there was a good deal of opposition to this social service in the trade union wing of the Labour party on the ground that it might be used to undermine wages, but during the war this hostility was overcome. No measure had, however, been introduced when the coalition broke up, and the reform reached the statute book in the brief period of Conservative government that followed. This happened also to an important measure laying down that no major new factory or extension of a factory might be built without an "industrial development certificate" from the Board of Trade, thereby making it possible for the government to guide new industry into areas of higher unemployment or other areas where it was socially desirable. Its general terms were settled during the coalition but put on the statute book under the subsequent period of Conservative rule.

On one other domestic topic of major importance agreement was reached between the parties during the coalition. This was embodied in a white paper of 1944 which stated: "The government accept as one of their primary aims and responsibilities the maintenance of a high and stable level of employment after the war." The war had demonstrated that mass unemployment could be abolished, and Keynes's advocacy of the injection of purchasing power by various devices into a stagnant or declining economy had by this time come to be generally accepted as showing how it could be avoided. In practice, not only has a high and stable level of employment been achieved throughout most of the subsequent years but full, or even over-full, employment. It would in 1944 have been considered rash to have laid down full employment as an objective always attainable—even Beveridge had made his proposals on the assumption that the unemployed would total three per cent of the insured population—and "a high and stable level" was the limit of the all-party agreement.

Some consideration of future Conservative policy was carried out by the Post-War Problems Central Committee headed by Butler and Maxwell Fyfe. By 1945 this committee had set up some sixteen sub-committees and issued half-a-dozen reports. But there was a group of younger Tories in Parliament who had more daring visions of social reform in the post-war age. The Tory Reform Committee, formed in 1943 "with the object of encouraging the government to take constructive action on the lines of the Beveridge scheme",[9] soon branched out in the whole field of domestic policy. Its chair-

man was Lord Hinchingbrooke, and it had Peter Thorneycroft and
Hugh Molson as its joint secretaries, but its most active and ebullient member was Quintin Hogg. Their subsequent careers have not
wholly been in accord with this early reputation for *avant-garde*
policies, but at the time their cavalier tactics and brilliance in
debate recalled the Fourth party, and they ran into similar trouble
with the leadership of the party. The climax was reached on 28th
March 1944 when Mrs. Cazalet Keir moved in committee an amendment to the Education Bill that in fixing salary scales the ministry
should not distinguish between men and women solely on the
grounds of sex. After a debate in which R. A. Butler protested that
he was as good a Tory reformer as anyone, the amendment was
carried by 117 votes to 116. On the following day Churchill himself
came down in great wrath and said the government would move to
delete the clause as amended. He announced that the vote would be
treated as a vote of confidence in the government, and the clause
was deleted by 425 votes to twenty-three—and eventually restored
in its original form on re-committal of the bill.

Over the centuries the machinery of Parliament had become so
geared to an opposition that when official opposition ceased it
became necessary to invent a fictional opposition. When the Labour
party joined the government in 1940 the post of leader of the
opposition, and the salary attached to it, lapsed, but certain privy
councillors not in the government sat on the opposition front bench
and one of them, the respected Labour leader, H. B. Lees-Smith, who
had been Postmaster-General in the second Labour government, put
the business question on Thursdays and discharged other formal
duties normally belonging to the leader of the opposition. At the
same time the executive committee of the Parliamentary Labour
party was dissolved (its leading members having gone into the
government) and an administrative committee of twelve non-
ministers (with representatives from the Labour peers) was set up in
its place. Lees-Smith was chairman of this committee, and when he
died in 1941 Pethick-Lawrence took his place there and on the
opposition front bench. In 1942 Arthur Greenwood lost his place in
the government and Pethick-Lawrence immediately ceded to him
both positions. Greenwood was styled deputy leader and acting
chairman of the Labour party. He discharged these functions till the
end of the war, and no breath of criticism of his former colleagues
came from him. More pungent criticism of the government came at
one period from two former ministers, one Labour and one Conservative, sitting beside him. The socialist, Emanuel Shinwell, and
the Tory, Lord Winterton, were men of totally contrasted upbring-
ing and outlook, and their temporary alliance won for them, after a
play then running in London, the name Arsenic and Old Lace.

What might have become a real opposition threatened sporadically to develop on the back benches. On the Conservative side, at a moment when the fortunes of war were at their lowest, Sir John Wardlaw-Milne moved on 1st July 1942 "that this house, while paying tribute to the heroism and endurance of the armed forces of the Crown, has no confidence in the central direction of the war". Wardlaw-Milne was a powerful figure in the Tory party and chairman of the Select Committee on National Expenditure. He was supported by Sir Roger Keyes, whose intervention in uniform had materially helped to displace Chamberlain. The Maldon by-election, where the government candidate had polled only 6,226 votes out of nearly 20,000, showed discontent with the fall of Tobruk. The occasion was critical, but Wardlaw-Milne lost the ear of the house when he suggested that the remedy might be found in making the Duke of Gloucester commander-in-chief of the British army. The danger passed, and so did any danger of a Conservative cave.

A more brilliant, persistent and malicious opposition to Churchill's government was sustained throughout the war from the Labour back benches by Aneurin Bevan. The fiery orator from Ebbw Vale passionately desired to see the defeat of nazism and fascism, but with equal vehemence he desired to see the triumph of socialism at home and abroad, and he regarded Churchill as the enemy almost as much as Hitler and Mussolini. Practically every major issue was used as a stick with which to belabour Churchill, and as the Labour leaders were so closely linked with the Prime Minister inevitably his blows struck them also and were bitterly resented. He came into special conflict with Herbert Morrison, whose attitude he described in debate as that of "a squalid backstairs Tammany Hall politician"; and he denounced Pethick-Lawrence, sitting in front of him, as "the crusted old Tory who still remains a member of this party".[10] Even more serious from the point of view of his position in the party was his clash with Ernest Bevin over a regulation making unofficial strikes among persons engaged in essential services punishable by fine or imprisonment.[11] After his speech in the Commons Greenwood said he had "gibbeted the trade union movement". Bevan mustered only twenty-three votes in the lobby against 314 for the government; but when the votes were analysed it was seen that the majority was almost wholly made up of Conservatives. Out of 165 Labour members, only fifty-six had voted for the regulation, and of them twenty-three were ministers, whips or parliamentary private secretaries. It was a situation that could not be ignored. Turning a blind eye to fifteen other Labour members who had supported him in the lobby, the administrative committee proposed to the party meeting that the whip should be withdrawn from Bevan. He would then have been reported to the National Executive committee for expulsion. At the first meeting a decision was postponed for a week, and at a week-end meeting in his constituency Bevan said: "Had the Labour leaders fought the Germans as hard as they have fought me, the war would have been over long ago." At the resumed meeting, Attlee gave all his authority to the recommendation for expulsion, but an amendment referring the matter to a joint meeting of the administrative committee and the National Executive was carried by seventy-one votes to sixty. A decisive part was played by a group of Labour members, on the whole of right-wing views, who had met over dinner the previous night and had decided to vote according to the way in which Bevan answered their question whether he still regarded the standing order of the party as binding on himself. Bevan's answer, "Yes, in the same way as other members," was accepted as satisfactory and their votes tipped the scale.[12] The question was still not settled. The National Executive itself demanded that within seven days he should give in writing an assurance that in future he would abide by the standing orders. He swallowed his pride, as he told his constituents, and signed. At the Trades Union Congress in October the reference back of the General Council's condemnation of "a most amazing attack on the trade union movement delivered by Mr. Aneurin Bevan" was defeated by only 3,686,000 votes to 2,802,000. At the Labour party conference that year the elections to the constituency section of the National Executive were headed by Laski and Shinwell, leading critics of the government in the country and in Parliament, while Bevan, standing for the first time, was elected in the fifth place. As the Delphic oracle said of Alcibiades, when you find you are rearing a lion cub you must either kill him or make him your ruler. The Labour party could not kill Bevan, and it had to admit him grudgingly to a share in the leadership.

Bevan's private war with Churchill was an embarrassment to the Labour leadership, but it could not in itself threaten the coalition. The existence of the coalition was, however, put to three major strains in the House of Commons when the Parliamentary Labour party decided on one occasion to vote against the government and on two other occasions to abstain from voting for it.

The vote against the government arose out of the Beveridge report. It was in June 1941 that an inter-departmental committee was appointed, under the chairmanship of Sir William Beveridge, to "undertake with special reference to the inter-relation of the schemes, a survey of the existing national schemes of social insurance and allied services, including workmen's compensation, and to make recommendations". The first sign of future trouble came with the announcement that in view of the issues of high policy involved, the representatives of the departments were to be regarded only as Beveridge's assessors and advisers. The report was published in December 1942. By the great mass of the people it was hailed with enthusiasm as ushering in a new era of security from "the womb to the tomb". Though many socialists distrusted the insurance principle and hankered for direct social payments out of taxation, the Labour party could not afford to lag behind the popular mood and Labour speakers came out in favour of the Beveridge report with hints of improvements on it in certain directions. Among Conservatives there were many misgivings about the financial implications, and the unorthodox action of its author in stumping the country advocating adoption of "my report", as he termed it, roused resentment. There were justifiable hesitations about two of the demands in the report, that the new plans should begin in July 1944, when it was virtually certain that the war would still be raging, and the automatic linking of benefits with the cost of living. In February 1943 Churchill circulated to the Cabinet a memorandum in which he stated: [13]

"This approach to social security, bringing the magic of averages nearer to the rescue of the millions, constitutes an essential part of any post-war scheme of national betterment . . .

"We cannot however initiate the legislation now or commit ourselves to the expenditure involved. This can only be done by a responsible government and a House of Commons refreshed by contact with the people."

In the light of these principles, a government motion was put down in the House of Commons welcoming the report as a comprehensive review of the present provisions and as a valuable aid in determining post-war legislation. This did not satisfy the rank and file of the Labour party either in the country or in Parliament, and the Parliamentary Labour party decided to support an amendment. On 18th February 1943 visitors to the House of Commons witnessed the undignified spectacle of Labour ministers walking into the "No" lobby with their Tory colleagues, while ninety-seven private Labour members divided into the "Aye" lobby. At the next party meeting Attlee made it clear that another scandal of this type would force the resignation of Labour ministers. The impression left in the public mind was that the Labour party wanted a big extension of the social services while the Conservative party was dragging its feet.

There was no exact repetition of the incident, but in June 1944 the Parliamentary Labour party decided to abstain from voting for the second reading of the Town and Country Planning Bill, which the Labour ministers were bound to support. Some such measure was urgently needed to enable the councils of bombed cities to plan their redevelopment, and in particular it was necessary to define their powers of compulsory purchase of land and the terms of compensation. A committee set up in 1941 under the chairmanship of Mr. Justice Uthwatt had dealt with the complicated question of the improvement in the value of land ("betterment") brought about by the action of local authorities in creating roads, sewers and so on.

The recommendation of the Uthwatt committee was that the state should acquire all development rights in undeveloped land in return for a global sum in compensation. This seemed to the property owners' organizations to savour of nationalization, and for the same reason it was welcomed in the Labour party. The bill, when introduced, did not carry out this recommendation of the Uthwatt committee, and Lewis Silkin, the Labour party's expert in such matters, denounced it as "a miserable and mean measure which represents a victory by the land-owning interests over the public interest". Persuaded by him, the Parliamentary Labour party decided against the advice of its ministers to abstain from voting on the second reading and to seek drastic changes in committee. A few Labour members actually voted against the bill. Mr. Michael Foot goes so far as to say: "The question of the ownership of land was the real rock on which the coalition was broken."[14]

The second occasion when the Parliamentary Labour party decided to abstain from supporting its ministers arose out of the Communist attempt to seize control of Greece at the end of 1944. When the crisis blew up, the debate on the address in reply to the King's Speech was in progress, and a group of Labour members together with Sir Richard Acland put down an amendment, "but humbly regrets that the Gracious Speech contains no assurance that his Majesty's forces will not be used to disarm the friends of democracy in Greece and other parts of Europe, or to suppress those popular movements which have valorously assisted in the defeat of the enemy and upon whose success we must rely for future friendly cooperation in Europe". The Parliamentary Labour party officially decided to abstain on this amendment, which was debated on 8th December. At the end of the day Labour ministers and one private Labour member voted with the majority of 279 against the amendment; the thirty who voted for included twenty-three Labour members.[15]

Such incidents as the three last described made it clear that the Labour party's association with the Conservatives was for the strictly limited purpose of waging war, and that as soon as the objective was achieved party strife would be resumed. Churchill himself hoped wistfully that the great coalition which he had led in war might hold together to solve the immense problems that war would leave behind. In a broadcast in March 1943 he had thrown out a suggestion for a four-year plan of post-war reconstruction. It was coldly received by the Labour party, which did not think that its views on post-war reconstruction would coincide with those of the Tories. The official Labour reply was given in a manifesto *Labour and the General Election* issued by the National Executive in October 1944. "It is in our view vital," said the manifesto,[16] "that the election should afford a real choice to the electors between candidates supporting definite policies." Failing in this grander objective, Churchill sought the more limited aim of keeping the coalition in being until Japan was defeated, which at that time was thought to require another eighteen months after the collapse of Germany. In October 1944 he said to the Commons: "Unless all political parties resolve to maintain the present coalition until the Japanese are defeated we must look to the termination of the war against nazism as a pointer which will fix the date of the general election." Somewhat sorrowfully, he added "the odour of dissolution is in the air".[17] Before going to San Francisco in April 1945 to help inaugurate the United Nations Attlee extracted from Churchill a promise that Parliament would not be dissolved in his absence. Germany surrendered on 10th May, and Churchill was under considerable pressure from within the Conservative party to have the election in June. At one meeting, he relates, he asked a gathering of Conservative ministers to write down the date they preferred, and all except two gave June.[18] In the absence of Attlee, Bevin and Morrison went to Churchill to find out what he had in mind. According to Morrison,[19] Bevin appeared to be ready to agree with Churchill's suggestion of a further two years of coalition or alternatively an election after the end of the war with Japan. Morrison himself considered that late October would be an appropriate time. A new register would by then be in operation and considerable numbers of troops and mobile war-workers would have returned home. (The same considerations led the Tory managers to prefer June.) Attlee returned a few days later, and was ready to agree that the coalition should last till the end of the Japanese war. The party soon assembled at Blackpool for its annual conference, and Churchill sent Attlee a formal proposal that the coalition should remain in being till the end of the war against Japan. The National Executive, swung by Morrison, asked him to reply in favour of continuing the coalition till October. Churchill rejected the suggestion, and on 23rd May tendered his resignation to the King. Thus the great coalition came to an end. As the Conservatives had a clear majority of one hundred over all other parties the King invited Churchill to form another government, and this he proceeded to do. It was composed mainly of his Conservative and National Liberal colleagues, but the non-party ministers who had served in the coalition—among them Sir John Anderson, Sir Andrew Duncan, Sir James Grigg and Lord Leathers—remained at their posts. The Liberals, with rather more misgivings, took the same line as the Labour party and decided against continuing in a coalition. As the task of the new administration was merely to carry on the King's government until the people expressed their views in a general election it became dubbed "the caretaker government", but as already noted it carried to the statute book two measures of great importance agreed upon in the coalition, one setting up the first national system of children's allowances and the other giving the Board of Trade powers to influence the location of industry. At a reception to ministers and ex-ministers given by Churchill at No. 10 Downing Street the break-up of the coalition seems to have aroused much genuine emotion, but in the House of Commons and on the platform it was surprising how quickly wartime colleagues slipped back into the ways of party politics. At the first sitting of the Commons after the end of the coalition the ferocity with which Morrison and Bevin sought to outdo each other in questioning ministers caused the Speaker to remind them gently that the election had not come yet.

According to an understanding that the King would grant a dissolution three weeks after the end of the coalition, Parliament was dissolved on 15th June, and polling day was fixed for 5th July. To allow time for the votes of men in the forces to be brought home, the votes were, exceptionally, not to be counted until 26th July. There were also provisions for proxy votes on behalf of serving men. On account of "wakes weeks" twenty-two constituencies polled on 12th July and two on 19th July.

The Conservative party managers hoped that an early election would enable them to benefit from the immense popularity of Churchill as the supreme war-leader and architect of victory. There is ample evidence that Churchill himself believed that he would receive the support of the great majority of electors. The circumstances were different from 1918, and the electors of 1945 were more concerned to take decisions about the future rather than to express a vote of thanks for past services. In any case, there was a sharp distinction in the minds of electors between Churchill and the party he led. The long years of fumbling and stumbling, fumbling with mass unemployment and stumbling ill-prepared into the greatest war in history, had stored up a wave of resentment against the Tory party which broke over the heads of Tory candidates and their blameless leader alike. The Conservatives paid at the end of the war the penalty for having been in office at the beginning with the same inevitability as the Liberals in 1918. As it turned out, in the course of the campaign Churchill blurred the image of himself as the national leader which voters in all parties had been prepared to concede. In a broadcast talk[20] he told the British people with great solemnity that socialism would require a Gestapo (venomously pronounced Jest-a-po) for its operation. "No socialist system can be established without a political police ... They would have to fall back on some form of Gestapo—no doubt very humanely directed in the first instance." In an academic analysis of theoretical socialism as expounded by Karl Marx this might have been arguable, but as a warning to the British people about the Labour party colleagues with whom he had been working so intimately for five years it could not be taken seriously. The national leader was felt to have sunk overnight to the position of a party politician.

In retrospect it is unlikely that the Conservatives would have fared better than they did if their machine had been in perfect order, but in fact it had been run down almost to nothing, and had virtually to be improvised in the few weeks before the campaign opened. A very high proportion of Conservative candidates, agents and officers of local associations spent the war years in the forces, and those left behind were too old or inexperienced to keep the party machine in good trim or could not give their mind to the task.

In contrast the Labour party machine was in good condition in 1945. There was nothing to choose in point of patriotism between the two major parties in the war, but many of the Labour party's candidates and organizers, being drawn from the ranks of trade unionists and other manual workers, had been encouraged or even required to stay at their civil occupations and were able to keep the party machine in good order. The selection of candidates by local Labour parties had been deliberately discouraged early in the war to avoid prejudicing the claims of candidates in the forces, but as victory drew nearer special efforts, for which Dalton deservedly took some of the credit,[21] were made to ensure that Labour would have an attractive line up when the election came. A vital step in organizing for victory was taken in March 1944 when James Middleton retired from the secretaryship of the party. He had served the party for forty-one years, almost the whole of its life, and had been secretary for nine years. He was a gentle and much-loved servant of the party, who had never fully recovered from the loss of MacDonald, but someone younger, more energetic and perhaps more ruthless was needed for the coming struggle. The National Executive decided to retain the ban on holding the post with a seat in Parliament, and after other candidates had been eliminated the post went to Morgan Phillips, an ex-miner from South Wales aged forty-one, who had already shown his administrative talents as a regional organizer and secretary to the policy committee of the executive.

The Labour party took care to conceal from the public as far as possible the divisions within its upper ranks, and gave the appearance of a united body. Those divisions were deep and frequently bitter, and were more personal than political. The mutual dislike of Arthur Greenwood and Herbert Morrison had manifested itself in 1943, when both were candidates for the office of party treasurer made vacant by the death of George Lathan. (The office was more important than it might appear as it gave the holder an *ex officio* seat on the National Executive.) Bevin, who had little love for Morrison, backed Greenwood, and secured for him the votes of the Transport and General Workers. By the vote of one delegate the vote of the National Union of Railwaymen was also given to Greenwood. Morrison had the support of the General and Municipal Workers. In the outcome Greenwood secured 1,253,000 votes, Morrison 926,000 and a third candidate, Glenvil Hall, for long the finance officer at Transport House, 519,000. In order to compete for the treasurership Morrison had not been nominated for the constituency section of the National Executive and was off that body until the next conference, delayed until December 1944.

Morrison was not, however, without his friends. At the party conference in May 1945 Ellen Wilkinson earnestly pressed upon Dalton, and no doubt on others, that Attlee should step down before the election began in favour of Morrison. She was at any rate consistent. According to Attlee himself, Laski pressed the same advice, but failed to get any response.[22]

The relations between Attlee and Laski during the election campaign are not only piquant but illustrate the complicated structure of the Labour party. As luck would have it, Laski, being the member with the longest service, became chairman of the National Executive after the 1945 conference and was thus chairman during the election campaign. ("It was a pity," Dalton observed caustically,[23] "that his name was Laski and not Smith, and that he was a member of the National Executive but not a member of Parliament.") Churchill had invited Attlee, though no longer in office, to accompany him to Potsdam for the discussions with Roosevelt and Stalin. Laski publicly commented: "It is essential that if Mr. Attlee attends this gathering he shall do so in the rôle of an observer only." Churchill drew Attlee's attention to the comment and said it was his idea that Attlee should accompany him as a "friend and counsellor". Attlee, in accepting, frigidly observed that there had never been any suggestion that he should attend "as a mere observer". Churchill could not let the matter rest there, and in an election broadcast he expressed his astonishment "that this hitherto almost unknown person, Professor Laski, who has never sought to face the electors and sits at the head of what is called the National Executive committee, of which the larger part are not even members of Parliament, should have the right to lay down the law to the leader of the Labour party and tell him that he could only go to the conference in the capacity of an observer and that no continuity in our foreign policy could be undertaken". In the subsequent acid exchanges between Attlee and Churchill honours may be considered equal.[24]

In the general desire to present so far as possible an appearance of unity at the election Bevan's vagaries were overlooked, and even Cripps was welcomed back to the fold. Churchill had thought that Cripps would make an acceptable ambassador to the Soviet Union, and when the German invasion brought Russia into the war on the allied side he gained a vicarious glory. On his return to London he was made Lord Privy Seal (with a seat in the War Cabinet) and leader of the House of Commons. He was not a success in that post, and Churchill, finding his messianic strain hard to endure, transferred him to the gruelling post of Minister of Aircraft Production outside the Cabinet. Throughout these years his relations with the Labour leaders remained cool, and he put the best face on his position by saying that so long as he remained in the government he would join no party, old or new. Nevertheless, in February 1945, after a local dispute in his constituency had been settled, the National Executive re-admitted him to the Labour party. It was a different Cripps who rejoined from the one who had been expelled. The experience of office, if not of the wilderness, had curbed the extravagances of his political philosophy, and the emphasis in his pre-election speeches was on the necessity for a mixed planned economy in which state ownership and controlled capitalism would exist side by side.

As the dissolution drew nearer, the struggle was instinctively felt by the nation to be a battle between the two giants. At that time few—it might almost be said no one—expected the result to be so clear-cut as it turned out to be. Among Conservatives there was general confidence that Churchill's war reputation would bring them back though with a reduced majority, and even in the ranks of Labour the general expectation was that the majority would be a small one either way. In this struggle even the Liberals failed to make any great impact on the nation, while the minor parties and the independents lost the adventitious glamour given to them by the electoral truce. The secession of the Liberals from the coalition was painful to Churchill, who had hoped that whatever the Labour party did they would remain with him. In his "Gestapo" broadcast he publicly appealed to Liberal voters:[25]

"Between us and orthodox socialists there is a great doctrinal gulf which yawns and gapes ... There is no such gulf between the Conservative and National government I have formed and the Liberals. There is scarcely a Liberal sentiment which animated the great Liberal leaders of the past which we do not inherit and defend."

Following a Speaker's Conference in 1944 a Redistribution Act and a Representation of the People Act had made changes in the mechanics of the election. The number of constituencies was temporarily increased to 640, and permanent boundary commissions were set up to report at intervals. The local government and parliamentary franchises were assimilated and the business vote reduced. The civilian register was based upon residence on 30th January 1945, but owing to the limitations of national registration and to the large number of removals at the end of the war it was far from accurate. The service register was even less accurate, and of those who were registered only fifty-nine out of every hundred succeeded in recording their votes. As it turned out, the result was so clear cut that these deficiencies could have made no difference to the overall picture. The campaign included the usual pattern of speeches and canvassing by candidates, but it was dominated by the relatively new phenomenon of the broadcast address by party leaders; and in that medium, which permitted the speaker to be heard but not seen, the quiet tones of Attlee made at least as effective an impression as the rumbustiousness of Churchill.

For the 640 seats the Conservatives put 573 candidates into the field, and their Liberal National allies fifty-one, a total of 624. The Labour total, at 604, was rather less, and included thirty-three standing as Labour and Cooperative. The Independent Labour party mustered only five candidates and there were five Labour Independents. The Liberals, making a heroic effort to regain their old position, threw no fewer than 306 candidates into the fight. No other party approached anything like these numbers. Common Wealth had twenty-three candidates, the Communist party twenty-one. There were nine Welsh Nationalists, eight Scottish Nationalists and three Irish Nationalists of various types. Seventy-four Independents and a motley band with strange labels brought the total number of candidates to 1,682, a large number, but less than in 1929.

The electors went quietly to the polls on 5th July, and the Churchill administration governed for another three weeks in blissful ignorance that the sealed black boxes contained a peremptory order of dismissal. When the results began to come in on 26th July it was soon obvious that this was no ordinary election. A landslide was the word inevitably used to describe what had happened. Out of a total electorate of over thirty-three millions, just over twenty-five millions recorded their votes. Of these 11,995,152 gave their votes to Labour candidates, and 9,988,306 to Conservative and Liberal National candidates. In round figures, twelve million voted Labour and ten million Conservative, but owing to the tendency of the British electoral system to reinforce success this gave Labour 393 members in the new House of Commons and the Conservatives only 213. Only one Labour seat held in Great Britain at the dissolution was lost, and that for special local reasons, and one in Northern Ireland. Harold Macmillan was the first of thirteen Conservative ministers to know that he was out of the House of Commons. The luck of the game had operated against Labour in 1931 and 1935, but now the luck was with the party. The 2,248,226 votes cast for Liberal candidates could secure the return of only twelve of them. The slogan "A Liberal vote is a wasted vote" had been effective; and whereas the presence of Liberal candidates in 1935 had generally been to the advantage of the Tories, in 1945 it generally helped Labour. Only three of the Independent Labour candidates were successful, all in Glasgow. Common Wealth lost two of its three

L

seats, including its leader's. Pritt kept his Hammersmith seat as a Labour Independent. The Communist representation increased from one to two. Two Irish Nationalists were successful, but no Welsh or Scottish Nationalist. There were twelve Independents, seven of them for university seats; it had come to be recognized by this time that the independence of university members was a necessary condition for the survival of university representation. Though the large vote cast for Labour was a minority of all the votes cast in the country— it was about one million less than the total vote of all other candidates—in the new House of Commons Labour had a majority of 146 over all other members; and of those other members about seven could normally be expected to vote with Labour. Inevitably the minds of older men went back to 1905; and, indeed, the regional pattern of voting for Labour and Conservative in 1945 bore some resemblance to that of voting for Liberal and Conservative forty years earlier. The Labour members included a far higher proportion of non-manual workers compared with the party's previous reputation. The trade unionists had the great majority of safe seats, but the trade unions sponsored only 126 candidates, of whom 121 became members. The divisional labour parties sponsored 437 candidates, of whom 248 were successful. The total of 393 Labour members was completed by twenty-three Cooperators (out of thirty-three candidates) and one success in Northern Ireland. It was not only by far the most numerous but also the ablest and most representative body of Labour members returned to Westminster. At last power as well as office was in the grasp of the Labour party.

30

LABOUR IN POWER 1945–1950: HIGH TIDE

Attlee becomes Prime Minister without waiting to be confirmed as Labour leader—and appoints ministers in the traditional manner—Bevin and Dalton switched—a liaison committee set up—Labour's opportunities and difficulties—the continuity of foreign policy—campaign by Labour dissidents against Bevin—expulsions—inter-party agreement on Commonwealth and Colonial questions—and on defence—clash on the repeal of the Trade Disputes and Trade Union Act—nationalization—a new Parliament Bill—an inter-party conference on reform of the upper house breaks down—the Parliament Bill becomes law—the Iron and Steel Bill carried—Conservative support for Labour's agricultural policy—controversy over national health service

ATTLEE has told in his laconic way how he became Prime Minister on 26th July 1945 after almost all the election results had come in:[1]

"Lord Portal, who was chairman of the Great Western Railway, gave the family tea at Paddington, and presently I was told by the Prime Minister that he was resigning. A summons to the Palace followed. My wife drove me there and waited outside for me. The King gave me his commission to form a government. He always used to say that I looked very surprised, as indeed I certainly was, at the extent of our success. We went to a victory rally at Westminster Central Hall, where I announced that I had been charged with the task of forming a government, looked in at a Fabian Society gathering and then returned to Stanmore after an exciting day."

The excitement was even greater than this bald narrative suggests. As the results flowed in, Morrison urged upon Attlee that if an invitation to form a government should be received from the King it should not be accepted until the Parliamentary Labour party had had an opportunity of expressing its views on the leadership. (A meeting of the parliamentary party was fixed for the Beaver Hall in the city of London for the morning of 28th July, that is, within forty-eight hours, for the purpose of selecting officers for the session in accordance with the normal practice.) Laski wrote to Attlee in a similar sense, and although he personally favoured Morrison for the succession he appears to have been persuaded by others to propose Bevin. At any rate, Bevin received a call from Arthur Deakin, who said he had come at the instigation of Laski to urge him to run for the leadership with Morrison as his deputy. Bevin's reaction, according to his own account next day to Dalton, was to exclaim : "How dare you come and talk to me like this!" He told Attlee that if the invitation to form a government came there must be no question of not accepting it immediately, and he, for one, would serve under no one else. When Attlee acquainted him of Morrison's move, Bevin said to more than one person : "If he goes on mucking about like this, he won't be in the —— government at all." Thus fortified, Attlee is reported to have replied to Laski : "I thank you for your letter, contents of which have been noted." Bevin refused from that point either to see Laski or to answer his letters.[2]

In the afternoon Attlee, Bevin, Morrison and Morgan Phillips met together in Bevin's room at Transport House. Laski and the other members of the National Executive were in Morgan Phillips's own room, listening to the late election results, in another part of the building. Morrison continued to put his view about the need to await the meeting of the parliamentary party, and after going out to receive a telephone call he announced that Cripps, to whom he had telegraphed for a comment, shared his opinion. At 3.30 p.m. a message arrived from Churchill conceding the result, congratulating Attlee and saying that he would soon be going to the Palace to resign and to recommend Attlee as his successor. Attlee went to his tea-party at the Paddington Hotel, where, according to his own account he received Churchill's message—it may very well have been sent to both addresses—and about 7.30 p.m. he received the summons to Buckingham Palace and accepted the King's commission to form a government. From the Palace Attlee went to the victory social at the Central Hall. Here Laski was in the chair and before Attlee's arrival Morrison had been trying to persuade M.P.s in conversation that the leadership of the party was still an open question. When Attlee in his quiet way told the meeting that he had just accepted the King's commission Laski's features could not conceal his surprise and annoyance, but he put the best face on the business by jumping to his feet and asking those present to join in congratulating "the Prime Minister".

It will be recalled that in 1932 and 1933 there had been fierce discussion within the Labour party on the procedure that should be followed when the party again found itself in a position to form a government, whether on a minority or a majority basis. Though it had not been laid down in so many words, "it was apparently assumed", as Mr. R. T. McKenzie says,[3] "that in the event of the Labour party being returned with a majority the Sovereign would await the meeting of the P[arliamentary] L[abour] P[arty] at which a new chairman and leader would be elected and that he would then call whoever had been selected and invite him to form a ministry". Morrison therefore had some justification for his view, and in his autobiography he denies that he was actuated by personal ambition. "What happened was that I was pressed by members of the Parliamentary Labour party to see that the democratic principles of the party were observed as regards choice of our leader and therefore of the nation's Prime Minister." When the occasion contemplated in 1933 actually arrived, neither King George VI nor Attlee waited. It is unlikely that the King of his own volition would have restricted his prerogative to send for anyone whom he thought capable of forming a government, but Attlee might have thought it politic, as Bonar Law did in 1922 in his very different position, to delay acceptance until he had been confirmed as leader. He did not, but behaved exactly as MacDonald or any Liberal or Conservative Prime Minister (Bonar Law excepted) would have behaved in similar circumstances. In the light of the shattering electoral victory gained under his leadership, he could afford to dismiss both criticisms of his personal qualities and the restrictions that the party conference had sought to impose on a person in such a position as that in which he now found himself.

This became even more manifest in the appointment of ministers, for on this subject the party conference of 1933 had been more explicit. While accepting that "final responsibility for ministerial appointments must rest with the Prime Minister", it had laid down that three members of the Parliamentary Labour party should be elected to advise the leader in the making of appointments, and that the secretary of the party should be associated with them.[4] When it came to the point in 1945, Attlee ignored this rule and proceeded to set about selecting members of his Cabinet in the same way as all his predecessors from Walpole onwards; and no one seems even to have raised this question. (It was certainly not raised at the meeting of the parliamentary party on 28th July.) When he came to deal with this matter in his autobiography, Attlee suavely observed: "The passage of time and further experience has led to these proposals being tacitly dropped."[5] It was he who did the dropping.

This does not mean that Attlee made the appointments, as MacDonald did in 1924, without consulting senior colleagues. It is known[6] that immediately after Churchill conceded defeat there was some discussion in Morgan Phillips's room. Bevin made known for the first time his wish to go to the Exchequer, and to a surprised Attlee's query suggested Dalton for the Foreign Office. Attlee had assumed after Bevin's speech at the party conference that he had marked out the Foreign Office for himself, but he seems at first to have acquiesced in the switch. That same evening, after Attlee had accepted the commission to be Prime Minister, the King wrote in his diary : [7]

"I told him he would have to appoint a Foreign Secy. & take him to Berlin. I found he was very surprised his Party had won & had no time to meet or discuss with his colleagues any of the Offices of State. I asked him whom he would make Foreign Secy. & he suggested Dr. Hugh Dalton. I disagreed with him & said that Foreign Affairs was the most important subject at the moment & I hoped he would make Mr. Bevin take it. He said he would but he could not return to Berlin till Saturday at the earliest."

The note made by the King's Private Secretary, Sir Alan Lascelles, immediately after the King told him what had passed, is not so emphatic : [8]

"Mr. Attlee mentioned to the King that he was thinking of appointing Mr. Dalton to be his Foreign Secretary. His Majesty begged him to think carefully about this, and suggested that Mr. Ernest Bevin might be a better choice."

The following morning Morrison saw Attlee in the presence of William Whiteley, the chief whip, and made known his wish to be Foreign Secretary. Attlee told him this was not possible and offered him the Lord Presidency; he was persuaded by Whiteley, while Attlee tactfully left the room, to accept a post which would also give him the leadership of the Commons and in effect make him deputy Prime Minister. Later that morning Attlee saw Dalton, who asked him where he was to go; Attlee replied, "Almost certainly the Foreign Office," and advised him to pack his bag for Potsdam. In the afternoon Attlee sent for Dalton again, and said to him : "I have been reconsidering it. I think it had better be the Exchequer." When Dalton asked whom he proposed to put at the Foreign Office he replied : "E.B." [9]

Both men accepted the transposition, but as both had made the original intention known fairly widely the curious episode could not be concealed. A story gained currency that Churchill had met Attlee privately and persuaded him that Bevin would handle foreign affairs more skilfully, but this has been denied by Attlee. Another story current in the American papers, namely that Churchill gave this advice to the King at his final audience, may have had more substance. The advice would have been palatable to the King for reasons which Dalton in his autobiography [10] made no attempt to conceal; but the King would have needed no prompting to reach the same conclusions. There would be no constitutional impropriety in the King making suggestions about the names for particular posts, particularly for the Foreign Office, but Attlee has denied [11] that the royal advice was as decisive as would appear from the official biography. "I naturally took into account the King's view, which was very sound, but it was not a decisive factor in my arrival at my decision." This must be so, as the following morning Attlee advised Dalton to pack for Berlin and Bevin was mentally drafting his first budget. Morrison claims that it was he who persuaded Attlee to make the change, on the ground that: "Dalton ... can have a temper, which is bad for diplomatic work."[12] Curiously, the only one of "various reasons" specified by Attlee for his change of mind "was that a very important and able man, Mr. Morrison, who was going to co-ordinate home matters, did not get on very well with Mr. Bevin. As Chancellor of the Exchequer Mr. Bevin would have been constantly in contact with Mr. Morrison, which might have led to friction on quite minor matters."[13]

The fact that Attlee had originally contemplated Bevin for the Foreign Office, that he had thought of putting Dalton there only when Bevin expressed a wish for the Exchequer, that he adhered to this view even after hearing the King's opinion and that he finally reverted to his original plan after reflecting on the dangers of conflict between Bevin and Morrison—this is a coherent sequence of events making sense. The episode is full of intense personal interest, and boded ill for the future of the Labour party, but on examination turns out not to possess the constitutional significance with which it has sometimes been invested.

Attlee was able to announce his first six appointments on the morning of 28th July by giving Greenwood the Privy Seal, Jowitt the Woolsack and Cripps the Board of Trade. After kissing hands and receiving their seals the new ministers went straight to the meeting of the Parliamentary Labour party. There were several hundred unfamiliar faces and the meeting had the character of a revivalist gathering. Bevin moved and Greenwood seconded a vote of confidence in, and thanks to, the Prime Minister. It was carried with enthusiasm. Morrison himself moved that Attlee be re-elected leader; there was no other nomination, or even breath of nomination, and he was elected with acclamation. Morrison was duly elected deputy leader. Attlee returned immediately to Potsdam, taking Bevin with him, and on his return completed his government. The only appointment that calls for comment is that of Aneurin Bevan, who had never previously held office, to be Minister of Health with a seat in the Cabinet. "I felt that he had it in him to do good service," was Attlee's later comment.[14] The full complement of ministers was accepted as skilfully representative of the party as a whole. "The trade unions, the Cooperative movement and the 'left wing'," as Morrison observes, "had their share of ministerial influence, but always with regard to their ability and experience."[15]

The elected members assembled on 1st August to choose a Speaker and take the oath. Much was made of an incident which took place before the Speaker was elected and technically therefore before the Parliament was in being. This was the singing of that dreary dirge, the *Red Flag*, by the Labour members. It was provoked by the singing of "For he's a jolly good fellow" on the Tory benches as Churchill entered. According to Morrison,[16] "Some did not know the words and some, judging by the rendering, the tune. The brief performance horrified some of the Tories and I must admit that it mildly disturbed me." It was, in fact, a high-spirited and spontaneous move with no revolutionary significance. The election of the Speaker that followed was significant in that the Labour party followed the custom of re-electing the Speaker in office, and Mr. Speaker Clifton Brown was deeply touched by this expression of confidence, which he ever afterwards retained.

The internal arrangements of the Labour party in this Parliament are of some interest. In place of the administrative committee of the days of coalition there was set up a liaison committee consisting of an elected chairman and an elected vice-chairman (later two elected vice-chairmen) from the back benches, the leader of the House of Commons, the chief whip and an elected back-bench Labour peer. This was meant to smooth the relationship between the back benches and the government, and to prevent the feeling of estrangement that had sprung up between back-benchers and ministers on the last occasion when Labour was in office. The usual groups of back-benchers were formed to occupy the energies of members interested in particular subjects, and ministers attended when invited. Most of them were innocuous, and Dalton even found the finance group helpful—he had taken great pains to ensure a good membership[17]—but two, those dealing with foreign affairs and civil aviation, were thorns in the flesh of the ministers concerned. It was from them rather than from the Conservatives that Ernest Bevin and Lord Winster met their real opposition. In view of the vast Labour majority, it was thought safe to suspend the standing orders of the party from session to session, and despite the relaxation of discipline the government's majority was never eaten into seriously.

Before the war the Labour party had been exercised by the thought of what the "capitalist class" would do when the will of the people voted Labour into office. It had been the argument of Cripps, Laski and their followers, that the "capitalist class" would not submit passively to the expropriation of its property and might even put up armed resistance. These fancies had always been laughable—and a source of great annoyance to the practical men whose minds were bent on winning the next election—and in the event the circumstances in which Labour took possession of the seats of power could not have been farther removed from such dreaming. It was not necessary to create the socialist state. It was there already. In order to win the war it had been necessary to make all property and all labour subject to state direction. Taxation had been raised to confiscatory heights, and a social revolution had brought the egalitarian state near. It was not a question of creating the socialist state; the question was how many of the wartime controls should be dismantled and how many made a permanent part of the economic structure of the nation.

The fact that Labour was put in a position to carry out its policies at the end of a great war therefore made the task easier in many respects than had been expected, but in other ways more difficult. The demobilization of millions of men and women, the switch-over in industry from the needs of war to those of peace, the shortage of houses and of all commodities except the bare necessities of life, and the sudden termination of the wartime American help known as lend-lease forced the problems of feeding, clothing and housing a great nation into the foreground and caused socialist experiments to be judged by the stern test of practical advantage rather than by the requirements of theory.

It is not possible to have a foreign policy unless there is continuity in relationships with other countries. Bevin's speech at the Blackpool conference of 1945 had been acceptable to the pro-Soviet elements of the party because it had been based on the thesis that "Left understands Left"; but a little noticed speech at Leeds, in which he emphasized the need for a bi-partisan foreign policy, was more proleptic.[18] When he and Attlee arrived at Potsdam there was more than a little curiosity, and even some anxiety, to see how he would behave. The anxiety soon disappeared. The American Secretary of State, James Byrnes, later wrote:[19]

"Britain's stand on the issues before the conference was not altered in the slightest, so far as we could discern, by the replacement of Mr. Churchill and Mr. Eden by Mr. Attlee and Mr. Bevin. The continuity of Britain's foreign policy impressed me."

Some commentators thought that Bevin was even more opposed to the Communist system than Churchill had been. Among them was Professor D. F. Fleming, who wrote:[20]

"Bevin was a Labour Churchill, still more volcanic and irascible, without Churchill's aristocratic graces ... His opposition to Russia was even greater than Churchill's, since to Sir Winston's defence of imperial positions vis-à-vis Russia he added the hatred of the democratic socialist for the dictatorial brand."

Laski put the same point more neatly when he said that Bevin looked on the Soviet Union as a breakaway from the Transport and General Workers' Union. Such an attitude endeared Bevin to the Foreign Office, which had been a little nervous before his arrival, and the staff came to regard him as the best Foreign Secretary they had ever known. His inquiries after their families, and his solicitude for their office and home comfort, increased their respect, nor can it be overlooked that his ignorance of foreign languages[21] and foreign countries made him more ready than most of his predecessors to accept the advice offered to him by his expert staff; but above all it was the shrewdness of his instinct and his pugnacity in defending his chosen positions that won him a respect seldom accorded to a Foreign Secretary. Only in one matter did his instinct possibly betray him. Not only did he accept the Foreign Office concern least the Arab world should be antagonized by the conversion of Palestine into a Jewish state, but his antipathy to the Zionists became irrational and emotional, though it must be admitted there was provocation. Though Churchill had been a supporter of Zionism, this did not disturb the admiration felt by Conservatives generally for Bevin's work, and in his long tenure of the office foreign policy was not an issue between the parties.

It became, however, an issue within the Labour party itself. The near-Communists and the Zionists in the party united to make Bevin's life as uncomfortable as they could, and though they never seriously threatened his position or his policy—for Attlee depended on him far more than he on Attlee in those years—their pin-pricks irritated him and consumed precious time. The foreign affairs group of the Parliamentary Labour party was their main instrument in baiting him. He was particularly incensed by Richard Crossman, a newcomer to Parliament who added to his other crimes that of being a Wykhamist intellectual, and who had not been given the junior office that would have disciplined his brilliant gifts and directed his ambitions into useful channels. In November 1946 Crossman headed a list of fifty-seven Labour members—inevitably in the light of a famous advertisement there were jests about the fifty-seven varieties among them—who put down an amendment to the address calling on the government to "recast its conduct of international affairs". Despite appeals by both Attlee and Morrison, Crossman moved his amendment, and had to move it on a day while the Foreign Secretary was in the United States. The Independent Labour party forced a division when it became obvious that Crossman himself was not going to do so, but none of the signatories voted for their own amendment. They thereby kept the letter, even though not the spirit, of the party rules, but Ernest Bevin did not forget. At the next party conference he turned savagely on his critics, declaring: "On the very day that I was trying to get the agreement with the Americans to prevent the bread ration going down, on that very day I was stabbed in the back." The need to ration bread, which had remained unrationed throughout the war, had been a bitter pill for the Labour government to take—the decision had been made in July 1946—and was the first major shock to its prestige.

Crossman came into further conflict with Bevin by his espousal of the Zionist cause. There was a substantial minority in the party who shared his opposition to the government's policy, and when the Palestine Bill, providing for the termination of the mandate, came before the House of Commons in 1948 both Crossman and W. N. Warbey put down reasoned amendments for its rejection. Only Warbey's was called. The Conservatives abstained from voting, and it was defeated by 240 votes to thirty.

The disagreements within the Labour party over foreign policy led to a series of expulsions in 1948 and 1949. In April 1948 a telegram was sent by—or at any rate in the names of—thirty-seven Labour members and the one Independent Socialist wishing Pietro Nenni, leader of the Italian Socialist party, success in the forthcoming elections. The Labour party was then supporting the Free Italian Socialist Party led by Giuseppe Saragat. The organizer of the telegram, J. Platts-Mills, was expelled from membership of the Labour party at a meeting of the National Executive presided over by that model of orthodox behaviour Emanuel Shinwell, and the twenty-one "Nenni-goats"—so they became known—who did not deny or withdraw their signatures were warned that if they did not individually retract within a week they also would be expelled. All complied with some grumbling.

In 1948 the National Executive expelled two more Labour members, Konni Zilliacus and L. J. Solley, who had made themselves notorious by their praise for puppet governments in Eastern Europe which the Labour leaders had condemned. Attempts to allow them to state their case at the party conference were defeated. In 1949 yet another Labour member, H. Lester Hutchinson, was put outside the party for his criticism of the government's foreign policy.

There was little conflict between the parties over developments in the British Empire and Commonwealth. As in the field of foreign affairs, there had to be a bi-partisan policy if there was to be policy at all. Ireland has always been *sui generis*, and the introduction in 1949 of the Ireland Bill, acknowledging the transformation in the previous year of Eire into the Republic of Ireland, did not fail to produce an internal quarrel within the Labour party. Sixty-six Labour members who were in sympathy with the southern Irish objection to the continuance of partition opposed the government in committee despite a three-line whip. The Prime Minister, reacting with unexpected tartness, required five ministers to dismiss their parliamentary private secretaries for joining in this revolt and all sixty-six were warned that if they again voted against the government in defiance of a three-line whip they would be reported to the National Executive.

This was an internal conflict. The Conservatives, while regretting the step, did not question the right of Eire to become a republic and to secede from the Commonwealth so long as the constitutional position of Northern Ireland as an integral part of the United Kingdom was left unchanged. Similar considerations governed the Conservative attitude to other parts of the Commonwealth. Though Churchill was full of nostalgia for the British *raj* in India, Conservatives generally, led by R. A. Butler, accepted the inevitability of the transfer of power; and the only serious ground of criticism was the decision, which appears to have been personal to Mountbatten and Attlee, to advance the date of independence from June 1948 to August 1947. This gave the British administrators no time to prepare for the vast and disorderly flight of refugees between India and Pakistan. Churchill was angered by the secession from the Commonwealth of Burma which his father had helped annex to the Crown, but most Conservatives could see no way of preventing it. In colonial affairs Oliver Stanley had already set in 1943 the pattern for future developments by the constitution which he had devised for Jamaica, and between him and the Labour Secretaries of State, Viscount Hall and Arthur Creech Jones, there developed a rare understanding that took colonial questions out of the era of dispute. Only when John Strachey as Minister of Food ransacked the beaches of the world to grow at vast expense in Tanganyika groundnuts that turned out not to be needed did the colonies enter the area of party strife; and "groundnuts" soon became the most blessed word in the Conservative vocabulary, calculated to cheer *morale* as nothing had done for many a month.

In the related field of defence there was also little conflict between the Labour government and the Conservative party. The Labour party decided to retain conscription and to develop nuclear weapons, and the Conservative party was not disposed to cavil at either of these decisions. Once more the real struggle was within the Labour ranks. When Attlee announced in 1946 that it would not be possible to depend on voluntary recruitment, forty-five Labour members voted against the government on an amendment to the address regretting the policy of conscription in peace and no fewer than 132 abstained. The Conservative party supported the National Service Bill, 1947, which provided for compulsory service of eighteen months with the colours and five and a half years with the reserves, but seventy Labour members voted against the second reading. In face of the revolt the government reduced the period to twelve months. The Conservatives forced a division, but the reduction was carried by 313 votes to 165. After the Communist *coup* in Czechoslovakia, the Russian blockade of Berlin and the Communist-inspired troubles in Malaya the government introduced in 1948 an amending bill which raised the period of service to eighteen months with the colours and four years with the auxiliaries. Despite a three-line whip, forty-five Labour members voted against the second reading and many more abstained. The bill was carried with

Conservative support. This number, forty-five, would appear to indicate the hard pacifist core in the party.

The clash between the parties was more marked in the field of domestic policy. The bill to repeal the Trade Disputes and Trade Unions Act of 1927 was not introduced until February 1946, but it sets the pattern of the whole party conflict. It was justified on third reading by the Attorney-General, Sir Hartley Shawcross, a newcomer to that Parliament and to active politics, with the argument used by Humpty Dumpty in *Alice Through the Looking Glass*: "The question is which is to be master. That's all." When Shawcross added, "We are the masters at the moment, and not only at the moment, but for a very long time to come,"[22] he was only expressing the realities of the situation, but pandemonium broke out both on the benches behind him and on those in front of him. Bevin could not resist the opportunity of taking a day off from the Foreign Office to jab his weapon into the hated measure, and repeal was carried by a large majority. The real purpose of the measure (and of the opposition to it) became clear over the next few years as the reversion to "contracting out" began to be reflected in the Labour party's membership and finances. The percentage of members of trade unions having political funds who were liable to contribute to those funds rose from forty-five at the end of 1945 to ninety-one at the end of 1947; and the affiliation fees paid to the Labour party by trade unions rose in the same period from £51,261 to £91,930.

It was inevitable that a Labour government should embark on a programme of nationalization, and just as inevitable that the Conservatives should oppose it, but the degree of opposition differed according to the service or industry selected. The nationalization of the Bank of England came first in the list and roused tremendous enthusiasm on the Labour benches as a symbol but no great antagonism among Conservatives. The struggle between the Treasury and the Bank had been settled in favour of the Treasury far back in 1917 when Bonar Law secured the removal of Cunliffe as Governor. Before that time, as Beaverbrook later recalled,[23] the Treasury was known as the West End branch of the Bank, but thereafter the Bank became the City branch of the Treasury. (Montagu Norman had referred to the relations of the Treasury and the Bank as those of Tweedledum and Tweedledee.)[24] With this background in his mind, Churchill had declared in his speech on the Address that the proposal to bring the Bank into public ownership raised no question of principle. The Conservatives did in fact divide, Churchill not voting, but it was a shadow fight and the bill received the royal assent on 14th February 1946. Lord Catto, the Governor, agreed to continue in that post, persuaded by Dalton over a cup of tea. Thus the Socialist revolution began in Great Britain in typically British manner. It was more significant and a source of annoyance to Labour's left wing, that no attempt was made to nationalize the joint stock banks, though they, too, had already become amenable to government influence and the instruments of Treasury policy.

The strength of the mine-workers in the Labour movement and the bitter history of their industry made it equally inevitable that the nationalization of the coal-mines should quickly follow that of the Bank of England. In earlier years this would have roused fierce hostility, but by 1945 passions were muted. There was a recognition on the Tory side, in the words of a famous advertisement, that the miner "won't be happy till he gets it". In the days of depression the mine-owners had naturally concentrated on the working of the best seams, and six years of war in which little could be done to counteract the wear-and-tear of equipment, much less to modernize the pits, made many owners willing to exchange their assets for cash compensation. The coal seams themselves, or at any rate the royalties on coal extracted, had already been nationalized by a Conservative government in 1938. After largely perfunctory opposition the Coal Industry Nationalization Act reached the statute book on 12th July 1946.

The Civil Aviation Act produced fierce controversy,[25] but almost entirely within the Labour party. British Overseas Airways had already been set up as a public corporation in 1940, and Lord Swinton as the Minister for Civil Aviation in the "caretaker government" had left behind plans for three corporations in which there should be a mixture of public and private elements. When Lord Winster succeeded him he accepted the general plan, but would have altered the balance in favour of the public element. Under pressure from his left wing exercised through his superiors he was compelled to make the three corporations wholly public and to give them a monopoly of scheduled services. This left charter services open to the independent air-lines, and also made it possible to employ the independents as agents of the corporations. The act reached the statute book on 1st August 1946. Lord Winster and his Parliamentary Secretary were not forgiven by the left wing, who soon afterwards secured from a weak Prime Minister their removal to other employment.

The Cable and Wireless Act, bringing telecommunications into public ownership, roused little controversy. It received the royal assent on 6th November 1946, and completed the nationalization achieved in the first session. So far there had been little to divide the parties seriously.

In the second session the Labour government turned to transport and electricity. The latter created no problem as the Conservatives had themselves set up the Central Electricity Board in 1926 to own the national "grid" of lines transmitting electricity at high tension and as over half the generating stations were municipally owned. It was hardly possible to resist seriously the extension of the principle of public ownership to the whole field, nor did the Conservatives do so. The Electricity Act, 1947, set up the British Electricity Authority to take over the generation and transmission of electricity and its distribution, through fourteen area boards. The North of Scotland Hydro-Electric Board was made responsible for generation, transmission and distribution in its area. During the passage of the bill Hugh Gaitskell, newly appointed Parliamentary Secretary to the Ministry of Fuel and Power, made his ministerial *début*.

The Transport Act, 1947, might have roused equally little controversy if it had been confined to the railways with their ancillary undertakings and the canals. Even before the war the railways had been giving a very low return on the capital employed and they had been necessarily run down during the war. An exchange for government bonds was not unwelcome to many railway stockholders. What roused controversy was the inclusion of long-distance road haulage, which was a flourishing new industry. This raised an important principle on which party division was legitimate and useful. The Labour party claimed that the inclusion of road haulage was desirable for the co-ordination of the different forms of transport, and also that it was right for the financially strong to support the weak. Conservatives argued that public ownership was not needed to secure co-ordinated services, and that it was contrary to the efficient working of the national economy to make a growing form of transport subsidize one that was no longer paying its way. Controversy settled particularly on the sections in the bill which limited the right of traders to carry their own goods (the "C" licence holders). This was not very palatable to the cooperative societies, which had large fleets of vehicles, and was anathema to the Conservatives; under the double pressure, one private and one public, it was dropped from the bill.

In the Town and Country Planning Act, 1947, the government made a renewed effort to do what had baffled Lloyd George and Snowden and had been avoided by the Churchill coalition, "to secure the recovery for the benefit of the community of development charges in respect of certain new developments", that is, in effect, to nationalize rights in the development of land. Under the measure provision was made for the state to acquire all development rights in land for a global sum of £300 million. All who lost the development value of their land by the measure were to apply for a share of the £300 million by the middle of 1953. The state was to recoup itself by levying, through the Central Land Board, a development charge every time development took place. The development charge was intended to be the amount by which the value of a piece of land was increased by the permission to develop it. In effect, the state was to buy up development rights wholesale and sell them back retail. It was a complicated measure, said to be under-stood only by the minister who introduced it, Lewis Silkin, but it was realized instinctively even by those who did not understand the clauses, that this was the real issue between the parties, and the Conservatives opposed it fiercely at all stages. The measure was carried, but the fixing and collection of the development charges proved unworkable. One reason was that the act destroyed the free market in land on which the assessment of development charges was based. The provisions were repealed, with very little opposition from the Labour benches, by acts passed in 1953 and 1954 after the Conservatives had returned to office.

By the third session of that Parliament the opposition was warm-ing to its task, and the nationalization of gas by the Gas Act, 1948, met with considerably more opposition than that of electricity. To those who do not follow closely the workings of the British party system this may have appeared odd, for about one-third of the gas industry was already in municipal ownership. In committee Gaitskell, now become Minister of Fuel and Power, endured a severe baptism of fire and drew attention to himself as a future leader.

To this point the nationalization programme of the Labour party had been moderate, except for development rights in land, and the opposition almost formal. The central bank and the public utilities were publicly owned in many countries that would have been shocked to hear themselves described as socialist, and the national-ization of the coal-mines was accepted as unavoidable. What had been done was made more palatable by the generally fair terms of compensation offered—though the £300 million for development rights was denounced by Conservatives as inadequate—and by the vesting of the nationalized industries and services in public corpora-tions, which gave the appearance, and to some extent the reality, of independence from state control. The independent socialist Pritt was disgusted with the failure of the Labour party to seize the oppor-tunity of achieving the socialist commonwealth, and regarded the terms of compensation as grossly excessive.[26] Left-wing members of the party who shared his outlook without having to endure his expulsion were of the same opinion.

What was not known to the general public or to more than a few members of Parliament was that inside the Cabinet a severe and protracted struggle was being waged between those who wished to see the steel industry nationalized and those who thought this would be asking for trouble. The steel industry was basic to the rest of the country's economy and, after its reorganization and re-equipment immediately before and during the war, was as efficient as any in the world. These were arguments to some Labour ministers that it ought to be brought into public ownership, to others that it ought to be left alone. It was certain that to lay hands on it would be to invite controversy of an entirely different order from that associated with coal and the public utilities. Morrison, supported by Greenwood, would have left out any reference to steel in *Let Us Face the Future* in 1945, and they acquiesced only when Dalton threatened to refuse to speak in favour of the policy declaration at the party conference and to leave it to them to explain "why this item, which had been enthusiastically adopted by conference only last December, had now vanished".[27] The document did not, in fact, specifically commit Labour to nationalizing the steel industry, but could be so interpreted by those who wished to do so. The actual words used, which could be severely criticized on the grounds of factual accuracy, were:[28]

"Public ownership of iron and steel.—Private monopoly has maintained high prices and kept inefficient high-cost plants in existence. Only if public ownership replaces private monopoly can the industry become efficient."

If so controversial a nettle were to be grasped, it was desirable to do it early in the life of the Parliament while the Labour members were still in high fettle and the Conservatives demoralized. This would also have allowed time for the measure to be passed under the Parliament Act of 1911 even if the House of Lords rejected it in two successive sessions. The divisions in the Cabinet prevented this course from being taken. Dalton was still strongly in favour of nationalization, and was supported by Bevin and Bevan, who on one occasion threatened resignation, and also by Alexander of Sheffield. Morrison remained opposed, and had reason to believe that Attlee was of the same opinion, but at the critical moment Attlee did not allow his personal opinion to deflect him from his established habit of siding with the majority.[29]

The responsible minister, John Wilmot, Minister of Supply and a close friend of Dalton, whose parliamentary private secretary he had been, was not himself a member of the Cabinet, which increased the difficulties of reaching a decision. He was, however, able to tell the House of Commons in April 1946 that the government, having considered the industry's own plans, had decided that a large measure of public ownership was necessary and desirable. Just a year later the Cabinet approved the heads of a bill drawn up by Wilmot for nationalizing sections of the industry. In the jargon of the day it was a proposal for "horizontal" nationalization, that is, for bringing into public ownership whole sections of the industry such as the smelting of the ore down to heavy rolling, while leaving the more sophisticated end products in private hands. Morrison was ill at the time, and when he returned Attlee deputed him to see Sir Andrew Duncan, head of the British Iron and Steel Federation, who had inquired about the possibility of some compromise. Morrison ascertained that the federation would agree to an iron and steel

M

board with wide powers, including the power to take over un-satisfactory undertakings. Attlee seemed relieved at the prospect of a compromise, but as there was opposition in the Cabinet he de-clared it to be unacceptable.

Wilmot proceeded with his bill, but the difficulties of separating those processes to be nationalized from those to be left in private hands proved intractable. In the summer of 1947 the government ran into severe economic difficulties, and at an emergency meeting of the Parliamentary Labour party in the holiday month of August it was agreed that the nationalization of steel might be delayed by twelve months. This opened the possibility that it might be killed by the veto of the House of Lords because there would no longer be time to pass the bill in three successive sessions in the House of Commons. The Labour party in its election manifesto had an-nounced that it would not "tolerate obstruction of the people's will" by the House of Lords, but to that point it had met no obstruction. The House of Lords had established its value as a debating and re-vising chamber, and in no single instance had it sought to override the considered view of the majority in the Commons. Those minis-ters who were keen to see steel nationalized decided, however, to take no chances and exacted a bill to amend the Parliament Act of 1911 as their price for acquiescing in postponement of the national-ization of steel. Under it a bill passed by the House of Commons in two successive sessions would automatically become law even though rejected by the House of Lords, and the effective delaying power of the upper house was reduced, and reduced retrospectively, from two years to one. The Conservatives did not oppose the measure with the same vehemence that their fathers had shown in 1910, but suggested an inter-party conference on the whole question of reform of the House of Lords. The government eventually agreed. The Labour party was represented in the talks by Attlee, Morrison, Addison, Jowitt and Whiteley, the Conservatives by Eden, Salis-bury, Swinton and Maxwell Fyfe, the Liberals by Samuel and Clement Davies. The conference reached agreement on some impor-tant principles—that the new second chamber should be based on a modification of the existing House of Lords, that there ought not to be an assured permanent majority for any one party, that an hereditary peerage should not by itself constitute a qualification for membership, but "Lords of Parliament" should be selected from hereditary peers or "Life peers" on grounds of personal distinction or public service, that women should be eligible for membership, that some remuneration should be paid to members, that peers who were not "Lords of Parliament" should be entitled to sit in the House of Commons if successful at an election and to vote in elections thereto, and that some provision should be made for disqualifying members of the second chamber who neglected or became incapable of performing their duties—but no agreement could be reached on the question of delaying powers. The Conservatives were willing to recommend a period of eighteen months, and the Labour representatives that the period of delay should not be less than nine months from third reading in the Commons. Both agreed that the difference between them on the subject of powers was fundamental, and not related only to the period of delay; the Liberals considered the difference a minor one which should have been capable of adjustment. Agreement not having been reached, the Lords rejected the bill in June and again in September 1948, and when it was once more passed by the Commons it received the royal assent in December 1949.

It was entirely in the British tradition that a constitutional change of permanent and major significance should have been devised to achieve a particular object in the party struggle. In fact, the measure reached the statute book too late in the life of that Parliament to affect the issue of steel. At long last the Iron and Steel Bill had been introduced, in October 1948. It was brought in by G. R. Strauss, Wilmot having been dropped from the ministry in a reconstruction just twelve months previously. In the previous spring a Labour member, Alfred Edwards, sitting for the steel town of Middlesbrough, had angered his political friends by attacking the nationalization of steel as "sheer madness"; he urged that if they were bent on doing a silly thing, there was no need to do it in a silly way, and declared that the right way, if it had to be done, would be to acquire the assets of whole firms working integrated processes from the raw material to the finished article, that is to say, to go for "vertical" rather than "horizontal" nationalization. The Labour party expelled him from its membership but took his advice.[30] When the bill was published—the mere announcement in the King's Speech had been enough to compel another Labour member, a former junior minister, to give up the Labour whip—it was seen to provide for the acquisition of the securities of whole firms. A total of nearly 250 firms was scheduled for nationalization under an Iron and Steel Corporation to be appointed by the Minister of Supply, and it was intended that they should retain the names under which they had previously traded. The Ford steel works at Dagenham was tactfully omitted from the list, no doubt to avoid international repercussions, though this was never admitted. The compensation to be paid was to be based on stock exchange prices before the announcement of the bill; this method had a superficial appearance of fairness, but was considered by the Conservatives to undervalue the assets of this flourishing industry. It was the only case apart from development rights in land where the scale of compensation proved a serious issue between the parties.

The steel bill was opposed energetically by the Conservatives at all stages in the House of Commons. When it went to the Lords a former colonial governor who had been ennobled, and who sat as a Labour peer, withdrew from the party and joined the Liberals. Lord Milverton's brief period in the Labour party was compared with the experience of a man wandering in the ladies' underwear department of a big store who suddenly realized where he was and beat a hasty retreat. The Lords, with the shadow of the Parliament Bill darkening their counsels, did not reject the measure outright but made substantial amendments. When these were referred to the Commons some were accepted and others sent back to the upper house. The only amendments on which the Lords insisted were a group postponing the vesting date from May 1950 to July 1951, and the date of operation of the bill to October 1950, that is, to dates after the last possible date for a general election. This action was justified on the ground that any mandate for the nationalization of steel given by the electors in 1945 was stale and the electorate should have another opportunity of expressing its views before the change of ownership was accomplished. The Labour government did not insist on the original dates and the bill received the royal assent. The difference from the earlier patterns of nationalization became evident when the minister set about constituting the Iron and Steel Corporation. He was unable to recruit more than one member having any direct connexion with a steel-making firm.

Though the Labour and Conservative parties divided on historical lines over the development of land for building, they were at one in their attitude to the use of land for farming. The submarine threat to imports from abroad had made it a matter of national survival to secure the maximum supplies of food and feeding stuffs from home sources and had brought the agricultural depression of the twenties and thirties to an end. While the war was still being waged, plans were worked out by the coalition government for putting British agriculture in peacetime on a permanently prosperous basis; and the need to conserve dollars secured in peace the same consideration for agriculture that the U-boat had gained in war. Owing to the change of government it fell to a Labour Minister of Agriculture, Tom Williams, to translate these plans into the Agriculture Act, 1947; and the former Tory Minister, R. S. Hudson, welcomed it as a measure which he would like to have introduced himself. The act continued the practice of holding annual price reviews in February, with special reviews at other times of the year, for the purpose of assuring fair remuneration to farmers. This fair remuneration was to be achieved by a guaranteed fixed price for any particular product, by a deficiency payment related to a standard price, by an acreage payment, by a subsidy, or by a price calculated in accordance with some formula. In practice, deficiency payments based on world prices have proved the most important instrument and have given the agricultural community a prosperity it has not known since the eighteenth century. This identity of view between the Labour and Conservative parties should cause no surprise—it had been foreshadowed by the Agricultural Marketing Act of 1931—for although both parties have occasionally been deflected from their philosophy by free-trade recruits basically they are both prepared to interfere with economic processes whenever the national interest, or indeed their own party interest, seems to them to require it. The nation as a whole has paid in higher taxes for the subsidies given to the farming community, for the Liberal party, which was still in a vague way the repository of the idea that money was best left to fructify in the pockets of the people, was out of favour in the immediate post-war years; and the nation as a whole has also had the benefits of relatively low costs for food compared with other countries.

Those years saw also an immense development of the social services paid for partly by the beneficiaries and partly by their employers, but to an increasing extent out of taxation. In Labour party propaganda the idea has not infrequently been cultivated that the Welfare State began with the general election of 5th July 1945; and the notion was encouraged when the National Insurance Act, 1946, was made to come into operation on 5th July 1948. In fact, with increases in the rates both of contribution and of benefit, the act followed the lines of a coalition white paper of 1944 arising out of the Beveridge report, and the white paper itself was in harmony with the Contributory Pensions Act of 1926 and a natural development from the National Insurance Act of 1911 in which the true fount of the Welfare State must be sought. The creation of a system of social security "from the cradle to the grave" has, indeed, been the combined work of Liberal, Conservative and Labour administrations, and no party can claim exclusive rights to it.

The related national health service roused deeper party strife. The necessity for big changes in the health services was universally recognized, and in particular it was accepted that the hospitals with their vastly increased expenditure could no longer rely on the casual gifts of the charitable. A comprehensive health service had been one of the three assumptions on which Beveridge based his report, and during the war the Conservative minister, Henry Willink, opened negotiations with the medical profession for such a service. When Aneurin Bevan took on the task in the Labour government, the sparks flew. Even his own supporters were sometimes outraged. Bessie Braddock has related[31] how he turned on an audience of Labour women, who had pressed for better representation on hospital committees, with the angry retort: "I'm not going to be dictated to by a lot of frustrated females." It would not have been easy for the most tactful of ministers to have persuaded the medical men to fall into line, and Bevan, not the most tactful of men, was spoiling for a fight. When his National Health Service Bill was introduced in 1946—and also timed to operate from the mystic date 5th July 1948—he met virulent opposition from the Conservatives. Fundamentally the difference between the parties was one of degree. The Labour party would have liked to see a state-salaried service available to all without charge at the time it was needed, but was willing to go some way to meet doctors who wished to continue their private practice and patients who wanted something better than the state would provide for all. The Conservative party accepted the need for a national service financed in the main by taxation and providing a basic minimum of attention for all, but did not wish to coerce any doctor into a state scheme and saw no reason why patients who wished to buy extra attention for themselves should be denied the means of so doing. The narrowness of the real difference was soon widened by the intransigence of the minister and the conservatism of the medical profession, and the opposition was led to vote for reasoned amendments on second and third reading in the Commons, which gave the impression to those who only take in headlines that the Labour party wanted a national health service while the Tories were against it. The bill was carried by large majorities, but after a plebiscite of medical practitioners in 1948 had shown eighty-six per cent to be against taking part in the service changes were brought about by an amending measure. It was, among other things, made impossible to introduce a full-time salaried service by regulation, which made the scheme more agreeable both to the profession and to the Conservative party. The mounting costs of the service soon gave rise to alarm, but it proved to be acceptable in the country at large, where freedom from medical bills in times of anxiety was welcomed with relief. Both the medical profession and the Conservative party dropped outright opposition and concentrated on improvements in detail.

31

LABOUR IN POWER 1945–1950: THE EBB

*Labour's troubles begin—an attempt to substitute Bevin for Attlee
—Dalton's resignation—the Conservative recovery—Butler's reshaping of policy—and Woolton's overhaul of organization—the
Maxwell-Fyfe reports—the faded glamour of nationalization and
controls—The Right Road for Britain and Labour Believes in
Britain—virtual end of the I.L.P.—the Liberal bid to come back—
the election manifestos—party broadcasts—the anti-nationalization
campaigns—the Liberals reduced to nine—and Labour scrapes back
with a majority of six*

THE first five years of "Labour in power as well as in office"
were years of swift and dramatic change. In no previous period
of British history had so many major bills found their way to the
statute book. The nation could never be the same after this experiment as before. These were the years of the triumph of Fabianism.
Though now living a Darby-and-Joan existence at Passfield Corner,
and having themselves passed beyond gradualism to Soviet Communism, the real authors of the revolution of 1945–50 were the
Webbs of Grosvenor Road. Yet all was not well. Foreign policy had
been conducted with an assurance that relieved allies, the British
Empire had been dismantled without loss of any territory save
Burma, the defences of the country had been maintained; the improvements in the social services and the support given to agriculture were beneficent and of permanent value; the programme of
nationalization, if not universally welcome, was in line with expectations; but by 1947 the Labour government was experiencing
difficulties against which its huge majority in the Commons was no
defence. In part these difficulties were its misfortune, in part of its
own creation.

In the volume of his memoirs entitled *High Tide and After* Dalton
called 1946 the *annus mirabilis* and 1947 the *annus horrendus*. The
year began with Bevin showing signs of ill-health, Morrison in hospital and Attlee becoming more nervy. Conscious of the drain on
the dollar loan negotiated in 1946, Dalton begged his colleagues to
reduce expenditure on the forces and to get more men into

productive industry. He warned Attlee that after a wonderful start they looked like finishing wonderfully badly, perhaps worse than in 1931.[1] A bitter winter brought a fuel crisis. Power was cut from domestic consumers and industry alike and the number of unemployed shot up from 397,000 to 2,300,000. The dollar reserves ran out at an even more alarming rate, but Dalton clung to his cheap money policy. In August convertibility of the pound had to be suspended.

Following a universal law of politics, members and ministers began to lay the blame for their troubles on lack of leadership at the top. Driving back from the Durham miners' gala with Bevin in July, Dalton had urged him to take over from Attlee, but a few days later Bevin spoke with anger of the idea that he should "betray Clem".[2] Early in September Cripps proposed to Dalton a new government in which Bevin should be Prime Minister, Attlee Chancellor and Dalton Foreign Secretary. He discussed it also with Morrison, now out of hospital, but failed with him because Morrison thought that he should himself be Prime Minister. On 9th September, by arrangement with Dalton, Cripps saw Attlee to discuss the plan with him. Attlee, assured by this time of Bevin's continued support, blandly explained why the plan would not do, and Cripps, who had entered the room a Cabinet-maker, went out having agreed to be Minister of Production, or, as the office came to be called, Minister of Economic Affairs. "The movement begun by Cripps, with my support," as Dalton recorded at the time, "to put Bevin in Attlee's place, has now turned into a movement to put Cripps in Morrison's place, or at least in the most important part of it";[3] and Attlee had survived another challenge to his leadership—the last, as it turned out, that he was to encounter.

The government was reconstructed in October, but the financial crisis did not abate, and for the first time in the history of the country potatoes had to be rationed. In November Dalton introduced an emergency budget to close the gap in the balance of payments. Unhappily for him, on his way into the chamber he had informed the lobby correspondent of the *Star* of some of his proposals, and against all probabilities the information had appeared in a late edition of that newspaper. The following morning, as soon as he learnt what had happened, Dalton offered to resign, and in response to a private notice question in the house accepted full responsibility. What follows is instructive as showing the intensity of the party struggle. Churchill's first reaction, as leader of the opposition, was to extend to Dalton "sympathy with him at the misuse of his confidence",[4] but later that evening, after discussion with his colleagues, he wrote to Dalton to say that, having received further information, he now felt it necessary that the incident should be the subject of an inquiry by a select committee. Dalton had in the meantime pressed his offer of resignation and Cripps had been appointed in his place.

It was too much to expect that the Conservative party should let such an opportunity pass. Dalton had gone out of his way time and time again to rub salt into Conservative wounds, and the gusto with which he did it, allied to the fact that as the son of a royal tutor and an old Etonian he was a "traitor to his class", had not created any affection between him and the Conservative ranks such as existed for Ernest Bevin or even for Clement Attlee.

The Conservative party by this time had recovered from its demoralization of 1945 and was once more in fighting trim. Two men had specially contributed to this recovery, R. A. Butler in the matter of policy and Lord Woolton in the matter of organization, though the formulation of ideas and their propagation cannot be rigorously separated.

From 1931 to 1945 Conservative ministers had been able to rely on the resources of the civil service to supply them with factual information and policy briefs. In July 1945 they were thrown upon their own resources, and at a time when the nation had made it unmistakably clear that the old Conservatism had lost its appeal. The result was a complete rethinking of Conservative policy in regard to all the main issues of the day, and the Conservative party came to present to the nation a more contemporary, forward-looking and even radical appearance.

In this rethinking a major part was played by Butler, partly through the force of his own personality and partly through the party organizations under his control. In 1945 he had become chairman of the Central Council of the National Union, and in November 1945 the Post-War Problems Committee of the union was reconstituted as the Advisory Committee on Policy and Political Education with Butler as its chairman. Its work was to be closely co-ordinated with that of the Conservative Research Department, and its chairman was to be the head of that department. At the end of 1945 the Conservative Political Centre was established as a virtually autonomous department of the Central Office and it embarked on a "two-way movement of ideas" for the purpose of ensuring "a continuing partnership between the party leaders and its rank and file in the formation of party policy on political issues". A further step was taken in 1948 when the Conservative Parliamentary Secretariat and the Central Office Library and Information Department were merged with it. Butler gathered a group of able young men in the Research Department and the Political Centre, and with their help there issued from the Central Office a stream of policy documents such as *The Industrial Charter* (1947), *The Agricultural Charter* (1948) and *Imperial Policy* (1949), which showed that the party had thoroughly adjusted itself to the new circumstances. The authors of *The Industrial Charter*[5] accepted frankly that it would be undesirable "to restore to private ownership the coal industry and the Bank of England", and confined themselves to freeing only "certain parts of civil aviation". They made the novel proposal that there should be a Workers' Charter guaranteeing "security of employment, incentive to do the job well and to get a better one", and "status as an individual, however big the firm or mechanized the job may be". The British farmers were offered guaranteed prices and markets "for all the food that they can produce in accordance with the rules of good husbandry and good estate management and up to the agreed levels", and farm-workers a charter providing for improved status, incentive and security of employment. It was reaffirmed that "self-government within the British Empire and Commonwealth is an aim to be achieved as soon as colonial peoples are ready for it". These declarations of principle were hailed not as a conversion to novel ideas, but as the return of Conservatism to those sound principles of Tory democracy enunciated by Beaconsfield and Randolph Churchill.

It became the task of Lord Woolton to see that the new Toryism found favour with the electorate. He had not, as it happened, been a member of the Conservative party until the general election of 1945. In his younger days he had even been a member of the Fabian Society, but had resigned in 1917 when his experiences as a wartime controller shook his faith in the ability of the gentleman in Whitehall to control the use of raw materials. As Minister of Food in the Second World War he had remained independent of party, but he had strongly supported Churchill during the election campaign of 1945, and at noon on 25th July, as the flow of results made it clear that defeat was inevitable, he wrote to Churchill "asking him if he would be good enough to honour me by allowing me to join him in the Conservative party, for I greatly feared the economic effect on the country of nationalizing the principal industries".[6] Out of office, he was taking up again the threads of his business life when he received a request to visit Churchill. The fallen statesman told him of his concern about the condition of the Conservative party organization. Woolton reflected that he had never before given much support to the Conservative Central Office, and Churchill unhesitatingly agreed. Churchill then asked him to take on the task of bringing it to a proper state of efficiency. Woolton was taken aback—he was sixty-five and the newest recruit to the party—but after a month of trying to find reasons for not accepting he agreed to become chairman of the Conservative party organization on condition that he could have a free hand and three months to set his personal affairs in order.

The invitation to Woolton was a stroke of genius. "Uncle Fred", as he became universally known in the party, had a benign personality that inspired confidence and he radiated cheerfulness around himself. These same qualities had made him a superb Minister of Food in the war, and the reputation he had gained in that vital department now won him the respect of the politically neutral and even of political opponents. But he found that he had accepted a difficult task. "The organization of the Conservative party," he wrote at a later date, "was the most Topsy-like arrangement that I had ever come across. It had grown up amidst conflicting and—it seemed—almost irreconcilable claims." As a businessman he felt the strongest temptation to urge the scrapping of the whole machinery and a new start, but after consultation with the local organizations he came to realize that, while he might create a machine that would be less wasteful of human effort, he might lose the interest roused by the feeling that success or failure depended on the individual efforts of large numbers of devoted supporters. He soon found that "the primary need of the whole of the Conservative party, but in particular of the Central Office, was that it should believe in itself, and in its capacity to convert the electorate to Conservatism". He rejected suggestions that the Conservative party should change its name or temporize with its principles, and addressed himself to the replenishing of the party coffers. He turned down a suggestion that he should appeal for a quarter of a million pounds on the ground that it might fail through being too unambitious. He asked for, and obtained, a million, and the achievement "gave the party a sense of accomplishment". He turned this new zest into "Operation Door-knocker", a great canvassing campaign designed to ascertain Conservative voters and increase their number. It was not the large public meetings addressed by important speakers, he realized, that would be the predominant power in winning the next election, but "the advocacy of people who, combining personal friendliness in their approach to individuals with a sense of high national purpose and deep political conviction based on knowledge, took these things to the houses of the voters". This, he said in his memoirs, "was the power that revolutionized the party". He was gratified to find that the new Conservatism was making a big appeal in the universities —ever ready to turn against established authority—and he gave encouragement to the Young Conservative organization designed to attract people of both sexes between the ages of fifteen and thirty. The Conservative party proved more successful than the Labour in organizing its young people; and this movement, in which the desire for social intercourse played its part no less than a thirst for political knowledge, ensured that a high proportion of persons coming on to the register would vote Conservative. As a further essential step in the recovery, Woolton persuaded Conservatives to play a more active rôle as a party in local government. "In the interests of the Conservative party," he argued, "it was necessary to accept the idea that local authority elections should be run on a political basis, that the machinery of the political party should be used for the purpose of selecting and nominating candidates, sharing with them the expenses of the election, undertaking canvassing on their behalf, in order to secure the highest possible interest in the work of the council and in the return of what we considered to be suitable candidates." He had two reasons, the first that the enemy, socialism, had its roots in local government, and the second that participation in local elections enabled the marking of the register to be perfected for parliamentary contests.[7]

The efficiency of the Central Office had suffered in the past because it had been largely regarded as a training-ground for political candidates. Woolton laid down that members of the staff must vacate their position on becoming candidates, and so gave a more professional note to the staff. The quality of candidates was of paramount importance if Conservatives were to recover their position, and under Woolton's leadership the party addressed itself to the problem in thoroughgoing fashion. A committee was set up by the Executive Committee of the National Union under the chairmanship of Sir David Maxwell Fyfe "to examine the constitution of the National Union and the relationships between the constituencies, the provincial areas, the National Union and the party as a whole". It was also required to study the reports of three special committees on party finance, financial arrangements of candidates and employment of agents. The Maxwell-Fyfe committee produced an interim report in 1948 and a final report in 1949. Its main recommendations concerned finance, and especially the financial arrangements between candidates and constituencies. The committee found that there was a gap of £200,000 a year between the annual income of the party's headquarters and the sum needed to do the job properly. It recommended that constituencies should pay a voluntary "quota" to the head office based on the number of Conservative votes at the last election. This was approved by the party conference and was adopted by nearly all constituencies in England and Wales. The party headquarters had previously depended exclusively on the contributions of wealthy firms or individuals. Turning to the relation between members or candidates and their constituencies, the Maxwell-Fyfe committee found it undesirable that they should be expected to meet the whole cost of their elections and to bear the whole or a substantial part of the cost of running the constituency organization. This limited the choice of candidates to wealthy men, who might not be the best for the purpose—apart from the fact that the supply of candidates able to meet these expenses was diminishing. The Maxwell Fyfe committee recommended that no member should be allowed to contribute more than fifty pounds a year, and no candidate more than twenty-five pounds a year, to the constituency funds; and that the constituency association should bear the whole of the election expenses of the candidate, including in suitable cases even his personal expenses. The committee, wrote Woolton,[8] "reported even more drastically than I dared to hope", and these democratic recommendations were accepted by the party and put into effect. The limits were far more drastic than those laid down by the Labour party for its members and candidates, and made it possible for many young men of ability who would previously have been unable to offer themselves as candidates to stand for Parliament. It was inevitable that among them should be a number of candidates of a more thrustful type than had been previously seen on Conservative platforms, but on balance the widening of the list was greatly to the advantage of the Tory party.

By the end of the war the close working together of Conservatives and National Liberals had made them virtually one party, and formal recognition was given to this fact in May 1947, when joint recommendations to constituencies were issued on behalf of the two party headquarters by Lord Woolton and Lord Teviot with the approval of the executive committee of the National Union of Conservative and Unionist Associations and the executive committee of the National Liberal Council. The Woolton–Teviot agreement, as these recommendations came to be known, was embodied in the following paragraphs:

(i) In constituencies where each party already has an organization a combined association should be formed under a mutually agreed title, which indicates their community of effort and purpose.

(ii) In constituencies where only one of the parties has an organization, that organization should consider including in its membership all those who support joint action against socialism, and extending its title accordingly.

(iii) In constituencies where combined associations are seeking a candidate a joint list will, if requested, be prepared by both party headquarters in consultation.

(iv) Combined associations would be eligible for affiliation both to the National Union of Conservatives and Unionist Associations and to the National Liberal Council.

(v) In constituencies where a combined organization has been formed, it is suggested that the most suitable designation for the prospective candidate may be "Liberal and Unionist".

These recommendations were not mandatory, but before the next general election united associations or combined committees were formed in sixty-two constituencies, that is, in almost all the constituencies where National Liberalism was an active force. The candidates selected by these joint associations or committees, whether their own antecedents were Liberal or Conservative, acknowledged a responsibility to both the Conservatives and the National Liberals in their division. To look ahead, seventeen such joint candidates were successful in 1950, and they formed a Liberal-Unionist group with its own chairman and whip. The group met weekly, and the members were eligible also to attend Conservative meetings. They acknowledged the leadership of the Conservative leader, and received a joint whip along with the Conservatives.

This reshaping of policy and recasting of organization made the Conservative party of 1949 a very different body from that which had been routed in 1945. The electors who sway elections tend to vote, however, against a party they temporarily dislike more than for one they positively favour. By the end of 1949 the glamour of the Labour party had faded. Nationalization, advocated as a panacea on so many Labour platforms, had been tried and had not proved conspicuously successful. In coal-mining and transport heavy losses had been made, prices had increased and labour relations were not better, but rather worse, than in the private sector of industry. The incautious dictum of a Labour member, later a minister, Douglas Jay, that "the gentleman in Whitehall really does know better what is good for people than the people know themselves",[9] was taken as a symbol of a general bureaucratic attitude, and was contrasted with the administrative failures of the Labour government in practice—the rationing in peacetime of bread and potatoes, which had remained unrationed all through the war, the power cuts, the groundnuts fiasco. In war a common danger had enabled the British people to endure shortages and hardships with firm resolve and cheerful good humour. With the end of the fighting many of the problems of supply remained, and some were intensified owing to the exchange problem, but the spirit to endure then disappeared. People expected an easing of their burdens and a brightening of their lives more quickly than Labour ministers could achieve these results; and when the austere Cripps succeeded the genial Dalton at the Exchequer there grew doubts whether the Labour government really wished to see a "merry England" once again. These doubts, both about the administrative competence of socialist ministers and their ultimate aims, reached a climax on 18th September 1949, when lack of confidence in sterling and the depletion of currency reserves compelled Cripps to announce a severe devaluation of the pound from 4·03 dollars to 2·80. He had made his position more humiliating by asserting categorically that no devaluation was contemplated.

A general election had to be held before July 1950, and as it was risky to run the full course the parties began their preparations the year before. In July 1949 a Conservative statement of policy, summing up the documents of the previous years, was issued under the title, *The Right Road for Britain*. With an eye to the widest support and a glance at his old party, Winston Churchill claimed in a foreword:[10] "We are not only reviving the Tory democracy of Lord Beaconsfield and after him of Lord Randolph Churchill, but are giving expression to the spirit of liberalism with its sense of progress, tolerance and humanity which has spread so widely throughout our island and indeed throughout the world." After a meeting of senior ministers with the National Executive the government party issued a statement of policy under the title *Labour Believes in Britain*, which was approved by the Blackpool conference in October. Owing to the mounting spirit of electioneering, Attlee took the unusual step of announcing that there would be no election before the end of the year, and when Parliament was prorogued in December it expected to meet again in January. That Parliament never met again. During the Christmas holidays Attlee finally made up his mind to ask the King for a February election. In earlier discussions Morrison had asked for a later date. Cripps wanted an early election. The difficulties of framing a budget in a deteriorating financial situation prevailed over fears of what February weather might be like.

The boundaries of constituencies had been so altered as to make comparison with previous elections misleading. Only eighty constituencies were left unchanged. The number of constituencies was reduced from its temporary number of 640 to 625. The twelve university seats were abolished, a matter for deep regret inasmuch as the universities had come to return independent-minded members of great distinction who added notably to the debates in the house. The business vote was abolished, and the cities of London and Westminster, previously returning two members each, were merged into a single constituency returning one member. This took away privileges that had been to the benefit of Conservatives. All two-member constituencies were abolished.

The Conservatives and their allies put up a candidate in 621 of the constituencies, that is, in every English constituency except that of the Speaker, himself a former Conservative, in every Welsh constituency save one, in every Scottish constituency except two and in every Northern Ireland division. The Labour party and its Cooperative ally put up candidates for 612 of the 613 seats in Great Britain, the Speaker's being respected, but the Northern Ireland Labour party contested only five of the twelve seats in that Tory stronghold. Of the Labour candidates, 140 were sponsored by trade unions and thirty-three by the Cooperative party. Pritt and the few Labour members expelled in 1948 and 1949 for criticisms of the government's foreign policy (J. F. F. Platts-Mills, L. J. Solley, K. Zilliacus and H. L. Hutchinson) stood as Labour Independents and were opposed by official Labour candidates. A new application for affiliation to the Labour Party had been made in 1946 by the I.L.P., but it was turned down by the National Executive and at the party conference nobody even bothered to query the decision. Instead the delegates, after turning down another Communist application, adopted an amendment to the constitution making such bodies having their own programme, principles and policy, or owing allegiance abroad, ineligible for affiliation. In the following year, wearying of isolation, McGovern, Campbell Stephen and Carmichael decided to conform to Labour party discipline—this was made easier by the suspension of standing orders—and were given the Labour whip. On Campbell Stephen's death in 1948 his Camlachie seat was contested by both official and Independent Labour candidates, and the split vote enabled a Conservative to win. This was virtually the end of the stormy history of the Independent Labour party, but an organization was kept in being, and in 1950 two I.L.P. candidates opposed McGovern and Carmichael in their Glasgow constituencies.

The Liberal party surpassed expectations by throwing no fewer than 475 candidates into the fight. This was the greatest number of Liberal candidates since 1917. Liberals were no doubt influenced by the argument, used to the full in propaganda, that only by intervention on this scale could they offer electors the possibility of voting a Liberal government into office. The Communists also made a big bid, putting forward 100 candidates. Seven Welsh Nationalists, one Welsh Republican, four Scottish Nationalists, one Scottish Self-government candidate, two Sinn Fein candidates, one Irish Nationalist and one Irish Anti-Partition candidate took the field. There were fourteen Independents. A motley band of thirty-two other candidates fighting under variegated labels brought the total figure to the unprecedented figure of 1,868.

The Labour and the Conservative policy documents were condensed into election manifestos under the titles *Let us win through together* and *This is the road*. This was an innovation for the Conservatives, as they had hitherto relied for a policy on the personal statement of their leader. Churchill kept a link with past customs by commending the manifesto in three sentences of introduction. The Labour document promised that beet sugar manufacture and sugar refining would be transferred to national ownership; that the cement industry would be converted from "a tightly organized private monopoly" to public ownership; that the chemical industry would be examined and "appropriate sections" transferred to public ownership; that where the job was too big for individual farmers to tackle, public ownership would be used as a means of bringing into sound cultivation good land not fully used; that all suitable minerals would be placed in public ownership; that water supply would become a wholly public responsibility; that there would be more markets for fruit and vegetables under municipal or other public ownership; that the development of cold storage would be effected through public ownership; that the existing system of distribution of meat through the Ministry of Food would become a permanent public service; and that industrial assurance would be "mutualized". The Conservatives appealed for "a true property-owning democracy ... based upon the wide distribution of private property, not upon its absorption in the state machine". They promised Scotland a new Minister of State with Cabinet rank and undertook that "a special responsibility for Wales should be assigned to a member of the Cabinet". The Liberal manifesto said the Liberal party was more likely to unite the nation than either the Conservatives or the socialists, "locked as they are in what is really a class struggle". The Communists proclaimed that their policy was to prevent the coming slump, to avert war and to end United States control of Britain.

As in 1945, the broadcast talks by party leaders dominated the election—and diminished still further the rôle of the ordinary candidate in comparison with his leaders. The Labour and Conservative parties were each allotted five talks of equal length, and the Liberals one long and two short talks. It was agreed that any other party with more than fifty candidates should have the right to a broadcast; the Communist party was the only one to win the right. It was significant of the new qualities brought to the fore by broadcasting that the Conservatives gave one of their places to Charles Hill, whose voice was already familiar to millions of listeners as "the radio doctor", and well he used his opportunity.

Churchill was more discreet in his utterances than in 1945, and played the part of the elder statesman to perfection. He engaged a special train for his electoral tour, and he addressed four great meetings at Cardiff, Edinburgh, Leeds and Manchester. At Edinburgh he threw out the suggestion of "another talk with Soviet Russia upon the highest level", which was dismissed—such is the working of the party system at election times—by Bevin as "stunt proposals" and by Morrison as "soap-box diplomacy".[11] Foreign policy, however, played little part in the election. The main issue in the minds of electors was whether there should be a further instalment of nationalization or not, and there can be no doubt that the miscellany of further proposals for public ownership made by the Labour party told heavily against it. Dalton in his memoirs blamed this "dog's dinner of new nationalization proposals" severely. It was the residue, he revealed, of a much longer list of "possibles" which had been worked over by the National Executive and its Policy Committee, presided over by Morrison.[12] Apart from the normal political propaganda of the revived Tory party, the case against nationalization had been powerfully made by some of the threatened industries with their vastly greater resources and technical skill in the field of public relations. The steel industry had

N

conducted a great advertising campaign to bring home the merits of British steel, which was not the less effective as a presentation of the case against nationalization for being indirect. When the Labour party's programme appeared, the sugar-refining and meat-distributing industries took more direct measures of self-protection, and "Mr. Cube" and "Sir Loin" began to appear on the hoardings and in the advertisement columns of the newspapers. The Labour party was enraged, and sought to get the cost of these campaigns reckoned among the election expenses of anti-nationalization candidates, but this was absurd as they were not designed to promote the candidature of any particular person but only to put before the public the case for the continuance of private enterprise in these threatened industries. None of Labour's proposals, according to Dalton, had been the subject of serious or prolonged propaganda. Trade Union organizers warned the party headquarters that the inclusion of sugar refining and chemicals was not popular with the workers of Tate and Lyle Ltd. and Imperial Chemical Industries Ltd. Even a large number of Labour voters who remained theoretically convinced of the case for the public ownership of the means of production, distribution and exchange would have preferred to see the country digest the first morsel of nationalization before inviting it to swallow another.

The Labour party entered the contest with seemingly good prospects. In the five years of that Parliament it had not lost at a by-election a single seat won at the previous general election, an achievement unprecedented in British political history, and the net result of expulsion, resignation and accession was to diminish its members in the House of Commons only by two—from 393 at the opening of Parliament to 391 at the dissolution. It would need a lot of acid to corrode away a majority of 142 over all others. Yet the Labour leaders knew that they had no easy task to retain their position. The majority in the House of Commons was no true reflection of voting in the country, and a swing of a few per cent in the votes cast could destroy their ascendancy. A speech by Aneurin Bevan at Manchester[13] in 1948 in which he had said, "No amount of cajolery can eradicate from my heart a deep, burning hatred for the Tory party . . . so far as I am concerned they are lower than vermin," was regarded with dismay by his senior colleagues. Morrison called him "the answer to the Tories' prayer", and calculated that the reference to vermin so increased the intensity of the Tory effort that it cost thirty to fifty Labour seats.[14] Attlee nevertheless expected to return with a majority of twenty to thirty. The public opinion polls, now becoming a major factor in the party struggle, indicated a closer result. On the eve of the election the Gallup poll gave the Conservatives a lead of one per cent.

The electors went to the polling stations quietly according to

Attlee, demurely according to Churchill,[15] but perhaps the right word is seriously. The knowledge that it was likely to be a close thing, and that one's personal vote might make all the difference between free enterprise and socialism, made for a high poll and compelled many of the normally uncommitted to vote Labour or Conservative without regard for candidates not belonging to the two major parties. The electorate had only slightly increased since 1945, but over two and a half million more electors recorded votes in an exceptional turnout of eighty-four per cent. Out of the 28,772,671 who dropped valid papers in the ballot boxes, 13,266,592 voted Labour and 12,502,567 Conservative, 2,261,548 for Liberal candidates, 91,746 for Communists, 93,421 for Nationalists and 196,797 for Independents and minor parties.

Not one Independent was returned except the Speaker, not even so well-liked a politician as W. J. Brown. Pritt, who had held Hammersmith North so easily in 1945, went down equally with the four other Labour Independents. The two Communists lost their seats and ninety-seven of the party's 100 candidates lost their deposits. Only in Northern Ireland were two Nationalists returned.

The solid array of Labour and Conservatives in the new house was broken only by nine Liberals. It was a poor return for the expenditure of money and effort that had gone into 475 candidatures. No fewer than 319 Liberal candidates lost their deposits. Fortunately the party had made an arrangement with Lloyd's by which all deposits lost after the first fifty up to a total of 250 were under-written. If the members elected are expressed as a percentage of the candidates, it was the biggest defeat ever in Liberal history. The leader, Clement Davies, was returned, but his chief whip, Frank Byers, was defeated, and so was the former leader, Sir Archibald Sinclair, standing again for Caithness and Sutherland. The only shafts of light to pierce the Liberal gloom were the victories of Joseph Grimond, a son-in-law of Lady Violet Bonham Carter, and A. J. F. Macdonald in ousting Conservatives in three-cornered fights.

The massive voting for the major parties resulted in the return of 315 Labour members and 298 Conservatives. Of the successful Labour candidates, 111 were sponsored by trade unions and eighteen by the Cooperative party. The Conservative total included seventeen who described themselves as National Liberal or added the name Liberal to Conservative in their description.

The Labour party had therefore won, but it was the closest election result for a hundred years. If the Labour victory of 1945 bore some resemblance to the Liberal triumph of 1906, so did the evaporation of its majority when put to the next electoral test, but on this occasion there was no third force in the shape of the Irish party. Labour's majority over all other members was a bare five—or six if the Speaker is not counted. It was too precarious for comfort.

32

UNSTABLE EQUILIBRIUM
1950–1951

The King's government carried on—Cripps's resignation and death
—Gaitskell appointed Chancellor—rising costs of defence and
national health service—Bevin's resignation and death—Morrison
made Foreign Secretary—Bevan's exclusion from higher office—he
resigns over charges for dentures and spectacles, and is followed
by Wilson and Freeman—Morrison's troubles at the Foreign Office
—the Conservatives wear down the government—and Attlee
obtains a dissolution—Bevanite successes in the elections to the
National Executive—election issues—"Whose finger on the trig-
ger?"—Conservative consideration for the Liberals—a Conservative
majority of seventeen

AFTER surveying the wreckage and consulting his colleagues
Attlee decided, in a phrase not heard for many years, that "it is
the duty of the present administration to continue in office, for the
King's government must be carried on".[1] Though the date for the
vesting of the steel industry was adhered to, clearly the additional
measures of nationalization in the election programme could not be
carried out; and the best the government could hope to do was to
cross bridges as it arrived at them. Only one Cabinet minister,
Creech Jones, had lost his seat, and at this time Attlee made few
changes. Before long, however, the illness of two senior ministers,
aggravated by the conditions under which the House of Commons
was now working, required changes that forced attention on the
question of Attlee's eventual successor, and in so doing reopened the
debate on the character and aims of the Labour party.

Cripps had taken severely the attacks on his honour for denying
that devaluation was on the way. Attlee's curious comment is:[2]
"Having to deny what was the truth was no doubt hard on a
Christian like Stafford"—is it easy for other people?—"but he
wouldn't have let it worry him if he'd had any sense." Cripps
carried through a budget in the spring, but ill-health was gnawing at
his vitals, and in the autumn he went to a sanatorium in Switzerland. In October he wrote to Attlee to say that he saw no alternative

but to hand in his resignation, and, in view of the narrow majority of the party in the House of Commons, to apply for the Chiltern Hundreds. Six months later he was dead.

Cripps had made known to Attlee that in his view the right successor was Gaitskell, and Dalton, warned by Douglas Jay that resignation was imminent, had pressed the same opinion upon the Prime Minister. It probably accorded with Attlee's own view, if Gaitskell's appointment in 1947 to be Minister of Fuel and Power was, as Shinwell believed,[3] "an early move by Attlee to sift through the recruits for the succession". In any event, Gaitskell was appointed. At the age of forty-five he was the youngest Chancellor of the Exchequer since Austen Chamberlain, who had been appointed to that great office in 1903 when only forty.

Shinwell, who had been made Minister of Defence when Gaitskell was appointed to supersede him as Minister of Fuel and Power after the fuel crisis of 1947, was asked by Attlee for his views. He advised Attlee to appoint Morrison "on grounds of his seniority and because such an appointment would cause less resentment among those colleagues who considered themselves capable of tackling the nation's financial problems".[4] There is no evidence that Morrison sought the position, and later he described the choice of Gaitskell as "a bold but wise move, though it displeased some of the old guard and infuriated a few of his own contemporaries, possibly including Nye Bevan and Harold Wilson".[5] He thought it was for Gaitskell "a chance which set him contemplating the leadership of the party", and that was undoubtedly how it appeared to Bevan. According to Dalton:[6] "Bevan was much vexed that Gaitskell, and not he, became Chancellor of the Exchequer." Shinwell is even more explicit:[7]

"The appointment produced a formidable result, affecting the party's future. It profoundly disturbed Nye Bevan, who, in length of service and as a minister senior to Gaitskell, considered he was due for promotion. In the view of a considerable section of the party, Bevan was regarded as the probable heir to the leadership when Attlee decided to retire."

For a while Bevan kept his counsels to himself, and in those months it became clear that Ernest Bevin could not continue much longer as Foreign Secretary. The invasion of South Korea by the North Koreans in July produced a situation out of which a third world war could easily arise, and Attlee had to assume Bevin's most important duties. To the dismay of its supporters, the government was obliged to introduce a big programme of rearmament and to increase the period of conscription from eighteen months to two years. Shortly before Cripps resigned the government had announced an expansion of the defence programme costing £3,600 million; in January 1951 this figure was revised to £4,700 million.

It was inevitable that there must be retrenchment in other

branches of government expenditure, and the Treasury criticism was particularly directed at the mounting costs of the National Health Service, which were getting out of control. From an original figure of £150 million for the net cost of the service in nine months of 1948–9 the estimate had leapt to £393 million for the twelve months of 1950–1. Power had been taken to make a charge for prescriptions and ineffectual attempts had been made by Cripps to impose a ceiling on expenditure.

This was the background to a reconstruction of the government in January 1951 when the Ministry of Health was shorn of many of its responsibilities and its minister ceased to be in the Cabinet. The reduced ministry was not considered to offer sufficient scope or prestige for Bevan. He was made Minister of Labour, but although this post ranked senior to the reduced Ministry of Health, "by any standard", as Shinwell observes,[8] "this was demotion for one of the outstanding personalities of the Labour movement". Moreover, it put Bevan on a side-track and left the Ministry of Health without a spokesman in the Cabinet at a time when the soaring cost of defence made it inevitable that some restraint should be placed on the health service. Bevan noted, but still bided his time.

Ernest Bevin was now clearly a dying man, and equally clearly he wished to die at the Foreign Office. With unnecessary clumsiness Attlee asked him in March for his resignation as Foreign Secretary, and five weeks later he was found dead of a heart attack among the red boxes of his new office as Lord Privy Seal.

The succession raised even more contentious issues than Cripps's resignation had done. On this occasion Morrison claimed the office for himself, and eventually his wish was gratified—it would have been well for him if he had been denied the pleasure—but not before a search had been made for all other possible incumbents, if only because Morrison was the last man Bevin would have wished to see at his great desk under George III's portrait. James Griffiths, who had taken Creech Jones's place at the Colonial Office, was not considered quite to measure up to the job, and Hector McNeil, who had been highly regarded as Minister of State, was thought too young. Attlee said ambiguously to Morrison, "It boils down to the fact that you are the inevitable choice," and later told Francis Williams: "He seemed to want it badly and turned down every other suggestion I made to him, so in the end I appointed him."[9]

Aneurin Bevan does not appear to have been seriously considered for the post, and the fact that he had been passed over in quick succession for the two senior departments of the government, and that Gaitskell was now obviously marked above him in the succession to the leadership, inflamed his mind. It was not entirely a personal question, though only a person very ignorant of the actual processes of politics could suppose that questions of personal ambition play no part in the evolution of party. Bevan indeed thought that his power to sway the masses by glowing oratory was a better qualification for leadership than Gaitskell's academic distinction and proficiency in the dismal science of economics. But he also argued, and rightly argued, that Gaitskell's type of socialism was being preferred to his own, and even that the Labour party was being asked quietly to jettison the socialism that it had hitherto proclaimed. He seemed to himself to be the guardian of the ark of the covenant, and, as Leslie Hunter has written, "saw his own exclusion from higher office as symbolizing a trend that would rapidly take the party on the road to mere Liberal reformism".[10]

The ground for a quarrel was soon found in a proposal by Gaitskell to make a charge for dentures and spectacles provided under the National Health Service. Bevan would not have a finger laid on his darling child, and in a speech at Bermondsey in April tried to coerce the government by publicly declaring: "I will never be a member of a government which makes charges on the National Health Service for the patient."[11] In Cabinet Gaitskell's quieter arguments prevailed, and in his budget a week after Bevan's speech he proposed a charge of fifty per cent of the cost of dentures and spectacles. A violent attack on these proposals in Bevan's newspaper, *Tribune*, prepared the way for his resignation on 23rd April, and this was followed by the resignation of Harold Wilson as President of the Board of Trade and John Freeman as Parliamentary Secretary to the Ministry of Supply. Attlee had been forced by a duodenal ulcer to go into hospital about that time and has hinted that if he had not been absent the resignations would have been avoided.[12] This is unfair both to Morrison's leadership and to Bevan's resolve. In his letter of resignation Bevan showed that teeth and eyes were the occasion rather than the cause of the breach by widening the area of contention to include the whole budget, and especially the expenditure on rearmament which he had previously defended. The budget, he wrote, was "wrong because it is based upon a scale of military expenditure, in the coming year, which is physically unattainable, without grave extravagance in its spending". It was wrong also "because it envisages rising prices as a means of reducing civilian consumption" and "because it is the beginning of the destruction of those social services in which Labour has taken a special pride".[13]

Troubles came in battalions for the Labour party that summer. Morrison soon had ample cause to regret that he had sought the Foreign Office. It is unlikely in any case that he would have made a good Foreign Secretary. One official summed up the contrast with his predecessor by saying, "Ernie didn't know how to pronounce the places either, but he did know where they were"; and Morrison's surprise that high officials should address each other by their Christian names, and even be so addressed by their political chief, shows how ill at ease he was in that department.[14] The appointment of Morrison, for whom the Tories felt a strong dislike, had the unfortunate effect of bringing foreign affairs once more into the realm of party controversy. He must be acquitted of any responsibility for the employment of Burgess and Maclean, but he soon had to incur the odium of their flight to Moscow. He had also soon after his appointment to handle the delicate situation created by the decision of the new and fanatical Prime Minister of Persia, Mossadeq, to nationalize the installations of the Anglo-Iranian Oil Company at Abadan. Morrison was personally in favour of what might be called a strong Tory line, and it is ironical that he should have come under so much Tory fire. He has recorded his view that there was "much to be said in favour of sharp and forceful action", but the Cabinet was told that an effective force could not be mounted in time. Dalton with a slightly different emphasis says that Morrison had to be restrained by the Cabinet from embarking on a policy that would have led to denunciation of Great Britain by the United Nations as an aggressor. The British government was caught in a dilemma. Having nationalized so much at home, it could hardly object to the Persian government nationalizing British property abroad; and Morrison was obliged to limit his demands to fair compensation and negotiations without duress. This linked Persian oil with party controversies at home, and made foreign policy an issue at the hustings. According to Morrison's sorrowful account: "The opposition was informed of what was going on, though regrettably they tried to make party capital out of our alleged running away and allowing valuable oil installations to be stolen."[15]

The Conservatives had naturally exploited the parliamentary situation to the full in the hope of wearing down the government. Four efforts to overthrow the government were made in the first month of the Parliament, one over the nationalization of steel and three on motions of censure. The government survived with majorities of from fourteen to forty-eight. In such a situation as then existed the opposition was in the stronger position because it was able to choose the times when it offered its challenges. A favourite tactic of Conservative members was to put down prayers against Orders in Council. These were taken at 10 p.m. after the close of the ordinary business of the sitting. It was an old device; and although there had been a great levelling in the private circumstances of members, a prolongation of the debate until the last trains and buses had gone still inconvenienced the Labour members more than their opponents. The Conservatives were reluctant to grant "pairs", even for ministers who had to be abroad. In such circumstances every division was a nightmare to the Labour whips. Dalton has related[16] how, when his two bills as Minister of Local Government and Planning were taken "upstairs", he had a majority of only one in a committee of sixty. This meant he could never risk a division, if even one of his supporters was temporarily absent, though it might be for only a few minutes. A hundred years earlier a narrow majority did not matter as governments were prepared to accept occasional defeat on unimportant issues, but by 1950 almost every vote had become a vote of confidence. The government were in fact outvoted five times, but not on issues which were regarded as appropriate for resignation. On all major issues the administration survived defeat, even when the Liberals voted with the Conservatives— as twice happened over the nationalization of steel. Twice there was a tie, upon which the chairman's vote was given for ministers, and once they escaped defeat by one vote. In its eighteen months of life the House of Commons divided 234 times.

In the early autumn of 1951 Attlee decided to put an end to a situation that had become intolerable. He took the risk of being taunted, as he was unfairly taunted, with running away from his responsibilities, and on 8th September he made known to his colleagues his decision to request a dissolution. He knew it would be granted. King George VI, who did not want an election during his projected tour of Australia and New Zealand in the spring of 1952, and who was troubled by the stalemate, was anxious to resolve it. Dalton was in favour of going to the country at once. Opposition came only from Morrison and Shinwell, who sent a joint telegram from the United States urging that the announcement should be held up till they could be consulted. Attlee was not deflected. In a broadcast he announced, in the tone of a man ordering the groceries, that there would be a general election on 25th October. It was the first time the radio was employed to make such an announcement.

This turned the Labour conference arranged for that month at Scarborough into a series of election meetings, and effectively silenced controversy in the debates. After the three ministerial resignations the Bevanites—for so they now became recognized—carried their campaign against the leadership to the country. Their organ was *Tribune*, and they made a forceful statement of their views in a pamphlet published in June by that journal under the title *One Way Only*. It found the "clue to the explosive world in which we live" not in Soviet militarism but in the poverty of the African and Asian peoples. By coincidence a further pamphlet, *Going Our Way*, was published on the very day that Attlee announced the general election. Such announcements, as already noted, have an effect similar to that which Dr. Johnson saw in a man's knowledge that he was to be hanged in a fortnight: they concentrate minds wonderfully. The Bevanites cancelled a meeting they were to have held at Scarborough on the eve of the conference, and their leader spoke on the same platform as Herbert Morrison. Their argument, Bevan explained, was giving way to a bigger one, and would have to wait until the bigger one was over. When the votes in the constituency section of the National Executive were announced to the conference it was impossible to conceal, however, the depth of the Bevanite rift. In Parliament Bevan's resignation had produced virtually no effect. Only three members voted against the clause imposing the charge on dentures and spectacles. In the trade unions, where his wartime attack had not been forgotten or forgiven, support was transferred unquestioningly to Gaitskell. But the constituency Labour parties took Bevan and Bevanism to their hearts even more warmly than before. In the annual popularity poll, as the elections to the constituency sections of the National Executive had become, Bevan once more headed the successful candidates, and next in order were his followers Barbara Castle and Driberg. Griffiths and Morrison followed them, and then another Bevanite, Ian Mikardo. Dalton was bottom of the successful candidates, and Shinwell, a special target as Minister of Defence for the Bevanites' hostility, lost his place altogether. The Bevanite candidates received substantially more votes than in previous years, the anti-Bevanites substantially less.

It was a warning, and Dalton and Sam Watson, the Durham miners' leader, between them concocted an election manifesto which satisfied, or at any rate was not disowned by, both Bevanites and anti-Bevanites. Four major tasks were declared to face the nation—to secure peace, to maintain full employment and increase production, to bring down the cost of living and to build a just society. No new measures of nationalization were proposed, and all the manifesto said on this subject was: "We shall take over concerns which fail the nation and start new public enterprises wherever this will serve the national interest." The Conservative manifesto once more took the form of a personal message issued by its leader. The prime need, Churchill said, was for a stable government with several years before it. He promised the repeal of the Iron and Steel Act and a housing target, as demanded by the Conservative conference, of 300,000 houses a year; this contrasted with Labour's promise to "maintain the present rate of 200,000 new houses a year and increase it as soon as raw materials and labour can be spared". By this time the pent-up demand, rising standards and earlier marriages had made housing a major issue in the party strife. A further statement of Conservative policy entitled *Britain Strong and Free* developed the thesis of the manifesto. The Liberal manifesto argued that the nation could not afford another Parliament based on open class division, bitter party strife and the remorseless friction of two great party machines. The Communist manifesto, based on "Britain's independence, not American control", urged that the return of Communists to Parliament would strengthen the militant Labour fighters inside and outside Parliament. The Independent Labour party asked for the end of conscription and for workers' control in industry.

Sound broadcasts again dominated the campaigning—there were thirteen of them, five Labour, five Conservative, three Liberal—but television made its entrance into electioneering. Samuel for the Liberals made the first appearance on the screen, Eden for the Conservatives displayed a graph to show that the cost of living had risen as sharply before the Korean War as after, while Christopher Mayhew for Labour showed a graph designed to assert the exact contrary.

It is rare for foreign affairs to become an issue in British general elections, but the nationalization of the Anglo-Iranian Oil Company's wells and Morrison's handling of the situation created thereby brought these topics into prominence. The one exception Woolton allowed to his rule that there must be "no personalities" in the Conservative election literature was a statement that if Eden had been in charge of the Foreign Office instead of Morrison it would not have been necessary to surrender Abadan.[17] Towards the end of the campaign the news that the Egyptian government intended to denounce the treaty of 1936 with Great Britain, providing for a British base in the Suez Canal zone, threw an even graver matter into the arena. Though Morrison "advocated a stiff line with Egypt", he used words that seemed to represent the Conservatives as warmongers. The climax came on the morning of the election, when the *Daily Mirror* appeared with a drawing of a pistol on its front page and the headline "Whose Finger?" (*sc.*, on the trigger). That same day Churchill, who had declared two days earlier that a lasting peace settlement was "the last prize I seek to win", issued a writ for alleged libel.[18]

The key to the electoral situation was held by the Liberals. With the recollection of their lost deposits still oppressive they nominated only 109 candidates in selected constituencies, and this made the Liberal vote in other divisions a prime consideration with the Conservative and Labour managers. Churchill in the previous Parliament would have gone to great lengths to secure an alliance of the Liberal and Conservative parties, of which he had been in turn the most shining living ornament, but the opposition within the Conservative party was too great for any formal approach. The Conservatives nevertheless, without any bargain, refrained from putting up candidates against the Liberal leader, Clement Davies, in Montgomeryshire, and three of his colleagues in the old Parliament, Hopkin Morris in Carmarthenshire, Roderic Bowen in Cardiganshire and Donald Wade in Huddersfield West, while the same consideration was extended Arthur Holt in Bolton West, to John Junor in Dundee and Lady Violet Bonham Carter in Colne Valley. Churchill even offered to speak at some effort to himself on behalf of Asquith's daughter in this last constituency, and the offer was accepted. The Liberal managers did not reciprocate these gestures. The party executive rejected a suggestion from Lord Teviot, chairman of the National Liberals, that Liberals should be advised to vote anti-Socialist where there was no Liberal in the field; and the party headquarters sought to profit from such concern by issuing a *questionnaire* to be put to candidates in divisions where no Liberal was standing seeking their views on such questions as co-partnership and profit-sharing.

The Communists, like the Liberals, put many fewer candidates in the field—only ten—but in their case no other party was anxious to have them as allies. The Independent Labour party, a poor shadow of its former self, could muster only three. There were eight Nationalists—four in Wales, one in Scotland, three in Northern Ireland—and twelve Independents. The short period since the last election militated against freak labels. More obviously than in any previous contest the nation was offered a choice between the Labour and Conservative parties, each of whom had 617 candidates for the 625 seats. (The Speaker had decided not to seek re-election, and no question of leaving him uncontested arose.)

There was once more a high turn-out of the electors as befitted the clarity of the issues, 82·5 per cent going to the polls. Labour candidates polled more votes than ever before in the history of the party, 13,948,605, while Conservative and allied candidates polled rather less, 13,717,538; but as more Labour than Tory votes were concentrated in divisions with abnormally high majorities, these figures sufficed to return only 295 Labour members against 321 Conservatives. Only six Liberals were returned, and the party's humiliation was increased by the knowledge that five of them owed their seats to the absence of a Conservative opponent. Only Joseph Grimond in the distant Orkneys triumphed over both Conservative and Labour opponents. Once more no Independent Labour and no Communist candidate was successful. The twelve Independents all went down. Apart from the six Liberals, only one Irish Labour member, one Anti-Partition candidate and one Irish Republican broke the Tory and Labour domination. Whereas only three Conservatives and one Labour candidate lost their deposits, sixty-six Liberals, all ten Communists and all three I.L.P. candidates did so, as well as six Nationalists. The Conservatives had a majority of twenty-six over Labour and of seventeen over all others. It was not much, but it was enough.

As soon as the results were clear, Attlee went to the Palace to tender his resignation. The Labour government, which came in with a bang in 1945, went out with scarcely a whimper six years later.

33

CONSERVATIVE REVIVAL
1951–1955

Churchill forms a Conservative government—Woolton's tenure of a salaried Cabinet post along with the chairmanship of the party organization—denationalization of steel and road transport—independent television—Eden succeeds—Attlee retains the leadership of the Labour party—and Morrison loses the chance to succeed—the Bevanite "party within a party"—Morrison and Dalton defeated for the National Executive Committee—Morrison defeats Bevan for the deputy leadership—Bevan's breach with Attlee and resignation from the "shadow Cabinet"—Wilson accepts his place—Gaitskell defeats Bevan for the treasurership—another clash between Bevan and Attlee over the hydrogen bomb—Attlee saves him from expulsion—Eden decides to go to the country—and Butler is accused of an election budget—television as a new electoral factor—the Conservatives increase their majority

WHEN Churchill accepted King George VI's commission to form a government few persons guessed that the new Parliament would run almost its full course, much less was it suspected that the Tories would return to Parliament in still greater numbers at two successive elections and still be in office thirteen years later. In these years the Labour leadership changed hands on two occasions, the Conservative on three. On both occasions in the Labour party, and on one in the Conservative the change of leadership was accompanied by violent dissension. A Labour Prime Minister and a Conservative Prime Minister were alike charged, rightly or wrongly, with so arranging their resignations as to prevent the succession passing to the man who had been generally regarded as the heir. While these controversies centred mainly on the personalities of the contenders for power, not far beneath the surface lay the questions, what sort of parties were the Conservatives and Labour to be, and in what way did they differ from each other. The Conservatives having successfully accomplished their internal adjustment in the years 1945–50, and being restrained from undue exuberance by the narrowness of their majority, were in the early years of the period less disturbed by such self-searching than Labour. The achievement of the task set before itself by the Labour party in 1945, and the chastening effect of defeat at the polls, led that party to embark on a process of self-examination that threatened to rend it asunder and lose the favour of electors; but before the end of the period, by which time some of the principal contenders were dead, these questions were resolved or shelved, and the movement's self-confidence was restored. Before that happened there were even a few years when it seemed that electors might turn from both the major parties in sufficient numbers to make the Liberal party once again a power in the state.

The intensity of the modern party struggle was shown as soon as Parliament assembled in a contest for the Speaker's chair. The Conservatives as the majority party put up W. S. Morrison, but the Labour members, arguing that they had accepted a Conservative when their numbers would have enabled them to claim someone drawn from their own ranks, and that Morrison was not a backbencher with no strong partisan record, as his predecessor had been, but the holder of a number of ministerial posts, nominated James Milner. Morrison was elected by sixty-seven votes. It was the first contest for the post since 1895.

Churchill had few difficulties in forming his first and only peacetime administration. Eden for the Foreign Office, Butler for the Exchequer, were appointments clearly indicated, and Macmillan as Minister of Housing and Local Government was given the task of producing the 300,000 houses a year that Woolton had promised to a vociferous party conference. It was Woolton's own appointment as Lord President that has most interest from the party point of view as he combined it with the chairmanship of the party organization.

He was the first chairman of the Conservative party—or officer of any party organization—to sit in the Cabinet and to draw a salary as a Cabinet minister. The latter point was of no great importance in Woolton's case—after taxation his salary was reduced to £125 a year—but it is one to which the House of Commons is peculiarly sensitive. He would willingly have renounced his salary, but did not do so, partly because he might prejudice a successor who did not have his private means and partly on principle. There was no question of neglecting his ministerial duties in favour of the party organization, for the Lord President has no great department and the Cabinet committees over which he presides allow him sufficient time for other activities. In the last resort the question of principle is the only one that matters. Woolton was emphatic that, far from there being any impropriety in the party chairman accepting office in the Cabinet, he ought to be there and to be paid for any services rendered in that capacity. In his memoirs he wrote:[1]

"When a government is returned to power, the country has decided that it approves of the principles that the government represents. It is the duty of the chairman of the party, under the leader of
the party, who is also the Prime Minister in these circumstances, to
endeavour to make the principles for which the party is striving
understood by the public and to secure a continuance of support for
them. In such circumstances it seems to me important that the person who has taken a leading part in submitting these principles to
the public should continue in the full confidence of the Prime Minister and of his colleagues, and should be publicly known to be sharing with his Cabinet colleagues responsibility for putting them into
practice.

"I cannot see any difference between the Prime Minister and the
other members of the Cabinet being paid by the Crown for ad-
ministering the principles on which they have been elected, and the
chairman of the party—acting as a volunteer in that capacity—
being paid for the administrative services that he renders in the
office that he holds in the government."

The way in which the Labour party represented the matter was
somewhat different; in effect, that public funds were being used to
finance the Conservative organization. The principle, once enunciated, took root, and several successors to Woolton as chairman of
the party organization have held Cabinet office. The crux of the
matter is that under modern conditions control of the party organization confers so much power on the holder that it has become a
means of political advancement. The occupant is no longer the
"cabin-boy" of Birkenhead's scorn.

The government's main preoccupation for some time was to
escape from the financial crisis under the shadow of which it had
taken office. A cut of £160 million in food subsidies was represented
by the opposition as a breach of an election promise by Woolton,
but Churchill, long inured to such charges, would not accept that
minister's proffered resignation. Compensatory increases were made
in pensions, national insurance benefits and family allowances. An
extension of charges for the National Health Service was also made
the subject of party contention. In 1952 the death of King George VI
and the accession of Queen Elizabeth II for a time stilled controversy, but at length the government addressed itself to the question of denationalizing steel and road transport to which it had
pledged itself in the election manifesto. This raised the question how
far it was appropriate for a government to undo the work of its
predecessor. From the time of the Reform Act of 1832 there had
grown up a tradition that changes brought about by a government
as a result of victory at the polls would be accepted by its successor.
This tradition had done much to ensure the smooth working of the
constitution and to make public life agreeable. It was not lightly to

be set aside. Conservatives argued that the Labour government had broken the tradition in 1946 by the straight repeal of the Trade Disputes and Trade Unions Act, 1927, but the Labour party retorted that the Conservatives had themselves broken the tradition in 1927 by amending the act of 1913. It would be difficult to argue that a question once settled by Parliament should never be reopened after the lapse of sufficient time, possibly in very changed circumstances, but the repeal by one government of measures initiated by its immediate predecessor raises considerations of a different order. It would play havoc with great industries to have them nationalized and denationalized, renationalized and again denationalized, according to the changing mood of electors. The Conservatives could argue that if the Labour party after an electoral victory was entitled to nationalize some industry, and the Conservative party in the day of its own success was by convention not to be allowed to denationalize it, in the course of time all industry would be nationalized, and the convention would amount to a tacit acceptance of the Labour thesis. In the particular cases of steel and road transport, it was further argued that as they were only two items in an omnibus programme no clear mandate for their nationalization had been given, and that as the process of nationalization had not gone far it could be undone without difficulty or damage. This the Conservatives proceeded to do. The Iron and Steel Act, 1953, repealed the act of 1949 and provided that on an appointed day the property, rights and liabilities of the Iron and Steel Corporation should pass to an Iron and Steel Holding and Realization Agency charged with the duty of returning the assets to private ownership in stages; an Iron and Steel Board composed of persons having experience in steelmaking or steel-using was set up to exercise a general supervision over the industry in such matters as development and maximum prices. Under the Transport Act, 1953, the operating limit of twenty-five miles on "A" and "B" licence holders was abolished, the Transport Commission was required to apply to the traffic courts for "A" and "B" licences for its vehicles like private operators, the nationalized road transport industry (British Road Services) was restricted to a number of vehicles equivalent to a twenty-five per cent increase on the number owned by the railways before nationalization, and surplus vehicles were sold in lots by tender to private enterprise.

These measures were strongly contested by the Labour party, as also was a decision by the government to introduce an element of private enterprise into the new and rapidly expanding service of television. This question had come up in 1951 while Labour was still in office, and at that time, while the Labour government was wholeheartedly in favour of continuing the monopoly of the British Broadcasting Corporation, the Conservative "shadow Cabinet" was divided. In the Commons W. S. Morrison gave general support to the continuance of the B.B.C. monopoly, but in the Lords Woolton expressed doubts and spoke prophetically of local stations operating on very high frequencies. Gradually the Conservative government came to the view that, while the B.B.C. might be allowed to retain its monopoly of sound broadcasting, an element of private enterprise and of competition could with advantage be introduced into television. The decision found expression in the Television Act, 1954, which set up an Independent Television Authority to provide television services additional to those of the B.B.C. The programmes were to be provided by companies under contract with it, and the programme companies were expected to derive their income from advertisements displayed on the screen between items of the programmes. The reason for the Conservative decision to introduce commercial television was not only a general preference for private enterprise, especially in a developing industry, and a belief in the virtues of competition but a fear that a monopoly of sound broadcasting and television put a power into the hands of the B.B.C. with which no body of persons, however high-minded, ought to be entrusted. The Labour party, supported by many educational and religious leaders, made light of this danger in their fear that dependence on advertising would lower standards and force the B.B.C. in competition with commercial television to lower its standards also. The Labour spokesman, Herbert Morrison, on second reading reserved "the right to modify, or indeed abandon, the entire scheme" when his party returned to power, and hinted that compensation might not be paid for the "know-how" and goodwill of the companies.[2] As no early opportunity arrived for the threat to be carried out, it cannot be said how much substance there was in it, and the proved popularity of commercial television with viewers may have induced a change of view.

By 1955 the grave external outlook when the Tories assumed office had gradually been transformed. The dispute with Persia over the nationalization of the oil-wells at Abadan had been resolved, and the dispute with Egypt was ended by an agreement to withdraw British troops from the Suez Canal base. It seemed as though Churchill was resolved to show that his hand was safer on the trigger than any other's, but the withdrawal from the canal base provoked among a section of the government's supporters a feeling of disquiet which might have led to open revolt if the majority had been less precarious. An agreement over Trieste removed a troublespot from the map, the war in Korea was at length brought to an end and the death of Stalin raised hopes for a new understanding between east and west. These relaxations were to some extent offset by the government's decisions to proceed with the federation of the Rhodesias and Nyasaland, which for the first time in many years brought colonial policy into the area of contention between the

o

parties. At home, not only was the financial crisis surmounted, but the Chancellor of the Exchequer, R. A. Butler, found it possible in his second budget in 1953 to make substantial reductions in taxation and to maintain them in the following year. The aim of producing 300,000 new homes a year was achieved under Macmillan's direction without such dislocation of the economy as had been feared. Industrial peace reigned, though purchased, some Tories thought, at the cost of too ready concessions to inflationary wage demands. A fall in the demand for cotton textiles in 1951 and 1952 led to short-time working and a rise in unemployment in Lancashire, but the vigorous measures taken by the government helped to bring about a recovery. It was the first real test of the Keynesian theories.

In this happy party atmosphere—"Conservative freedom works" said the posters—Churchill decided that the time had at last come to lay down the burden of high office. At a unique ceremony in Westminster Hall in November 1954 members and former members and peers of all parties had joined to pay tribute to him on his eightieth birthday. Though he still possessed astonishing vigour for his years, increasing deafness made it difficult for him to transact business, and a minor stroke that temporarily paralysed him had been a warning not to be ignored. On 5th April 1955 he resigned office as Prime Minister, and the next day the Queen sent for Anthony Eden to be his successor. The great commoner of the age, he declined the offer of an earldom and kept his seat in the House of Commons.

There was never any doubt that Eden would succeed him. He had groomed himself for this part for many years and had been waiting in the wings for this moment as long as many statesmen spend in public life. During the wartime coalition Churchill had designated him as his successor if he should himself be laid low by enemy action, and the choice of the leader had been tacitly endorsed by the party. There were no contenders for the post. All the leading figures in the party expected Eden to be their leader and gave him unquestioned loyalty. No Prime Minister ever entered into his inheritance in such happy circumstances.

The new Prime Minister made only a few changes necessitated mainly by his own move to higher office. There had been a major reconstruction the previous year. Macmillan, who had been a most successful Minister of Housing and Local Government, and who had since been for a short time Minister of Defence, took Eden's place at the Foreign Office. Selwyn Lloyd became Minister of Defence, and the Earl of Home, who had been Minister of State at the Scottish Office, now entered the Cabinet as Secretary of State for Commonwealth Relations. Barely a week later, employing the same technique that was used by Attlee in 1951, the Prime Minister announced over the radio that Parliament was to be dissolved. The circumstances were propitious. Not only had the government not

lost a by-election, but it had even won a seat from the Labour party
—Sunderland South in 1953—the first time a government had
wrested a seat from the opposition for twenty-nine years. The Con-
servative party was in high fettle, and, equally important, the
Labour party was torn, as it had been throughout the whole of that
Parliament, by fratricidal strife.

It has been urged in retrospect that Attlee should have stood
down after the Labour defeat of 1951 and allowed a new leader to
rally the party. At that time the most likely successor was Morrison,
but his reputation had suffered as a result of his brief spell at the
Foreign Office, and Attlee later gave this as a reason in conversation
with Francis Williams why he remained leader: [3]

"It was hard on Herbert to have this on his plate when he hadn't
been in the Foreign Office five minutes. It hurt his reputation all
round. That was one of the reasons why I agreed to stay on as leader
after the election. I wanted to go, but everybody said, 'No, you must
stay, you are our biggest asset,' and apart from everything else it
seemed a bit unfair, when I thought it over, to raise the issue of the
leadership when Herbert, who naturally had expectations, was in
this position. Other things being equal, it seemed right to leave time
for his reputation to recover. As it turned out, it didn't make any
difference. When I did go in 1955, the party decided it didn't want
Herbert and chose Gaitskell. I hadn't anything to do with that. The
leadership of the Labour party isn't an hereditary position, one
doesn't choose one's successor. But Herbert's chance would have
been even smaller in 1951 than it turned out to be in 1955."

This was not how it appeared to Morrison himself, and to other
commentators, and the evidence for what happened in 1955 will be
given in its proper sequence; but at this point it would seem certain
that Attlee's assessment of what might have happened in 1951 is not
correct. At that time he was re-elected leader and Morrison deputy
leader without a contest. Gaitskell did not enter the lists, and at that
time he had not achieved sufficient standing in the party to offer a
challenge to Morrison with any hope of success. He needed several
more years in which to consolidate his position. The only person
who could or would have challenged Morrison in a contest for the
leadership was Bevan, then riding high in the favour of the constituency parties but still distrusted by his parliamentary colleagues, and
what would have happened is shown by what did happen a year
later. Morrison won without difficulty.

Bevan had, however, set his sights high and was leading what was
in effect "a party within a party". It was so described by many of
his parliamentary colleagues,[4] and fairly described inasmuch as the
Bevanites met regularly to decide the line they would take at party
meetings and in debates in the house. The Bevanite group did not
arise through Bevan gathering a band of disciples round him, but

through the old "Keep Left" group approaching Bevan, Wilson and Freeman and inviting these ex-ministers to join them.[5] The first serious clash with the leadership came on 5th March 1952. The government had on the order paper the motion: "That this house approves the *Statement on Defence, 1952*, Cmd.8475." The "shadow Cabinet", to which Bevan had not sought election the previous autumn, sought to add the words, "but has no confidence in the capacity of her Majesty's present advisers to carry it out". The party meeting, mindful of the damage done to the movement by voting against defence estimates in the past, decided to vote for the amendment and, when this was defeated, to abstain from voting on the government motion. Sensing that trouble was brewing, the leader (Attlee), deputy leader (Morrison) and chief whip (Whiteley) signed a letter sent to every Labour member of Parliament saying that he would be expected to vote in this way. When the division came, sixty Labour members voted against the amendment because the amended motion would have approved the defence programme of which they disapproved, and when this was defeated fifty-seven of them—the same mystic number as an earlier revolt of many varieties—voted against the government motion while the party officially abstained.

The immediate consequence of this revolt was the reimposition, with some amendments, of the standing orders of the Parliamentary Labour party, which had been suspended since 1946. About a third of the membership voted against the reimposition. The standing orders as revised in March 1952 required acceptance of decisions of the party meeting, gave the parliamentary committee of the party power to withdraw the whip for things said or done in the House of Commons and provided that members guilty of serious or persistent breaches of discipline might be reported to the National Executive, but allowed members to abstain from voting on "matters of deeply-held personal conscientious conviction". This attempt to tighten up discipline had no effect on the Bevanites, who were encouraged by further striking successes in the elections to the constituency section of the National Executive at the party conference at Morecambe in September. Not only did Bevan, Barbara Castle and Driberg win the first three places, but Wilson, Mikardo and Crossman took the fifth, sixth and seventh positions. Barbara Castle's success was astounding in that there is a separate women's section of the National Executive filled by the votes of the whole conference; she had sat in this section the previous year, but conscious that trade union votes were to be denied her she decided to defy the trade union leaders by standing for the constituency section. Only James Griffiths, in the fourth place, broke a complete Bevanite sequence, and the veterans Morrison and Dalton both lost their places on the committee. These elder statesmen of the party, though neither was very old in years, had both been on the executive for over a quarter of a century. It was the first time Wilson and Crossman secured election. Gaitskell, standing for the first time, secured barely more than half the votes of his fellow-Wykhamist, Crossman, and Shinwell, making a vain attempt to get back, less than half of Gaitskell's. After the results were announced Arthur Deakin, appearing as a "fraternal delegate" from the Trades Union Congress, strongly attacked the Bevanites. He asked "those people within the party who have set up a caucus . . . to realize that the ordinary rank-and-file party member or trade unionist has no time, or use, for such tactics or for their disregard of those principles and loyalties to which our movement has held so strongly through the whole course of its existence".[6] He stuck to his theme through a chorus of boos. That afternoon Morrison wound up a debate on home affairs with a speech in which he excelled himself—the "speech of his life" it was called—and made people wonder what sort of party it was that could reject him and elect six Bevanites for seven places. This result, as gradually became known, was due as much to careful organization, especially by Ian Mikardo, as to any other factor. It did not alter the fact that the Bevanites were in, and Morrison and Dalton were out, at any rate for twelve months. In Dalton's case it was for ever, as he did not stand again. Morrison was persuaded the following year to try to recover his seat by once more standing against Greenwood for the treasurership of the party, as he had done in 1943. The preliminary line-up of the trade unions before the Margate conference in 1953 made it likely that he would again be defeated, but at the last moment he was saved from this humiliation. The National Executive decided to recommend to the conference an amendment to the constitution providing that the deputy leader of the party should *ex officio* have a seat among its members. Morrison withdrew from the contest for the treasurership, the conference accepted the amendment, and Morrison was again assured of a place on the executive so long as he could retain the support of his colleagues in Parliament for the deputy leadership.

This is to look ahead by twelve months. When Parliament reassembled in October 1952 after the Morecambe conference, the Labour leaders secured by 188 votes to fifty-one the passage of a resolution banning "all group organizations within the party other than those officially recognized". Attlee had made the issue one of confidence in himself, and in November he was re-elected leader without a contest. In formal rather than real obedience the Bevanite group was disbanded, and Bevan himself challenged Morrison for the deputy leadership. Morrison prevailed by 194 votes to eighty-two, but the support for Bevan was ominously large. The Bevanites, having agreed to disband their group, accepted the argument that they should stand for the "shadow Cabinet". A new method of voting was introduced by which every member was required to vote for twelve candidates, only those who obtained over fifty per cent of the votes cast were to be declared elected, and a second ballot was to be held to complete the places. Bevan himself was the only one of his group to secure election—in the twelfth place after a second ballot with 137 votes out of 273. The result was perfectly calculated to deprive Bevan of the relative freedom of the back-benches without allowing him to give himself airs, but it made little difference in practice.

Recrimination continued throughout 1953, especially over the acceptance by Lincoln Evans, general secretary of the Iron and Steel Trades Confederation, first of a knighthood and then of a place on the Iron and Steel Board. The autumn pattern of events was re-peated. At the Margate conference in September the six Bevanites retained their places on the National Executive, along with Griffiths; Gaitskell and Shinwell were again defeated. In the parliamentary party a month later Bevan again stood against Morrison, and lost by seventy-six votes to 181. Their relative support had changed little in twelve months. In the elections to the "shadow Cabinet" Bevan moved up from twelfth to ninth place. Soon afterwards in an article in the Bevanite organ, *Tribune*, J. P. W. Mallalieu pictured himself as being asked by a constituent a very pertinent question: How was it that at the conference the constituency parties voted virtu-ally the straight Bevanite ticket, while the constituency party repre-sentatives in Parliament put Bevan three places from the bottom of the "shadow Cabinet" and excluded all his associates?[7] The answer of the majority in the parliamentary party would probably have been that they knew Bevan and his associates better than the con-stituencies could do, but Mallalieu's answer was that the constitu-ency parties as a whole supported a more aggressive socialist policy, while the parliamentary party as a whole supported consolidation. His constituent said it looked "as though some of these chaps say one thing in public in the country and another thing behind closed doors in the party meetings", and suggested that voting lists should be published after party meetings. When the matter was discussed at the "shadow Cabinet" and Gaitskell referred to "the dangers of indiscipline", Bevan, according to Dalton's account, fixed him "with a glare of concentrated hatred" and said: "You're too young in the movement to know what you're talking about."[8] Mallalieu was censured by the National Executive. Mikardo was also censured for an article attacking trade union leaders—the first time the executive had ever censured one of its own members.

The controversy deepened in 1954. The question of German re-armament brought a new bone of contention, and in February a motion favouring it was carried by only nine votes in the parlia-mentary party. Dalton, who might have swung the decision the other way, was in a nursing home—thus can a slipped disc determine great issues. In April Bevan had a public breach with Attlee in the House of Commons. Eden announced that he and Dulles had agreed to discuss with representatives of countries in south-east Asia "a collective defence, within the framework of the charter of the United Nations, to assure the peace, security and freedom of south-east Asia and the western Pacific".[9] Attlee made a cautious comment appropriate to the occasion, but Bevan rose in his place and said the statement would be universally regarded as a surrender to American pressure; unless it were clarified it would be regarded as a plan to impose European colonial rule on certain people in that area, and would estrange Commonwealth members in that part of the world. Attlee, not unnaturally, resented this attempt to give a lead to the party over his head; he rebuked Bevan in the "shadow Cabinet" and proposed to report the rebuke to the party meeting. Bevan forestalled him by resigning from the "shadow Cabinet". Will Lawther, the miners' leader, made a pointed reference to a "group of people with anarchistic tendencies and highly inflated egos".

Under the rules of the party, the place vacated by Bevan would be filled by the runner-up in the elections the previous November. This was Harold Wilson, who had resigned office with Bevan and had subsequently worked closely with him. He wished to accept, but would prefer to do so with Bevan's approval. Crossman offered to act as an intermediary, and Bevan made clear to him that he would regard acceptance of a place in the "shadow Cabinet" by any member of the Bevanite group as an act of "gross personal disloyalty". "So you regard Harold as expendable?" said a surprised Crossman. "Yes, and you too," came the angry retort.[10] Wilson accepted. He and Crossman, in Leslie Hunter's phrase, "had set foot on the main Brighton road".[11]

Bevan himself was still far from that track. The death of Greenwood reopened the question of the treasurership. Morrison, already possessed of an *ex officio* place on the executive, had no reason to stand. The occasion was critical in the history of the party. The right-wing leaders in the parliamentary party and the trade union movement decided that this was the proper time to bring Gaitskell forward. In open competition he had not so far won a place for himself on the National Executive, but he had all the prestige of a former Chancellor of the Exchequer, and he had quietly been building up his reputation in the party. The news of Gaitskell's nomination angered Bevan and his friends. They rightly saw in it an attempt to place Gaitskell on the road to the leadership. In the inflamed state of his mind Bevan's judgement deserted him. He had no need of the treasurership, as Gaitskell did, to get on the executive. He had topped the constituency section for three years. Yet he decided to embark on a contest that must inevitably cost him his seat on the executive—for he had to stand down for the constituency section and Gaitskell was backed by the big unions—and also lose for him the seniority that would give him the chairmanship of the party in what might easily be an election year. Some of his friends were aghast at this apparently suicidal rashness. When the votes were counted, Gaitskell had 4,338,000 to Bevan's 2,032,000. The Bevanites were more successful in getting support for their policies than for their personalities. Endorsement of the National Executive's policy in favour of German rearmament was carried by only 3,270,000 votes to 3,022,000, and even that modest victory would not have been achieved but for a last minute switch by the Woodworkers. At times of weakness in the Parliamentary Labour party it is inevitable that the trade union leaders should play a preponderant rôle, and Arthur Deakin had worked hard behind the scenes to secure both the defeat of Bevan and the acceptance of German rearmament. In the contest for the National Executive the five remaining Bevanites were re-elected, and with their help Anthony Greenwood secured fourth place; once more Griffiths was the only non-Bevanite to secure election in the constituency section. At a *Tribune* meeting during the conference Bevan declared: "I know now the right kind of leader is a desiccated calculating machine who must not allow himself in any way to be swayed by emotion."[12] Later he explained that this did not refer to Gaitskell, who could not in any case calculate as he was three hundred millions out.

In March 1955 there was another public clash between Bevan and Attlee in the House of Commons. The annual white paper on defence had included the momentous announcement that Great Britain was to embark on the production of the hydrogen bomb. The government had put down a motion approving the white paper. To it the Labour party proposed an amendment "recognizing . . . that until effective world disarmament has been achieved it is necessary, as a deterrent to aggression, to rely on the threat of using thermo-nuclear weapons". As Attlee finished speaking Bevan demanded to know if this associated the Labour party with a policy of using hydrogen bombs even if they had not first been used against this country. He had ended his own speech earlier in the debate by turning to his followers and saying, "If we cannot have the lead from them, let us give the lead ourselves"; and sixty-two Labour members abstained from voting for the amendment.[13] The party, in Dalton's sorrowful recollection,[14] then "succumbed to one of those fits of suicidal mania to which it is so often prone". The "shadow Cabinet" decided to recommend the parliamentary party "to withdraw the whip from Mr. Bevan because of his conduct in challenging the party leaders during the recent defence debate". An amendment to censure him without withdrawal of the whip was lost by fourteen votes, and the recommendation was carried by 141 votes to 112. It was reported to the National Executive that Bevan was no longer in receipt of the whip, and that body then had to consider whether he should again be expelled from the party. At this point Attlee, bearing in mind the smallness of the majority for withdrawal of the whip, moved as an amendment to the motion for expulsion that Bevan should be seen by a sub-committee, which should seek assurance for his future conduct. Though Attlee's retreat angered the right-wing trade unionists who were bent on getting rid of Bevan, his amendment was carried by fourteen votes to thirteen, the sub-committee professed itself satisfied by Bevan, and by sixteen votes to nine the National Executive decided not to expel him. To add to the confusion, Sir Richard Acland, founder of Common Wealth, who had returned to the house as a Labour member in 1947 when Garry Allighan was expelled, announced that he would resign his Gravesend seat to fight a by-election as an opponent of the use of the hydrogen bomb. The by-election did not take place because the new Prime Minister, Eden, not surprisingly judged that the time was opportune to ask for a dissolution, and at the ensuing general election the divided Labour vote made a present of the seat to the Conservatives. As Parliament was already in its fourth year, and there was a general expectation of an appeal to the country at the end of an era marked by Churchill's retirement, the Queen considered it proper to grant the new Prime Minister's request, and polling was fixed for 25th May 1955.

The Conservatives issued a manifesto, *United for Peace and Progress*, prefaced by a personal statement from their leader, thus following the pattern set in 1950 except that the introduction was longer. "I have no doubt that we are right to make the hydrogen bomb," wrote Eden, and threw his own grenade into the opposite camp by adding, "and it is a source of strength to the country that the opposition should support us in that step." The manifesto proclaimed that "the British people have a real chance during the coming twenty-five years to double their standard of living", and offered the country "peace and prosperity in the nuclear age". This was heartening, but the real election manifesto of the Conservatives was the budget, which Butler opened four days after Eden had announced the date of polling. Early in the year signs of economic difficulties had led the Chancellor to put up the bank-rate and place restrictions on hire purchase, but in April he took another sixpence off the income-tax, increased allowances and to help Lancashire took off the purchase-tax on non-woollen textiles.

The National Liberals claimed in their separate manifesto that their alliance with the Conservatives was not simply a matter of convenience; it arose naturally because in general terms Liberalism and modern Conservatism had common aims.

The Labour manifesto, *Forward with Labour*, asked for high-level talks to deal with the situation created by the hydrogen bomb. The party was thrown out of gear during the campaign when Russia not only agreed to sign a treaty with regard to Austria but accepted a four-power meeting, and a poster "Top Level Talks Now" had to be hastily changed to "Top Level Talks—Send Attlee". The Labour leader suggested in a television broadcast that there was "a strong case for a reduction in the length of national service", and Eden was forced to drop a hint that if the negotiations went well some reduction might be possible.[15] The Labour manifesto promised that the cost of living would be kept steady and that a Ministry of Social Welfare would be created. It offered the renationalization of steel and road haulage, but limited promises of further measures of public ownership to "sections of the chemical and machine tools industries". It was realized that nationalization had ceased to have a vote-catching appeal. A new note was struck in the statement: "Where necessary we shall start new public enterprises." The Labour party was encouraged early in the campaign by the adhesion to its ranks of Lady Megan Lloyd George, who had sat for Anglesey as a Liberal for twenty-two years until her defeat in 1951. She balanced her brother, Gwilym Lloyd-George, who had been defeated as a Liberal and Conservative in 1950 in Pembroke, had won Newcastle-upon-Tyne North under that label in 1951, and was again standing for that constituency as a Liberal and Conservative.

The divergence of Lloyd George's children was typical of the movement among Liberals everywhere, but a solid core remained, and to them the Liberal manifesto, *Crisis Unresolved*, offered a defence of the "fundamental freedoms". The Cooperative manifesto, while of course supporting the Labour case, struck an independent note by asking for a new major ministry with special responsibility for consumers' welfare. The Communists in their manifesto attacked Tories and right-wing Labour leaders equally for the decision to make the hydrogen bomb, rearm the Nazis and prepare for atomic war as allies of the American millionaires.

An extensive redistribution of seats had taken place a few months previous in pursuance of reports by the Boundary Commissions, and the membership of the house was brought up to 630. Charges of "rigging" and "jiggery pokery" were freely made by both sides, though not supported by headquarters, and there was general agreement that the interval between reviews must be extended. In all 1,409 candidates took the field, and for the first time since the Reform Act of 1832—and probably for the first time in the history of Parliament—no seat was uncontested. The Conservatives and their allies had 624 candidates. It is instructive to consider their labels. Of the total 579 were described as Conservative and Unionist, or simply Conservative or simply Unionist; eight were called Conservative and Liberal, thirteen Conservative and National Liberal, four simply National Liberal, eight National Liberal and Conservative, twelve Liberal and Conservative. The differences of the names, or order of the names, arose out of the history of the constituency associations or of the candidates themselves, and, though these differences are often jealously guarded, for practical purposes they were all Conservative candidates. The only six seats not contested by the Conservatives or their allies were those of five Liberals, who had sat in the last Parliament, and Pembrokeshire, where an Independent was given a clear run against a Labour member, Desmond Donnelly, with a small majority. The Labour party and its Cooperative ally put up 617 candidates in Great Britain, leaving only the Speaker's seat uncontested—but an Independent candidate of Labour background stood there—and the Northern Ireland Labour party contested three of the twelve Northern Ireland seats, a total of 620. The Independent Labour party could put only two candidates in the field, one in Glasgow and one in London. The Liberals managed to run 110 candidates, just one more than in 1951. The Communists could muster only seventeen. The Nationalist candidates numbered thirteen, and twenty-three Independents and candidates of variegated labels made up the total.

In this election for the first time television ranked with sound broadcasting as a factor, and in both media the parties were greatly concerned to see that they received their fair share of time and used it to the best advantage. The public opinion polls had also become by this time a factor of concern to the parties. In the first four months of the year the Gallup poll had shown the Conservatives only one point ahead of Labour, but during the campaign the Conservatives drew ahead to a three-point advantage. The percentage of those who said they would vote Liberal dropped from seven to two as the opportunity of doing so drew nearer.

The year 1929 had left a belief among socialists that a May election was favourable to the Labour party. It is dangerous to base laws on single instances. The general election of 1955 followed closely on the local government elections of that year, which showed a marked swing towards the Conservatives both in the boroughs, where the Tories made a net gain of 783 seats, and in Lancashire, where the textile industry had been passing through great difficulties which the budget was intended to relieve. The public opinion polls confirmed the local elections, and the voting figures showed that neither had been a false pointer. The turnout, at 76·7 per cent, was normal, but small compared with the two previous elections, a factor which in itself favoured the Conservatives as on the whole Labour does best in a big poll—another way of saying that Labour sympathizers tend to abstain from voting more readily than Conservatives however indignant they may be with their party. The Conservatives and their allies received 13,286,569 votes, Labour and its allies 12,404,970. The

Conservative vote was 430,969 less than in 1951, but on this occasion it was decisively more than the Labour vote, which dropped by 1,543,635. For the first time since 1935 the Conservatives had secured more votes than Labour. The Liberals obtained 722,405 votes, slightly less than four years previously, and the Communists remained fairly steady at 33,144.

When these figures were translated into seats, it meant that the Conservatives could count on 344 votes in the House of Commons (the Speaker, W. S. Morrison, being excluded) and Labour on 277. The Liberals retained their six seats—all of them except one, as both Tories and socialists did not fail to point out, thanks to Conservative votes. Joseph Grimond in the distant Orkneys again came through both Labour and Conservative opposition. Two Sinn Fein candidates broke the Conservative phalanx in Northern Ireland, but as in 1950 and 1951 the other Nationalists, the Independent Labour party and the Communists failed to get a single member elected, nor was a single Independent returned. The grip of the two major parties on the House of Commons, and through the house on all the machinery of state, was almost complete.

The Conservatives had twenty-three more members than in the old house, the Labour party eighteen less. The Tory majority over all others had increased from seventeen to fifty-nine. It would be necessary to go back a long time to find an example of a government increasing its majority after several years in office. No one complained that the result was not fair. The internecine quarrels of the Labour party had invited defeat. The Conservatives had governed well, and several pieces of good fortune that came their way, even during the election campaign itself, merely confirmed a verdict that was already implicit in voters' intentions. The country relaxed to see what Sir Anthony Eden would make of his great victory.

CHANGES AT THE HELM
1955–1959

Wilson's inquiry into Labour party organization—Dalton's cam-
paign for younger men—the leadership deflected towards Gaitskell
—Attlee resigns—and Gaitskell is elected leader in preference to
Bevan and Morrison—Woolton's resignation as Conservative chair-
man—the Suez episode unites the Labour party—fall in Eden's
popularity—he resigns—and Macmillan is chosen Prime Minister in
preference to Butler—his rapid mastery of the international situa-
tion and of his party—effect of the Rent Act and deflationary
measures on Conservative standing—resignation of the Treasury
team—new harmony of Gaitskell and Bevan—a Liberal revival—
the tide of Conservative unpopularity turns—and at the general
election of 1959 the Conservative majority is increased

IT is the habit of defeated parties to blame their organization
rather than their policies or personalities, and Labour in 1955 was
no exception. Harold Wilson was appointed by the National Executive to preside over an inquiry into the alleged deficiencies. The sub-
committee's report attracted attention by its picturesque admission :
"Compared with our opponents we are still at the penny-farthing
stage in a jet-propelled era, and our machine at that is getting rusty
and deteriorating with age."[1] The diagnosis was unfair to the
machinery of the Labour party both at headquarters and in the
constituencies, the changes recommended were not of great significance, and the most fundamental of them—the appointment of a
standing committee of the National Executive to supervise party
organization from which the secretary of the party would be
excluded—was not carried out. It was decided to retain the existing
sub-committee on organization, of which Wilson became chairman.
Some practical help was given to the constituencies by the allocation of £50,000 a year to assist marginal constituencies to appoint
full-time agents and to train voluntary workers in such tasks as the
marking of registers.

The Wilson committee had noted, "With the exception of a small
number of constituencies, mainly marginal, all reports have confirmed that voluntary workers were fewer and less enthusiastic than

at any previous time," but this was not primarily due to defects of organization. Shinwell expressed the opinion that an examination of policy should have preceded the *post mortem* into organization, and delivered himself of the dictum: "Given the right policy and effective leadership, organization will follow."[2] In his memoirs Dalton analysed the *malaise* more closely. After praising "the five shining years of majority Labour rule", he discerned "a political time-bomb deep in the rapidly changing social pattern of British society" which "exploded violently against the Labour party in the nineteen-fifties".[3]

"From 1950 onwards [he wrote] the Labour party lost its unity. The drive and self-confidence, the will to use power and to compromise rather than split, which had carried us through the shining years, were gone. Factions fought and slanged each other in public, seeming to think that public opinion, which sways voters, neither saw nor heard them. And failure to agree became a chronic posture. But, in truth, public opinion was alert and thoughtful. First it sensed deep division in the Labour party and deep hatreds and unreliability. Then it lost interest, and then it turned away."

Dalton's remedy was to sweep out the old men and to let in the young ones, and he cheerfully sacrificed himself for this purpose. On 1st June 1955 he sent a letter[4] to Attlee pointing out that the "shadow Cabinet" was becoming more a shadow of the past and less a Cabinet of the future. Of its fifteen members when Parliament was dissolved, no fewer than nine were over sixty-five years of age that year. He informed Attlee that he had decided not to be a candidate for the "shadow Cabinet" in the new Parliament, and added: "I hope that a number of my fellow-veterans will decide likewise." In a private covering letter he named Whiteley (the chief whip), Ede, Shinwell, Will Glenvil Hall and Noel-Baker as among those he had in mind.

Apart from Hall, who saw the force of Dalton's reasoning, this well-meant advice was ill-received. "We have all recognized and deplored Dalton's failing physical powers and can sympathize with him," said Ede with a well-developed power of sarcasm, "fortunately these signs of senility are not infectious."[5] Shinwell talked at large about his bodily and mental vigour. Nevertheless, both of them did not stand again for the "shadow Cabinet". Noel-Baker did not take the advice, and Whiteley, though now forgetful of appointments and given to falling asleep in his office chair, was determined to carry on even though faced with the prospect of a contest with two other candidates equally determined that he should not.

In his letters Dalton did not mention Morrison, and he specifically exempted Attlee himself. It might have been expected that Attlee, who had led the party in two successive defeats, would now resign. He had shown irresolution in dealing with the Bevanite faction, and at seventy-two was well above the age limit set by Dalton. But Dalton ended his public letter to him by saying: "Your own position is a very special one. It is my strong hope that, in the interests of party unity, you will continue as leader when the new Parliament meets. This hope is shared, I know, by many of our colleagues. No one else among us, of whatever age, can do this difficult job so well as you can."

At that time it was expected that the government would content itself with clearing away in a short session business disturbed by the general election and start its real work at a new session in November. When the "shadow Cabinet" met on 6th June Attlee raised his own position at the outset by saying that he could not go on much longer. If Labour had won the election, he would have gone back to Downing Street, but not for longer than a year. If the party wanted him to do so, he would go on for that short session. At the party meeting the next morning Attlee made the same point, and in the expectation that the session would be brief no one cavilled at the suggestion that he should carry on till the end of it. Two days later, 9th June, the Queen's Speech made it clear that the session would not be a short one. There would be no break in the autumn of 1955, and the session would run on till the autumn of 1956. This upset many calculations, and at the Labour party meeting held that same morning it precipitated Whiteley's resignation; the unpleasantness of a contest was avoided, and his deputy, Herbert Bowden, was unanimously voted into his place. Attlee then spoke of his own position. Now that it was to be a long session, he told members, he would be willing, if they wished, to go on till the end of it, but then he must finish and they must choose a younger leader. At that point Bevan astonished members by making an emotional appeal to Attlee not to fix a date for retirement. "Clem, I implore you," he cried, according to Dalton's recollection, "put no limit. Just go on." When Attlee asked, "Is that the general wish?", there were cheers from all parts of the room. His question "Anyone against?" brought no sign of dissent. "Very well," he said.

In his diary that night Dalton wrote: "This is almost certainly the end of Morrison as possible future leader. He'll be sixty-eight next January and sixty-nine in January 1957. Too old to succeed Attlee now." Seven years later he summed up the situation in the words: "The thought in many minds that day was that Bevan had ditched Morrison by prolonging Attlee's reign beyond the next twelve months, and that, when Attlee finally went, Bevan might, perhaps, succeed him."[6] It was without doubt the thought in Bevan's own mind, mingled with gratitude for the protection that Attlee had given him. In fact, Attlee went within six months, and neither Morrison nor Bevan was the successor. Attlee must have realized at least as clearly as Dalton that by staying he was depriving Morrison of the chance of succeeding him; but he was able to say that he had offered to go and stayed only by the general wish of the party. Whether he shared the belief that Bevan would succeed him, or already hoped that it would be Gaitskell, and was deliberately working to that end, is an enigma on which his uncommunicative autobiography throws no light.

A mild stroke in August and an attack of eczema, a condition often caused by worry, made the question of the succession more urgent. Morrison's speeches in Parliament that session had not added lustre to his reputation. It was his misfortune to lose his sparkle just when he most needed it. Bevan was behaving with a mildness that surprised friends and enemies alike, as though he were determined not to set a foot wrong. But eyes were increasingly turned to Gaitskell. His speeches on finance and economics, always acknowledged to appeal to the head, were beginning to appeal to the heart also. Winchester and New College did not suggest the background of a Labour leader, but he had been drawn to the party by the general strike of 1926 while still an undergraduate, and some trade unionists began to wonder whether he might not be more reliable than any other possible candidate. His friend and patron Hugh Dalton, whose personal assistant he had been in the war at the Ministry of Economic Warfare, had no hesitations. "Towards this most exceptional young man I decided that I would do my best to deflect the leadership."[7] Without naming Gaitskell, Attlee made a statement that was even more decisive in deflecting the leadership towards him as it travelled from mouth to mouth and into the newspapers. "We are now more than halfway through this century, and it's time the Labour party had a leader who was born in this century and not in the last."[8] A glance at the books showed that Morrison was born in 1888, Bevan in 1897, Gaitskell in 1906.

Gaitskell's improved position was shown at the party conference at Margate in October, when Bevan again ran against him for the treasurership and lost by 1,225,000 votes to 5,475,000. A year earlier Bevan had told his followers that it would take him three years to capture the trade union votes, but instead of capturing them he was seeing them fall away to his younger rival. At a secret session to consider internal party matters Bevan returned to his old style and flayed the Wilson report. What was wrong was not the machinery but the failure to put over a socialist policy. Those who had tried to throw him out of the party were not even socialists. His supporters were beside themselves with delight. Unfortunately, the loudspeakers had not been turned off and transmitted his caustic comments to anyone in Margate who cared to listen. The next day both Morrison and Gaitskell had to address the conference in public. Morrison won respectful applause, but it was Gaitskell, speaking for the first time from the platform, who captured their enthusiasm. In an obvious reply to Bevan, he jested about himself as a "calculating machine", and, dropping his notes, told his hearers how he had become a socialist thirty years ago, not so much because he was a passionate advocate of public ownership, but because at a very early age he came to hate and loathe social injustice.

The conference performances led to a notable marking up of Gaitskell's stock and marking down of Morrison's and Bevan's. Gaitskell let it be known that he would be willing to stand for the leadership when Attlee wished to go, Attlee dropped hints that perhaps the time had come, and members began to align themselves. On Wednesday, 7th December, Attlee told the party meeting that before the main business he had a personal statement to make. There was no question now of placing himself in the party's hands and being willing to stay until the end of the session. "He merely announced that *he* thought the party was ready for a change and that consequently he was resigning."[9] Though he had seemed the least likely of leaders, and though attempts without number had been made to remove him, he had in fact led the Labour party for more than twenty years, a period of office far longer than that of any other party leader in the century. Later that day it was announced that he had accepted an earldom.

The timing of the resignation forced the Labour party to choose a new leader when Gaitskell's star was in the ascendant, Bevan's in the middle heaven and Morrison's sinking towards the horizon. All three were duly nominated, and then an astonishing thing happened. Morrison and Bevan were seen dining together by themselves, and the next day Bevan announced[10] that he had been approached by ten named Labour members of Parliament, who had suggested to him that it was desirable in the interests of the party to avoid a contest for the leadership. They had asked whether, if the other persons nominated withdrew, he would also withdraw in order to give an unopposed return to Morrison, the deputy leader. He informed them that he would certainly be willing to fall in with their suggestion. Thus, as each saw the prize slipping from his grasp, was the fiery Welsh orator reconciled to the man whom he had once called a "squalid backstairs Tammany Hall politician".

The manoeuvre failed. When Gaitskell was told of it, he issued the following statement:[11] "A number of my colleagues have been good enough to nominate me. They have made it plain to me that they would greatly regret it if I were to withdraw. I propose to allow my name to stand. I have the highest regard for Mr. Morrison, but I think the party should have the opportunity of choosing." The public failure of the manoeuvre based as it obviously was on the expectation that Gaitskell would win, threw waverers into his camp. When the votes were counted on 14th December the result was seen to be: Gaitskell, 157; Bevan, seventy; Morrison, forty.

P

Gaitskell had not only a majority over both opponents, which was more than Attlee had achieved in 1935, but a decisive majority. After only ten years in Parliament it was a tremendous personal success. The election of Bevan in the second place was hardly less surprising. No doubt those whose primary thought was to "stop Gaitskell" believed that Bevan had a better chance of so doing than Morrison. For Morrison the humiliation was complete. After congratulating Gaitskell, Morrison announced his own resignation as deputy leader. Gaitskell begged him to reconsider his decision— "Don't listen to him, Herbert," called out Shinwell's voice from the back of the room[12]—but he would not be persuaded. Bevan responded to Gaitskell's appeal to let bygones be bygones by promising support in maintaining the *mystique* of the Labour movement.

Some commentators, Dalton noted in his memoirs, had suggested that Attlee delayed his resignation through the critical months, when opinion was building up in favour of Gaitskell, in order to ensure that Morrison should not be his successor. He added: "I know not whether this was true. But I do know that he did not regard Morrison as likely to make a good Prime Minister or to make the Labour party a happy ship." The chief of these commentators was Leslie Hunter, a close observer of the persons concerned as the former lobby correspondent of the *Daily Herald*, who devoted no little part of his book, *The Road to Brighton Pier*, to the theme. "Attlee's dislike and distrust of Morrison seemed more emotional than reasonable," he wrote, "but they were none the less real for that. Equally real was his determination to destroy Morrison's hopes of succeeding him." Shinwell, after noting that Attlee had remained in office long after his anticipated retirement as party leader, commented: "His motives were doubtless to await an easing of the party's internal tensions and to reach a personal decision on his successor ... He undoubtedly considered that vigorous leadership demanded a man who could shoulder the burdens for at least a decade. This was the source of his misgivings quite as much as any feeling that Morrison was unsuited for the position of leader." Attlee's view that he "hadn't anything to do" with the party's preference for Gaitskell over Morrison has already been noted. This seems altogether too modest. Morrison himself in his autobiography observed that he had been asked more than once if he felt it to be true that Attlee deferred retirement until it was over-late for him to succeed. "My answer has always been," he wrote, "regretfully but inevitably in view of the evidence, that this in my view is a correct interpretation." It is difficult to dissent from this conclusion.[13]

Dalton has recorded[14] that if Morrison had accepted the deputy leadership "he would have met with an immense acclaim, and become the most popular, most highly respected and most influential figure in the party, quite overshadowing the new leader, for a time at least". He would have retained his key positions in the "shadow Cabinet" and on the National Executive, but, human nature being compounded of feelings as well as reason, he preferred to throw these prospects away and virtually retired from active politics. Though Bevan's promise of support in maintaining the *mystique* of the movement was not unambiguous, it looked like a pledge that, if elected deputy leader, he would work loyally with Gaitskell. He was duly nominated in January 1956, but the thought was too much for those whom he had fought so bitterly over many years. Various names to stop him were canvassed. Wilson was dismissed, for it would not do to have "intellectuals" in both the leading positions. Alfred Robens and George Brown won some support, and when it proved inconclusive Dalton launched a campaign in favour of giving the deputy leadership to the ex-miner James Griffiths, whom everyone liked, until the young men proved themselves and it was clear whether Bevan intended to discipline himself. When the votes were counted, Griffiths had 141 and Bevan 111. Though Bevan maintained that he had stood mainly as a proof of his readiness to serve as a subordinate to Gaitskell, the intoxication of a mass meeting at Manchester two days later was too much for him. If the Labour party was not going to be a socialist party, he declared, he did not wish to lead it. When people said they would investigate industries one by one to see whether they qualified for nationalization, that was a retrograde step; he would make private enterprise justify itself. He had been advised to "play inside the team", but when a man joined a team in the expectation that it would play rugger he could not be expected to be enthusiastic if asked to play tiddlywinks. He attacked the whole system of private party meetings, for "to enforce upon public representatives policies, votes and conduct arrived at behind locked doors, secretly from the people, is basically antagonistic to democratic principles of any sort whatsoever". He ended defiantly by saying: "I know these are words that are going to get me into trouble, but I am not a communist; I am a democratic socialist."[15] On returning to Westminster he obeyed with the air of a martyr approaching the faggots a summons to the room of the leader of the opposition, but wisely the only pyre that Gaitskell offered him was the oversight of colonial affairs in place of Griffiths. The promotion of Gaitskell and Griffiths had left the posts of "shadow Chancellor" and "shadow Colonial Secretary" vacant. Bevan would have no doubt preferred the former, but it had gone to his erstwhile disciple, Wilson, and he took the latter.

It turned out later that what he really wanted was to be "shadow Foreign Secretary", but that post had been held since the general election by Robens. In the meantime another conference had come round and another contest for the treasurership. Though Gaitskell was no longer a candidate, Bevan was not allowed a walk-over.

There were unprecedented efforts to find a candidate who would muster enough votes to stop him, but the variety of the efforts proved self-defeating, and Bevan just slipped through on a minority vote. He had 3,029,000 votes to 2,755,000 for George Brown, with 644,000 for Charles Pannell and 42,000 for a long-odds choice, D. Rydderch. At least four trade union or parliamentary leaders who could have stopped Bevan had declined to be drafted, and Brown would have done so but for the loss of the votes that went to Pannell. It was at this same conference that Bevan let it be known discreetly that he would like to be the party's spokesman on foreign affairs. Gaitskell had his doubts, others were aghast, but when the elections to the "shadow Cabinet" put Bevan in the third place he tried him out in a foreign affairs debate. The subject was the Suez expedition, on which Sir Anthony Eden had just embarked, as will soon be related. There is nothing like a common enemy for restoring unity, and the Labour party found in Suez the unity for which it had so long been searching. Robens made matters easier by offering to step down, and Bevan was at length offered the post that he coveted, a post that marked him out, despite Griffiths's titular position, as second in the party hierarchy only to Gaitskell. The party organizers in the constituencies breathed a sigh of relief that their leaders would now give up fighting each other in favour of fighting the Tories.

Woolton had supervised the conduct of the 1955 election for the Conservatives with the same quiet efficiency as in 1950 and 1951. A different technique, he noted,[16] was required for running an election with Sir Anthony Eden from running one with Sir Winston Churchill. The latter had revelled in controversy; the former "had never wavered in his Conservatism, but had propounded Liberal principles". There was an opportunity to gather round "this new young Prime Minister" a great deal of "middle of the road support". Woolton was certain that much of the success achieved was due to the feeling of confidence in his personal sincerity which the Prime Minister created as he spoke for a short time in as many constituencies as possible. The victory won, he insisted on resigning the chairmanship of the party organization, and at the party conference at Bournemouth that year, the tenth he had attended, when many deserved tributes were paid to his work, he had some salutary words for those who find all ills and all remedies in organization:[17]

"From the outset, when Sir Winston Churchill told me that I must become the chairman of the party, I had no doubt as to what the party needed. The problem was not primarily one of building a well-oiled machine—whatever that may mean in terms of politics. The Conservative party needed a revival of faith in its duty, and in its capacity to do that duty: and I knew that if we were to gain the responsibility for government of the country the party would have to be revitalized as a broad-based democratic party, embracing all sections of society, and its inspiration drawn from the full meaning of the phrase, 'Tory democracy'. Ladies and gentlemen, we have made that phrase into a reality."

On Woolton's resignation Eden reverted to the earlier practice and appointed as chairman of the party organization Oliver Poole, the member of Parliament for Oswestry, who had been joint treasurer of the party since 1952. Poole was a man with considerable interests in the city and had no ambition to enter the Cabinet. Woolton's deputy had been another Tory member of Parliament, John Hare, but though later to enter the upper house as Lord Blakenham he then preferred a ministerial career in the Commons, and even Woolton agreed that the chairmanship could not be held by a minister tied by attendance in the House of Commons. At Eden's insistence, Woolton kept his seat in the Cabinet till December.

By that date the reputation of the Conservative government and its Prime Minister had begun to lose the lustre of the spring. Eden's reluctance to embark on a major reconstruction meant that Butler stayed at the Exchequer, and this was his undoing. If he could have gone out in June he would have left behind a shining record as Chancellor, but in the summer of 1955 the country began to suffer from inflationary pressures, and it became necessary to introduce an autumn budget—Butler's fifth—to curb demand. By reason of various changes in purchase-tax it became known as the "pots and pans budget", a term that in itself bore a derisory sense. Labour taunted him with having made an autumn budget necessary by an electioneering budget in the spring, and Gaitskell delivered a tremendous attack which consolidated his newly won leadership. For the first time since 1951 Labour began to look like an effective opposition.

Towards the end of 1955 Eden acknowledged that reconstruction could no longer be delayed. Butler was allowed at last to escape from the Treasury and became Lord Privy Seal; he continued to be leader of the House of Commons as he had been since the previous April. Macmillan took his place at the Exchequer. According to Kilmuir,[18] "he accepted the Treasury on the strict understanding that this was to be regarded as a step towards, and not away from, the premiership; it is ironical to recall that at the time this caused a considerable amount of amusement among his colleagues, most of whom strongly supported him for the position some thirteen months later". The general public had even less suspicion at this time that Macmillan harboured thoughts of becoming Prime Minister. Selwyn Lloyd succeeded him at the Foreign Office. He was himself succeeded as Minister of Defence by Sir Walter Monckton, but the latter gave up the office on grounds of health on 18th October 1956—the date was to become significant—and an ex-soldier, until then Secretary of State for War, Brigadier Antony Head, thus became Minister of Defence on the eve of the Suez operations to be described. One other important change in Eden's reconstruction was to bring in Edward Heath as chief whip. He was to prove himself in a testing time one of the great whips.

No Prime Minister in modern times had assumed office with such general support as Eden, but between the autumn of 1955 and the spring of 1956 the percentage of electors approving his work, according to the Gallup poll, dropped from seventy to forty. In part this was due to his inexperience in home affairs, which engage the feelings of electors much more immediately than do foreign issues, and he had to take his share of blame for the miscalculations that led to the autumn budget. He became the subject of press rumours, and in January, when he had been in office barely nine months, his office took the unusual, and indeed unprecedented, step of denying that he intended to resign. His followers became more disturbed when he began to falter also in his own specialist field. In a debate in the House of Commons in March 1956 on King Hussein's dismissal of General Glubb from Jordanian service, Eden's speech was re-garded (according to his own account[19]) as "one of the worst in my career". He sighed for the days "when the fixing of a foreign affairs debate was related to concern for British interests abroad" and "speeches were even sometimes couched in moderate terms so as not to increase the difficulties of her Majesty's ministers". Due allowance was not made at the time for the fact that Eden was not only temperamentally impulsive but had been weakened by illness. He had been obliged in 1953 to have three operations for an internal complaint. (In the same year Churchill, as already noted, suffered a stroke, but could not resign because it would have meant denying Eden the reversion which he had every right to expect—by such accidents is the course of politics determined.) These operations had left their toll. To what extent his condition was purely physical and to what a consequence of his anxieties must be a matter for con-jecture. It was a measure of the falling popularity of the govern-ment that in a by-election at Tonbridge in the summer of 1956 a Conservative majority of 10,196 was clipped to 1,602.

The standing of the government and the Prime Minister had there-fore already deteriorated with alarming suddenness when in the autumn of 1956 the Suez crisis burst upon the country. It can be argued that the decisive step in the termination of British responsi-bilities in Egypt had been taken in 1954 when Eden as Foreign Secre-tary had signed the treaty by which Great Britain agreed to give up its military base in the Suez canal zone. A body of Conservatives, twenty-five to forty in number and generally known as the Suez group, had expressed their discontent with this agreement, but the government's majority was tiny and only one, E. A. H. Legge-Bourke, went to the length of renouncing the Conservative whip. In July 1956 the withdrawal of the offer of American help for the Aswan dam was quickly followed by President Nasser's decision to national-ize the Suez canal. By this time Conservative dislike of the revolu-tionary régime in Egypt had hardened, and the feeling was almost universal that firm action must be taken to maintain the inter-national character of the Suez waterway. The delicate situation created by nationalization was at first met by attempts to negotiate and then by the formation of a users' association and reference to the Security Council of the United Nations. In these measures the Labour party, though unable to object to nationalization in prin-ciple, supported the government, and Gaitskell even went beyond Eden in the strength of his language, comparing Nasser with Hitler and Mussolini.[20]

The situation was transformed on 29th October when Israelian troops invaded Egypt. Only the barest skeleton of events need here be given. The British and French governments issued an ultimatum requiring both Israel and Egypt to withdraw their forces and to allow Anglo-French forces temporarily to occupy key positions. Egypt rejected the ultimatum; in the morning of 31st October bomb-ing of Egyptian airfields began, and on 5th November British and French troops landed in Egypt. Commonwealth governments were perturbed because they had not been consulted. The United States government did not conceal its irritation. John Foster Dulles, with whom Eden had been getting increasingly testy, took the lead in condemning the Anglo-French action in the Security Council, where the British delegate was obliged to use his power of veto for the first time. The Soviet Union's attitude was even more menacing. In a letter to Eden the Russian Prime Minister, Bulganin, asserted that the war in Egypt could grow into a third world war, and ominously added: "There are countries now which need not have sent a navy or air force to the coasts of Britain, but could have used other means, such as a rocket technique."[21] A run on sterling which de-veloped in the financial centres of the world was an even more immediate danger. With the gradual build-up of a United Nations Emergency Force the British and French governments announced their intention to withdraw from Egypt. Three days before Christ-mas the last British troops left.

Such in outline was the astonishing episode that brought foreign policy into the centre of the party struggle and made Eden, once the darling of the League of Nations Union, assume the mantle of Palmerston and embark on a military expedition wholly out of character with the times and with his own previous reputation. Here we are concerned only with the consequences for the party system.

The effect on the Labour party was to give it a sense of unity, purpose and confidence that it had not known for six years. In that hour Gaitskell and Bevan sank the last of their differences and threw themselves with ardour into the fight against the old enemy, the Tory party. On 31st October, immediately after the expiry of the ultimatum, Gaitskell declared: "I must now tell the government and the country that we cannot support the action they have taken and that we shall feel bound by every constitutional means at our disposal to oppose it." In a later broadcast he denounced the use of British troops as "a betrayal of all that we have stood for", and said that Eden was "utterly, utterly discredited".[22] When the government's ultimatum to Egypt was debated in the House of Commons on 30th October Labour forced a division. The house was again divided on 1st November on a Labour motion of censure, and on 8th November, when a cease-fire had been accepted, there was a further division during the debate on the Queen's speech. With a single exception the whole of the Parliamentary Labour party rallied to Gaitskell's call, not even the seventeen Jewish Labour members dissociating themselves from the general condemnation. The exception was Stanley Evans, the member for Wednesbury, who had a reputation for a rugged individuality. A speech in which he had described farm subsidies as "featherbedding" for the farmers had cost him in 1950 the office of Parliamentary Secretary to the Ministry of Food.[23] It did not therefore come altogether as a surprise to his friends when he spoke against the Labour policy and abstained from voting on the motion of censure despite the three-line whip. The general management committee of the Wednesbury party demanded his resignation and he complied.

The Liberal party, though reminded how Gladstone had authorized the bombardment of Alexandria, also came out officially against the government's Suez policy, but in the small band of six Liberals in the House of Commons there was nevertheless one who abstained from voting against it.

In the nature of things it was the Conservative party whose unity was most threatened by the government's action over Suez, and that from opposite directions—from those who wished the government had not gone so far and from those who wished it had gone a great deal farther. Whatever feelings they may have entertained in private, the great majority of Conservative members rallied at once to the support of the government. The fact that British troops were in action would in any case have silenced most criticism, but in truth most Conservative members were relieved that a stand was at last being made; and the virulence of the Labour attacks made the Tory ranks close with a snap. There was manifested a degree of bitterness in the House of Commons such as only a few living parliamentarians could remember. "The scenes in the House of Commons," writes Kilmuir,[24] "were the worst since the bitter clashes between Liberals and Unionists in 1911. A storm of booing would break out as soon as Anthony entered the chamber, and would rise to a crescendo of hysteria when he actually rose to speak. At one point the chances of fighting actually breaking out between members was very real, so intense were the passions on each side." On 1st November the Speaker felt obliged to suspend the sitting for half an hour to let tempers cool.

The virtual unanimity of the Conservative party in the House of Commons has deeply impressed an American commentator who has made a close study of what took place. Mr. Leon D. Epstein has written:[25]

"The crucial political fact about the Suez crisis was the support of the government by Conservative M.P.s, including some who never wanted to go into Egypt and some who never wanted to come out. The nearly solid party voting meant that the parliamentary system did not operate in the classical nineteenth-century manner to defeat the government on grounds of either the Suez action or its failure. Yet here, if on any occasion, M.P.s might have been expected to break with their governmental leadership."

Of those Conservatives who objected to strong action against Egypt, two ministers outside the Cabinet resigned their offices— Anthony Nutting as Minister of State for Foreign Affairs and Sir Edward Boyle as Economic Secretary to the Treasury. Nutting, who had already given offence in the Quorn country by his opposition to hunting and was in matrimonial difficulties, gave up his seat at Melton Mowbray, but Boyle was soon forgiven by the Handsworth association for his deviation and returned to office. In the division on 8th November eight Conservatives who disagreed with the government's action conspicuously abstained from voting. Their case histories are worth close study for the working of the party system.[26] Three of them—Nigel Nicolson, Sir Frank Medlicott and Cyril Banks—were disowned by their constituency associations, which selected different candidates for the next election. The others met much criticism from their local associations, but survived.

The old Suez group naturally supported the government's military action against Egypt and were correspondingly displeased when the British troops were withdrawn. Fourteen of them abstained on 16th May 1957 from the vote approving the government's decision to advise British shipowners to use the canal on the terms laid down by Egypt; and of them eight took the extreme course of renouncing the Conservative whip. One had the whip restored in 1957, and two gave up their seats in Parliament to pursue work abroad, but five of them constituted an independent conservative group under the leadership of Lord Hinchingbrooke until June 1958. It is significant that they did not incur nearly so much criticism from their local associations as the anti-Suez abstentionists, and none of them was asked to give up his seat by reason of his attitude to Suez.[27]

The assertion by two French journalists[28] in a book translated into English that the Suez operation was terminated by Eden partly because "Butler had wrested the arms from his grasp by threatening to resign on 5th November with seven other ministers, taking from the Conservative majority forty hostile votes" is not supported by evidence and seems at variance with the facts. In his memoirs Eden subsequently commented:[29]

"There were reports at this time of a dissident minority in the Conservative party in the House of Commons. I was told that if a cease-fire were not announced that day, some of them would not vote with us. I was not influenced by these reports, or by the knowledge that there had been some contacts between one or two members of our party and the opposition leaders. The overwhelming majority was firmly loyal. There are always weak sisters in any crisis, and sometimes they will be found among those who were toughest at the outset of the journey."

The failure of the Suez operation and the vicious criticism to which he was subjected in the House of Commons destroyed Eden's confidence and contributed to bring about a recurrence of his physical complaints. In October, after visiting his wife in hospital, he was seized by a high fever and was ignominiously placed in a room adjoining hers. A holiday in Jamaica brought only a temporary alleviation of his troubles. In January 1957 the attacks recurred, and he was warned that they would become more frequent. He decided that he could not with this liability carry out the duties of a Prime Minister, and on 9th January, after informing the Cabinet of his intention, he tendered his resignation to the Queen. After applying for the Chiltern Hundreds he went to the House of Lords as the Earl of Avon.

What followed Eden's resignation shows more than anything else in recent years how easy it is for anyone not in the inner counsels of the Conservative party to err in predicting or interpreting its actions. When the readers of the morning newspapers of 10th January saw that Eden had resigned, almost everyone assumed that Butler would be his successor. *The Economist* had gone much too far in asserting that "if Sir Anthony were to lay down the premiership tomorrow, there is really no doubt that the Queen would be constitutionally bound to send for Mr. Butler",[30] but almost all the morning newspapers of 10th January predicted fairly confidently that the choice would fall on him. He had been both Chancellor and Foreign Secretary, he had moulded the post-war Conservative party more than anyone else, he had long been recognized as second only to Eden in the hierarchy, and during Eden's absence in Jamaica he had presided over the Cabinet. Yet there were reservations in some of the better-informed quarters. *The Times* made clear to its readers that the merits of both Butler and Macmillan were being canvassed, and although a leading article urged that on balance Butler was "the more likely to lead the nation in its present straits and the party at the next general election", the political correspondent argued that "he may not be acceptable as leader to the strong right-wing element of Conservative M.P.s and Mr. Macmillan might prove a more acceptable choice". He was right. That afternoon Harold Macmillan kissed hands as Prime Minister. On 22nd January, at a meeting attended by Conservative and National Liberal peers, members of Parliament and candidates, and by members of the executive committee of the National Union, he was unanimously elected leader of the party. The motion was moved by Salisbury and seconded by Butler, who won much sympathy by his declaration : "I would like to say simply to you what I have said to him [Macmillan] : That is that he can count on my loyal support, and that any influence I have will be exerted on his behalf ... The question of who is to be Prime Minister is decided."[31]

In his subsequent memoirs Eden gave no hint of what passed between him and the Queen on 9th January when his resignation was accepted. It would have been in accordance with normal practice if her Majesty had sought his advice on his successor, and if she did so Eden could hardly have failed to disclose that the party was divided between the merits of Butler and Macmillan; and as the Queen could not have failed to be apprised of this fact already it may be that she refrained from putting a question that might have been embarrassing to the outgoing Prime Minister. Lord Kilmuir has written : [32]

"I do not know for certain, but am fairly sure that the advice of Sir Anthony Eden concerning his successor was not invited, just as Queen Victoria did not invite that of Mr. Gladstone in 1894, although for very different reasons. There is no obligation upon the Sovereign to seek the advice of a retiring Prime Minister on the matter of his successor, although this normally occurs. Had Eden advised her Majesty to send for Butler, and had this advice been [given and] accepted, an extremely delicate and difficult situation might have arisen. I am sure that the great majority of the Cabinet would have agreed to serve under Butler out of loyalty, but there would have been some conspicuous and highly damaging resignations, and the parliamentary party might well have disintegrated in public."

Kilmuir, who was Lord Chancellor at the time and "keeper of the Queen's conscience" has also written : [33] "Having considered the constitutional position very carefully I had come to the conclusion that the Queen was entitled to ask for advice from anyone she chose in order to discover who would command the support of a majority in the House of Commons. I took the view very strongly that she need and ought not to wait for a party meeting. To do so would be to abandon the most important remaining part of her prerogative, whose maintenance might be of immeasurable value to the country in the later years of her reign should a political crisis develop." This was undoubtedly sound constitutional doctrine at the time, though the constitution is always evolving and it might not be asserted so confidently today; and in pursuance of this doctine the Queen decided to seek the advice of two senior statesmen held in high respect in the Conservative party, one a commoner and the only surviving ex-Prime Minister apart from Eden himself, the other the leader of the House of Lords—Sir Winston Churchill and Lord Salisbury.

Churchill's advice may have been based in the main on his own unrivalled study of the political scene, but Salisbury went to the Palace armed with the individual opinion of each Cabinet minister. Before the meeting at which Eden announced his intention to resign, Kilmuir and Salisbury, as "the senior members of the Cabinet, whose position in the Lords left us unconcerned in the succession", agreed that they would "consult all Cabinet ministers one by one and get their views as between Harold Macmillan and Rab Butler". Immediately after the meeting the two peers asked their colleagues to see them one by one in Salisbury's room in the Privy Council offices, which could be reached without leaving the building before the eyes of waiting journalists. Kilmuir has painted a fascinating picture of the succession of interviews:

"There were two light reliefs. Practically each one began by saying: 'This is like coming to the headmaster's study.' To each Bobbety said: 'Well, which is it, Wab or Hawold?' "

According to Kilmuir, "An overwhelming majority of Cabinet ministers was in favour of Macmillan as Eden's successor," and in emphasizing the constitutional importance of certain features of this ministerial crisis he says: "The most significant was that the ex-Cabinet virtually selected the next Prime Minister."[34] When Salisbury went to the Palace he was in possession, however, of the views not only of the Cabinet but of back-benchers and organizers of the party. He and Kilmuir interviewed, not only their Cabinet colleagues, but the chief whip, Edward Heath, and the chairman of the party organization, Oliver Poole; and the following morning Kilmuir received a telephone call from John Morrison, the chairman of the 1922 committee of Conservative private members. Back-bench opinion, as reported to them, strongly endorsed the view that Macmillan rather than Butler should be Eden's successor. According to Kilmuir, "party feeling in the House of Commons was running very strongly against Butler at this time, and at one point there was even a serious proposal by a number of Conservatives to walk out of the chamber when Rab entered it".

The whips and officers do not appear to have sought the views of back-benchers in any systematic way, but they made notes of what they were told. From the date of Eden's return from Jamaica many Conservative members had felt doubtful whether he could continue as leader, and not a few made known to the whips their views on the succession. One of them, Dame Irene Ward, stated in the *Daily Telegraph* of 15th January: "I would have preferred to have served under Sir Anthony Eden to the end of the road, but as a realist I took steps to inform our most admirable whips before the Christmas recess that in the event of a change of Prime Minister I preferred Mr. Macmillan." On the same day another Conservative member, Martin Lindsay, wrote: "It was quite apparent to the majority of us that Sir Anthony was a very sick man when he returned from Jamaica. Most of us, therefore, anticipated the situation which we considered was likely to arise during the parliamentary recess and wrote to the chief whip expressing our individual opinions as to whom the Queen should send for. To my knowledge Mr. Heath received a large number of such letters and was therefore in a position to state authoritatively that the greatest measure of agreement would be found in support of Mr. Macmillan." It is possible that the whips themselves sounded some members, but there was no general canvassing of members' views, and the correspondence in the *Daily Telegraph* began with a complaint from T. L. Iremonger, then a relatively new member, that "matters were handled so that the Sovereign has in effect chosen the party's leader for it without the will of the party itself having found expression".[35] This was a novel point of view in the Conservative party, which had on many previous occasions been content to allow the Sovereign to choose its leader for it, but it was to recur in the future and indicated a new trend of opinion. On this occasion it would appear that back-bench opinion was not unimportant, but that the views of Cabinet ministers were decisive.

If they had not reinforced each other, Salisbury—and the Queen —would have had a more difficult problem. As it was, Salisbury, who arrived at the Palace about eleven o'clock in the morning of 10th January, had been left in no doubt about the advice he should tender. About half an hour later, while he was still in audience, Churchill arrived. Salisbury left at ten minutes before noon, Churchill a few minutes after noon. The Queen would thus have had the opportunity of receiving their individual and collective advice. Two years later Churchill made known that he had recommended the Queen to send for Macmillan,[36] and though Salisbury has not disclosed his own advice there can be no doubt that it was identical. The Queen sent for Macmillan barely two hours after their departure.

There remains the question on which subsequent speculation has chiefly settled, why the Conservative preference (and therefore the

Queen's choice) fell on Macmillan rather than on the public favourite, Butler. This must be considered briefly, for it bears on the nature
of the Conservative party.

There is no evidence of any difference between Butler and Macmillan in their attitude to the Suez campaign. Eden has testified:[37]
"I had interviews with a number of colleagues individually, during
the weeks which passed after the seizure of the canal. There was no
friction of any kind between us." Though Eden was obsessed by the
parallel that he saw between appeasing Hitler and appeasing Nasser,
the theory that Butler was regarded at this time as an appeaser on
account of his under-secretaryship in the Chamberlain government[38] is most improbable; Conservative memories are elephantine,
but not so long as that, and it is well understood that junior ministers are not to be held responsible for the sins of their seniors. (The
coup de grâce to this theory was given in 1963 when the Earl of
Home was preferred as Prime Minister to Butler for, as Lord Dunglass, he had been parliamentary private secretary to Neville
Chamberlain at the time of Munich, but we must not use the benefit
of hindsight.) The view that Butler's progressive policies had given
offence to the right-wing section of the party needs closer examination. It was this, as we have seen, that led the political correspondent of *The Times* even before the choice was made to wonder
whether Macmillan might not prove the more acceptable. The idea
that Butler belonged to the left wing and Macmillan to the right is
not, however, a theory that can be long sustained. The pre-war
Macmillan may have been the foe of appeasement, but he was also
the advocate of the middle way and the enemy of unemployment.
He had been called a "socialist" by the extremists of the party at
least as much as Butler. In the light of Macmillan's subsequent
career, especially his shedding of imperial responsibilities, it is impossible to regard him as a man of the right and Butler as a man of
the left, but even on the evidence available in 1957 the contrast is
not one that could be made by anyone with a close knowledge of
the two men.

Kilmuir has given his reasons for the sharp decline in Butler's
personal fortunes at the end of 1956 and beginning of 1957. "Many
at that time," he has written,[39] "considered that his habit of
publicly hedging his political bets was too great a weakness and this
had accordingly damaged his position both in the Conservative
hierarchy and in the parliamentary party." A leader has to lead, and
there frequently come occasions when he has to say, in language
free from ambiguity or misunderstanding: "This is my policy and
by it I stand or fall." Butler's convoluted thought and mastery of
intricate forms of expression won admiration for him as a dialec-
tician, but simpler minds began to ask whether a more direct
approach to political problems was not needed.

Though commentators have been reluctant to accept so obvious an explanation, the plain fact is that at the beginning of 1957 Conservative ministers and members of Parliament saw more of the stuff of a Prime Minister in Macmillan than in Butler. Both had first-class brains, the one trained at Eton and Oxford, the other at Marlborough and Cambridge, but Butler's coldly analytical mind would have made him the ideal civil servant whereas Macmillan possessed the fire to kindle the imagination. Both had held the two greatest offices of state, but Macmillan had the credit of an achievement that weighed still more, that of having produced 300,000 houses a year when the Labour party said it could not be done. The delay in the reconstruction of the government after Eden's appointment as Prime Minister, as we have seen, had been greatly to Butler's disadvantage. There was a further personal factor that gets overlooked. Butler had never been quite the same man since the death of his wife in 1954; he had been sick himself, and it was uncertain whether he would recover the same confident grip on affairs. Nor could it be overlooked, in an age when television had become a dominating factor in electioneering, that Butler was unhappy before the cameras—not photogenic as the jargon is. Though it is hard to explain why, those Conservatives who opposed Butler's selection felt more strongly against him than those who opposed Macmillan's. In the end this factor probably proved decisive. Even before the decision was taken *The Times* perceptively commented that, while Butler had a powerful body of support, those opposed to him were more likely to make trouble than those opposed to Macmillan.[40] At a time when the great need was to restore the unity of the party, this was a consideration that could not be neglected. Analysing the reports they received, the chief whip, Salisbury and Churchill could not fail to come to the conclusion that in the dark hour following Suez Macmillan was more likely to rally the party than Butler. They advised accordingly.

The Labour party "shadow Cabinet" was not prepared to treat these changes as a matter concerning the Tory party alone. It met immediately and agreed to meet again to consider "the constitutional implications of the way which the change was brought about". That same evening Griffiths, in the absence of Gaitskell abroad, declared in a broadcast talk that the Conservatives had "placed the Crown in a very difficult and embarrassing position". When the "shadow Cabinet" met again Gaitskell had returned, and it was decided not to pursue this line, but to state the party's view of what should happen if a vacancy occurred while it was in power. Holding up the example of Bonar Law in 1922 as a precedent—it must have gone against the grain to quote such an enemy of socialism—the "shadow Cabinet" asserted that the Queen should not be

required to choose a new Prime Minister before the party in power
had elected a new leader.

There was little sympathy for this view at that time in the Conservative ranks, though it has since gained a rather wider acceptance. The Conservatives had so often chosen as their leader a man
on whom the Sovereign's choice for the post of Prime Minister had
already fallen that it had become the rule rather than the exception.
On the whole Conservatives preferred to have it that way. Usually
there was no doubt whom they wished to see as their leader—and as
Prime Minister—and when there was a doubt, as in 1923, there was
much to be said for allowing it to be resolved by the Crown rather
than to have an unseemly wrangle at a party meeting. In 1923 there
was a real sense in which King George V chose the leader of the
Conservatives for them. In 1957 Queen Elizabeth II showed no disposition to abandon the royal prerogative of choosing the Prime
Minister. "The Queen's government must be carried on", and there
seems to have been no thought of delaying the resignation, or doing
without a titular head of the government, until a party meeting
could be summoned. But although Queen Elizabeth presented the
Conservatives with a *fait accompli*, she did not choose their leader
to the same extent that King George V had done thirty-four years
earlier. By a careful process of consultation she chose as Prime
Minister the man whom the Conservatives were most likely to
choose if they had an unfettered choice.

There was no recrimination on the Conservative side. Butler bore
his disappointment with fortitude and maintained throughout the
years the generosity and loyalty of speech he made in seconding
Macmillan's election. His supporters followed his example. That
loyalty to the man in charge which has always been the strongest
party asset of the Tories was never seen to better advantage than in
the Suez crisis. Macmillan, too, soon showed that he fully justified
the confidence placed in him by the Queen and the party. At that
time he confined himself almost entirely to necessary changes.
Thorneycroft took his own place at the Exchequer. Butler added the
Home Office and Welsh Affairs to the duties of Lord Privy Seal.
Head, who as Minister of Defence had a special share of responsibility for the execution of the Suez venture, dropped out of the
government and Sandys took his place. Hailsham entered the
Cabinet as Minister of Education. Good relations with the United
States were restored with consummate ease. Sterling rapidly recovered in the markets of the world. The Prime Minister's com-
posure in the face of difficulties set an example to the country and
won for him a reputation for "unflappability". He soon had opportunities to show that he was completely master of the Conservative
party. On 29th March Salisbury offered his resignation as a protest
against the release of Archbishop Makarios from exile in the hope of

bringing about a settlement of the Cyprus question; Macmillan accepted it, and thereby showed that he was not dependent on the man who had conveyed the advice that made him Prime Minister. In May he simply ignored the renunciation of the whip by the eight Conservative members who objected to the government's "capitulation" to Nasser. By every practical test he showed that as Prime Minister he did not differ from the "middle of the way" member for Stockton-on-Tees of the nineteen-thirties. It is true that he allowed himself to be pictured as an aristocrat of Edwardian tastes who delighted in nothing more than in shooting grouse on ducal moors; but though the son-in-law of a duke he never forgot that he was the grandson of a crofter. As shrewd a politician as had occupied No. 10 Downing Street since Baldwin, he found it useful to assume the pose of aristocratic grandeur to balance the essential liberalism of his views. He continued to guide the Conservative party in the path of Tory democracy that Churchill and Eden had indicated, though more surely and at a gathering speed; and although throughout 1956 and 1957 and for the greater part of 1958 the Conservative party seemed to be heading for electoral massacre, by the summer of 1958 it was again in confident mood.

In the index of voting intentions provided by the Gallup poll the Labour party gained a one-point lead over the Conservatives in November 1955 and did not lose the lead until August 1958. The Suez operation was not the most crucial factor in the swing of opinion—indeed, it won for the government a good deal of support from uncommitted electors—for in the critical month of December 1956 the Labour lead was no more than one point, whereas it rose to a peak of thirteen in September 1957. The decision of the government in the autumn of 1956 to remove the protection of rent control from a large number of dwellings weighed more heavily with voters. Though amply justified by the large number of new houses built since the war and by the artificially low figures of rents based on 1939 values, which made it impossible for owners to carry out repairs of controlled property, the Rent Act, 1957, which Henry Brooke had the unpleasant task of piloting through the Commons, could easily be, and was, represented as a measure passed in the interest of rapacious landlords grinding the faces of the poor. At a by-election at Lewisham North in February 1957 the socialist candidate turned a Conservative majority of 3,236 into a Labour majority of 1,110. It was the first time a government had lost a seat at a by-election since 1939.

Inflationary pressures on the economy, leading to doubts about the stability of sterling and speculative pressure on the pound, with a consequential heavy loss of gold, increased the government's troubles in the summer of 1957 and led the Chancellor, Thorneycroft, to bring in a drastic set of measures to cope with the situation.

Q

Bank-rate was raised to the high level of seven per cent—by this time readiness to rely on interest rates as against physical controls had become one of the marks distinguishing a Tory from a socialist. A ceiling was set on public investment and restrictions placed on bank advances for private investment. The estimates for the coming year were severely pruned, but still showed a rise of £50 million on the previous year's figures. Thorneycroft demanded further economies. At this point Macmillan declined to give him his head and thereby showed that in such matters as social welfare he still remained in the middle of the road. In January 1958 Thorneycroft resigned, and was followed by two other Treasury ministers, Nigel Birch and Enoch Powell. It was the type of incident that could bring down governments. Macmillan, just about to leave on a Commonwealth tour, dismissed "these little local difficulties"[41] and appointed Heathcoat Amory in Thorneycroft's place. The appearance of pockets of unemployment in some of the old familiar places soon made it clear that what the economy needed was not further restriction but the injection of more purchasing power, which Heathcoat Amory sought to provide. Unemployment rose to a peak of 2.8 per cent in February 1959, and although this was below the level of three per cent which Beveridge had assumed as normal it concealed a much higher incidence in certain areas and was no longer acceptable to the public conscience. The Conservative party suffered accordingly at the by-elections.

The Labour party profited by its rival's discomfiture. The reconciliation between Gaitskell and Bevan which came about at the time of the Suez operation matured into a harmonious partnership. When the party conference assembled at Brighton in September 1957, a large number of resolutions calling for the unilateral renunciation of the manufacture, testing and use of hydrogen bombs were amalgamated into a composite resolution. Gaitskell urged that Bevan must oppose this resolution on behalf of the National Executive; otherwise it would be manifest that he, as the party's spokesman on foreign affairs, was in conflict with the party leadership. He hesitated, and sought compromises, but in the event he argued powerfully from the platform that to vote for unilateral renunciation would send a Labour Foreign Secretary "naked into the conference chamber" and that for Great Britain to contract out unilaterally without even consulting the Commonwealth would not be statesmanship but "an emotional spasm". For the first time, Bevan led the opposition to the Bevanites, and he carried the conference by the big majority of 5,836,000 to 781,000. By this time he had had enough of sterile opposition, and decided not to compromise the road to power that was opening before him.[42] The erstwhile Bevanites revived the group known as "Victory for Socialism", but bereft of their leader they made little headway; and the novel spectacle of unity at the top increased the standing of the Labour party in the country and brought it increasing success at the by-elections. In March 1958 Kelvingrove followed the example of North Lewisham and returned the Labour candidate in place of a Tory.

What was more surprising was the spectacle of a modest Liberal revival. The party's fortunes had seemed at their nadir in 1957 when Lady Megan Lloyd George and Dingle Foot, who had some time previously resigned their membership of the party, secured election in the Labour interest for Carmarthenshire and Ipswich respectively. When two such prominent Liberals publicly announced their loss of faith it seemed that there could not possibly be any future for the party. But there were many electors, disgruntled by the Conservative performance yet not prepared to vote Labour, who saw in support for Liberal candidates a method of expressing their protest. At Rochdale early in 1958 a Liberal candidate forced the Conservative into a bad third place; and at Torrington a little later Mark Bonham Carter, grandson of Asquith, actually won the seat from a Conservative candidate. The margin was only 219 votes, but as the first Liberal gain since 1929 it was hailed by the party as the dawn of a Liberal revival. In a by-election at Southend in January 1959 Liberal hopes ran high when their share of the poll increased by 9·2 per cent and the Conservative share fell by 9·2 per cent, with Labour's share virtually stationary. Galloway told the same tale in March.

It was deceptive, for about the same time the tide of Conservative fortune began to turn, and when it turned it came in rapidly. A visit to Russia by Macmillan began a round of visits that established his reputation as a world statesman. At home the measures to put new life into the economy began to have effect. The pockets of unemployment disappeared, and in his April budget Heathcoat Amory reduced the standard rate of income-tax, cut purchase-tax, took twopence a pint off beer and made a start in the earlier repayment of post-war credits. It was denounced as an electioneering budget, and it certainly improved the disposition of the country towards the Tory party. On 8th September Macmillan judged that the time was ripe, and in an announcement from Downing Street—reverting to the practice before Attlee's use of the radio in 1951—he gave out that Parliament would be dissolved on 18th September and a general election held on 8th October.

Every seat was contested. The Conservatives and their allies fought 625 out of the 630 elections; Sir David Robertson, who had renounced the Conservative whip at the beginning of the year to express dissatisfaction at the government's treatment of Highland affairs, was given a straight fight with his Labour opponent, and four Liberals were allowed the same privilege. Except for those who did not stand again, the Suez rebels were official Conservative candidates; one of them, Patrick Maitland, who echoed at Lanark

Churchill's 1945 charge that a Labour victory would lead to a police state, had the unusual experience of having his views first circulated and then repudiated by the Central Office.

The Labour party was seriously split by the issue of the hydrogen bomb, and Conservatives exploited this to the full, but otherwise the party was relatively free from dissension. It put 621 candidates into the field, leaving nine constituencies uncontested in Northern Ireland; of these the odd twenty-one were sponsored by the Cooperative party. A disappointed man was Morgan Phillips, who was prepared to give up the party secretaryship in order to stand for Parliament, but was not selected as a candidate in North-east Derbyshire. The Liberals, encouraged by their by-election successes, had 216 candidates. Lady Megan Lloyd George and Dingle Foot were not exempted from the Liberal challenge by any consideration of past affection. The Communists mustered eighteen candidates, but the Independent Labour party only two. There were on this occasion no fewer than thirty-seven Nationalist candidates. *Plaid Cymru*, making the most determined effort in its history, contested five of the ten Welsh boroughs and fifteen of the twenty-six Welsh county seats. Scottish Nationalists in comparison made a half-hearted showing with five candidates, but Sinn Fein showed the flag in every one of the twelve Northern Ireland constituencies. Seventeen Independents and candidates with unusual labels brought the total to 1,536, the largest entry since 1950.

The Conservative manifesto followed the pattern set in the two previous elections—a party document with a preface by the leader. It was entitled *The Next Five Years: Conservative Programme for Peace and Prosperity*, and offered "to double the British standard of living in this generation", but the keynote of the Conservative campaign was struck in the poster-slogan, "Life's better with the Conservatives, Don't let Labour ruin it".[43] The Labour manifesto, *Britain belongs to you*, declared that "as part of our planned expansion, it will be necessary to extend the area of public ownership", specifically promised the renationalization of the steel industry and commercial long-distance road haulage, and vaguely announced that "road building must be related to a national plan". It added, "We have no other plans for further nationalization," but reserved the right to nationalize any industry "shown, after thorough inquiry, to be failing the nation". For the most part the manifesto concentrated on expansion of the economy and of the social services. A new system of retirement pensions called national superannuation and based on graduated contributions was intended to be a main feature of the Labour programme. The Conservatives stole some of its attractions by writing their own scheme of graduated pensions on the statute book, to come into effect in 1961, but the Labour plan seems to have gained votes among the older people. In a preface to the Liberal manifesto, *People Count*, Grimond took comfort in the increase of support at by-elections "as a first stage to the eventual formation of a Liberal government".

The 1959 general election was fought more professionally than any previous contest. In the Woolton era the Conservatives had employed a firm of public relations consultants, Messrs. Colman, Prentis and Varley, to advise on short pre-election advertising campaigns in 1949 and 1951, but with the goal of office won the advertising ceased. In 1957 the Central Office once more engaged their services for a more sustained and carefully planned presentation of the Conservative case. It drew from R. H. S. Crossman the complaint that the Prime Minister was being sold to the country "like a detergent", though neither his name nor photograph was used, but Labour was stirred into a "glossier than thou" policy, in Hailsham's phrase.[44] In these pre-election campaigns great emphasis was laid on the need to create a favourable "party image". The reasons why people vote as they do had in recent years been subjected to much closer and much more scientific analysis than ever before—D. E. Butler and Richard Rose observed "a new level of psephological sophistication"[45]—and it was accepted that the general impression left on the minds of the public by a party was more important than the details of its policy. This was indeed no new discovery, for without using the term (like M. Jourdain speaking prose for forty years without knowing it) the parties had always tried to create favourable pictures of themselves and unfavourable ones of their opponents; but the terminology was new and the image-making more deliberate. The rise in the number of homes with television sets— seventy per cent in 1959 compared with forty per cent in 1955— made it inevitable that the television screen should dominate the election, and in this branch of electioneering the Labour party showed themselves more professional, or as some said more slick, than the Conservatives. The Labour managers also showed themselves more adept at public relations in holding a daily press conference at Transport House. Morgan Phillips's skill at providing the press with news ensured that his party always made a good show in the next day's newspapers. It was an innovation likely to become a permanent part of British electioneering—the daily "battle of Smith Square".

The great talking points of the campaign nevertheless came in more conventional forms of electioneering. At a meeting in Newcastle-upon-Tyne Gaitskell made the promise, "There will be no increase in the standard or other rates of income-tax under the Labour government so long as normal peacetime conditions continue"; and a statement from Transport House pledged Labour to abolish purchase-tax on essential goods. Macmillan accused Labour of "the biggest budget leak in history" and turning the election into a mock auction.[46]

At eve of poll meetings in Leeds Gaitskell announced: "The Tories have got the wind up, and they have the right to have the wind up, because we are going to win."[47] This was the general expectation in the Labour party, but the Gallup poll had shown a Conservative lead over Labour since the previous May, and the prediction was not falsified. When the ballot papers came to be counted it was seen that the Conservatives and their allies had obtained 13,749,830 votes and 365 seats in the House of Commons, while Labour had only 12,215,538 votes and 258 seats in the Commons. Far from losing the election, the Conservatives had increased their strength in the house by twenty-one, and the Labour strength had fallen by nineteen. The Conservative majority was increased to 100 over all others—comfortable enough for even the most anxious of whips. The Liberals remained stationary at six. The only other successful candidate was the dissident Conservative Sir David Robertson. He and four Liberals owed their election to the absence of a Conservative candidate; Joseph Grimond and Clement Davies, leader and ex-leader of the Liberal party, alone triumphed in three-cornered fights.

The Liberal revival was conclusively demonstrated to be no more than a protest vote, and the British party scene was once more shown to be essentially a struggle between two powerful and nearly equal groups. The interesting question raised by the general election of 1959, following that of 1955, was whether a party in power need ever be defeated. We have noticed that until 1830 no government was ever defeated at a general election, and that, far from elections making governments, it was governments who made elections. The crude methods of bribery and patronage used to achieve that result had long since been put outside the law, but the power to regulate the economy vested in modern governments has given the party in power a potent instrument in creating an atmosphere favourable to success in the months preceding an election. The Parliaments of 1951–5 and 1955–9 had shown the same cyclical pattern. The middle years of each Parliament were marked by a tight hand at the Exchequer, high taxation, restriction of credit, the tarnishing of the "image" of the party in power and a decline in the government's popularity, whereas in each case the pre-election year was marked by a looser rein at the Treasury, reliefs in taxation, the easing of credit, the refurbishing of the governing party's "image" and a return in the popularity of the administration. How often could this process be repeated? The control of governments over elections before 1830 was acceptable because governments could be changed in other ways; and the power of governments since 1950 to influence the economic climate is unlikely by itself to prevail over other considerations.

The Labour party failed to win the election of 1959, not because the Conservatives had the advantage of being in office, but because it had failed to come to terms with the great social changes of the nineteen-fifties. The rise in standards of living had taken large numbers of the manual workers into the ranks of the middle classes, and they found the philosophy of Conservatism more attractive than the class warfare and egalitarianism which still played a big part in Labour speech and writing. Anthony Crosland in his *Future of Socialism* published in 1956 had warned his Labour colleagues about the significance of these changes, but few took his warning to heart, and most continued to address the engineers and automobile workers of Birmingham as Keir Hardie had talked to the steel workers of Merthyr Tydfil. In the moment of truth after defeat Patrick Gordon Walker sadly acknowledged the reason: "The simple fact is that the Tories identified themselves with the new working class rather better than we did."[48]

35

NEW LEADERS AND POLICIES
1959–1964

Gaitskell tries to get clause four revised—and is attacked by the left wing—the attempt abandoned—Labour divisions over nuclear weapons—Wilson unsuccessfully challenges Gaitskell—who persuades the conference to abandon unilateral nuclear disarmament —two major reorientations in Conservative policy—the "wind of change" in imperial affairs—the European common market—Gaitskell comes out against the common market—and gains the support of the left—his death opens a new struggle for the leadership —Wilson defeats Brown—the Conservative party runs into trouble —the Liberals capture Orpington—Macmillan's massive reconstruction—Selwyn Lloyd's inquiry into the party organization—the Profumo case—demands for Macmillan's resignation—the Peerage Bill—Home emerges as the leader—he succeeds in forming a government—and after disclaiming is elected to the Commons—he is chosen Conservative leader—the Conservatives seek the end of resale price maintenance

A PARTY defeated for the third time in succession was bound to ask the reason why, and Gaitskell had no illusions. It was the identification of the Labour party in the minds of electors with the policy of the nationalization of all the means of production, distribution and exchange. Whatever economic or social arguments there might be for nationalization, it had become a political liability. At the general elections of 1951, 1955 and 1959 the controllers of the Labour party had muted the call for public ownership as much as they dared, but so long as it remained the declared goal of the party the Conservatives would be able to hold it up as a bogey. With his usual clarity of mind Gaitskell decided that the only course was to delete or modify that paragraph of clause four of the party constitution which laid down among the party's objects:

"To secure for the workers by hand or by brain the full fruits of their industry and the most equitable distribution thereof that may be possible, upon the basis of the common ownership of the means of production, distribution and exchange, and the best obtainable system of popular administration and control of each industry or service."

The party conference, postponed on account of the election, was held in shortened form on 28th and 29th November. With a direct-ness that bore witness more to the guilelessness of his character than to his acumen as a politician, Gaitskell determined to unburden his thoughts to the delegates. On account of the unusual nature of the conference it had been decided that members of the National Executive would speak without necessarily committing their col-leagues, and he began by saying: "This afternoon I speak for myself alone." He never spoke truer words. He was virtually thinking aloud, with little preliminary consultation, and an astonished con-ference which had that morning cheered its chairman, Barbara Castle, for asking, "Why should we be frightened at this moment of all moments about public ownership?", listened with rising anger and dismay as Gaitskell developed the contrary theme.[1]

"I do think that we should clear our minds on these fundamental issues and then try to express in the most simple and comprehensive fashion what we stand for in the world today.

"The only official document which embodies such an attempt is the party constitution, written over forty years ago. It seems to me that this needs to be brought up to date. For instance, can we really be satisfied today with a statement of fundamentals which makes no mention at all of colonial freedom, race relations, disarmament, full employment or planning? The only specific reference to our objec-tives at home is the famous phrase: 'To secure for the workers by hand or by brain the full fruits of their industry and the most equit-able distribution thereof that may be possible, upon the basis of the common ownership of the means of production, distribution and exchange.'

"Standing as it does on its own, this cannot possibly be regarded as adequate. It lays us open to continual misrepresentation. It im-plies that common ownership is an end, whereas in fact it is a means. It implies that the only precise object we have is nationaliza-tion, whereas we have in fact many other socialist objectives. It implies that we propose to nationalize everything; but do we? Everything?—the whole of light industry, the whole of agriculture, all the shops, every little pub and garage? Of course not. We have long ago come to accept, we know very well, for the foreseeable future, at least in some form, a mixed economy; in which case, if this is our view—as I believe it to be of ninety per cent of the Labour party—had we better not say so instead of going out of our way to court misrepresentation?"

Gaitskell did not appear to realize that he had laid impious hands upon the ark of the covenant, and the anger of the conference was kindled against him. The most significant attack came from Frank Cousins, general secretary of the Transport and General Workers' Union, and it brought to light a big change that had taken place at the top of the Labour party. Attlee had been able to maintain his position as leader because he could always count on the support of a body of right-wing trade union leaders whom R. T. McKenzie aptly calls the "Praetorian guard".[2] Among them a pre-eminent position was held by the general secretary of the million-strong Transport and General Workers' Union, firstly Ernest Bevin and then Arthur Deakin. They were wise enough to allow a political figure to lead the movement while keeping the realities of power in their own hands, and Attlee was careful to ensure that he carried their support for any major course of action and, if necessary, to defer to their judgement. Deakin's opposition to Communism and left-wing in-filtration was so great that at the Margate conference in 1953 he threatened that the trade unions might break with the party; but he died in 1955, and his successor, who had been groomed to follow the same course, died unexpectedly in the same year. The man who eventually became general secretary of the Transport and General Workers' Union, Frank Cousins, stood well to the left of Bevin and Deakin, and by virtue of his position was frequently able to swing the votes of the union in directions of which they would have dis-approved. A powerful link in the alliance between the political and trade union heads of the Labour movement had been broken, and when Cousins rose to comment on Gaitskell's plea for a revision of clause four it was to say:[3]

"We have all accepted in the past that, whilst we can have nationalization without socialism, we cannot have socialism with-out nationalization. Those who make any other form of approach are doing a disservice to the Labour movement . . .

"I was a bit disturbed by Hugh's reference that, whilst we are going along as we are now, there may be need to revise the con-stitution in the modern circumstances in which we find ourselves. It seemed a bit peculiar that there had been no consultation with the National Executive committee. I think I am a fairly powerful man in my own organization, but if I were going to give a public airing to a change in the constitution of my union I should wait until I had talked to the executive before doing it. If the idea is that all we need to do is to add something to our constitution there could be something to be said in favour of that. But if, as I gather, rule four is likely to be revised to make a different reference to our attitude towards public ownership, I would suggest, with the greatest respect to our leader, that no way—Douglas Jay's or any other way—is going to change that one."

The debate was wound up by Aneurin Bevan who had just been elected deputy leader by the parliamentary party on the retirement of James Griffiths. He was one of the few persons to whom Gaitskell had shown the text of his proposed remarks. He had then made no comment, but in his speech to the conference, also talking for himself, he passionately argued the case for keeping public ownership in the Labour programme. At the end he was paid a tribute of loud and sustained applause such as the annual conference has seldom given to any speaker. It is possible that if he had lived he would have seen Gaitskell repudiated and himself rewarded for his fidelity to socialism by the free gift of the leadership which he had so often failed to seize, but it was not to be. Soon he was striken by a mortal illness.

Despite the hostile reception, Gaitskell continued to press for revision of clause four. The mass of the party was equally resolved that it should not be weakened. On 16th March 1960 the National Executive tried to reach a compromise by issuing a statement which, it was said, "reaffirms, amplifies and clarifies party objects in the light of post-war developments and the historic achievements of the first majority Labour government". It was proposed to include in the restatement of the party's aims the following paragraph : [4]

"It [the Labour party] is convinced that these social and economic objectives can be achieved only through the extension of common ownership substantial enough to give the community power over the commanding heights of the economy. Common ownership takes varying forms, including state-owned industries and firms, producer and consumer cooperation, municipal ownership and public participation in private concerns. Recognizing that both public and private enterprise have a place in the economy it believes that further extensions of common ownership should be decided from time to time in the light of these objectives and according to circumstances, with due regard for the views of the workers and consumers concerned."

The "clarification" led to worse confusion, some laying emphasis on the "reaffirmation", some on the assurance given to private enterprise. The fight grew in bitterness. Cousins told the Scottish conference of his union that Gaitskell's views were not socialist, and the "Victory for Socialism" group called upon Gaitskell to resign. The National Executive thereupon unanimously passed a vote of confidence in him, and the parliamentary party by 179 votes to seven affirmed its "full confidence in the leader of the party". Nevertheless, Gaitskell realized that he would have to abandon the attempt. On 13th July the National Executive passed the following resolution : [5]

"The National Executive resolves not to proceed with any amendment of or addition to clause four of the constitution, but declares the statement which it adopted on 16th March is an invaluable expression of the aims of the Labour party in the second half of the twentieth century and commends it to the conference accordingly."

It had been a gallant effort on Gaitskell's part, but he had misjudged the devotion of the party to its shibboleths and had failed to prepare the ground even in the smallest degree for the great change he was proposing. At the party conference he said it had become obvious that there was throughout the party and the movement very strong feelings about the 1918 constitution, and in the National Executive they felt bound to take note of the obvious feelings that existed.

There was another good reason for dropping the issue before fingers became too badly burnt, and Gaitskell did not conceal it. "It was quite clear that we were going to have a major division over defence, and we did not want to add to the divisions in the party unnecessarily."[6] This battle had, in fact, been joined at the previous day's sitting of the conference. A new statement of Labour's defence policy had been drawn up in June 1960 by the Trades Union Congress, the National Executive and the Parliamentary Labour party. It laid down that Great Britain, while continuing to support the North Atlantic Treaty Organization, should not attempt to maintain an independent nuclear deterrent but should rely on the United States for this weapon. This policy was put to the party conference in October along with three other resolutions—one from the Woodworkers adding that "the realities of international politics make imperative our continued membership of NATO", another from the Transport and General Workers which called "for a complete rejection of any defence policy based on the threat of the use of strategic or tactical nuclear weapons", and yet another from the Amalgamated Engineering Union asking for "the unilateral renunciation of the testing, manufacture, stockpiling and basing of all nuclear weapons in Great Britain". By one of those quirks of procedure under which the Labour party is governed, many unions had committed themselves to unilateralism before the new policy statement was adopted, and it was known that the National Executive's resolution was in danger. It was, in fact, defeated by 3,339,000 votes to 3,042,000, and the Woodworkers' resolution was also defeated, while the resolutions from the Transport Workers and the Engineers were carried by similar majorities. Before this happened Gaitskell asked the delegates to contemplate the position of the parliamentary party:[7]

"It is not in dispute that the vast majority of Labour members of Parliament are utterly opposed to unilateralism and neutralism. So what do you expect them to do? Change their minds overnight? To go back on the pledges they gave to the people who elected them in their constituencies? And supposing they did do that. Supposing all of us, like well-behaved sheep, were to follow the policies of unilateralism and neutralism, what kind of an impression would that make upon the British people? . . .

"We may lose the vote today and the result may deal this party a grave blow. It may not be possible to prevent it, but I think there are many of us who will not accept that this blow need be mortal, who will not believe that such an end is inevitable. There are some of us, Mr. Chairman, who will fight and fight and fight again to save the party we love. We will fight and fight and fight again to bring back sanity and honesty and dignity, so that our party with its great past may retain its glory and its greatness."

The threat to "fight and fight and fight again" was a deliberate challenge that the parliamentary party would ignore the decision of the conference, and in throwing it down Gaitskell raised an issue that had always been implicit in the party's constitution but which most Labour leaders had preferred to keep dormant. As it happened, the issue had been debated the previous day on the basis of two resolutions.[8] One of them stated bluntly, "This conference reaffirms its belief that in a democratic organization decisions should be the result of a majority vote by the membership and instructs the Parliamentary Labour party to carry out fully the decisions arrived at by the party conference"; this was rejected by 5,627,000 votes to 767,000. The other resolution ran:

"This conference reaffirms that the policy of the Labour party to be pursued nationally and in Parliament on questions of principle shall be determined by annual conference. While acknowledging that the day to day tactics in Parliament must be the job of the Parliamentary Labour party, this conference declares that Labour policy is decided by the party conference, which is the final authority."

The National Executive thought it politic to accept this resolution, but the deputy general secretary, Len Williams, in announcing the acceptance made a number of qualifications to emphasize the autonomous nature of the parliamentary party, and the issue was left ambiguous. It was still ambiguous a year later, for Gaitskell was so successful in his threat "to fight and fight and fight again" that he persuaded the conference to reverse its decision, and a direct clash between the conference and the parliamentary party was thus avoided. In the meantime deep waters had been stirred. On 13th October 1960, in the week following the conference that rejected the official policy on the nuclear deterrent, Anthony Greenwood, a leading unilateralist, resigned from the "shadow Cabinet" and the following day he made known that, if no stronger candidate were forthcoming, he would stand against Gaitskell for the leadership; he added, a little curiously, that he would do so for the sake of unity in the party. The stronger candidate was not long in appearing. Within a week Harold Wilson announced that he was willing to stand, also as a unity candidate, and Greenwood withdrew. The unopposed return of Hugh Gaitskell, he declared, would be taken "as a mandate from his parliamentary colleagues to defy conference, to ignore the National Executive committee, and plunge the movement into still worse conflict". His own remedy for re-establishing unity was "a willingness to restate the National Executive committee's defence policy on a basis which could be accepted with dignity by Labour

M.P.s but which at the same time reflected the fact that important pronouncements had been made at the Scarborough conference".[9]

Gaitskell thus became the first leader of the Labour party to be challenged for re-election; but Wilson was still regarded at that time with some suspicion, and collected only eighty-one votes to his 166. It was much the same as Aneurin Bevan's following when he was the darling of the left. To fill the place left vacant by Bevan, the right-wing trade unionist George Brown was elected after a challenge from Barbara Castle. The moderate chief whip, H. W. Bowden, defeated a challenge from Ben Parkin. In the elections to the parliamentary committee that followed, Wilson dropped from first to ninth place, and of the other eleven elected members only one, Fred Lee, was opposed to Gaitskell's decision to "fight" against the Scarborough decision.

Fortified by the almost unanimous support of the parliamentary party, Gaitskell took the fight to the country. At meetings he was often greeted by an organized barrage of heckling and shouts of "Gaitskell must go". To counter this movement W. T. Rodgers and others organized a Campaign for Democratic Socialism, and won a measure of success among the constituency parties. What was more important was that the unions who had defeated the platform at Scarborough began gradually to change sides. In February 1961 the National Executive, the parliamentary party and the General Council hammered out a new statement on defence called *Policy for Peace*. The essential element in it was that the West could not renounce nuclear weapons so long as they were in the possession of the Communist *bloc*, but Great Britain should give up the attempt to be an independent nuclear power. During the spring of 1961 the Union of Shop Distributive and Allied Workers, the Amalgamated Engineering Union and the National Union of Railwaymen approved the new statement of policy. The example proved contagious, and in all thirteen unions which had cast 1,551,300 votes in favour of unilateralism at Scarborough decided to change. The Transport and General Workers' Union, under Cousin's leadership, remained obdurate, but the card vote of the Electrical Trades Union was no longer available for unilateralism as that union was expelled from the Trades Union Congress and disaffiliated from the Labour party after the "fraudulent and unlawful devices" used by Communists to obtain control over it had been exposed in a High Court action.[10] When the vote to approve *Policy for Peace* was taken at the party conference in October the figures were 4,526,000 for and 1,756,000 against. "Sanity and honesty and dignity" had been brought back, but the unilateralists had some satisfaction in persuading the conference to pass resolutions demanding the removal of the United States Polaris base from Great Britain and condemning the training of German troops in Great Britain.

Gaitskell ignored these resolutions in his subsequent actions in Parliament, as he could well afford to do, for his success in routing the advocates of unilateral disarmament and reversing the conference decision gave him an unassailable position in the movement. Yet he seems to have realized that he must not try his opponents' patience too far, and when the next great issue arose, the question whether Great Britain should enter the European common market, he took a line at variance with his general outlook that delighted his old enemies in the party as much as it perplexed most of his friends. To understand how this issue arose, it is necessary to return to Macmillan's leadership of the Conservatives.

The surprisingly massive Conservative victory of 1959, against all the rules of form, gave Macmillan a commanding position in the party. Heathcoat Amory's resignation from the Exchequer in July 1960, wisely timed before the economic winds turned unkind, gave him the opportunity to remould the Cabinet nearer to his desire. Selwyn Lloyd was asked to fill the vacant place at the Exchequer, while the Earl of Home took his place at the Foreign Office, and displayed an immediate mastery of that department. Hailsham became Lord President, and Edward Heath took his place as Lord Privy Seal, with new Foreign Office responsibilities. Butler remained Home Secretary and chairman of the party organization until 1961. In that year he was succeeded in the latter post by Iain Macleod, who gave up the full-time office of Colonial Secretary to which he had been appointed in 1959 and took the sinecure of the Duchy of Lancaster. Macleod combined his party and ministerial duties with the leadership of the Commons. In these years Macmillan used his undisputed position in the party to bring about two major reorientations in Conservative policy. One was in the Conservative attitude to the British Empire, the other in the Conservative attitude to continental Europe. They were not entirely unconnected.

From the time of Beaconsfield, as we have noticed, the imperial vision had taken possession of the Conservative party, and devotion to the British Empire had assumed almost an equal place with devotion to the Crown among the tenets of Conservatism. Yet, in fact, the men who built up the British Empire were pursuing two irreconcilable ideals. One was to create a nation-wide political and economic entity of which Great Britain should be the centre, the other to advance the peoples of the dependent territories until they were capable of self-finance, self-defence and self-government. Owing to the geographical separation of the component parts of the British Empire and the wide disparity of its races and creeds, it was inevitable that the second conception should prevail. When the dominions peopled mainly by British stock achieved the complete management of their own affairs, the British Empire became the British Commonwealth and Empire, and this was recognized in 1926. It was not yet evident that the territories peopled by non-British stocks would go the same way, but we have already noticed how a lead was given in 1943 when, under a Conservative Secretary of State, Oliver Stanley, Jamaica was given a new constitution on the basis of universal adult suffrage. The example was not lost upon other dependent territories, and it soon became as much out of the question to delay as to deny the march to independence. In this process of evolution from Empire to Commonwealth Conservative statesmen were not one whit behind their Labour counterparts, but Conservative thought and Conservative language about the Empire, especially in the constituencies, lagged behind Conservative action at Westminster and in Whitehall.

It was one of the achievements of Harold Macmillan's period as Prime Minister to lead the Conservative party to adjust itself to the new currents and thereby to accelerate the transformation of the British Empire into the British Commonwealth. Whereas Churchill had declared[11] that he had "not become the King's first minister in order to preside over the liquidation of the British Empire", Macmillan recognized that in the old sense of the word the Empire must die to be reborn as a Commonwealth of free nations. With typical courage he chose the occasion of a speech to the South African Parliament at Cape Town on 3rd February 1960 to enunciate his thoughts:[12]

"In the twentieth century, and especially since the end of the war, the processes which gave birth to the nation-states of Europe have been repeated all over the world. We have seen the wakening of national consciousness in peoples who have for centuries lived in dependence on some other power.

"Fifteen years ago this movement spread through Asia ... Today the same thing is happening in Africa. The most striking of all the impressions I have formed since I left London a month ago is of the strength of this African consciousness. In different places it may take different forms, but it is happening everywhere.

"The wind of change is blowing through the continent. Whether we like it or not, this growth of national consciousness is a political fact."

The wind of change soon developed gale force. The Union of South Africa felt obliged to leave the Commonwealth and became a republic. Iain Macleod, as Secretary of State for the Colonies, made clear that Kenya would become an African state. The white settlers in Southern Rhodesia saw the writing on the wall; and throughout all the dependent territories from Fiji to British Guiana the wind of change blew old ideas of empire away. Under Macmillan's leadership the Conservative party accepted these momentous changes with hardly a tremor. The League of Empire Loyalists, formed mainly out of dissident, right-wing Conservatives, organized some heckling at meetings, but this was no more than a pin-prick. The Conservative party, as always in its long history, accepted the inevitable with good grace and assured itself that this had always been its aim—that the end of Empire in one sense of that ambiguous word had also been its end in the other.

As the dream of imperial political and economic unity faded, it became natural in a world dominated by super-states to look in other directions for means of strengthening British trade and British influence in the world, and in no direction more naturally than to Great Britain's geographical neighbours across the North Sea and the English Channel who were already organizing themselves into a greater unity. Tentative moves in the direction of closer association among the countries of Europe reached a decisive stage with the signing of the Treaty of Rome in 1957 by "the Six" (Belgium, France, Germany, Italy, Luxembourg and the Netherlands) which established the European Economic Community. Great Britain and six other countries outside the European Economic Community then established the European Free Trade Association, but it was never meant to be a rival to the community, and efforts were made to see how the two could be reconciled. When Heath was appointed Lord Privy Seal in 1960 this was made his main responsibility. After a full study of alternatives the government came to the conclusion that the only way forward was for Great Britain to seek membership of the European Economic Community and sign the Treaty of Rome. On 3rd August 1961 the following motion was voted upon in the House of Commons: [13]

"That this house supports the decision of her Majesty's government to make formal application under Article 237 of the Treaty of Rome in order to initiate negotiations to see if satisfactory arrangements can be made to meet the special interests of the United Kingdom, of the Commonwealth and of the European Free Trade Association; and further accepts the undertaking of her Majesty's government that no agreement affecting these special interests or involving British sovereignty will be entered into until it has been approved by this house after full consultation with other Commonwealth countries, by whatever procedure they may generally agree."

It was a historic departure from policy, and the drama was heightened by the consciousness that the decision was being taken forty-seven years to the day after the famous debate in which Edward Grey led a virtually united House of Commons into a great European war. That decision was in the grand line of British policy from Tudor times onwards—the maintenance of the balance of power in Europe, and in particular the prevention of control over the Low Countries falling into the hands of a major continental power. Throughout its long history the Conservative party had identified itself wholeheartedly with this policy, which was indeed

R

considered by statesmen and diplomatists alike as an axiom of British existence. A second great war in 1939, which was really a continuation of the first, demonstrated the need to find a better way, and Macmillan had come to the conclusion that the better way lay, not in the division of Europe, but in its unification; and that British interests were better served, not by standing aloof from the continent but in becoming part of it.

This had not been a sudden discovery. He had accompanied Churchill to the congress at The Hague in 1948 when European unity first began to take shape. When Churchill returned to office in 1951 and nothing was done to carry out the ideals of The Hague, it was alleged that the Tory enthusiasm for European unity had been only a stick with which to beat the Labour government. In truth there was a great deal of educational work to be done, and not least within the Conservative party itself, before statesmen could make practical proposals to other governments or to the British Parliament. For centuries suspicion of foreigners had been a leading trait of the average Englishman in the isolation of his island home. "Frogs, wops, wogs and dagoes" were a few of the choice epithets with which they were distinguished. It needed a revolution in British thinking to regard continental Europeans as brothers and potential fellow-citizens. The establishment of the common market hastened the process by making it a matter of self-interest. Even so, Macmillan and Heath had to walk warily in their advocacy of seeking entry. There were three matters on which the Conservative party would specially need to be reassured. One was that the interests of the British Commonwealth were not being sacrificed to Europe, for although Commonwealth trade was becoming a smaller fraction of the whole, sentimental attachment to the Commonwealth was still strong. A second was the position of British agriculture, and this was the chief of the "special interests of the United Kingdom" mentioned in the House of Commons resolution. The third was the maintenance of British sovereignty. These were delicate matters, but Macmillan and Heath were able to convince the Conservative party both in Parliament and in the country. The House of Commons motion was approved by 313 votes to five, the Labour party officially abstaining after its reasoned amendment had been rejected by 318 votes to 209. In carefully framed resolutions put before the less sophisticated audiences of the party conferences of 1961 and 1962, the Conservative leadership emphasized the special conditions for British entry and won overwhelming majorities. At the 1961 conference the resolution asked for a "form of closer association with the 'Six' compatible with our Commonwealth and European Free Trade Association responsibilities, economic and political, and our pledges to British agriculture".[14] The 1962 conference expressed "confidence in the government's determination to find adequate safeguards for our special interests and those of our partners in the Commonwealth and the European Free Trade Area".[15] Though the Conservative party would not have agreed to entry without safeguards, it had taken a decisive and historic turn in its attitude to continental Europe. There was opposition ably led by two former Ministers of Health, R. H. Turton and Sir Derek Walker-Smith, but it was listened to with more respect than conviction. The respective attitudes of the Conservative and Labour parties to the question of European union make a fascinating and somewhat paradoxical study. It might have been expected that the Labour party with its professions of international solidarity, its many links with socialist parties and trade union movements abroad and its frequent denunciations of the evils of nationalism and unrestricted sovereignty would have taken the lead in promoting European unity, whereas it would not have been surprising if the Tory party, with its long tradition of flag-wagging and beating the nationalist and imperialist drum and "making the foreigner pay", had looked askance at all advances towards closer association with other countries. In fact, it was the Conservative party that adjusted itself more quickly to the necessities of a new international order, whereas the old insular prejudices against foreigners found their strongest continued expression in the Labour party. Though Ernest Bevin, by reading more into General Marshall's words than they really contained, had initiated the Organization for European Economic Cooperation, his motive was primarily to get American aid, and he frowned upon the congress at The Hague. Labour members were asked not to take part, and only a few defied the ban. The Brussels treaty of 1948 was limited to defence and cultural and social cooperation. In opposition the Labour party, while still advocating international brotherhood in general, was almost chauvinistic in its attitude to this particular form of it. Nevertheless, many of the most gifted members of the party, especially Roy Jenkins, were warm advocates of Great Britain's adhesion to the common market, and it came as a shock to them when Gaitskell at the party conference of October 1962 at Brighton came out strongly against the plan.

"What exactly [he asked[15a]] is involved in the concept of political union? ... It may mean that there is no obligation upon the government of Britain to do more than talk, to consult more frequently with the President of France and the Chancellor of Germany ... The second possibility is majority decisions on political issues, just as we are to have majority decisions on economic issues . . . Then, of course, there is the idea and ideal of federal Europe ... We must be clear about this: it does mean, if this is the idea, the end of Britain as an independent European state. I make no apology for repeating it. It means the end of a thousand years of history."

Gaitskell's previous record had not prepared anyone for so

vehement an expression of hostility. In the crucial debate in the House of Commons, as we have noted, the Labour party abstained from voting when its own reasoned amendment was rejected. It is difficult to avoid the conclusion that Gaitskell's feeling against the common market hardened precisely as the Conservatives warmed towards it, and that this hardening had an element of political calculation in it. The change certainly won back for him the support of the left that he had alienated by his attitude to clause four and nuclear weapons. His prestige in the party stood higher than ever at the close of the Brighton conference, and outside the party he had gained the support of that amorphous mass of public opinion which took its lead from the Beaverbrook press. At the November elections in the Parliamentary Labour party he was not opposed, and this time Wilson discreetly reserved his challenge for the post of deputy leader. He was decisively beaten by George Brown by 133 votes to 103. The members of the parliamentary party may have thought that Gaitskell and Brown would make a more harmonious team than Gaitskell and Wilson. It seemed that the party reunited under Gaitskell's leadership must go forward irresistibly to victory at the next general election. Once more fate took control of the situation. Within a few months Gaitskell was battling for his life with a kidney infection and did not survive.

The question of the leadership of the Labour party was again thrown wide open by Gaitskell's death. As deputy leader George Brown had a claim to the succession but no right of pre-emption. The qualities needed for a deputy leader are very different from those needed in a leader. Wilson, then in America, hastened back and left no doubt that he would be a candidate. The right and the left wings of the party began to range themselves round Brown and Wilson respectively. Wilson's conduct in the Labour party to that date—his resignation along with Bevan, his acceptance of Bevan's place in the "shadow Cabinet", his challenge to Gaitskell in the name of unity—had left an impression of opportunism that did not endear him to the solid mass of trade union and right-wing opinion. Unfortunately for them Brown was not the strongest candidate that they could have wished to oppose to Wilson. He was a likeable man of sound common-sense instincts and patriotism, and with a lively untrained mind, but liable to emotional outbursts which made even his admirers wonder whether he could safely be placed in supreme charge of the nation's affairs. At this moment the right-wing element missed Alfred Robens, who had been persuaded to leave the House of Commons in 1961 to become chairman of the National Coal Board. In 1961 and 1962 the Labour party in the House of Commons lost not only Robens but three other of its best men—Geoffrey de Freitas, who became High Commissioner to Ghana, Hilary Marquand, who was appointed Director of the International Institute for Labour Studies, and Kenneth Younger, made Director-General of the Royal Institute of International Affairs. It was inevitable that able men, wearying of a long period in opposition, should welcome the opportunity of addressing themselves to executive tasks worthy of their powers. Some commentators saw in Macmillan's invitation to Robens and de Freitas—he had no responsibility for the others—a generous impulse towards political opponents typical of the British party system, others detected a Machiavellian cunning in removing the ablest rivals. There can be little doubt that if Robens had been available the trade union and right-wing members of the Parliamentary Labour party would have ensured his election as leader. Brown did not command the same support, but he looked, nevertheless, like being a formidable opponent to Wilson when the entry of James Callaghan, the "shadow Chancellor", into the contest upset previous calculations. He had no possibility of winning, and it is hard to see what he had to gain from his candidature except staking out a claim for future years. As he was generally on the right of the party in his policies though occasionally on the left in his language, any votes that he gained would be likely to be taken from Brown. The right-wing members had reason to be disturbed by his candidature for the results of the first ballot, announced on 7th February 1963, were: Wilson 115, Brown eighty-eight, Callaghan forty-one. By the rules of the election Callaghan dropped out and a second ballot was held. If all Callaghan's votes had gone to Brown, the latter would have won by a comfortable margin, but by this time the principle of the band-wagon had come into play and many who had voted for Brown or Callaghan hastened to rally to the victor of the first ballot. The final figures, announced on 14th February, were: Wilson 144, Brown 103. Brown accepted the result graciously and remained deputy leader. As leader of the party Wilson showed adroitness and subtlety. In the game of parliamentary tactics he rarely lost a trick, and he proved himself a master of the biting phrase, but he seldom stirred the depths of feeling as MacDonald or Gaitskell had done.

His task was made easier by the fact that the Conservative government had by this time run into heavy weather. The good fortune that led to Macmillan being described by the cartoonists as "Super-Mac" and "Macwonder" had evaporated. The spur to economic activity given in the election year, 1959, had been so successful that a curb to restrain excessive demands became necessary. In January 1960 the bank-rate was raised to five per cent, and a tough budget in 1960 was followed by a still tougher one in 1961. The pressure on sterling nevertheless increased, and in July the bank-rate was raised to the exceptional level of seven per cent, a large sum was borrowed from the International Monetary Fund, import duties were increased, the banks were called upon to restrict advances and the Chancellor called for a pause in wages and salaries (the "pay pause") until productivity caught up and there was room for further advances. These measures proved successful in stopping the drain on sterling, but were in some danger of braking the home economy too sharply, and by 1962 the bank-rate was brought down to $4\frac{1}{2}$ per cent, tax remissions were made in the budget and hire purchase restriction eased.

The severity of the economic measures produced a sharp fall in the Conservative party's popularity which benefited the socialists but advantaged the Liberals even more for a season. A by-election at Orpington on 14th March 1962 gave a sharp jolt to the government. At the general election the Conservative candidate had a majority of 14,760 over his Labour opponent with the Liberal just behind in third place. At the by-election the Liberal, E. R. Lubbock, was returned with a majority of no less than 7,855 over the Conservative with Labour beaten well into third place. The Liberal vote increased from 9,092 to 22,846, the Conservative decreased from 24,303 to 14,991, and the Labour vote from 9,543 to 5,350. All the national discontents with the Conservative party, and a good many local ones as well, were thrown into the ballot-boxes at Orpington. It was evident from the figures that many who had voted Conservative at the general election had transferred their votes to the Liberal, and that not a few who then voted Labour had also switched their votes, not necessarily because they had changed their beliefs, but in the justified expectation that the Liberal had a better chance of winning. At a by-election in the mid-term of a government electors will take liberties with their party that they would not take at a general election. Orpington was nevertheless hailed as the beginning of another Liberal revival, and Grimond held before his followers the prospect of becoming, instead of Labour, the second party in the state. The Liberals retained Montgomeryshire with an increased vote at a by-election following the death of Clement Davies, and in a few Labour-held seats beat the Conservative into second place, but their success at Orpington was not repeated. As the statutory term of Parliament drew near, fewer disgruntled Tories or calculating socialists allowed themselves the luxury of voting Liberal. The reality of the party system as a struggle between two giant organizations again became obvious, and Orpington fell into perspective as a protest by a middle-class dormitory town against local and national grievances.

The protest was not disregarded in the quarter to which it was specially directed. On 12th July 1962 the Conservative candidate in a by-election at North-east Leicester was beaten into a bad third place by the Liberal. The following day Macmillan carried through the most sweeping reconstruction of the Cabinet recorded in British political history. Awed commentators spoke of the night of the long knives. Of the twenty-one Cabinet ministers, no fewer than seven went out of office, and among them were the Chancellor of the Exchequer, Selwyn Lloyd, and the Lord Chancellor, Kilmuir, who by any standard must have been reckoned among the first six men of the Tory party. It was not only the deed but the manner in which it was done that rankled. Only in the case of Lloyd was there time for the customary exchange of letters before a public announcement— for this the danger of premature disclosure by the press was blamed. It is not usual for a former Prime Minister to comment on his successor's reconstructions, but Lord Avon, speaking in his old constituency, took it upon himself to say: "I feel that Mr. Selwyn Lloyd has been harshly treated, but I have no doubt that he will serve the nation again in high office."[16]

The changes were not confined to the Cabinet. On 16th July nine other ministers were removed. Mr. Gladstone's saying, "A Prime Minister has to be a bit of a butcher", has often been quoted by his successors, but no one previously had carried out butchery on this scale. The reconstruction brought home the great constitutional change in modern times by which the Prime Minister was ceasing to be merely *primus inter pares* and was on the way to becoming a president on the American model. Macmillan no doubt wished to indicate to the country in unmistakable terms that a new approach would be made to the problems that had given rise to discontent. In particular, he wished to indicate in the clearest possible way that the policy of restraint and restriction was finished, and that growth and expansion were the order of the day. The former member for Stockton-on-Tees must have found it increasingly difficult to acquiesce in the policy of the heavy hand at the Exchequer, which he had found even before the war to be as damaging to the Tory party's reputation as it was to the nation's economy. Sensing the change, Lloyd in his letter accepting dismissal expressed his anxiety that "the growth of public expenditure, so much of it highly desirable in itself, should not outstrip our resources".[17] He was assured that the government would continue on the path he had prepared; and, in truth, Lloyd's own foot had already been transferred from the brake to the accelerator even before the reconstruction. The accelerator was now to be pressed down harder.

In the course of the changes, Butler's position as the second man in the government was recognized with the formal title of Deputy Prime Minister; he ceased to be Home Secretary and was given the new post of First Secretary of State with the oversight of Central African affairs (then a contentious question between the parties) and the problems of joining the common market. Maudling took Lloyd's place at the Exchequer, and Manningham-Buller, with the title Lord Dilhorne, went to the Woolsack. Henry Brooke took Butler's place at the Home Office. While heads were rolling all around them,

Home, Macleod and Hailsham were undisturbed. Like Sieyès, they could claim that they had survived. Along with Butler and Macmillan himself they had become the hard core of the Conservative party.

The changes, for all their drama, did not result in an immediate improvement in the Conservative party's fortunes. When Macmillan next entered the House of Commons, he was coldly received by his party. An isolated act of ruthlessness may lead to a wave of admiration for a Prime Minister's strength, but on this occasion the victims were too numerous and too influential. What had been the lone voice of Sir Harry Legge-Bourke calling for Macmillan's resignation early in 1961 now became an under-current in the party, and the cry was taken up by more powerful men, notably Nigel Birch, who had resigned office for much the same reasons that led to Lloyd's displacement.

The changes might still have succeeded in their intention if the new economic policies could have had an instantaneous effect, but there is an inevitable delay of several months in such matters. The old deflationary policies were still working their way through the economy when the Conservatives met in conference in October, and members of that once sedate body could not resist the onomatopoeic satisfaction of chanting, "Stop daudling, Maudling." In that month the number of unemployed in Great Britain rose above half a million for the first time since the winter of 1958–9—a figure that would have given satisfaction at any time up to the Second World War, but had now become unacceptable to the public conscience— and the number rose in January to a peak of 814,632, the highest since the disastrous winter of 1947 which had helped to undo the Labour government. The incidence of unemployment in particular areas was much higher than the national average. It was no satisfaction to the unemployed of Scotland and the north-east coast that there was plenty of work in Birmingham and London.

Domestic difficulties might have been compensated by a success in the field of foreign policy, and the common market might have provided the best stimulus for the sluggish home economy. If Macmillan had been successful in leading this country into new arrangements with continental Europe, it would have been a great historic event on which he might have ridden to fresh triumphs at an early general election, but he was cheated of the hope. In January 1963 General de Gaulle put his veto finally upon British entry, and Macmillan, broadcasting on a decision that was "bad for us, bad for Europe, and bad for the whole free world",[18] had to confess that he had no ready-made alternative plan.

A party in difficulties generally looks to its organization, and this gave an opportunity of offering some amends to Selwyn Lloyd, who had loyally refused either to lead a rebellion or to form a cave. At the Conservative conference in October 1962 it was announced[19] that he had accepted an invitation from the chairman of the party, Macleod, to conduct a one-man inquiry into "the relationship and liaison between members of the party in Parliament, the party headquarters, the National Union and the party in the constituencies", and "to review the reports of the committee on Party Organization 1948 and 1949 [Maxwell-Fyfe Committee] and to recommend any changes made necessary to meet present conditions". His recommendations made in May 1963[20] were of a minor character, and rightly so; it was not defects in organization that had led to the fall in the Conservative party's popularity.

In the spring of 1963 the expansionary measures taken by Maudling began at last to have their effect. Bank-rate had been reduced to four per cent in January, unemployment and sickness benefits had been increased in March, reliefs were given to income-tax payers in the April budget and pensions were raised in May. Unemployment fell, productivity increased, exports increased and the gross national product began to grow at a satisfactory rate. It looked as though the pattern of events before the 1959 election might be repeated, but a wholly unexpected and cruel turn of fortune thrust the Conservative party back into the shadows just as it was hoping to emerge.

On 14th March there began the trial of a West Indian accused of shooting with intent to murder a young woman named Christine Keeler. She was not to be found when the proceedings began. On 21st March a Labour member of Parliament, George Wigg, invited the Home Secretary to deny rumours linking Christine Keeler with a member of the government front bench. At 3.30 a.m. that night the Secretary of State for War, John Profumo, who had been summoned from his bed, met the leader of the House of Commons (Macleod), the chief whip (Redmayne), the Attorney-General (Sir John Hobson), the Solicitor-General (Sir Peter Rawlinson) and the Minister without Portfolio (William Deedes). His solicitor was also present. They accepted what he told them and helped him to draft a statement to be made in the Commons later in the day. In the course of the statement[21] he said: "My wife and I first met Miss Keeler at a house party in July, 1961, at Cliveden. Among a number of people there was Dr. Stephen Ward, whom we already knew slightly, and a Mr. Ivanov, who was an attaché at the Russian embassy ... There was no impropriety whatsoever in my acquaintanceship with Miss Keeler." On 4th June he wrote to the Prime Minister tendering his resignation, which was accepted, on the ground: "In my statement I said that there had been no impropriety in this association. To my deep regret I have to admit that this was not true, and that I misled you, and my colleagues, and the house."[22]

There is no spectacle so ridiculous, as Macaulay said, as the British public in one of its periodical fits of morality, and it is not necessary here to discuss the ethical issues of a case that shook British politics as nothing had done since Parnell and Dilke were ruined by their association with women not their wives. The main point of political interest lay in the fact that Profumo admitted impropriety with a young woman who had also been friendly with a Russian attaché. It was soon established that no secret information had passed, but the incident came after a series of trials in which persons had been convicted of spying or violating the Official Secrets Act. A junior minister whose private secretary had been sent to prison had resigned so as not to be an embarrassment to the government—he was later most properly restored to office—and the removal of his chief had been most unfairly demanded by a section of the press. The government were therefore vulnerable on this issue, and the Prime Minister, being responsible for the security services, was the special target for attack. Upon Macmillan was cast, not only the morals of his ministers but the discretion of every clerk in the Civil Service. The Labour party could be expected to seize every opportunity of using the incident to bring down the government; and now for the first time there arose within the Conservative party itself a serious move to bring about Macmillan's resignation. In the debate on the Profumo affair on 17th June the government's normal majority of nearly 100 fell to sixty-nine; twenty-seven Conservatives abstained, and in debate one of them, Birch, compared Macmillan to "The Lost Leader" of Browning's poem and savagely said,[23] "Let him never come back to us," for there could be "never glad confident morning again". Macmillan could justly have asked his colleagues to relieve him of the burden of office. He was sixty-nine years of age, he had been Prime Minister for a longer period than anyone in the century save Asquith, he had earned the gratitude of his country for restoring Anglo-American relations after Suez, and he had carried through momentous changes in British policy towards the dependent territories and towards Europe. If he seemed to others to be tiring, he may himself have been conscious that he was suffering from a debilitating complaint common to men of his age. Two years earlier he had said:[24] "I do not intend 'to live after my flame lacks oil to be the snuff of younger spirits'." Yet it was manifest that he, whose name had never been blown upon by the hot breath of scandal, could not possibly resign of his own volition upon the issues that had been raised. He reacted to speculation about his future in a vigorous, even jaunty way. At the annual luncheon of the 1922 Committee on 10th April he told Conservative back benches: "I shall be leading you into the general election and I shall be with you in the new Parliament." This was before Profumo's resignation, but he repeated the assurance, with an important qualification, in a television interview on 28th June: "All being well, if I keep my health and strength, I hope to lead the party into the election . . . Of course, I must have the support of the party and I think I have it."[25] In the meantime he had taken measures to try to ensure that he did have the support of the party. On 17th April he appointed Lord Poole to be joint chairman of the party organization with Macleod. Poole's work as chairman in 1955–7 and as deputy chairman to Hailsham from 1957 to 1959 had won him a high reputation among Conservative workers, by whom he was regarded as a main architect of the Tory victories of the past two general elections. Macleod had inevitably received much of the blame for the Tory decline during his chairmanship, a not unimportant consideration with an election in the offing, and his radical views were not popular, as those of Poole were, in those financial circles which still provided a substantial part of the backing for the Central Office's activities. In his care for organization Macmillan did not neglect policy. On 10th June he asked Hailsham to go to Moscow for the closing stages of the negotiations for a treaty banning nuclear tests on which he had set his heart; at a meeting of the 1922 Committee on 25th July he was able to tell back-benchers that the treaty had been initialled an hour before, and critics were silenced.

There took place in the summer of 1963 a seemingly irrelevant constitutional change that was to prove of major import in the party struggle. The unwillingness of Anthony Wedgwood Benn, a member of the House of Commons, to go to the upper house as Lord Stansgate on the death of his father had led to the setting up in 1962 of a committee on House of Lords reform which was authorized to consider among other topics whether a peer should be allowed to renounce his peerage. At one of its meetings a Labour member, G. R. Mitchison, moved that hereditary peers, who might have been glad to exercise such a right had it existed, should be allowed to renounce within a reasonable time along with the heirs to peerages. His proposal was accepted in the committee by eleven votes to ten, and eventually by Parliament. Furthermore, the Peerage Bill as introduced would come into force at the dissolution of that Parliament. Moving to bring it into force immediately, Gordon Walker taunted the government with wanting "to keep Lord Hailsham out as long as they possibly can". Hailsham, as was well known, had been most reluctant to leave the House of Commons, even to the point of asking the Prime Minister of the day, Attlee, for special legislation, and he had sent to the committee a powerful argument for giving peers who had already taken their seat the right of disclaiming. In the Commons the government secured the defeat of Gordon Walker's amendment, but the Lords by a majority of 105 to twenty-five accepted a similar amendment, making the bill come into force with the royal assent, which had been moved by a Labour peer, Silkin. The government yielded with good grace when the measure returned to the Commons, and the proposal became law.

In the inscrutable workings of providence this Labour-sponsored proposal in a Labour-originated bill was to be the means of solving the problem of the leadership in the Tory party. By August Macmillan had come to realize that the possibility of his leading the Conservative party into the next election was diminishing. If he were not to do so, it was desirable to resign at a fairly early date so as to give the new man an opportunity of playing himself in on a tricky wicket. But who was to be the new man? Butler regarded himself, and was regarded by a large section of the press and the public, as having a natural claim to the succession. In addition to his qualifications of ability and experience, he was now formally Deputy Prime Minister. He was generally regarded as having staked out a claim in a television interview on 8th July when he said:[26] "I did a lot in the years 1945 to 1951 when in opposition, and I think I am pretty well aware that people want us to give a fresh impression of vigour and decision before the next election." But the press and public do not choose the leader of the Conservative party, and among those who do the objections that ruled out Butler in 1957 still told. "Donnish, dignified and dull" was the verdict of one of the jury, Sir Gerald Nabarro.[27] In a subsequent review Macleod has written:[28] "The truth is that at all times, from the first day of his premiership to the last, Macmillan was determined that Butler, although incomparably the best qualified of the contenders, should not succeed him." This is remarkably similar to the charge that Attlee clung on to the premiership in order to keep Morrison out, but the only evidence Macleod gives to support it is that he, Maudling and Heath were advanced to positions of importance by Macmillan and asked to preside over three sessions of a much-publicized week-end at Chequers on the modernization of Britain. This is not convincing. A Prime Minister has always to be looking for talent, and the three ministers invited to chair the Chequers week-end were the obvious three: they had to be concerned with home affairs and they had to be young. Randolph Churchill, whom Macleod is controverting, went perhaps too far in saying:[29] "It can be argued that Macmillan did all he could during his seven years as Prime Minister to advance the fortunes of Butler." The truth is intermediate. A large section of the Conservative party in Parliament did not consider that Butler had enough "fire in his belly" to be their leader; and Macmillan, having already been preferred over Butler for that reason, may be forgiven if six and a half years later he was of the same opinion.

When Butler was ruled out, Macmillan's thoughts turned to Hailsham as the successor likely to be most acceptable to the party. The Peerage Act made it possible for him to be considered, and throughout the early part of 1963 a strong wave of support for him had been reported from the constituencies. To intellectual gifts of the first order he added an oratorical talent that stirred Conservative audiences to enthusiasm and sometimes to frenzy. He had been the darling of the 1958 conferences; and the party looked on him with affection for his part in winning the 1959 election against all odds. If he roused the ire of his Labour opponents more than anyone else on the Tory side, that was a qualification rather than the reverse in the eyes of Tory associations; and anyway it was not the Labour party that chose the Conservative leader. There were objections, however, in quarters that could not be ignored. They were summed up by Nabarro in his series of vignettes of potential Tory leaders as "Ebullient, erudite and erratic", though it is fair to add that he would have been Nabarro's own choice. An interview in which he had dealt censoriously and even angrily with his late colleague, Profumo, was held up as an example of these alleged faults in temperament.

That Hailsham was favoured by Macmillan for the succession was then known to few beyond themselves, and in the ranks of the party other names were also being canvassed. There was Maudling —described by Nabarro as "matey, manly and moneywise"—who held what was generally regarded as the second post in the government, and the joint party chairman, Macleod, neither of whom would have refused a call. A few were asking for Heath, and a much wider circle looked on him as the right man for the next time. No one at this stage appears to have considered Home as a possibility, and he gave no hint that he would be willing to renounce his ancient title to become a candidate.

The approach of the party conference, fixed to open on Wednesday, 9th October, at Blackpool, made it imperative for Macmillan to reach a decision on the question of resigning or continuing. In accordance with custom, he was due to speak at a mass rally on the Saturday after the close of the conference, and he would be obliged in his speech to give some indication. Throughout the week-end and preceding the conference, fortified by the advice of his son, Maurice Macmillan, and his son-in-law, Julian Amery, he inclined to stay. On Tuesday, 8th October, illness intervened. He woke in great pain, and the doctor who arrived at five in the morning diagnosed obstruction of the prostate gland. He nevertheless presided over a Cabinet that morning without revealing to his colleagues, except by the pallor of his countenance, the pain from which he was suffering, and at the end told them he would give his decision in his speech at Blackpool on Saturday. That night his medical advisors decided that he must enter hospital immediately and have an operation. A formal announcement said: "It is expected that this will involve his absence from official duties for some weeks, and he has asked the First Secretary, Mr. R. A. Butler, to take charge of the government while he is away."[30]

It was with this knowledge that delegates assembled at Blackpool on the morning of 9th October. Though the announcement made no suggestion that Macmillan intended to resign—rather the reverse—inevitably canvassing for his successor was heightened. From the traditional Tory point of view it was most unfortunate that Macmillan's illness should have coincided with the conference, for it meant that the conference would take on the character of an American party convention, and the process of evolving a leader, normally carried out in great privacy, would be conducted in a blaze of publicity. An example was seen in the first hour of the conference. As the chairman introduced in order those on the platform, her eye came to an empty chair, and at that very moment Hailsham emerged from the wings to occupy it. He received a tremendous ovation from the delegates, but one man of high standing in the party deplored to the representative of the *Daily Telegraph* "democracy by decibels".[31] The "stop Hailsham" movement had begun. It was to grow in intensity as the week proceeded.

A "stop Butler" movement was also soon under way. On his arrival he had naturally moved into the rooms reserved for the Prime Minister and prepared to make the speech to the mass rally in place of Macmillan. There was some opposition from those who thought it would give him an undue advantage in the struggle for the leadership. The decision lay with the senior officials of the National Union responsible for the conference, and they eventually decided that Butler should make the speech.

On the Wednesday of this fateful week Macmillan was being prepared for his operation, but was visited by the Lord Chancellor and the Foreign Secretary who had remained in London. At this point Macmillan appears for the first time to have told Home that in some circumstances it might be necessary for him to become the leader of the party. Home was reluctant and thought that if enough time were allowed someone would emerge. That same day the correspondent of the *Daily Telegraph* at Blackpool sent a message to his paper saying: "A comparatively new name is beginning to be 'talked up' in the conference and hotel lobbies: the Earl of Home, Foreign Secretary." Yet in the same issue of the *Daily Telegraph* a Gallup poll gave the following answers to the question: "If Mr. Macmillan were to retire, who [sic] would you like to see take his place?"—Hailsham 18 per cent of Conservative voters, Butler 15, Maudling 11, Heath 9, Macleod 6, Selwyn Lloyd 5, Home 3, Don't know 33.[32]

Before going to bed that Wednesday night, Macmillan finally made up his mind to resign, and dictated a letter to Home who, as it happened, was President of the National Union, to read to the conference when he went to Blackpool. The following morning he sent the letter to the Foreign Office and submitted himself to his operation. In the afternoon delegates streamed back into the conference hall as Home read out:[33]

"It is now clear that, whatever might have been my previous feelings, it will not be possible for me to carry the physical burden of leading the party at the next general election. If the operation, which I am to undergo tomorrow, proves successful, it is clear that I will need a considerable period of convalescence. I would not be able to face all that is involved in a prolonged electoral campaign. Nor could I hope to fulfil the tasks of Prime Minister for any extended period, and I have so informed the Queen.

"In these circumstances I hope that it will soon be possible for the customary processes of consultation to be carried on within the party about its future leadership."

Macmillan's letter was a warning to the Conservative party that it must be ready with an agreed new leader for the moment when he resigned. On this occasion the Queen must not be left, as she was in 1957, with the necessity of finding out for herself whom the Conservative party wanted as its leader. It would seem probable that this course was agreeable also to the Crown, which could not in an increasingly democratic age relish the prospect of, in effect, selecting the leader of the Conservative party for it, either by consultations of its own, or by trial and possible error. The phrase in Macmillan's letter that attracted most attention was "the customary processes of consultation". That there were such processes of consultation was not doubted, but no one could describe the nature of the processes or say who were consulted. The words of Ernest Pretyman in moving the invitation to Austen Chamberlain to lead the Conservative party in 1921 were often in men's minds: "Great leaders of parties are not elected, they are evolved."[34]

They could not, however, add, as Pretyman had done: "The leader is there, and we all know it when he is there." The blunt fact was that the customary processes of consultation within the party had broken down, and Macmillan's challenge to the party to agree on a successor let loose a struggle for power in the full view of the nation. To wish to be Prime Minister is an honourable ambition of which no politician need be ashamed, and in modern times the Prime Minister commands so much more power than any of his colleagues that the other great offices of state no longer satisfy as they used to do. In a monastic community Butler, Hailsham, Maudling and Macleod might have exposed themselves to censure if they could not agree on which of them should be the next abbot, but the Conservative party was not a monastery nor were they monks. Their open struggle for the highest position in the state nevertheless temporarily damaged the reputation of the Conservative party and rejoiced the hearts of its opponents.

All four of the principal contenders were due to make speeches at or during the week of the Conservative conference, and each of their speeches could not fail to be regarded as a bid for power by which they would be judged. Macleod opened the "singing competition" on Thursday morning with an appeal for confidence that left the conference in good heart and certainly did nothing to injure his prospects, but he was always regarded as an outside chance rather than a favourite. On Thursday evening Hailsham followed with a rousing speech to the Conservative Political Centre. The content was good, but what chiefly roused the enthusiasm was his reply to a vote of thanks. After explaining that hitherto he had felt it contrary to duty to do any act calculated to undermine the authority of the Prime Minister of the day he added: "It must be obvious to you that that situation no longer obtains just now. I shall continue to try and serve my country honourably as a friend to my colleagues, but I ought to say tonight that my intention is, after deep thought, to disclaim my peerage."[35] The applause that followed his announcement was tumultuous, and the audience began singing: "For he's a jolly good fellow." Hailsham had thrown his coronet into the ring with the approval of Poole, the joint chairman, and in the belief that he was still the choice of Macmillan (as Maurice Macmillan and Amery had assured him the night before), but the old guard of the party were alarmed at the thought of having a leader chosen by public acclaim, and behind the scenes the "stop Hailsham" movement grew.

Maudling's speech was delivered on Friday morning to the conference. It contained plenty of meat from the Treasury counter, but as a bid for the leadership it was uninspiring, and Maudling ceased to be regarded as a serious contender. On Saturday Butler gave the address to the mass rally, and it was broadcast to the nation. It was perhaps the most testing occasion of his life, and he made a polished and competent speech, but not one inspiring enough to mark him out from the others as the obvious person to succeed. Normally the speaker at the mass rally has the whole meeting behind him from the first word, but Butler suffered from the disadvantage of knowing that many of the representatives present did not wish him to shine too brilliantly.

The party managers breathed a sigh of relief when the struggle for the leadership could be transferred from the hot-house atmosphere of the Blackpool conference to the more "customary processes of consultation" in London. Until these years the Conservative party had been regarded as possessing an instinct for survival, whereas the Labour party seemed possessed by an instinct for suicide; but now the Conservative party seemed bent on self-destruction, whereas the Labour party carefully avoided any step that would jeopardize its bid for power. The conference had settled nothing, though some deduced that the local associations would have chosen Hailsham, that Butler would have been the choice of his Cabinet colleagues, and that Maudling or Macleod might have been the choice of the party in Parliament. When it was clear that no one among them was prepared to stand down, and that no one had a clear lead or was universally acceptable, an increasing number of eyes began to look towards Home as the solution of the party's dilemma. Though he had made no suggestion that he would be willing to become a candidate, and had even let it be known discreetly that he thought Hailsham the right man, his readiness to await a call rather than to advance his claims was considered a becoming qualification in the competitive atmosphere of Blackpool. His claims were, in fact, considerable, for apart from his ancient lineage, seldom a disadvantage in the Tory ranks, his speeches as Foreign Secretary had impressed the party by their forthrightness; and during the Friday morning session of the conference he made a speech on foreign affairs that increased still further his standing in the eyes of the representatives present. Though he offered "a prize to any newspaper man this morning who can find any clue in my speech that this is Lord Home's bid for leadership",[36] the purely adventitious fact that he was President of the National Union that year, and as such the bearer of Macmillan's letter and the chairman for Butler's speech at the mass rally, concentrated eyes on him and made representatives think of him as a leader. By the close of the Blackpool conference it was clear to many commentators that Home was already emerging as the leader whether he wished it or not. Nigel Birch, who had made such a devastating attack on Macmillan, saw Home as the successor with unique clarity, and he made a special journey to Blackpool towards the end of the conference to communicate his discovery to others. He found willing ears.

When the problem was transferred to London, Macmillan, though still in hospital, had recovered from the sedatives administered for his operation and once more took command of the situation. It was clear to him by this time that the opposition to Hailsham was too formidable for that resourceful minister to succeed, and other ways had to be found of resolving the situation. On the Monday afternoon, 14th October, according to Churchill,[37] he dictated "a memorandum ... of a magisterial character" in which he recommended to Butler that the Lord Chancellor (Dilhorne) should sound the Cabinet, that the chief whip in the Commons (Redmayne) should sound Conservative members of that house, that the chief whip in the Lords (St. Aldwyn) should gather the opinions of Conservative peers who regularly took the whip, and that three officers of the party (Lord Poole, Mrs. Shepperd and Lord Chelmer) should sound the constituency parties as best they could. According to Churchill, on the following day the Cabinet unanimously approved the course proposed by the Prime Minister. Redmayne's account

S

given in a B.B.C. interview is in accord save possibly on the question of date:[38] "As soon as he [Macmillan] was beginning to recover from his operation, he sent out a directive to the Cabinet that there was to be a system of selection which he carefully detailed, in which I as chief whip was to sound the whole of the party in the Commons, the chief whip in the Lords was to sound the active peers in the Lords, the Lord Chancellor was to sound the Cabinet, and the leaders of the National Union were to collect opinion in the country, through the agents, through chairmen, and the Young Conservatives, and candidates and so forth. And all this information was collated and put together." Some of these consultations had already begun even before Macmillan requested them. Dilhorne had been sounding the Cabinet on his own, and John Morrison, chairman of the 1922 Committee, had been trying to ascertain the wishes of backbenchers.

Before the selection of Macmillan in 1957, as we have seen, an effort had been made to ascertain the preferences of members of the Cabinet, Conservative members of the House of Commons, and active Conservative peers. The processes initiated by Macmillan in 1963 were similar, but were made more formal and more complete. An attempt was made to get the views of all Conservative peers and members, even those abroad, while candidates, chairmen and agents were included for the first time, though necessarily in their case the gathering of opinion was more haphazard. Macleod has complained that he and others failed to get a meeting of the Cabinet to consider the leadership, but Dilhorne was constitutionally correct in seeking the views of individual members and was acting within his instructions.

In all such inquiries a great deal depends on the way questions are framed. Such evidence as is available suggests that questions were put in very general terms leaving the persons interrogated free to say anything they thought relevant. The argument that most persons concerned did not at this stage know whether Home would accept a "draft" is not therefore of importance; if they thought he would make the best leader they were free to say so. Redmayne has explained with some precision how he discharged his allotted share of the task. "As far as the Commons was concerned it was done by my whips, each of them taking on their own area of thirty or forty members. They gave me just a simple note of the preferences of each man, of any second or third preference, and of any particular objection he might have to any of the known candidates, plus a great deal of other detail, some of it personal, some of it political, and so forth."

The evaluation of such answers and the reporting of it to the Prime Minister raised problems of their own. In his B.B.C. interview Redmayne was asked, "Did every back-bench M.P. count for one or did some count for more than one," and he replied: "When one came to assess this mass of opinion one had to start by getting what I call a numerical guide about what the situation was; one then had to consider carefully the shade of opinions expressed in various letters and reports." The interviewer observed: "Therefore you would attach more weight to the opinion of some M.P.s than to the opinions of others?" Redmayne acknowledged: "It sounds a little disparaging to the others to say that that is necessarily true, but it would surely be human that, having a fairly comprehensive knowledge of the House of Commons, and since in every organization there must be people on whose opinion one would more strongly rely than on others, one should take a certain objective view of the opinions expressed."

On Tuesday and Wednesday, 15th and 16th October, Macmillan saw almost all his Cabinet colleagues in hospital, individually or in small groups. They may have expressed their personal views, but these had little significance now that the organized collection of opinions was proceeding. By the morning of Thursday, 17th October, the processes were complete. At intervals during the morning Macmillan saw the three officers of the party to get their report of feeling in the country, Dilhorne for the views of Cabinet ministers, Redmayne and Morrison for the views of back-benchers, and St. Aldwyn for the peers. The chief point emerging from the report of the party officials was that the selection either of Butler or of Hailsham would lead to strong resentment in the other camp and disunity in the party. According to Churchill, Dilhorne reported a switch of opinion in the Cabinet so that "the overwhelming consensus now pointed to Home". Macleod has challenged this assessment, saying that some eleven members of the Cabinet were to his knowledge at that time in favour of candidates other than Home. It is not disputed that St. Aldwyn reported an overwhelming majority of the peers in favour of Home. The report that matters most was brought from the House of Commons by Redmayne, and it is fortunately available in his own words. After noting, as quoted above, that it was necessary to take "a certain objective view of the opinions expressed", Redmayne went on: "At the same time I want to make it clear that even on a straight numerical assessment Lord Home was, although marginally, the leader on first choice, and outstandingly the leader as you took it further through the field."[39]

In the afternoon Macmillan saw his morning visitors once more, this time collectively, and asked them to repeat to each other the reports they had made to him. In this way he made sure that there was no misunderstanding and that he could not be accused of distorting the recommendations. With these reports in his hands Macmillan could not fail to come to the conclusion that if, on resigning, he was asked for advice about his successor the answer was bound to be Home—on condition, of course, that he renounced his peerage and found a seat in the House of Commons. By this time, though exactly when is uncertain, Home had agreed to accept the call if it came and to renounce his title. Macmillan prepared a letter of resignation and a memorandum for the Queen collating the four reports made to him.

Macleod had learnt in the afternoon that the choice had been made and would fall on Home. He found this astounding, and according to him Maudling was equally in the dark. "It is some measure of the tightness of the magic circle on this occasion," he has observed,[40] "that neither the Chancellor of the Exchequer nor the leader of the House of Commons had any inkling of what was happening." The suggestion of deliberate exclusion is not justified. As contenders themselves, they could not be invited to take part in such matters as the gathering and assessment of opinion, but although the newspapers predicted until Friday morning that the choice would fall on Butler there were not lacking ample signs for experienced politicians that Home was in fact emerging as the leader. Once he did become aware of what was happening, Macleod did his utmost to prevent it. He believed that the appointment of a peer would create a bad image for the Tory party. After dinner he went round to Enoch Powell's flat, and both spoke to Home on the telephone, trying to persuade him against acceptance. Lord Aldington and Erroll joined them, and Hailsham kept in touch by telephone. "Before long," according to Macleod's account, "it was established that Maudling and Hailsham were not only opposed to Lord Home but believed Butler to be the right and obvious successor, and would be ready and indeed happy to serve under him." This news was communicated by telephone to the chief whip, who came round to see them and promised to convey it to the Prime Minister. The decision came too late. If Hailsham and Maudling had expressed themselves at the opening of the Blackpool conference as ready to serve under Butler, undoubtedly Butler would have become Macmillan's successor and the Conservative party would have been spared a great deal of storm and stress. It was their rivalry to Butler that brought about the emergence of Home. What would have been hailed as an act of statesmanship eight days earlier now appeared merely as a "stop Home" movement.

The following morning, Friday, 18th October, the Prime Minister's private secretary set out for the Palace with a letter conveying his resignation, which the Queen accepted. She intimated that she wished to consult him that morning at his hospital, and arrangements were accordingly made for this unique audience. When she sought his advice on the question of a successor, he begged leave to read the memorandum he had prepared the night before. On returning to the Palace the Queen sent for Home, and afterwards the announcement was made: "The Queen has received the Earl of Home in audience and invited him to form an administration."[41]

The formula, though common enough in older days, was unusual in modern times. Home had not kissed hands as the new Prime Minister, and had merely undertaken to investigate the possibilities of forming a government under himself as Prime Minister. This was no mere archaism, but a measure of the real difficulties that still lay ahead.

Home's first interviews were naturally with Butler, Maudling and Hailsham. The two latter declined to serve unless Butler did so, and Butler at first reserved his position. While waiting for his final word, Home obtained an assurance of support from most of his former colleagues, but Macleod and Powell could not be persuaded to join. Macleod took the line that, having told Home that it would be wrong to accept an invitation to form an administration, he could not honourably serve in that administration. On the Saturday morning Butler agreed to serve, convinced that it was the only way to unite the party, and Maudling and Hailsham then gave their consent. This allowed Home to go to the Palace that morning and kiss hands as Prime Minister. By Sunday afternoon he had completed his Cabinet. Butler took his own place as Foreign Secretary and there were few other changes. Macleod's withdrawal enabled him to bring back Selwyn Lloyd as leader of the House of Commons and so repair one serious rift in the party. Thus ended the most desperate struggle for the leadership ever known in the long history of the Tory party.[41a]

There were consequential changes in the party organization. As Poole had been backing Hailsham, and Macleod was opposed to Home's acceptance of the leadership, they could hardly continue to hold the chairmanship jointly. John Hare, who was ennobled as Viscount Blakenham, was brought back as sole chairman of the party organization, and made Chancellor of the Duchy of Lancaster instead of Minister of Labour. The holding of a paid Cabinet post along with the chairmanship of the party, despite Woolton's justification, was to bring him into trouble with the Labour party.

A by-election in Kinross and West Perthshire gave Home the opportunity of disclaiming his peerage and returning to the House of Commons as Sir Alec Douglas-Home. Some time later the elevation of Sir Wavell Wakefield to the House of Lords provided a vacancy for Hailsham in his father's old constituency. He disclaimed and reverted to the name of Quintin Hogg with which he first appeared in these pages. The Peerage Act had worked in a way hardly intended by the Labour sponsors of the critical amendments that enabled both Home and Hailsham to leave the red benches. Their departure showed the reality of the fears that the act might lower the debating ability of the House of Lords and its effectiveness as a second chamber. Carrington was made leader of the Lords in place of Hailsham and given a place in the Cabinet.

Sir Alec Douglas-Home was formally elected leader of the Conservative and Unionist party at a meeting of peers, members of Parliament, prospective candidates and members of the Executive Committee of the National Union at a meeting held at Church House on 11th November. The motion was proposed by Carrington and seconded by Butler. Discharging this duty for the second time in his life, Butler did it felicitously, and there was no one present who failed to realize that without his readiness to subordinate his personal feelings to the unity of the party the Conservative administration would have disintegrated.

The great question left by the change of leader was whether the Tory party had taken a lurch to the right. This was naturally the line taken by the leader of the Labour party. Speaking at Manchester on the same day, 19th October, that Sir Alec Douglas-Home kissed hands, Harold Wilson said:[42]

"The message that has gone out to the world is that in 1963 the government party in Britain selects its leader and the country's Prime Minister through the machinery of an aristocratic cabal. In this ruthlessly competitive, scientific, technical, industrial age, a week of intrigues has produced a result based on family and hereditary connexions. The leader has emerged, an elegant anachronism. In this so-called opportunity state, in democratic Britain, no one in 1963 can become Conservative Prime Minister unless he has been to Eton, the third in succession. In 350 M.P.s, we are told, there is no one fitted to lead them."

Wilson's strictures were echoed almost word for word from within the party by Macleod. "The only interesting part of Churchill's book," he has written,[43] "is the account of the advice Macmillan tendered: of how, having first supported Hailsham in the decisive days, he switched to Home; of how he organized the collection of opinions by Lord Dilhorne, Lord St. Aldwyn, Lord Poole, Mr. John Morrison and Mr. Martin Redmayne. Eight of the nine men mentioned in the last sentence went to Eton." The one who did not was Redmayne, and it is a curious contradiction in Macleod's argument to ascribe to Redmayne a rôle in the evolution of Home second only to that of Macmillan. It is clear from what has been written above that Home did not become leader because he was an Etonian, but because he offered the best prospect of producing unity in the party, that Butler was not rejected because he was a Marlburian or Maudling because he went to the Merchant Taylors' School, and that Hailsham was turned down despite the glamour of an Eton and Christ Church education which he shared with Home. If the Conservative political families in modern times send their sons mainly to Eton, there will inevitably be many Etonians on the Conservative front bench and in a Conservative Cabinet. "We have confessed," Macleod has said in agreement with Wilson, "that the Tory party could not find a Prime Minister in the House of Commons at all." The struggle for the leadership has left on the minds of others a different impression, namely, that the Conservative party had in the House of Commons at least four members who had the stuff of a Prime Minister in them—Butler, Maudling, Heath and Macleod himself—but a former member of the house was considered to be even better.

The gravamen of Macleod's charge was "that the Tory party for the first time since Bonar Law is now being led from the right of centre". He added: "That this chimes with the wishes of many good Tories who were disturbed and angered by some aspects of our policies these last twelve years need not be doubted. Nor need it be doubted that there is anxiety among those Tories who believed most fiercely in those policies." Wilson made the same point more forcefully in the Manchester speech already quoted:

"How can a scion of an effete establishment appreciate and understand, above all read, the scientific revolution, the mobilization of the skill and talents of all our people in the struggle to restore Britain's position in the world? . . . This is a counter-revolution. After half a century of democratic advance, of social revolution, or rising expectations, the whole process has ground to a halt with a fourteenth earl."

The debating point about his ancestry was neatly answered by Sir Alec himself on television when he observed:[44] "As far as the fourteenth earl is concerned, I suppose Mr. Wilson, when you come to think of it, is the fourteenth Mr. Wilson." A historian might point to the notable contributions to British science made by such scions of effete establishments as Boyle, Cavendish and Rayleigh. Two criticisms would appear to be mutually destructive—that Sir Alec Douglas-Home knew little about home affairs and that he was pursuing a policy to the right of centre.

The question whether a government led by a Prime Minister of patrician descent will pursue a forward- or a backward-looking policy is not one that can be settled by a priori arguments but only in the light of experience. The first test of the new government's policies did not suggest that it was wedded to outworn economic theories, for this was nothing less than the abolition of resale price maintenance, in other words, the abolition of price-fixing by manufacturers. The reason given was the stimulus to efficiency that would be given to British industry by the extension of competition to a wide range of goods of which the price to the consumer had previously been fixed. It represented a further invasion of the Conservative party by the doctrines of laisser faire, and was a substitute for the stimulus that would have been provided by the common market. It was perhaps significant that the minister who had been in charge of the common market negotiations was also in charge of the bill, but he received throughout the backing of the Prime Minister. Under previous legislation it had been possible for the Monopolies Commission and the Restrictive Practices Court to argue that an agreement fixing minimum selling prices was against the public interest, but the new measure, introduced in March 1964, threw on to the manufacturers the onus of proving that such an agreement was in the public interest. When the wind of competition blew more freely through retail trade the government hoped to see a substantial reduction in the cost of living, and in this way trusted to avoid the inflationary tendencies inherent in the pursuit of an expanding economy under conditions of full employment. The Labour party could not very well oppose the measure on principle, as it had declared in 1951 that it would have brought in such a measure itself if it had remained in office[45]—indeed, this could be looked upon as a case of the Conservatives stealing the socialists' clothes while they were bathing—but it hoped to harass the government in committee. The government's main trouble came from its own supporters, and especially from those who argued that under the measure small shopkeepers would be driven out of business by the big stores. On the second reading twenty-three Conservatives in the House of Commons voted against the bill, and nearly forty abstained. There were anxious consultations between the rebels and the government, and some changes were made, but the rebellion continued in committee. The Conservative party still seemed bent on self-destruction.

THE FOURTH LABOUR
GOVERNMENT
1964

Recovery of Conservative unity—and support in the country as measured by the public opinion polls—Parliament allowed to run its full term—the party manifestoes—end of the Daily Herald—*the candidates—a close result indicated—a low turnout—Labour's overall majority of four—Liberal disappointment despite a strong position in the Commons—Labour vote not increased—Conservative defeat due to withdrawal of support—Conservatives resign and Wilson forms the fourth Labour government—"the endless adventure"*

IN the summer of 1964, partly through the avoidance of further controversial issues, partly through consciousness that an election could not be delayed beyond the autumn of 1964, the Conservative party recovered its unity and began to gain in popular esteem. The public opinion polls confirmed the general impression that the Conservatives were cutting down the Labour lead; and the great question for the Conservative managers was whether the election could be held off long enough for them completely to close the gap. The latest statutory date at which the election could be held fell in November, and the problem before the Conservative managers was complicated by the knowledge that their policy of a growing economy was leading to an increase in imports which was not balanced by a compensating increase in exports and might cause a crisis in the balance of payments in the autumn. For this reason the Chancellor of the Exchequer, Maudling, favoured an election in June, but defeat at that time would have been unavoidable and those who urged an extension of time prevailed. In September Douglas-Home made his choice; and an announcement from No. 10 Downing Street in the traditional manner confirmed the general calculation that polling would take place on 15th October.

The Labour party's electoral programme had been broadly settled in *Signposts for the Sixties*,[1] which had been approved by the annual conference at Blackpool in 1961. Its keynote was "planning for expansion". Though the fact of increased prosperity was not denied, it was argued that "our rate of industrial advance has been faltering; and the rapid and continuous expansion required to keep abreast of our competitors has been frustrated". The same note was struck in the party's election manifesto, *The New Britain*, which made a call for "mobilizing the resources of technology under a national plan; harnessing our national wealth in brains, our genius for scientific invention and medical discovery; reversing the decline of the thirteen wasted years;[2] affording a new opportunity to equal, and if possible surpass, the roaring progress of other western powers while Tory Britain has moved sideways, backwards but seldom forward". The manifesto pledged a Labour government to propose the re-negotiation of the Nassau agreement to buy Polaris missiles from the United States, to oppose national nuclear deterrents, and also to oppose the American plan for a nuclear surface fleet manned by crews drawn from different nations. The fury of the great struggle to retain clause four in the constitution was echoed in only two sentences in the manifesto. One of these merely promised to re-organize under full public ownership the water-supply industry, most of which was already publicly owned. The other introduced the most contentious subject of the campaign: "Private monopoly in steel will be replaced by public ownership and control."

Douglas-Home promptly dubbed the Labour proposals "a menu without prices", and their cost was soon queried on every Conservative platform. The Conservative manifesto, *Prosperity with a Purpose*, was introduced in a manner that had now become standard with a personal commendation from the leader. In its title it sought to protect the party from the charge of seeking mere material affluence that had been levelled at it since the days of the slogan attributed to it: "The British people have never had it so good." Like the Labour party, the Conservatives pledged themselves to economic growth—in their case to a steady four per cent a year—and they claimed, in answer to the charge of wasted years, that "in thirteen years of Conservative government the living standards of the British people have improved more than in the whole of the previous half-century". In sharp contrast with the Labour manifesto, the Conservatives laid down that "Britain must in the ultimate resort have independently controlled nuclear power to deter an aggressor".

The Liberal manifesto, *Think for Yourself*, offered the electorate "a radical, non-Socialist alternative"; and as in the manifesto of the two chief parties, economic expansion was assigned "top priority". Claiming Lloyd George and Beveridge as the pioneers of the social security system, it urged that the minimum state pension should be fixed at half the average national earnings. The Communist manifesto, *Britain for the People*, alleged that the Labour, Conservative and Liberal parties were alike dodging the great question, which was "whether big business—the monopolies and the speculators—will continue to dominate our lives or whether the people will challenge monopoly rule and open up a new era of abundance for Britain". A theme common to all the manifestos was that prosperity could be obtained through the ballot-box if only the right choice of party was made.

The Labour party opened its campaign without having the *Daily Herald* as an official organ. The system of dual control established in 1929 whereby the publishers were bound to follow the political and industrial policies laid down by the General Council of the Trades Union Congress had never worked satisfactorily. The editor's necessity of looking over his shoulder to find out what the Trades Union Congress might say had led to a dull paper, and although it had a solid core of over a million loyal readers who bought it because it was the official organ, most Labour voters preferred to seek their news, and sometimes their views, elsewhere. In 1957 the company formed jointly by Odhams Press and the Trades Union Congress to publish the *Daily Herald* handed over publication to Odhams, but as the obligation to follow the policies laid down by the Congress remained there was no improvement. Three years later the T.U.C. reluctantly agreed to abandon their control of political and industrial policy, and gave Odhams a free hand for twenty-five years to develop the paper as they pleased. Odhams undertook to give general support to the Labour movement. When the International Publishing Corporation, owners of the *Daily Mirror* and other papers, acquired control of Odhams, the future of the *Daily Herald* again came under discussion. An agreement was made in 1961 that it should be published under licence by the *Daily Mirror* company, and an undertaking was given that it would be kept going for at least seven years, but still no improvement came. Three years later the decisive step of bringing the *Daily Herald* to an end was taken by agreement. On 14th September the last issue of the *Daily Herald* appeared. On the following day, which by a coincidence was the day on which the dissolution of Parliament was announced, the first number of the *Sun* came off the Odhams presses. Though it resembled the old *Daily Herald* to some extent in appearance, and proclaimed itself "a radical paper", it differed in being free of political control. It was, in fact, published in the same way as any other newspaper. The experiment of a party newspaper was finally admitted to have been a failure.

The Conservative party contested every seat save that of the Speaker. Labour candidates appeared in every division except two in Northern Ireland. The Liberals, making their greatest effort since 1950, put up 365 candidates, not quite equal to the four hundred they had hoped to field, but enough to make a serious challenge. No other party could muster fifty candidates, and under the agreed arrangements no other party was therefore allowed a sound or television broadcast. *Plaid Cymru*, contesting twenty-three of the thirty-six Welsh seats, protested that it never could qualify under the rules made by the larger parties. Scottish Nationalists fought fifteen of the seventy-one seats north of the border, and Irish Nationalists (under the label Republican) contested every one of the twelve Northern Ireland seats. (There was one Republican Labour candidate also.) Communist candidates numbered thirty-six. The Independent Labour party at last faded from the national scene, not fielding a single candidate, but the Socialist Party of Great Britain reappeared with one. A few new party names appeared—the Patriotic party with two candidates, the National Democrats with one, the Taxpayers' Coalition party with one, and there was a Christian Progressive as well as a Social Credit candidate—but it would be rash to assign them any permanent place in the British political scene. The remaining forty-eight candidates represented varying types of independence, sometimes with qualifying labels, sometimes without. Tory dissidence was represented not only by three unofficial Conservatives fighting official candidates for local reasons but by two candidates from the Anti-Common Market League, two Independent Loyalists representing the views of the League of Empire Loyalists, one candidate standing in the name of the British and Commonwealth party, and an Independent Conservative Trade Unionist candidate. There was a Radical Liberal who took on an official Liberal as well as the Labour and Conservative candidates, and even Communism had an Anti-Revisionist candidate representing a breakaway movement. The two candidates of the Independent Nuclear Disarmament Committee represented dissatisfaction with all parties on one major issue. The British National party had one candidate. In all there were 1,757 candidates for the 630 seats, the biggest field since 1950.

More than any other election it was a trial by television, but the candidates still felt obliged to go through the ritual of indoor and outdoor meetings, and a disquieting feature was the refusal of some loutish youthful audiences to give the Prime Minister a hearing.[3] Wilson sought to dominate electioneering to such an extent that his party was chided as a one-man band; and his efforts to bring about a personal confrontation on television between himself and Douglas-Home were rejected on the grounds that his was not a presidential election but a choice between two parties. So indeed it was, but the personality of candidates, usually a negligible factor in the twentieth-century party struggle, seemed to count for rather more than it had done in recent elections, and in some constituencies local issues were paramount. This was particularly true of the control of immigration in areas where coloured persons had settled in large numbers.

As the odour of dissolution grew stronger, the opinion polls had indicated that the election might be the closest-run thing since Waterloo. The *Daily Express* poll gave the Conservatives a lead of 2·3 per cent over Labour as early as the end of August. At that time the Gallup poll conducted for the *Sunday Telegraph* still gave Labour a 6·5 per cent lead, but on 20th September the figure was down to 2·5 per cent and a week later it gave the Tories a lead of 0·5 per cent. The National Opinion poll conducted by the *Daily Mail* was virtually in agreement in putting the Tories ahead by one-fifth of one per cent. Such figures were within the admitted margin of error of the polls, but clearly a Tory victory, the fourth in a row, was again a possibility. The politicians on both sides professed themselves indifferent to the polls, but the psephologists were beside themselves with excitement. It was, however, the high point of the Conservative recovery as measured by the polls. On 4th October Gallup showed Labour back in the lead by a margin of 4·5 per cent, and a week later, with only four days to go, the margin had increased to six per cent.

Much can happen in four days,[4] and the psephologists recollected that Labour needed a lead of nearly three per cent to achieve equality owing to the waste of votes in constituencies with abnormally large majorities. A great deal would clearly depend on the turnout of voters. The electorate had risen by half a million to 35,894,307, and the first of many surprises that the electors provided on 15th October was that the total poll increased by less than half of that figure. Despite all, the percentage of those voting dropped from 78·8 to 77·0. As the first results began to come out, it became manifest that there were considerable local variations in the pattern of voting—to the confusion of those pollsters who claimed on the strength of the swing shown in the first declarations to be able to forecast the majority in the House of Commons. There was undeniably a swing to Labour in most constituencies, but in some there was a swing to the Conservatives, and notably in Smethwick, where Patrick Gordon Walker, already indicated as Labour's Foreign Secretary, lost his seat over the contentious issue of the control of coloured immigration.[5] When all the declarations had come in for the night, Labour had a lead of sixty-seven over all other members elected. As these were mainly urban declarations, the lead would clearly be whittled down as the country results came in the following day; and there was mounting excitement as one county declaration after another bit into the Labour lead. When all the votes were counted, it was seen that the new house would have 317 Labour members, 303 Conservatives, nine Liberals and one non-party member (the Speaker). Labour had a majority of four over all others, or five if the Speaker is omitted. Not since the election of 1847, which produced a Whig majority of one, had there been such a close result; but the election of 1950, which gave Labour a majority of six, was a closer analogue, and recollections of the difficulties of that Parliament diminished the Labour rejoicings and consoled the Conservatives in their disappointment.

These figures deserve a closer analysis. The fact that no Independent (other than the Speaker) and no candidate from a party other than the three principal parties secured election confirmed the dominance of the party system in modern times. Deposits were forfeited by 187 of the defeated candidates, including all thirty-six Communists, all but two of the Welsh Nationalists, all but three of the Scottish Nationalists and seven Irish Republicans. The Liberals increased their representation from six to nine, and although the prospect of being courted by both sides, and almost holding the balance of power, was exhilarating the modest size of the increase was a disappointment to them. With 365 candidates in the field compared with 216 in 1959, they secured 3,101,103 votes against 1,640,760. They were entitled to point out that under proportional representation their share of the popular vote would have given them seventy seats in the House of Commons, but the painful thought remained that the average Liberal vote in constituencies where there was a Liberal to vote for had increased from 7,596 to only 8,496. The increased Liberal vote in by-elections was once again proved to be a protest vote against the other parties rather than evidence of a genuine revival. They held Orpington despite a strong Tory challenge, and they actually registered four wins at Bodmin, Ross and Cromarty, Inverness, and Caithness and Sutherland; but they lost Huddersfield West and Bolton West because the local Tories declined any longer to give them a straight fight with Labour, and they failed to recover Torrington or to capture other seats in the west country where their hopes were high. When the electoral map was redrawn, it was seen that all the Liberal victors were in the Celtic fringe except for Eric Lubbock at Orpington.

Though Labour had scraped home, it also had its disappointments. Its net increase of fifty-six seats was made up of sixty-one gains and five losses, and concealed wide variations in local support. Over the country as a whole there was a swing to Labour of 3·2 per cent of the votes in comparison with 1959, but in Liverpool it was as high as 8·1 per cent and in the west Midlands as low as 2·2 per cent, while in Norfolk and Suffolk it was only 1·6 per cent. There were seven seats in the Midlands that swung away from Labour, and the Conservatives actually gained one seat in Norfolk. Labour's most satisfying gain was at Kemp Town division of Brighton, won by seven votes after seven recounts, which gave the party its first footing ever in the county of Sussex. The first glow of enthusiasm over the seats gained was cooled as the figures for the total popular vote became available. Despite the increase in the electorate, Labour's total vote was ten thousand down on its 1959 figure—12,205,581 instead of 12,216,172; and Labour's share of the total votes cast increased only slightly from 43·8 to 44·1 per cent. It was clearly not a positive increase of support for Labour policies and personalities that had put Harold Wilson and his colleagues in the lead. The Labour vote was, in fact, the lowest that the party had received since the war.

The Conservatives lost sixty-three seats but gained five. One of their losses was Tottenham, which had returned in 1959 a Labour man, Alan Brown, who subsequently crossed the floor of the house and stood again in the same constituency as a Conservative. Another former Labour member, Evelyn King, was successful in restoring Conservative representation to South Dorset, which had gone Labour at a by-election in 1962 when Viscount Hinchingbrooke succeeded his father as Earl of Sandwich.[6] So great was Hinchingbrooke's opposition to the common market that he supported an unofficial Conservative against the official candidate and the Labour candidate slipped in for two years. At Carlisle the sitting Conservative member, Dr. Donald Johnson, who had lost the support of his association, stood as an Independent Conservative, but the Labour candidate would just have won the seat even without the 1,227 votes that he collected. The presence of the Independent Conservative Trade Unionist candidate at Wokingham scarcely affected the outcome—he was given 645 votes—but it gave practical expression to a demand frequently heard that the Conservative party should foster more trade union candidates. John Paul, a former Conservative candidate, had little support at Bexley against Edward Heath in the interest of the Anti-Common Market League, of which he was founder and chairman. If the 1,263 votes he obtained may be taken as a guide, opposition to the proposal to join the common market did not play a big part in the Conservative decline; nor would the votes obtained by the several Independent Loyalists suggest that there was grave discontent with the "wind of change" in the Commonwealth.

It was, however, a marked decline in Conservative votes rather than an increase in support for Labour that put Labour at the head of the poll. Votes cast for Conservative candidates fell from 13,750,875 in 1959 to 11,980,783; and the Conservative share of the poll fell in the same period from 49·4 to 43·4 per cent. It was the biggest fall for either of the chief parties since the Conservative rout in 1945. The falling away in Conservative support was not due in any marked degree to Liberal intervention. The fact that in divisions contested by the Liberals there was a swing of 4·2 per cent to Labour compared with the national average of 3·6 per cent suggests that

Liberal candidates lost the Conservatives on balance 0·6 per cent of the votes. The statistical reduction in the Tory vote may indicate some abstention on the part of electors who had voted Conservative in 1959, but a bigger element is probably the failure to recruit a sufficient share of the new voters who had since come on the register. The Labour party's claim to be the better guide in modernizing Britain for the new technological age probably had more success with such voters than the Conservative party's achievements in office, which were taken for granted by young people to whom the harsh realities of the inter-war years were unknown. This failure to win acceptance for the Tory party as the party for the second half of the twentieth century, rather than discontent with policies actually pursued, would appear to be the root cause of the Conservative inability to rally as many voters as in 1959. It is certain that housing difficulties also lost the Conservatives votes, especially among the new voters; for although new homes had been built at the unprecedented rate of 300,000 a year for twelve years, this vast total did not match the demand created by rising prosperity, a growing population, the increasing expectation of life and the falling age of marriage. Failure to grapple with the related problem of the high cost of land was undoubtedly held against the Conservatives by many voters. In analysing the results, the Conservatives could reflect that if the election had been held twelve months earlier they would have been out with a majority of at least a hundred against them. The recovery in the party's fortunes since the nadir of the struggle for the leadership had been impressive; but time had run out before they could complete the recovery, and even if there had been more time economic difficulties might have begun to tell against them.

When it was clear that Labour had a small majority Douglas-Home did not quibble. The old doctrine that a Prime Minister should take his dismissal from Parliament rather than from the electorate was no longer in favour. That same afternoon he submitted his resignation, and a little later Wilson accepted her Majesty's commission to form a government.

Thus thirteen years of Conservative rule came to an end, on a strict computation the longest consecutive period of party rule since the Tory defeat in 1830, and a new chapter opened in the "endless adventure"[7] that began with the parliamentary struggles of Whigs and Tories in the Restoration Parliament. It might be easier to discern Danby in Sir Alec Douglas-Home than Shaftesbury in Mr. Grimond, and Mr. Wilson would disown the ancestry of either, but the essentials of the party struggle remain as they were laid down nearly three hundred years ago in the debates over the Exclusion Bill. The topics of party interests have changed out of all recognition; party organization has been extended from Westminster to every constituency in the kingdom, and has been intensified to a degree that would not have been thought credible; but the reasons why men join parties are the same as they were three centuries ago. Though the system has its defects, and is cruel to those who do not fit easily into its patterns, no way that is both equally fair and equally efficient has yet been found for deciding how the nation's affairs shall be transacted and who shall conduct them. It may be improved from time to time, and the parties will certainly change as much in the future as they have done in the past, but it is unlikely that a system which has stood the test of three centuries will be wholly discarded.

T

NOTES

Chapter 22 LABOUR IN OFFICE 1924

1. Royal Archives, Windsor, K.1918,30, cited by Harold Nicolson, *King George the Fifth*, p. 382.

2. *Spectator*, 15th Dec. 1923.

3. G. M. Young, *Stanley Baldwin*, p. 70.

4. The Earl of Oxford and Asquith, *Memories and Reflections*, vol. 2, p. 209.

5. Royal Archives, Windsor, King George V's Diary, 22nd Jan. 1924, cited by Harold Nicolson, *King George the Fifth*, p. 384.

6. J. R. Clynes, *Memoirs 1869–1924*, p. 343.

7. Clynes, (*op. cit.*, pp. 341–2) relates that at a luncheon to discuss policy one person suggested that Labour should form a government, but draw up a King's Speech of such a socialist character that the Liberals would immediately put them out again; he denounced this as a theatrical gesture.

8. George Lansbury, Speech at Shoreditch Town Hall, 5th Jan. 1924 (Harold Nicolson, *King George the Fifth*, p. 385).

9. Viscount Snowden, *An Autobiography*, vol. 2, pp. 596–8. Webb's account has been subsequently published in the *Political Quarterly*, Jan.–March 1961, pp. 6 ff.

10. *The Times*, 12th Feb. 1924. There is an account from one who was present as a defeated candidate in W. A. S. Hewins, *The Apologia of an Imperialist*, vol. 2, p. 282.

11. *Gleanings and Memoranda*, March 1924, pp. 227–37.

12. And on the whole, we may now add, though with occasional lapses, did shake itself free.

13. *Beatrice Webb's Diaries 1924–1932*, edited by Margaret Cole, under entry for 24th Sept. 1924, p. 43.

14. L. MacNeill Weir, *The Tragedy of Ramsay MacDonald*, p. 181.

15. Harold Nicolson, *King George the Fifth*, p. 401.

16. L. MacNeill Weir, *The Tragedy of Ramsay MacDonald*, p. 185.

17. *Ibid.*, p. 187.

18. *The Times*, 25th Oct. 1924.

19. In a minute dated 26th Oct. 1924 on a copy of Sir Eyre Crowe's letter to the Prime Minister, Royal Archives, Windsor, K.1958,34, cited by Harold Nicolson, *King George the Fifth*, p. 402

20. J. H. Thomas, *My Story*, p. 78; Geoffrey Blaxland, *J. H. Thomas: A Life for Unity*, p. 178. Thomas had been speaking the night before for Snowden in the Colne Valley and they were staying at the same Huddersfield hotel.

21. L. MacNeill Weir, *The Tragedy of Ramsay MacDonald*, p. 194.

22. *Ibid.*, pp. 193–4.

23. J. D. Gregory, *On the Edge of Diplomacy*, p. 216.

24. Royal Archives, Windsor, King George V's Diary, 4th Nov. 1924, cited by Harold Nicolson, *King George the Fifth*, p. 403.

Chapter 23   TORIES *versus* SOCIALISTS 1924–1929

1. Personal information from Bevil Rudd. According to the present Lord Birkenhead, he declined to return to the Woolsack (*The Life of F. E. Smith*, p. 504).

2. G. D. H. Cole, *A History of the Labour Party from 1914*, pp. 176–7.

3. The Earl of Oxford and Asquith, *Memories and Reflections*, vol. 2, pp. 213–17, 223–8.

4. The facts about the Lloyd George Political Fund are fairly set out by Frank Owen, *Tempestuous Journey*, pp. 684–93, and his conclusion is: "It did him (Lloyd George) deep, if disproportionate and undeserved harm." He compares him with Sir Henry Morgan, who was bitterly reviled in his day, not for the sack of Panama, but because the loot was so unevenly distributed.

5. House of Commons, 6th March 1925, *Hansard*, Fifth Series, vol. 181, cols. 840–1; G. M. Young, *Stanley Baldwin*, pp. 91–4.

6. G. M. Young, *Stanley Baldwin*, p. 95.

7. Derek Walker-Smith, *Neville Chamberlain*, p. 148.

8. *Evening Standard*, 22nd, 23rd and 24th July 1925. For Churchill's budget speech announcing the return to the gold standard, see *Hansard*, Fifth Series, House of Commons, 28th April 1925, vol. 183, cols. 52–8.

9. G. M. Young, *Stanley Baldwin*, p. 99.

10. House of Commons, 6th Aug. 1925, *Hansard*, Fifth Series, vol. 187, col. 1613.

10a. The course of the general strike can be followed in W. H. Crook, *The General Strike: A Study of Labour's Tragic Weapon in Theory and Practice*; Julian Symons, *The General Strike: A Historical Portrait*; and Lord Citrine, *Men and Work: An Autobiography*, which includes the author's diary as acting secretary of the Trades Union Congress during the critical days.

11. The speech is reproduced in Viscount Simon, *Retrospect*, pp. 291–6.

12. Frank Owen, *Tempestuous Journey*, p. 705.

13. Lord Oxford and Asquith, *Memories and Reflections*, vol. 2, p. 236.

14. *Ibid.*, p. 237.

15. *Ibid.*, p. 240. I have corrected "expansive" to "expensive".

16. *Ibid.*, p. 245.

17. G. M. Trevelyan, *Grey of Fallodon*, pp. 358–9.

18. G. D. H. Cole, *A History of the Labour Party from 1914*, p. 198.

19. *Ibid.*, p. 205.

20. *Ibid.*, p. 214.

21. He returned to the Labour fold, stood unsuccessfully as a Labour candidate in 1931 and 1935, and after representing North Islington from 1937 was made a peer in 1950.

Chapter 24 SECOND LABOUR GOVERNMENT 1929–1931

1. Frank Owen, *Tempestuous Journey*, p. 692.

2. In his memoirs Lord Kilmuir, as Maxwell-Fyfe became in 1954, says: "I managed with some difficulty to convince my supporters that I should not fight the 1929 election. I then had the difficult task of keeping the organization together when I knew I couldn't fight" (*Political Adventure*, p. 34).

3. Fuller details of the Nationalist parties may be found in *The Party System in Great Britain*, ed. 1953, pp. 72–9.

4. Lloyd George to C. P. Scott, 30th April 1929, cited by Frank Owen, *Tempestuous Journey*, p. 710.

5. Frank Owen, *Tempestuous Journey*, p. 714.

6. Harold Nicolson, *King George the Fifth*, p. 504 and *n*; Earl of Birkenhead, *The Life of F. E. Smith*, pp. 510–11.

7. Alan Campbell Johnson, *Viscount Halifax*, p. 222; Viscount Templewood, *Nine Troubled Years*, p. 45. The announcement was made in the form of a *communiqué* to the Indian Gazette.

8. Viscount Simon, *Retrospect*, p. 152; *ibid.*, p. 153.

9. Viscount Templewood, *Nine Troubled Years*, p. 49.

10. Sir Evelyn Wrench, "Churchill and the Empire", in Charles Eade (editor), *Churchill by his Contemporaries*, p. 199.

11. Philip Guedalla, *Mr. Churchill: A Portrait*, p. 246.

12. G. M. Young, *Stanley Baldwin*, p. 149.

13. *Ibid.*, p. 152.

14. H. R. S. Phillpott, *The Right Hon. J. H. Thomas*, p. 206.

15. Sir Robert Topping to Neville Chamberlain, 25th Feb. 1931, cited by Iain Macleod, *Neville Chamberlain*, pp. 139–41, with the omission of a few "wounding phrases".

16. G. M. Young, *Stanley Baldwin*, p. 156.

17. *Ibid.*, p. 158.

18. Stanley Baldwin, Speech at the Queen's Hall, London, 17th March 1931 (*The Times*, 18th March 1931). Disraeli coined the phrase "power without responsibility" in *Endymion*, and Baldwin had already employed it against the extreme socialists.

19. Iain Macleod, *Neville Chamberlain*, p. 143.

20. Frank Owen, *Tempestuous Journey*, pp. 714–15; Michael Foot, *Aneurin Bevan*, vol. 1, pp. 115–18.

21. Winston S. Churchill, House of Commons, 28th Jan. 1931, *Hansard*, Fifth Series, vol. 247, col. 1022. Churchill was quoting from "the junior member for Treorchy", the columnist of the *Western Mail*.

22. Winston S. Churchill, House of Commons, 21st Jan. 1931, *Hansard*, Fifth Series, vol. 247, col. 267.

23. Viscount Snowden, *An Autobiography*, vol. 2, pp. 885–6.

24. Frank Owen, *Tempestuous Journey*, pp. 715–17.

25. Viscount Simon, *Retrospect*, p. 163.

26. House of Commons, 3rd July 1931, *Hansard*, Fifth Series, vol. 254, cols. 1628–35, 1659–68. It was in this speech that Lloyd George observed that other men who had changed their opinions "did not leave behind the slime of hypocrisy in passing from one side to the other". He "was always ready to give a Roland for an Oliver", Simon commented (*Retrospect*, p. 166).

27. Margaret Cole, *Beatrice Webb's Diaries, 1924–1932*, under date 2nd Dec. 1930, p. 230.

28. Beatrice Webb commented: "Thomas made the same old speech—just the sort of 'statement of policy' which might be made by any slow-going Conservative employer who happened to be in Thomas's position" (*ibid.*, 21st May 1930, p. 243).

29. "Has MacDonald found his superseder in Oswald Mosley? MacDonald owes his pre-eminence largely to the fact that he is the only artist, the only aristocrat by temperament and talent in a party of plebeians and plain men. Hitherto he has had no competitor in personal charm and good looks, delightful voice and the gift of oratory. But Mosley has all these with the *élan* of youth, wealth and social position added to them. Like Mosley, MacDonald began as a Utopian, but today he is a disillusioned Utopian while Mosley has still a young man's zeal—and is, I think, more able to use other men's brains. Whether Mosley has Mac's toughness of texture—whether he will not break down in health or in character I have doubts" (*ibid.*, under date 29th May 1930, pp. 243–4).

30. G. D. H. Cole, *A History of the Labour Party from 1914*, p. 203.

31. *Ibid.*, pp. 246–7.

Chapter 25 FALL OF THE SECOND LABOUR GOVERNMENT

1. All the facts ascertainable in 1958, the year of publication, are set out with great skill by R. Bassett, *Nineteen Thirty-one*, and his interpretations can generally be relied upon, especially against the detractors of MacDonald, but he shows himself a little blind, or indulgent, to the failings on MacDonald's part. He makes use of two documents prepared for the use of Labour ex-ministers shortly before the reassembly of Parliament on 8th Sept. 1931—the "Graham memorandum" drafted by Graham and agreed with Henderson regarding the proceedings of the Cabinet Economy Committee, and the "ex-ministers' memorandum", drafted by Greenwood, relating to the subsequent Cabinet proceedings. Webb wrote an account "What Happened in 1931: A Record" in the *Political Quarterly*, Jan.–March 1932, vol. 3, no. 1, pp. 1–17 (subsequently reprinted as Fabian Tract No. 237). *Beatrice Webb's Diaries 1924–1932* is an important contemporary source for some details. Among the memoirs published by ex-ministers, Snowden's *An Autobiography*, published in 1934, is indispensable, but needs to be used with care; Dalton's *Call Back Yesterday* (1953) and Shinwell's *Conflict without Malice* (1955) add a little authentic information, but the others are disappointingly meagre. Of the memoirs or biographies of the other chief participants, Samuel's *Memoirs* (1945) and Nicolson's *King George the Fifth* (1952) are of outstanding im-

portance; *The Life of Neville Chamberlain* (1946) by Keith Feiling is useful for its citations from his subject's diary, and John Bowle, *Viscount Samuel* (1959) adds some details to the *Memoirs*. The section in the most recent of the memoirs of participants, Lord Citrine, *Men and Work: An Autobiography*, is surprisingly brief, but contains a good study of MacDonald. The chief gap in the material is MacDonald's own case, and this may be remedied when Mr. David Marquand writes the official biography.

2. Viscount Snowden, *An Autobiography*, vol. 2, p. 938.

3. R. Bassett, *op. cit.*, p. 88.

4. Walter Citrine, Speech to the Trades Union Congress, Bristol, 7th Sept. 1931 (*The Times*, 8th Sept. 1931; R. Bassett, *Nineteen Thirty-one*, p. 97).

5. Margaret Cole, *Beatrice Webb's Diaries 1924–1932*, under date 22nd Aug. 1931 *iterum*, p. 281.

6. Raymond Postgate, *The Life of George Lansbury*, p. 269.

7. House of Commons, 14th Sept. 1931, *Hansard*, Fifth Series, vol. 256, col. 546; R. Bassett, *op. cit.*, p. 105.

8. Margaret Cole, *Beatrice Webb's Diaries 1924–1932*, under date 23rd Aug. 1931, p. 282.

9. *Ibid.*, p. 282.

10. R. Bassett, *op. cit.*, p. 120.

11. Viscount Templewood, *Nine Troubled Years*, p. 18; Keith Feiling, *The Life of Neville Chamberlain*, p. 193.

12. *The Times*, 24th Aug. 1931.

13. John Evelyn Wrench, *Geoffrey Dawson and our Times*, p. 291.

14. Harold Nicolson, *King George the Fifth*, p. 461; Wrench, *op. cit.*, p. 292.

15. Royal Archives, Windsor, K.2330(1)/18, cited by Harold Nicolson, *King George the Fifth*, p. 461.

16. House of Lords Record Office, Samuel Papers; John Bowle, *Viscount Samuel*, p. 271.

17. Viscount Samuel, *Memoirs*, p. 204.

18. Sir Henry Clay, *Lord Norman*, p. 390.

19. Harold Nicolson, *op. cit.*, p. 463, using personal information from Sir Ernest Harvey, see p. 462 n.

20. Sir Henry Clay, *Lord Norman*, pp. 391–2.

21. There is some disagreement in the sources about the names, and a legend grew up in the Labour party that a majority (expanded by L. S. Amery, *My Political Life*, vol. 3, p. 59, into a "large majority") had voted against the cuts, but Bassett's analysis (*op. cit.*, pp. 138–41) leaves no doubt that the supporters and dissentients were as stated. There would not have been a formal vote.

22. Royal Archives, Windsor, K.2330(1)7, cited by Harold Nicolson, *King George the Fifth*, p. 464.

23. Keith Feiling, *The Life of Neville Chamberlain*, p. 193.

24. Neville Chamberlain, Speech at Dumfries, 11th Sept. 1931 (Viscount Snowden, *An Autobiography*, vol. 2, pp. 951–2); Malcolm MacDonald to Lord Passfield, 6th Jan. 1932, cited by R. Bassett, *op. cit.*, p. 413.

25. Royal Archives, Windsor, K.2330(1)/7, cited by Harold Nicolson, *King George the Fifth*, pp. 465–6.

26. John Bowle, *Viscount Samuel*, p. 273.

27. *The Times*, 25th Aug. 1931.

28. Harold Nicolson, *King George the Fifth*, pp. 467–8; L. MacNeill Weir, *The Tragedy of Ramsay MacDonald*, pp. 386–90; Hugh Dalton, *Call Back Yesterday*, pp. 272–3.

29. *Political Quarterly*, Jan.–March 1932, vol. 3, no. 1, p. 1. The "plot theory" is dissected in Appendix 5 to R. Bassett, *Nineteen Thirty-one*, pp. 408–21.

30. House of Commons, 2nd July 1929, *Hansard*, Fifth Series, vol. 229, cols. 64–5.

31. Viscount Snowden, *An Autobiography*, vol. 2, p. 957.

32. Hugh Dalton, *Call Back Yesterday*, p. 278. In its election manifesto issued on 14th Oct. the General Council of the Trades Union Congress borrowed Dalton's words: "Fellow workers, the first Labour government was destroyed by a 'Red Letter'. The second Labour government has been destroyed by a Banker's Order."

33. Leonard Wolff, *Political Quarterly*, Oct.–Dec. 1931, vol. 2, no. 4, pp. 476–7; Harold Laski, *The Crisis and the Constitution*. Mr. Herbert Morrison in his *Government and Parliament*, p. 80, took the more moderate view: "On a balance of considerations, therefore, my own view is that in this instance King George V received bad advice and that he himself made a mistake in accepting it, though I would not go so far as to assert that his action was unconstitutional."

34. Viscount Samuel, *Memoirs*, pp. 221–2. What Samuel wrote was formally correct, and discussion must be suspended at this point until further evidence comes to light, as it may possibly do when the official life of Mac-Donald is published. There are clearly gaps in the information at present available, especially about the extent to which a National government had been discussed between the King and Mr. MacDonald before the critical week-end. The statements in Beatrice Webb's diary for 23rd Aug., and the ex-ministers' revelations of the discussion in Cabinet on 19th Aug. raise more questions than they answer.

35. In conversation with Citrine in 1933 MacDonald said: "If I had only been able to carry my colleagues with me what we could have achieved! What a chance we had! But we threw it away. If they had only been straight enough to stand by what they had initiated, not what finally resulted from it—I am not saying that—I could have helped them. When they ran away and began to deny that they had ever had anything to do with our proposals, well, I thought to myself that politics had become too degraded for me". (Lord Citrine, *Men and Work: An Autobiography*, p. 288.)

Chapter 26 LABOUR ROUT 1931

1. *The Times*, 28th Aug. 1931; R. Bassett, *Nineteen Thirty-one*, pp. 182–3.

2. Snowden forgot this when he came to write *An Autobiography*, vol. 2, p. 953.

3. *The Times*, 8th Sept. 1931; R. Bassett, *op. cit.*, p. 209.

4. R. Bassett, *op. cit.*, p. 187. A letter from MacDonald to Lloyd George on 26th Aug., and Lloyd George's reply of 30th Aug., are reproduced in Frank Owen, *Tempestuous Journey*, pp. 718–19.

5. *The Times*, 29th Aug. 1931.

6. House of Commons, *Hansard*, Fifth Series, vol. 256, col. 43.

7. Hugh Dalton, *Call Back Yesterday*, p. 290. Keynes's *Essays in Persuasion* was published towards the close of 1931.

8. *Vide supra*, p. 63.

9. R. Bassett, *op. cit.*, p. 247.

10. Keith Feiling, *The Life of Neville Chamberlain*, p. 195.

11. Viscount Simon, *Retrospect*, pp. 169–71; R. Bassett, *op. cit.*, p. 255.

12. Royal Archives, Windsor, K.2331(1)18, cited by Harold Nicolson, *King George the Fifth*, p. 491.

13. The decision was not published immediately; it was first reported in the *Daily Herald* of 30th Sept. and made public officially on 1st Oct., when the national agent sent to Snowden the interesting letter which he reproduces in *An Autobiography*, vol. 2, p. 987.

14. Mary Agnes Hamilton, *Arthur Henderson*, p. 399.

15. *The Times*, 29th Sept. 1931; R. Bassett, *op. cit.*, pp. 261–2.

16. L. S. Amery, *My Political Life*, vol. 3, pp. 68–9; Keith Feiling's *Neville Chamberlain*, p. 195.

17. *The Times*, 3rd Oct. 1931.

18. Royal Archives, Windsor, King George V's Diary, 2nd Oct. 1931, cited by Harold Nicolson, *King George the Fifth*, p. 492.

19. Memorandum by Sir Clive Wigram, 3rd Oct. 1931, Royal Archives, Windsor, K.2331(1)29, cited by Harold Nicolson, *King George the Fifth*, p. 493.

20. Viscount Samuel, *Memoirs*, p. 211.

21. L. S. Amery, *My Political Life*, vol. 3, p. 69; Thomas Jones (on the authority of Philip Kerr, Lord Lothian), *A Diary with Letters*, p. 15; but Snowden makes no claim in *An Autobiography* to have been the author. There is no supporting evidence for the statement by C. L. Mowat, *Britain Between the Wars*, p. 408, that the author was Chamberlain.

22. "He was beside himself with rage. He had been betrayed! For years his resentment of Samuel was not assuaged. As for the Liberal M.P.s who had agreed with Samuel's decision and were rash enough to pay a visit to Lloyd George immediately afterwards, the gale of his denunciation nearly blew them out of the house. 'You have sold every pass that we held,' he shouted" (Frank Owen, *Tempestuous Journey*, p. 720).

23. L. S. Amery, *My Political Life*, vol. 3, p. 70.

24. Keith Feiling, *The Life of Neville Chamberlain*, p. 195.

25. Viscount Simon, *Retrospect*, p. 171.

26. Broadcast Talk, 15th Oct. 1931.

27. Ramsay Muir, Letter to Liberal associations and candidates, 10th Oct. 1931 (R. Bassett, *Nineteen Thirty-one*, p. 298).

28. The pioneer use of broadcasting by MacDonald and Baldwin in 1929 has already been noted.

29. Walter Runciman, Speech at Newcastle, 24th Oct. 1931; Viscount Snowden, *An Autobiography*, vol. 2, p. 996.

30. Viscount Snowden, *An Autobiography*, vol. 2, p. 995.

31. Reproduced in *An Autobiography*, vol. 2, pp. 1059–64; and R. Bassett, *Nineteen Thirty-one*, pp. 444–9. It shows how much Snowden had ceased to be in touch with his old working-class associates that he should not be able to get the name of the Trades Union Congress right and should speak to men on the "dole" of "your investments".

32. Mary Agnes Hamilton, *Arthur Henderson*, p. 401.

33. Mr. Alan Bullock points out that the political defeat of 1931 marks the end of a period in Bevin's career as sharply as the industrial defeat of 1926. He adds the penetrating comment: "His reaction to the fall of the second Labour government was quite the opposite to that which followed the fall of the first. After the election of 1924 he had been disillusioned with politics and had turned back to industrial action as the only reliable means of improving working-class conditions. His experience in the intervening years, however, confirmed by the defeat of 1931, convinced him that the trade unions must commit themselves more, not less, to political action and draw closer to the Labour party. In the period beginning with the crisis of 1931, Bevin played a part in Labour politics which, as Francis Williams has justly pointed out, entitles him to be regarded as one of the architects of the Labour party as much as of the trade-union movement" (*The Life and Times of Ernest Bevin*, vol. 1, p. 499).

34. Margaret Cole, *Beatrice Webb's Diaries 1924–1932*, p. 294.

Chapter 27 "NATIONAL" GOVERNMENT 1931–1935

1. John Bowle, *Viscount Samuel*, p. 285.

2. Lloyd George to Reading, 14th Aug. 1929, cited by Frank Owen, *Tempestuous Journey*, pp. 689–90.

3. Neville Chamberlain, Speech at Dudley, 26th Oct. 1931 (*The Times*, 27th Oct.).

4. House of Commons, 4th Feb. 1932, *Hansard*, Fifth Series, vol. 261, col. 296. The "nineteen years" of the text appear in *Hansard* as "seventeen years", but was corrected in the autograph of this passage which Chamberlain wrote for the Duke of York (the future King George VI), which is reproduced facsimile in Keith Feiling, *The Life of Neville Chamberlain*, between pp. 204 and 205.

5. John Bowle, *Viscount Samuel*, p. 288.

6. John Bowle, *Viscount Samuel*, p. 292.

7. MacDonald to King George V, 11th Sept. 1932, Royal Archives, Windsor, K.2357,1, cited by Harold Nicolson, *King George the Fifth*, p. 498.

8. Keith Feiling, *The Life of Neville Chamberlain*, p. 216.

9. Frank Owen, *Tempestuous Journey*, p. 728.

10. *Ibid.*, p. 727.

11. *Ibid.*, p. 729.

12. Macmillan had been elected for a northern industrial constituency, Stockton-on-Tees, in 1923, lost it in 1929, and was again returned in 1931. In *Reconstruction* he urged that "the great need for the moment is not only for a policy of action to deal with a pressing situation, but for a new theory of social and economic organization which will facilitate the evolution towards a new economic system suitable to the changed circumstances of the modern world". He devoted a chapter to the case for planning "through the intelligent direction of production by a central authority for each industry guaranteed against redundancy, duplication and disorderly competition by the grant of monopoly powers in return for the acceptance of certain social responsibilities". This was a new note in Conservative thought—though in harmony with such Conservative actions as the setting up of the Central Electricity Board in 1926—and there was no surprise when Macmillan joined with members of other parties, or of none, in drafting *The Next Five Years: An Essay in Political Agreement*, which appeared in 1935.

13. Harold Nicolson, *King George the Fifth*, p. 494, n. [2].

14. Hugh Dalton, *Call Back Yesterday*, p. 297; *The Fateful Years*, p. 19.

15. C. R. Attlee, *As It Happened*, p. 75.

16. Baldwin later paid a generous tribute to him.

17. Sir Stafford Cripps, Speech at Nottingham, 6th Jan. 1934; Eric Estorick, *Stafford Cripps*, p. 124; Hugh Dalton, *The Fateful Years*, p. 41.

18. In a letter in *The Times*.

19. G. D. H. Cole, *A History of the Labour Party from 1914*, p. 298.

20. House of Commons, 17th April 1934, *Hansard*, Fifth Series, vol. 288, cols. 905–6.

21. Keith Feiling, *A History of England*, p. 1115.

22. Blanche E. C. Dugdale, *Arthur James Balfour 1906–1930*, pp. 379–80; Harold Nicolson, *King George the Fifth*, p. 471.

23. Viscount Templewood, *Nine Troubled Years*.

24. *Ibid.*, p. 98.

25. Harold Nicolson, *King George the Fifth*, p. 473.

26. So, at least, the story ran at the time. See, for example, Eric Estorick, *Stafford Cripps*, p. 114.

27. Eric Estorick, *op. cit.*, pp. 114–15.

28. House of Commons, 10th Nov. 1936, *Hansard*, Fifth Series, vol. 317, col. 742, quoting *Joel* 2, 25.

29. S. Baldwin, House of Commons, 8th March 1934, *Hansard*, Fifth Series, vol. 286, col. 2077.

30. Hugh Dalton, *Hitler's War: Before and After*, pp. 58–60; *The Fateful Years*, p. 47.

31. House of Commons, 12th Nov. 1936, *Hansard*, Fifth Series, vol. 317, cols. 1144–5.

32. R. Bassett has emphasized this in an article in the *Cambridge Journal*, Nov. 1948, vol. 2, no. 2, pp. 84–95; and the words "supposing I had gone to the country" taken in their context can bear no other meaning.

33. Baldwin cannot be blamed for thinking in 1933–5 that the advent of Labour to power would have led to even less rearmament; this was the only conclusion that could be drawn from Labour speeches and actions at that time. He can be blamed for not giving a more decisive lead to the country. Sir Winston Churchill, *The Second World War*, vol. 1, *The Gathering Storm*, p. 169, takes a severe view of the speech: "This was indeed appalling frankness. It carried naked truth about his motives into indecency. That a Prime Minister should avow that he had not done his duty in regard to national safety because he was afraid of losing the election was an incident without parallel in our parliamentary history." G. M. Young, though frequently severe in his censure of Baldwin, on this occasion acquits him of anything worse than clumsiness, *Stanley Baldwin*, p. 229: "Never I suppose in our history has a statesman used a phrase so fatal to his own good name, and at the same time so wholly unnecessary, so incomprehensible." Mr. A. W. Baldwin, *My Father: The True Story*, p. 272, agrees: "Whether it was sheer fatigue of mind following his breakdown of August and at the brink of the abdication, or a search for a fresh angle on the years-long argument, it seems that in the language of the card-room Baldwin over-played his hand that day in the House of Commons. . . . With but six months to go he had slipped badly. Words, with which he had always striven to be more precise than most, played him false." On the House of Commons principle that the best construction should be put on its proceedings, it would appear that Baldwin should be found guilty of a clumsy use of language rather than of deliberate deceit for the purpose of frustrating a Labour victory. The speech has been not unsympathetically examined by a historian with no prejudice in favour of Baldwin—C. L. Mowat, *Journal of Modern History*, June 1955, vol. 27, no. 2.

34. House of Commons, 30th July 1934, *Hansard*, Fifth Series, vol. 292, col. 2325; Attlee, col. 2349; Cripps, col. 2431; Samuel, cols. 2360–1; and House of Commons, 13th July 1934, *Hansard*, Fifth Series, vol. 292, col. 675.

35. The figures are taken from the official report of the Peace Ballot.

36. Lord Cecil of Chelwood, speech at the Albert Hall, London, 27th June 1935 (*The Times*, 28th June).

37. Baldwin, Speech at Glasgow, 23rd Nov. 1934 (A. W. Baldwin, *My Father: The True Story*, p. 207). The pamphlet is also cited by G. M. Young, *Stanley Baldwin*, p. 178 n., as being used at a by-election. Baldwin commented on it: "A more nauseating and lying document I have never read— not even in the days of Chinese slavery."

38. C. R. Attlee, House of Commons, 11th March 1935, *Hansard*, Fifth Series, vol. 299, col. 46.

39. Samuel Hoare to Neville Chamberlain, 18th Aug. 1935, cited in Viscount Templewood, *Nine Troubled Years*, pp. 164–5; *ibid.*, p. 166.

40. *The Times*, 13th Sept. 1935; Viscount Templewood, *Nine Troubled Years*, p. 170.

41. Hugh Dalton, *The Fateful Years*, pp. 63–4.

42. The 1918 constitution had said in Clause Six: "The secretary . . . shall devote his whole time to the work of the party, but this shall not prevent him being a candidate for or a member of Parliament." The amendment was made at the Southport conference in 1934.

43. Hugh Dalton, *The Fateful Years*, p. 66.

44. Accounts of this memorable conference may be found in Hugh Dalton, *The Fateful Years*, pp. 67–9; Francis Williams, *Ernest Bevin*, pp. 190–6; Alan Bullock, *The Life and Times of Ernest Bevin*, pp. 565–71; Eric Estorick, *Stafford Cripps*, pp. 142–5.

Chapter 28   LABOUR'S AND CHURCHILL'S ROAD BACK 1935–1940

1. House of Commons, 22nd Oct. 1935, *Hansard*, Fifth Series, vol. 305, col. 46.

2. G. M. Young, *Stanley Baldwin*, pp. 213–15.

3. Lord Morrison of Lambeth, *Herbert Morrison: An Autobiography*, p. 163. The chapter in which this judgement occurs is entitled "Leadership from the rear".

4. Emanuel Shinwell, *Conflict without Malice*, pp. 128–30.

5. House of Lords, 22nd May, 1935, *Hansard*, Fifth Series, vol. 96, col. 1017.

6. Winston S. Churchill, *The Second World War*, vol. 1, *The Gathering Storm*, p. 140.

7. Hugh Dalton, *The Fateful Years*, pp. 79–82; Lord Morrison of Lambeth, *Herbert Morrison: An Autobiography*, pp. 163–5.

8. Emanuel Shinwell, *Conflict without Malice*, p. 133; *The Labour Story*, pp. 155–6.

9. Emanuel Shinwell, *The Labour Story*, p. 156. The attempts to unseat Attlee are briefly summarized in *Conflict without Malice*, pp. 133–4.

10. House of Commons, 19th Dec. 1935, *Hansard*, Fifth Series, vol. 307, cols. 2032–5.

11. Sir Charles Petrie, *The Life and Letters of the Right Hon. Sir Austen Chamberlain*, vol. 2, pp. 403–6; Keith Feiling, *The Life of Neville Chamberlain*, p. 274.

12. C. R. Attlee, House of Commons, 19th Dec. 1935, *Hansard*, Fifth Series, vol. 307, cols. 2028–9.

13. Neville Chamberlain, Speech to the 1900 Club, London, 10th June 1936 (Keith Feiling, *The Life of Neville Chamberlain*, p. 296).

14. House of Commons, 18th June 1936, *Hansard*, Fifth Series, vol. 313, col. 1232.

15. Sir Walter Citrine, speech at Trades Union Congress, Plymouth, 10th Sept. 1936.

16. Michael Foot, *Aneurin Bevan*, vol. 1, p. 218.

17. *Forward*, 3rd Oct. 1936.

18. Hugh Dalton, *The Fateful Years*, p. 100.

19. *Report of the Thirty-sixth Annual Conference of the Labour Party*, Edinburgh, 1936, pp. 103, 182–4, 203, 207; Hugh Dalton, *The Fateful Years*, pp. 101–4.

20. The moving phrase used by the King's physician, Lord Dawson of Penn, in the final bulletin, 20th Jan. 1936.

21. A. W. Baldwin, *My Father: The True Story*, p. 307, gives Baldwin's determination as not to "speak to the man at the wheel". A new life of Baldwin by John Barnes and Keith Middlemass is in preparation.

22. Chamberlain had written in his diary for 7th Oct. 1936: "On October 2 I took S.B.'s place at the mass meeting after the party conference at Margate. . . . The main result . . . appears to be a general acceptance of my position as heir-apparent" (Keith Feiling, *Neville Chamberlain*, p. 287).

23. R. T. McKenzie, *British Political Parties*, ed. 1963, p. 46, n. 1.

24. He has given his own story in *The Mist Procession*, and Ian Colvin, *Vansittart in Office*, may also be consulted.

25. Neville Chamberlain's diary, 19th Feb. 1938, cited by Keith Feiling, *The Life of Neville Chamberlain*, p. 330.

26. Earl of Avon, *The Eden Memoirs* [vol. 1], *Facing the Dictators*, p. 549.

27. Winston S. Churchill, *The Second World War*, vol. 1, *The Gathering Storm*, p. 199.

28. The circumstances—largely accidental—in which this leading article, wrongly assumed to be inspired by the Foreign Office, came to be written are revealed in *The History of The Times*, vol. 4, pt. 2, pp. 926–34.

29. Neville Chamberlain's diary, 19th Sept. 1938, cited by Keith Feiling, *The Life of Neville Chamberlain*, p. 367.

30. Neville Chamberlain, Broadcast Talk, 27th Sept. 1938 (Keith Feiling, *The Life of Neville Chamberlain*, p. 372; *ibid.*, p. 381); speech from window of No. 10, Downing Street, 30th Sept. 1938 (*The Times*, 1st Oct.).

31. Winston S. Churchill, *The Second World War*, vol. 1, *The Gathering Storm*, p. 253.

32. A. Duff Cooper, House of Commons, 3rd Oct. 1938, *Hansard*, Fifth Series, vol. 339, col. 34; Winston S. Churchill, 5th Oct. 1938, *ibid.*, vol. 339, col, 360.

33. R. J. Minney, *The Private Papers of Leslie Hore-Belisha*, pp. 196–7; Winston S. Churchill, *The Second World War*, vol. 1, *The Gathering Storm*, p. 278.

34. G. D. H. Cole, *A History of the Labour Party from 1914*, pp. 340–1.

35. *Ibid.*, pp. 347–50.

36. Stafford Cripps, Speech at Newcastle-upon-Tyne, 5th Feb. 1939. The petition is cited in Eric Estorick, *Stafford Cripps*, pp. 165–6.

37. *Report of the Thirty-eighth Annual Conference of the Labour Party*, Southport, 1939, p. 235.

38. C. R. Attlee, *As It Happened*, p. 105; Hugh Dalton, *The Fateful Years*, pp. 222–5.

39. Duff Cooper, *Old Men Forget*, p. 239; Hugh Dalton, *op. cit.*, p. 264.

40. Eric Estorick, *Stafford Cripps*, p. 175; Winston S. Churchill, *The Second World War*, vol. 1, *The Gathering Storm*, p. 279.

41. Winston S. Churchill, *op. cit.*, p. 320.

42. Winston S. Churchill, *op. cit.*, p. 318.

43. The text is given in the *Report of the Forty-second Annual Conference of the Labour Party*, London, 1943, p. 8.

44. The term was used by Keith Feiling as the heading of Chapter 33 of *The Life of Neville Chamberlain* and borrowed by Churchill for the title of Book 2 of *The Gathering Storm;* no doubt it was preferred by that lover of good language to "the phoney war" of popular speech.

45. Keith Feiling, *The Life of Neville Chamberlain*, p. 434.

46. Neville Chamberlain, Speech to the Central Council of the National Union of Conservative and Unionist Associations, London, 5th April 1940, cited by Winston S. Churchill, *The Second World War*, vol. 1, *The Gathering Storm*, p. 461; House of Commons, 7th May 1940, *Hansard*, Fifth Series, vol. 360, col. 1075.

47. L. S. Amery, House of Commons, 7th May 1940, *Hansard*, Fifth Series, vol. 360, col. 1150.

48. Neville Chamberlain, House of Commons, 8th May 1940, *Hansard*, Fifth Series, vol. 360, col. 1266.

49. D. Lloyd George, *ibid.*, col. 1283.

50. Hugh Dalton, *The Fateful Years*, p. 311.

51. These are Chamberlain's words as recorded by Churchill (*The Gathering Storm*, p. 523) and if exactly recorded would be an admission on Chamberlain's part that the government over which he presided was not national in the full sense of the term.

52. Keith Feiling, *The Life of Neville Chamberlain*, p. 441; Hugh Dalton, *The Fateful Years*, pp. 306–7. There appears to be no truth (Dalton, *op. cit.*, p. 309 *n.*) in the story of a meeting between Attlee and Bracken (L. S. Amery, *My Political Life*, vol. 3, p. 371, E. S. Spears, *Prelude to Dunkirk*, pp. 130–1) when Attlee was alleged to have said his people had never forgiven Churchill for Tonypandy and would expect a new government to be under Halifax; yet in 1950 Tonypandy was still an evocative name and in a general election speech at Cardiff on 8th Feb. 1950, Churchill felt obliged to deny that he had called out troops to put down miners (*The Times*, 9th Feb.). There were even echoes in 1964–5 when it was urged in a few quarters that the Churchill memorial fund should not be supported on account of Tonypandy.

53. Hugh Dalton, *The Fateful Years*, p. 313.

54. Emrys Hughes, *Macmillan: Portrait of a Politician*, pp. 47–52, is the tribute of a Labour opponent in the House of Commons.

55. Macmillan to Baldwin, 29th June 1936, cited by Emrys Hughes, *Macmillan*, pp. 45–6.

56. Keith Feiling, *The Life of Neville Chamberlain*, pp. 447–8.

57. Hugh Dalton, *The Fateful Years*, p. 316.

58. House of Commons, 13th May 1940, *Hansard*, Fifth Series, vol. 360, col. 1502. Churchill would not have thought it necessary to tell his hearers, or sub-

sequent readers, that he was echoing Garibaldi's words in the Piazza di San Pietro as he set out on the retreat from Rome—*Fame, sete, marcie forzate, battaglie e morte*—but it is curious how many have supposed he was using these words for the first time.

Chapter 29 ELECTORAL TRUCE AND LABOUR TRIUMPH 1940–1945

1. G. D. H. Cole, *A History of the Labour Party from 1914*, p. 374.

2. The protracted and illuminating exchange of letters between Harry Pollitt, secretary of the Communist party of Great Britain (British Section of the Communist International) and J. S. Middleton, secretary of the Labour Party, is reproduced in the *Report of the Forty-second Annual Conference of the Labour Party*, London, 1943, pp. 9–18.

3. *Ibid.*, p. 19.

4. *Ibid.*, pp. 161, 168.

5. G. D. H. Cole, *A History of the Labour Party from 1914*, p. 398.

6. The exchange does not seem to have found its way into *Hansard*.

7. *Report of the Forty-second Annual Conference of the Labour Party*, London, 1943, pp. 19, 152–3.

8. The constitution of the National Council of Labour as settled on 21st July 1941 is given in the *Report of the Forty-second Annual Conference of the Labour Party*, London, 1943, p. 226.

9. *Forward—By the Right!*, p. 1. This was a statement of aims by the committee, and its early activities can be further studied in Quintin Hogg, *One Year's Work*.

10. House of Commons, 27th Oct. 1943, in a speech on the Workmen's Compensation (Temporary Increases) Bill, *Hansard*, Fifth Series, vol. 393, col. 301; House of Commons, 1st Dec. 1944, in a debate upon the allied ban on Count Sforza as Italian Foreign Minister, *Hansard*, Fifth Series, vol. 406, col. 307.

11. Michael Foot, *Aneurin Bevan*, vol. 1, pp. 451–63.

12. Michael Foot in his autobiography appears to be unaware of this intervention. The mediating members were led by G. M. Garro Jones (later Lord Trefgarne), and the group's spokesman in the meeting of the parliamentary party was Hubert Beaumont.

13. Winston S. Churchill, *The Second World War*, vol. 4, *The Hinge of Fate*, p. 862.

14. Michael Foot, *Aneurin Bevan*, pp. 473–4.

15. House of Commons, 8th Dec. 1944, *Hansard*, Fifth Series, vol. 406, cols. 908–1014.

16. G. D. H. Cole, *A History of the Labour Party from 1914*, p. 411.

17. House of Commons, 31st Oct. 1944, *Hansard*, Fifth Series, vol. 404, cols. 666–7.

18. Winston S. Churchill, *The Second World War*, vol. 6, *Triumph and Tragedy*, p. 511.

19. Lord Morrison of Lambeth, *Herbert Morrison*, p. 234.

20. Winston S. Churchill, Broadcast Talk, 4th June 1945 (*The Times*, 5th June).

21. Hugh Dalton, *The Fateful Years*, p. 476.

22. *Ibid.*, p. 460; C. R. Attlee, *As It Happened*, p. 145.

23. Hugh Dalton, *The Fateful Years*, p. 464.

24. Winston S. Churchill, *The Second World War*, vol. 6, *Triumph and Tragedy*, pp. 521–2; C. R. Attlee, *As It Happened*, pp. 138, 145; Winston S. Churchill, Broadcast Talk, 30th June 1945; R. B. McCallum and Alison Readman, *The British General Election of 1945*, pp. 144–50; and for the constitutional and party-structural significance, Ivor Bulmer-Thomas, *The Party System in Great Britain*, pp. 191–5.

25. Winston S. Churchill, Broadcast Talk, 4th June 1945 (*The Times*, 5th June).

Chapter 30   LABOUR IN POWER 1945–1950 : HIGH TIDE

1. C. R. Attlee, *As It Happened*, p. 148.

2. Hugh Dalton, *The Fateful Years*, p. 467–8; Francis Williams, *Ernest Bevin*, pp. 238–9; Lord Morrison of Lambeth, *Herbert Morrison*, pp. 245–6; Francis Williams, *A Prime Minister Remembers*, pp. 3–4. Morrison denies that Bevin's vigorous comment was made in a telephone call to himself, as recorded by Dalton; it was, in fact, made to third parties.

3. R. T. McKenzie, *British Political Parties*, ed. 1963, p. 321, *n.* 1.

4. *Report of the Thirty-third Annual Conference of the Labour Party*, Hastings, 1933, pp. 8–10, 166–8.

5. C. R. Attlee, *As It Happened*, p. 156. The need to return to the Potsdam conference gave him a special motive for making his senior appointments quickly, but it is clear from the passage cited that this was not his sole or even chief reason for not carrying out the 1933 requirements.

6. Hugh Dalton, *The Fateful Years*, p. 473.

7. King George VI's diary, 26th July 1945, cited by J. Wheeler Bennett, *King George VI: His Life and Reign*, p. 638.

8. Royal Archives, Windsor, G. VI Conf./254, cited by J. Wheeler Bennett, *op. cit.*, p. 638, *n.*.

9. Hugh Dalton, *The Fateful Years*, pp. 474, 468, 469.

10. Hugh Dalton, *High Tide and After*, pp. 9–10.

11. C. R. Attlee, "The Role of the Monarchy", *Observer*, 23rd Aug. 1959. He had made a similar denial earlier, *Daily Herald*, 20th Feb. 1952.

12. Lord Morrison of Lambeth, *Herbert Morrison*, p. 247.

13. C. R. Attlee, *Observer*, 23rd Aug. 1959. He also told Francis Williams: "Ernie and Herbert didn't get on together. If you'd put both on the home front there might have been trouble, therefore it was better that Ernie should operate mainly in foreign affairs" (*A Prime Minister Remembers*, p. 5).

14. C. R. Attlee, *As It Happened*, p. 154. Bevan, who had never previously held office, had steeled himself to refusing anything but "a major Cabinet post" (Michael Foot, *Aneurin Bevan*, vol. 1, pp. 509–10).

15. Lord Morrison of Lambeth, *Herbert Morrison*, p. 249.

16. *Ibid.*, p. 251. A vivid account of this incident as seen from the press gallery is given in Guy Eden, *Portrait of Churchill*, pp. 194–5.

17. Hugh Dalton, *High Tide and After*, pp. 22–3.

18. Ernest Bevin, Speech at Blackpool, 23rd May 1945 (*Report of the Forty-fourth Annual Conference of the Labour Party*, Blackpool, 1945, p. 119); Speech at Leeds, 7th April 1945 (*The Times*, 16th April).

19. James F. Byrnes, *Speaking Frankly*, p. 79. He expressed the same sentiments in *All in One Lifetime*, pp. 298–9.

20. D. F. Fleming, *The Cold War and its Origins 1917–1960*, vol. 1, pp. 291–2.

21. When asked if he spoke any foreign languages he replied: "I can't even speak my own."

22. Sir Hartley Shawcross, House of Commons, 2nd April 1946, *Hansard*, Fifth Series, vol. 421, col. 1213.

23. Lord Beaverbrook, Letter to *The Times*, 10th Oct. 1955, commenting on the account given by Robert Blake, *The Unknown Prime Minister*, pp. 351–5.

24. In his evidence to the Macmillan Committee.

25. D. N. Pritt, *The Labour Government 1945–51*, p. 41, shows himself blissfully ignorant of the bitter dispute behind the scenes in saying: "Of the Civil Aviation Act and the Cable and Wireless Act I need not write. They were necessary and useful measures, and scarcely controversial." This is true of the Cable and Wireless Act.

26. *Ibid.*, pp. 41–5.

27. Hugh Dalton, *The Fateful Years*, pp. 432–3.

28. *Let us Face the Future*, p. 7.

29. Lord Morrison of Lambeth, *Herbert Morrison*, p. 296; Hugh Dalton, *High Tide and After*, pp. 248–53. An American student of British politics, George W. Ross, *The Nationalization of Steel*, pp. 64–68, 156, is critical of what he regards as the indecision of the Labour government, and is especially severe on Morrison's attempt at compromise.

30. The opportunity to expel Alfred Edwards provided by such remarks was no doubt taken in May 1948 as a sop to those left-wing critics who had been offended by the expulsion of J. Platts-Mills on 21st April; *vide supra*, p. 165.

31. Jack and Bessie Braddock, *The Braddocks*, p. 212.

Chapter 31   LABOUR IN POWER 1945–1950: THE EBB

1. Hugh Dalton, *High Tide and After*, p. 197.

2. *Ibid.*, pp. 238–40.

3. *Ibid.*, p. 246. Discussing these manoeuvres with me expansively in his great room at the Foreign Office Bevin observed: "I could never be leader of this party; it's too disloyal."

4. House of Commons, 13th Nov. 1947, *Hansard*, Fifth Series, vol. 444, col. 551.

5. *The Industrial Charter*, pp. 28, 39; *The Agricultural Charter*, pp. 12–13, 22; *Imperial Policy*, p. 55. The committee which drew up the *Industrial Charter*

U

included Butler, Oliver Stanley, Oliver Lyttelton, David Eccles and Maxwell-Fyfe, and the last-named has given an account of its genesis in his memoirs (the Earl of Kilmuir, *Political Adventure*, pp. 162–3). See also J. D. Hoffman, *The Conservative Party in Opposition, 1945–51*, pp. 143–66. This thesis by a Canadian student gives a useful documented record of the Conservatives from the end of the war to their return to office.

6. *The Memoirs of the Rt. Hon. the Earl of Woolton*, pp. 304–5.

7. *Ibid.*, pp. 331, 334, 337, 340.

8. *Ibid.*, p. 345. Maxwell-Fyfe's own comments on the report at a later date, when he had become Lord Kilmuir, are both objective and perceptive: "The report had several important minor defects, but its main results were the establishment of a system of trained, paid, and experienced agents throughout the country, the absolute removal of financial burdens upon candidates, the careful definition of the rôles of the various party organizations to ensure that there was no serious overlapping of effort or mutual jealousies—which had caused considerable difficulties in the past—and the unequivocal endorsement of the independence of the constituency organization, particularly in the selection of candidates. Looking back, with all the advantage of hindsight, I am not sure that the last recommendation has had a wholly beneficial effect on the party's fortunes. At the time, we considered —and rightly—that the party would not have accepted any other proposal, but the effect has been for the party to virtually abrogate its control over the selection of parliamentary candidates. The retention of the power of veto by the Central Office is, of course, a negative approach, and Central Office has naturally been very reluctant to exercise this power except in extreme cases" (the Earl of Kilmuir, *Political Adventure*, pp. 157–8).

9. Douglas Jay, *The Socialist Case*, ed. 1949, p. 258.

10. *The Right Road for Britain*, p. 5.

11. Winston S. Churchill, Speech at Edinburgh, 14th Feb. 1950 (*The Times*, 15th Feb.); Ernest Bevin, Broadcast Talk, 15th Feb. 1950 (*The Times*, 16th Feb.); Herbert Morrison, Speech at Lewisham, 16th Feb. 1950 (*The Times*, 17th Feb.).

12. Hugh Dalton, *High Tide and After*, pp. 338–40.

13. Aneurin Bevan, Speech at Manchester, 4th July 1948 (*The Times*, 5th July).

14. Herbert Morrison, *Socialist Commentary*, May 1954. In his autobiography, *Herbert Morrison*, p. 264, Morrison quoted an estimate by Laski that the "vermin" slight cost the Labour party two million votes. This, like his own estimate in terms of seats, is almost certainly a gross exaggeration.

15. Lord Morrison of Lambeth, *Herbert Morrison*, pp. 268–9.

Chapter 32   UNSTABLE EQUILIBRIUM 1950–1951

1. He repeated the phrase in *As It Happened*, p. 196, "The King's government had got to be carried on, whatever the difficulties."

2. Francis Williams, *A Prime Minister Remembers*, p. 227.

3. Emanuel Shinwell, *The Labour Story*, p. 184.

4. *Ibid.*, p. 188.

5. Lord Morrison of Lambeth, *Herbert Morrison*, p. 271.

6. Hugh Dalton, *High Tide and After*, p. 358.

7. Emanuel Shinwell, *The Labour Story*, p. 188.

8. *Ibid.*, p. 189.

9. Lord Morrison of Lambeth, *Herbert Morrison*, p. 273; Francis Williams, *A Prime Minister Remembers*, p. 243.

10. Leslie Hunter, *The Road to Brighton Pier*, p. 220.

11. Aneurin Bevan, Speech at Bermondsey, Town Hall, 3rd April 1951 (*News Chronicle*, 4th April 1951). He had himself, nevertheless, piloted through the House of Commons a bill authorizing a charge of one shilling on prescriptions.

12. Francis Williams, *A Prime Minister Remembers*, pp. 245, 246.

13. *Ibid.*, p. 247.

14. Hugh Dalton, *High Tide and After*, p. 361; Lord Morrison of Lambeth, *Herbert Morrison*, p. 274.

15. Lord Morrison of Lambeth, *op. cit.*, p. 281; Hugh Dalton, *op. cit.*, p. 377.

16. Hugh Dalton, *op. cit.*, p. 357.

17. *The Memoirs of the Rt. Hon. the Earl of Woolton*, p. 353; but by a trick of memory he has attributed this to the 1950 election, when Morrison had not become Foreign Secretary.

18. Lord Morrison of Lambeth, *Herbert Morrison*, p. 282; Herbert Morrison, Speech at Labour Party Conference, 3rd Oct. 1951: "Would Mr. Churchill say whether in his judgement the government should have gone to war with Persia or not? The Conservatives still lived in that world, and it was a dangerous one" (*The Times*, 4th Oct.); *The Daily Mirror*, 25th Oct. 1951; Winston S. Churchill, Speech at Plymouth, 23rd Oct. 1951 (*The Times*, 24th Oct.). Churchill's action for libel was not pursued after he had again become Prime Minister.

Chapter 33 CONSERVATIVE REVIVAL 1951–1955

1. *The Memoirs of the Rt. Hon. the Earl of Woolton*, p. 394.

2. House of Commons, 25th March 1954, *Hansard*, Fifth Series, vol. 525, cols. 1473–4.

3. Francis Williams, *A Prime Minister Remembers*, p. 255.

4. For example, Patrick Gordon Walker, Speech at Dorking, 29th July 1952: "We have to take into account that there is a deliberately organized party within the parliamentary party, which plans out every step and seeks to take advantage of legitimate differences within the party". Richard Stokes, Speech at Leiston, 1st Aug. 1952: "There has grown up in the Parliamentary Labour party a party within a party. It holds its own meetings, organizes the action of its own members and really tries to dictate policy. It should not be allowed. It is something quite different from the traditional group idea." Lord Pakenham, *Tribune*, 8th Aug. 1952: "Bevanism to-day is organized as a 'party within a party'."

5. Leslie Hunter, *The Road to Brighton Pier*, p. 42, attributes the move to Harold Davies, M.P. for Leek.

6. *Report of the Fifty-first Annual Conference of the Labour Party*, Morecambe, 1952, pp. 126–7.

7. *Tribune*, 13th Nov. 1953.

8. Hugh Dalton, *High Tide and After*, p. 395.

9. House of Commons, 13th April 1954, *Hansard*, Fifth Series, vol. 526, col. 969.

10. Hugh Dalton, *High Tide and After*, p. 409; Leslie Hunter, *The Road to Brighton Pier*, p. 79. There are slight differences in the words reported to be used, but the substantial truth of the account is not in doubt.

11. Leslie Hunter, *op. cit.*, p. 79.

12. Leslie Hunter, *op. cit.*, pp. 81–2.

13. House of Commons, 2nd March 1955, *Hansard*, Fifth Series, vol. 537, cols. 2176, 2122, and for the division lists, cols. 2189–200.

14. Hugh Dalton, *High Tide and After*, p. 409.

15. C. R. Attlee, Television Talk, 11th May 1955; Anthony Eden, Television Talk, 12th May 1955.

Chapter 34   CHANGES AT THE HELM 1955–1959

1. *Interim Report on the Party Organization* (Wilson Report), p. 7; Dudley Smith, *Harold Wilson*, p. 162.

2. *Star*, 6th Oct. 1955.

3. Hugh Dalton, *High Tide and After*, pp. 352–3.

4. *Ibid.*, pp. 413–14.

5. Leslie Hunter, *The Road to Brighton Pier*, p. 121.

6. Hugh Dalton, *op. cit.*, p. 422.

7. *Ibid.*, p. 429.

8. *Ibid.*, p. 426. Attlee said in an interview with Percy Cudlipp for the *News Chronicle*: "We must have at the top men brought up in the present age and not, as I was, in the Victorian age" (Leslie Hunter, *The Road to Brighton Pier*, p. 134).

9. Leslie Hunter, *The Road to Brighton Pier*, p. 172.

10. Hugh Dalton, *High Tide and After*, p. 431; Leslie Hunter, *The Road to Brighton Pier*, p. 173.

11. Hugh Dalton, *op. cit.*, p. 431.

12. *Ibid.*, p. 433. For Shinwell's own account see *The Labour Story*, pp. 200–1: "Morrison's defeat in what had been a most successful career in the sphere of British politics caused him much offence. It wounded his feelings and was an affront to his integrity. Consequently, when asked to stand for the deputy leadership, he declined." Morrison himself says: "I declined, not through sulkiness, but because I had had a long run in the No. 2 position under Attlee, partly enjoyable, partly not so enjoyable. There was no point in continuing in this position" (*Herbert Morrison*, p. 305).

13. Hugh Dalton, *High Tide and After*, p. 429; Leslie Hunter, *The Road to Brighton Pier*, p. 131; Emanuel Shinwell, *The Labour Story*, pp. 199–200; Francis Williams, *A Prime Minister Remembers*, p. 255; Lord Morrison of Lambeth, *Herbert Morrison*, p. 293.

14. Hugh Dalton, *High Tide and After*, pp. 434–5.

15. Aneurin Bevan, Speech at Manchester, 4th Feb. 1956; Leslie Hunter, *The Road to Brighton Pier*, p. 181.

16. *The Memoirs of the Rt. Hon. the Earl of Woolton*, pp. 417–18.

17. *Ibid.*, p. 421.

18. Earl of Kilmuir, *Political Adventure*, p. 256.

19. Sir Anthony Eden (the Earl of Avon), *The Eden Memoirs*, [vol. 3], *Full Circle*, p. 352.

20. "It is all very familiar. It is exactly the same that we encountered from Mussolini and Hitler in those years before the war" (Hugh Gaitskell, House of Commons, 2nd Aug. 1956, *Hansard*, Fifth Series, vol. 557, col. 1613).

21. Sir Anthony Eden (the Earl of Avon), *op. cit.*, p. 554.

22. Hugh Gaitskell, House of Commons, 31st Oct. 1956, *Hansard*, Fifth Series, vol. 558, col. 1462; Broadcast Talk, 4th Nov. 1956.

23. "No other country featherbeds its agriculture like Britain. I think the time has arrived to ask ourselves whether the cost of providing farmers with guaranteed prices and assured markets has not now reached a level which neither the consumer nor the taxpayer can afford" (Stanley Evans, Speech at Manchester, 14th April 1950).

24. Earl of Kilmuir, *Political Adventure*, pp. 273–4.

25. Leon D. Epstein, *British Politics in the Suez Crisis*, p. 87.

26. This has been attempted by Mr. Epstein in the work cited, and on the whole successfully, though as an American he is unaware of certain relevant facts well appreciated inside the party (as was pointed out in the review in *The Times Literary Supplement*, 19th March 1964). The most important of the cases is that of Nigel Nicolson, who incurred additional displeasure with many of his right-wing constituents in Bournemouth East and Christchurch because of his hostility to capital punishment, and because a firm in which he was a director published the book *Lolita*. By 298 votes to ninety-two a special meeting of the local Conservative association decided to seek a new candidate for the next election, and actually chose a new candidate, Major J. A. Friend, who had, however, to be disowned when he was found to have connexions with the League of Empire Loyalists. With support from the Central Office, Nicolson demanded a postal ballot of members, but just failed to carry the day, the voting being 3,762 to 3,671. He did not stand again. He has given his own account up to the penultimate stage in *People and Parliament*.

Sir Frank Medlicott had sat as a Liberal National for East Norfolk from 1939 to 1950 and as a National Liberal and Conservative for Central Norfolk from 1950. The prominent part he played in the temperance movement and his opposition to capital punishment and blood sports reflected his Liberal and Nonconformist antecedents, but Mr. Epstein is mistaken in thinking they had any bearing on his loss of the constituency. When he wrote to the Prime

Minister dissociating himself from the Suez policy his action was badly received by his local association, but his resignation was not demanded, and if he had handled the situation more tactfully he could have remained the member. In fact, he announced himself that he would not stand again, and eventually he joined the Liberal party. His successor, R. C. M. Collard, secured election as a "Conservative and National Liberal", inverting Medlicott's order, and his successor Ian Gilmour, stood in 1964 simply as a "Conservative".

Cyril Banks, Conservative member for Pudsey from 1950, differed in being a personal friend of Nasser and in holding that it was necessary to come to terms with him. After abstaining on 8th Nov. he gave up the Conservative whip, and his local association seized the opportunity to look for another candidate for the next election.

None of the other critics of the Suez operation lost his seat as a result, though Michael Astor had already announced that he would not stand again for East Surrey (his *Tribal Feeling* acknowledges his dislike of political life) and Robert Boothby, after riding a mild storm in East Aberdeenshire, accepted a life peerage and eventually left the Conservative party. William Yates, who resembled Banks in that he was a supporter of the Arab cause, escaped with no more than criticism in his very marginal constituency of the Wrekin. Peter Kirk, also in a marginal constituency at Gravesend, and Sir Alexander Spearman were severely criticized for expressing their hesitations, even though they had voted with the government on all critical occasions, but their resignation was not demanded.

27. The eight were John Biggs-Davison, Anthony Fell, Lord Hinchingbrooke, Patrick Maitland, Angus Maude, Victor Raikes, Lawrence Turner and Paul Williams. Maitland had the whip restored to him in 1957; Raikes left Parliament in 1957 to pursue business interests in Africa, and Maude in 1958 to edit the *Sydney Morning Herald*. Turner did not stand again, but the reasons were health and financial. All eight except Raikes received assurances of support from their constituency associations, and in Raikes's case the matter does not seem to have been raised.

The moral of both sets of Suez rebels seems to be that nobody was repudiated by his constituency association simply for his attitude to Suez, but Suez provided an opportunity of dispensing with the future services of some members with whom their local associations had already become restive on other grounds.

28. Merry and Serge Bromberger, *Secrets of Suez*, p. 159.

29. Sir Anthony Eden (the Earl of Avon), *The Eden Memoirs*, [vol. 3], *Full Circle*, p. 557.

30. *Economist*, 22nd Dec. 1956; in the light of what actually happened there was an unsuspected aptness in the title of the note in which the comment appeared, "The Heir Too Apparent."

31. *The Times*, 23rd Jan. 1957.

32. Earl of Kilmuir, *Political Adventure*, pp. 286–7.

33. *Ibid.*, p. 285.

34. *Ibid.*, p. 286.

35. *Daily Telegraph*, 12th Jan. 1956.

36. *Manchester Guardian Weekly*, 8th Jan. 1959.

37. Sir Anthony Eden (the Earl of Avon), *The Eden Memoirs*, [vol. 3], *Full Circle*, p. 520. Lord Lambton, M.P., writing in the *Evening Standard* two years later, attributed Butler's failure to the fact "that he was never enamoured of the Suez plan and that he openly and perhaps indiscreetly expressed these views", and he is supported by Emrys Hughes from the other side of the house, but it is more probable that Butler spoke ambiguously rather than openly. (Emrys Hughes, *Macmillan*, p. 132.)

38. R. T. McKenzie, *British Political Parties*, ed. 1963, p. 591.

39. Earl of Kilmuir, *Political Adventure*, p. 286.

40. *The Times*, 10th Jan. 1957.

41. *The Times*, 8th Jan. 1958.

42. *Report of the Fifty-sixth Annual Conference of the Labour Party*, Brighton, 1957, p. 181. He resented suggestions made in newspapers "that some of my actions could be explained only on the basis that I was anxious to become Foreign Secretary".

43. In retrospect, the Conservatives were accused of having fought the election on the slogan, "You've never had it so good", but, as D. E. Butler and Richard Rose point out (*The British General Election of 1959*, p. 22): "Those planning the campaign were so determined to emphasize the party's interest in the future that they never used the slogan frequently attributed to them, 'You've never had it so good', because it was negative and because it was looking backwards. Instead, the idea was adapted in an election poster which read: 'You're having it good. Have it better. Vote Conservative.'" The offending phrase was used on one occasion only, and then quite innocuously, in a speech by Macmillan at Bedford, 20th July 1957, in the course of which he said: "Indeed, let's be frank about it; most of our people have never had it so good."

44. D. E. Butler and Richard Rose, *The British General Election of 1959*, p. 27 and *n*.

45. *Ibid.*

46. Hugh Gaitskell, Speech at Newcastle-upon-Tyne, 28th Sept. 1959 (*The Times*, 29th Sept.); Transport House press statement, 1st Oct. 1959 (*The Times*, 2nd Oct.); Harold Macmillan, Speech at Nottingham, 1st Oct. 1959 (*The Times*, 2nd Oct.); D. E. Butler and Richard Rose, *op. cit.*, pp. 59–60.

47. Hugh Gaitskell, Speech at Leeds, 7th Oct. 1959. Roy Jenkins in *Hugh Gaitskell 1906–1963*, edited by W. T. Rogers, confirms that he expected to win until the returns began to come in.

48. D. E. Butler and Richard Rose, *op. cit.*, p. 147.

Chapter 35 NEW LEADERS AND POLICIES 1959–1964

1. *Report of the Fifty-eighth Annual Conference of the Labour Party*, Blackpool, 1959, pp. 85, 112.

2. R. T. McKenzie, *British Political Parties*, ed. 1963, p. 599.

3. *Report of the Fifty-eighth Annual Conference of the Labour Party*, Blackpool, 1959, p. 131.

4. *The Times*, 17th March 1960.

5. *The Times*, 14th July, 1960.

6. *Report of the Fifty-ninth Annual Conference of the Labour Party*, Scarborough, 1960, p. 219.

7. *Ibid.*, p. 201.

8. *Ibid.*, p. 161.

9. *The Times*, 14th, 15th and 21st Oct. 1960.

10. Mr. Justice Winn's findings were announced on 28th June and 3rd July 1961. The union was expelled from the Trades Union Congress on 4th Sept., and disaffiliated from the Labour party on 2nd Oct. 1961. No longer under Communist control, it has since been re-admitted to membership of both bodies.

11. Winston S. Churchill, Speech at Mansion House, London, 10th Nov. 1942 (*The Times*, 11th Nov.).

12. *The Times*, 4th Feb. 1960. Lord Egremont, who, as Mr. John Wyndham was Macmillan's private secretary at the time and accompanied him on the trip, has pointed out in an article in *The Sunday Times Weekly Review*, 10th May 1964, that Macmillan had developed the theme and even used the term "wind of change" without rousing much comment in Ghana on the way to Cape Town. He rightly exempts Macmillan from being responsible for creating the wind of change. "That speech was a diagnosis, not a prescription."

13. House of Commons, 3rd Aug. 1961, *Hansard*, Fifth Series, vol. 645, cols. 1785–6.

14. *National Union of Conservative and Unionist Associations, 80th Annual Conference*, Brighton, 1961, pp. 5, 46.

15. *National Union of Conservative and Unionist Associations, 81st Annual Conference*, Llandudno, 1962, pp. 6, 46.

15a. *Report of the Sixty-first Annual Conference of the Labour Party*, Brighton, 1962, pp. 158–9.

16. Earl of Avon, Speech at Leamington Spa, 21st July 1962 (*The Times*, 23rd July). The other Cabinet ministers to be dismissed, besides Lloyd and Kilmuir, were Eccles (Education), Hill (Housing), Maclay (Scotland), Mills (Minister without Portfolio) and Watkinson (Defence). Kilmuir has left no doubt in his memoirs that the reconstruction severely shook the party: "I once remarked to a young historian . . . that 'loyalty was the Tories' secret weapon'. I doubt if it has ever had to endure so severe a strain" (*Political Adventure*, p. 324).

17. *The Times*, 14th July 1962.

18. Harold Macmillan, Television Talk, 30th Jan. 1963 (*The Times*, 31st Jan.).

19. *National Union of Conservative and Unionist Associations, 81st Annual Conference*, Llandudno, 1962, p. 126.

20. *The Selwyn Lloyd Report 1963*. The terms of reference as given in the text are given on p. 3 of this document and were laid down by the Executive Committee of the National Union.

21. House of Commons, 22nd March 1963, *Hansard*, Fifth Series, vol. 674, cols. 809–10.

22. *The Times*, 6th June 1963.

23. House of Commons, 17th June 1963, *Hansard*, Fifth Series, vol. 679, col. 99.

24. *Daily Mirror*, 14th June 1963.

25. *The Times*, 11th April 1963; *ibid.*, 29th June 1963.

26. *Ibid.*, 9th July 1964.

27. Sir Gerald Nabarro, Speech at Bolton Town Hall, 9th Oct. 1963 (*The Times*, 10th Oct.). The speaker's thumb-nail sketches of Maudling and Hailsham are given in this text below.

28. *Spectator*, 17th Jan. 1964.

29. Randolph S. Churchill, *The Fight for the Tory Leadership*, p. 94. This chronicle of the events leading to the emergence of the Earl of Home as the Conservative leader is a document of major importance in that its source for parts of the narrative could only have been, and is virtually admitted to have been, Macmillan himself. It has been used, along with newspaper reports, by John Dickie in *The Uncommon Commoner: A Study of Sir Alec Douglas-Home*.

30. *The Times*, 9th Oct. 1963.

31. *Daily Telegraph*, 10th Oct. 1963.

32. *Ibid.*

33. *The Times*, 11th Oct. 1963; *National Union of Conservative and Unionist Associations, 82nd Annual Conference*, Blackpool, 1963, pp. 80-1.

34. *Gleanings and Memoranda*, April 1921, p. 301.

35. *The Times*, 11th Oct. 1963.

36. *The Guardian*, 12th Oct. 1963.

37. Randolph S. Churchill, *The Fight for the Tory Leadership*, pp. 125-6.

38. *The Listener*, 19th Dec. 1963.

39. Randolph S. Churchill, *The Fight for the Tory Leadership*, p. 133; *Spectator*, 17th Jan. 1964; *The Listener*, 19th Dec. 1963.

40. *Spectator*, 17th Jan. 1964.

41. *The Times*, 19th Oct. 1963.

41a. *The Making of the Prime Minister*, by Anthony Howard and Richard West, two journalists who describe themselves as "lazy supporters of the Labour party and wary admirers of Mr. Harold Wilson", is a study of the rise of Wilson and Home to the supreme position. It has been aptly termed "a political thriller". In *The Greasy Pole* Reginald Bevins, a Liverpool man of working-class origins who had become the Conservative Postmaster General but lost his seat in 1964, reveals himself as a believer in the "magic circle" theory and a supporter of Macleod.

42. *The Times*, 21st Oct. 1963.

43. *Spectator*, 17th Jan. 1964.

44. Television Talk, 21st Oct. 1963 (*Daily Telegraph*, 22nd Oct.).

45. It was embodied in *A Statement on Resale Price Maintenance, being a trade practice which prevents shopkeepers from reducing certain prices to*

the public, Cmd. 8274, 1951. Hugh Dalton says that, "it would have been great fun pushing a bill, containing this proposal, through Parliament" (*High Tide and After*, p. 372).

Chapter 36   THE FOURTH LABOUR GOVERNMENT 1964

1. There were subsidiary documents, *Signposts for Scotland* and *Signposts to the New Wales*.

2. This became a favourite theme of Labour propaganda: *Twelve Wasted Years* was the title of a book prepared by the Labour Party Research Department and published in 1963.

3. Notably in the Rag Market at Birmingham on 8th Oct. (*The Times*, 9th Oct. 1964).

4. There was dismay and anger among Conservative candidates fighting with their backs to the wall when R. A. Butler was reported as saying, in an unaccountably detached manner a few days before the election in an interview in a train with Mr. George Gale of the *Daily Express*: "Things might start slipping in the last few days . . . Yes. They won't slip towards us." (*Daily Express*, 9th Oct. 1964.)

5. It is likely that the veteran champion of the coloured races, Fenner Brockway, lost his seat at Eton and Slough to a Conservative for the same reason.

6. Another former Labour member, Aidan Crawley, was returned as a Conservative for West Derbyshire, which he had first won at a by-election in 1962. After renouncing his peerage, the new Earl of Sandwich contested Accrington as Mr. Victor Montagu in the Conservative interest, but he was unsuccessful. *The British General Election 1964*, by David Butler and Anthony King, is now available for a detailed study of the contest.

7. The title of F. S. Oliver's great work on politics, *The Endless Adventure*, featuring Walpole as its star character, may fitly conclude, if that word may be used, a story that can have no end until the final dissolution of human polities.

WORKS CITED

THE author and publisher acknowledge with gratitude permission to publish extracts from the following copyright works:

Lord Beaverbrook, *Politicians and the War 1914–1916* (Oldbourne Book Co. Ltd.)

Lord Beaverbrook, *The Decline and Fall of Lloyd George* (Cassell & Co. Ltd.)

The Second Earl of Birkenhead, *F.E.: The Life of F. E. Smith, First Earl of Birkenhead* (Eyre and Spottiswoode (Publishers) Ltd.)

Robert Blake, *The Unknown Prime Minister* (Eyre and Spottiswoode (Publishers) Ltd.)

John Bowle, *Viscount Samuel* (Victor Gollancz Ltd.)

John Carswell, *The Old Cause* (The Cresset Press)

Lady Gwendolen Cecil, *Life of Robert Marquis of Salisbury* (Hodder & Stoughton Ltd.) (by permission of the owner of the copyright and Hodder & Stoughton Ltd.)

J. R. Clynes, *Memoirs* (Hutchinson & Co. (Publishers) Ltd.)

Margaret Cole (Editor), *Beatrice Webb's Diaries 1924–1932* (Longmans, Green and Co. Ltd.) (by permission of the owners of the copyright, the Passfield Trustees)

Hugh Dalton, *Call Back Yesterday, The Fateful Years, High Tide and After* (Frederick Muller Limited)

Sir Anthony Eden [The Earl of Avon], *Full Circle* (Cassell & Co. Ltd.) (by permission of the owners of the copyright, The Times Publishing Co. Ltd.)

Sir Keith Feiling, *A History of England* (Macmillan & Co. Ltd.)

Sir Keith Feiling, *A History of the Tory Party 1604–1714* (Oxford: Clarendon Press)

Sir Keith Feiling, *The Second Tory Party 1714–1832* (Macmillan & Co. Ltd.)

Sir Keith Feiling, *The Life of Neville Chamberlain* (Macmillan & Co. Ltd.)

Archibald A. S. Foord, *His Majesty's Opposition* (Oxford: Clarendon Press)

Roy Jenkins, *Mr. Balfour's Poodle* (William Heinemann Ltd.)

The Earl of Kilmuir, *Political Adventure* (Messrs. Weidenfeld and Nicolson) (by permission of the owner of the copyright, the Kilmuir Literary Trust)

Sir Lewis Namier, *The Structure of Politics at the Accession of George III* (Macmillan & Co. Ltd.)

Sir Lewis Namier, *Monarchy and the Party System* (Oxford: Clarendon Press)

Sir Lewis Namier and John Brooke (Editors), *The History of Parliament: The House of Commons 1754–1790*, Introduction by John Brooke (Her Majesty's Stationery Office)

Sir Harold Nicolson, *King George the Fifth: His Life and Reign* (Constable & Co. Ltd.)

David Ogg, *England in the Reign of Charles II* (Oxford: Clarendon Press)

The Earl of Oxford and Asquith, *Memories and Reflections* (Cassell & Co. Ltd.)

Henry Pelling, *The Origins of the Labour Party* (Macmillan & Co. Ltd.)

Henry Pelling, *A Short History of the Labour Party* (Macmillan & Co. Ltd.)

Donald Southgate, *The Passing of the Whigs 1832–1886* (Macmillan & Co. Ltd.)

G. M. Trevelyan, *History of England* (Longmans, Green and Co. Ltd.)

Sir John Wheeler-Bennett, *King George VI: His Life and Reign* (Macmillan & Co. Ltd.)

The Earl of Woolton, *The Memoirs of the Rt. Hon. the Earl of Woolton* (Cassell & Co. Ltd.)

The Crown copyright in the Official Report of Parliamentary Debates (*Hansard*) is vested in the Controller of Her Majesty's Stationery Office, to whom thanks are extended for permission to quote a number of passages.

INDEX TO VOLUME II

The principal entry for persons known by different names at different stages of their careers will be found under the title by which they were known when politically most active, but with cross-references when desirable. Thus, the Conservative leader from 1963 to 1965 may be found under Douglas-Home, Sir Alexander Frederick, with cross-references from Dunglass, Lord, and Home, 14th Earl of. In order to increase the utility of the index, a few references in square brackets to events not recorded in the text are given.

x